"X/1999 DEMANDS YOUR ATTENTION…THIS TITLE IS A SELF-CONTAINED, INTELLECTUAL

SERIES THAT, WHILE [IT] BEGRUDGINGLY GIVES THE READER PLENTY OF GRATUITOUS

ACTION AND VIOLENCE, MANAGES TO STAND APART FROM THAT AND ENTICE READERS WITH

THE BEAUTY OF ITS ART AND THE SERIOUSNESS OF THE STORY."

—EX: THE ONLINE WORLD OF ANIME & MANGA

This volume contains the X/1999 installments from Animerica Extra, the Anime Fan's Comic Magazine, Vol. 3, No. 1 through Vol. 3, No. 7 in their entirety.

STORY & ART BY CLAMP

ENGLISH ADAPTATION BY FRED BURKE

Translation/Lillian Olsen
Touch-Up Art & Lettering/Wayne Truman
Cover Design/Hidemi Sahara
Graphics and Layout/Carolina Ugalde

Publisher/Seiji Horibuchi
Editor in Chief/Hyoe Narita
Managing Editor/Annette Roman
Editor/Julie Davis

VP of Sales and Marketing/Rick Bauer

Printed in Canada

Published by Viz Communications, Inc.
P.O. Box 77010 • San Francisco, CA 94107

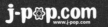

www.viz.com
www.j-pop.com
www.animerica-mag.com
www.pulp-mag.com

10 9 8 7 6 5 4 3 2 1
First printing, May 2002

X/1999 GRAPHIC NOVELS TO DATE

X/1999: PRELUDE
X/1999: OVERTURE
X/1999: SONATA
X/1999: INTERMEZZO
X/1999: SERENADE
X/1999: DUET
X/1999: RHAPSODY

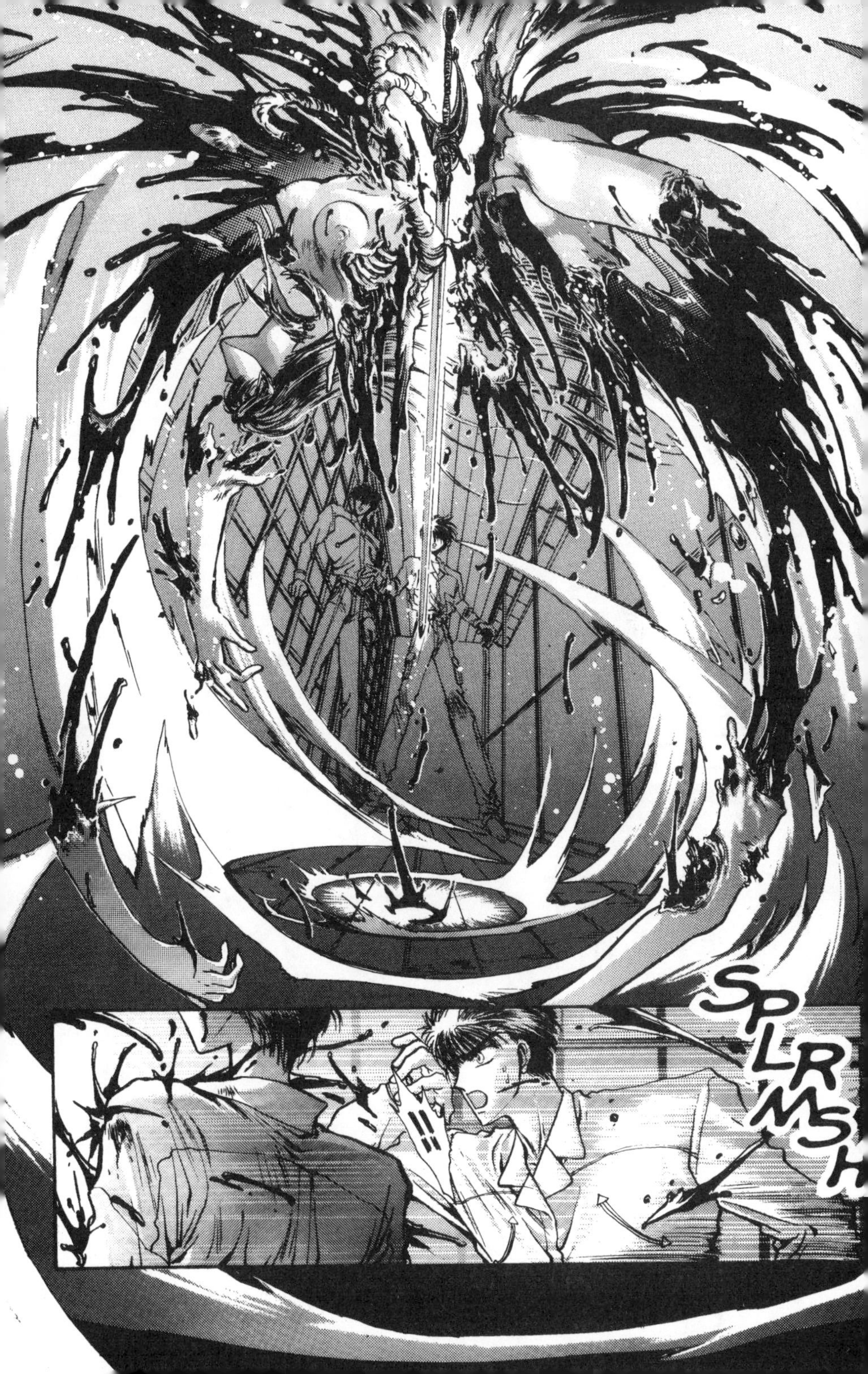
SPLRMSH

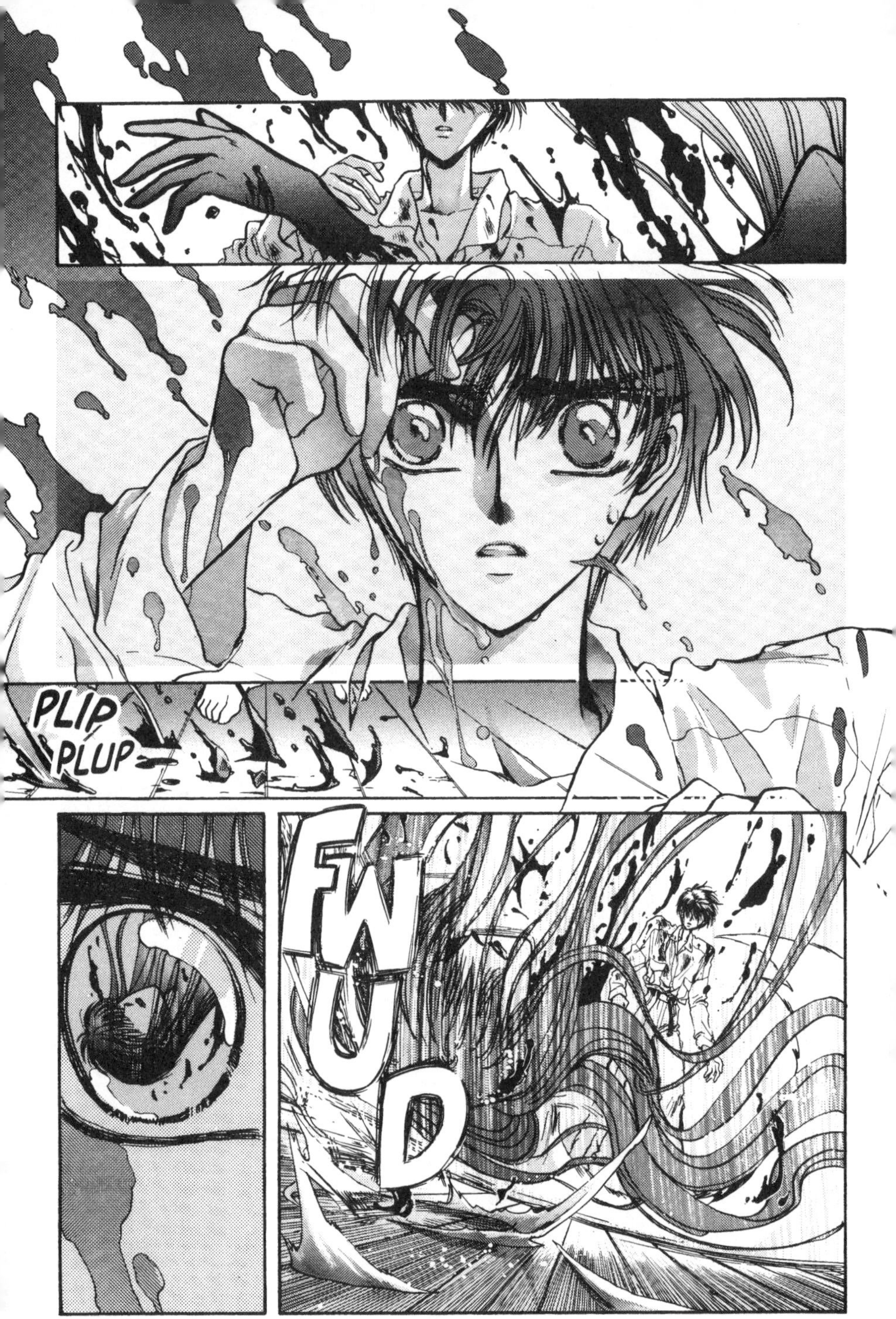
PLIP PLUP
FWUD

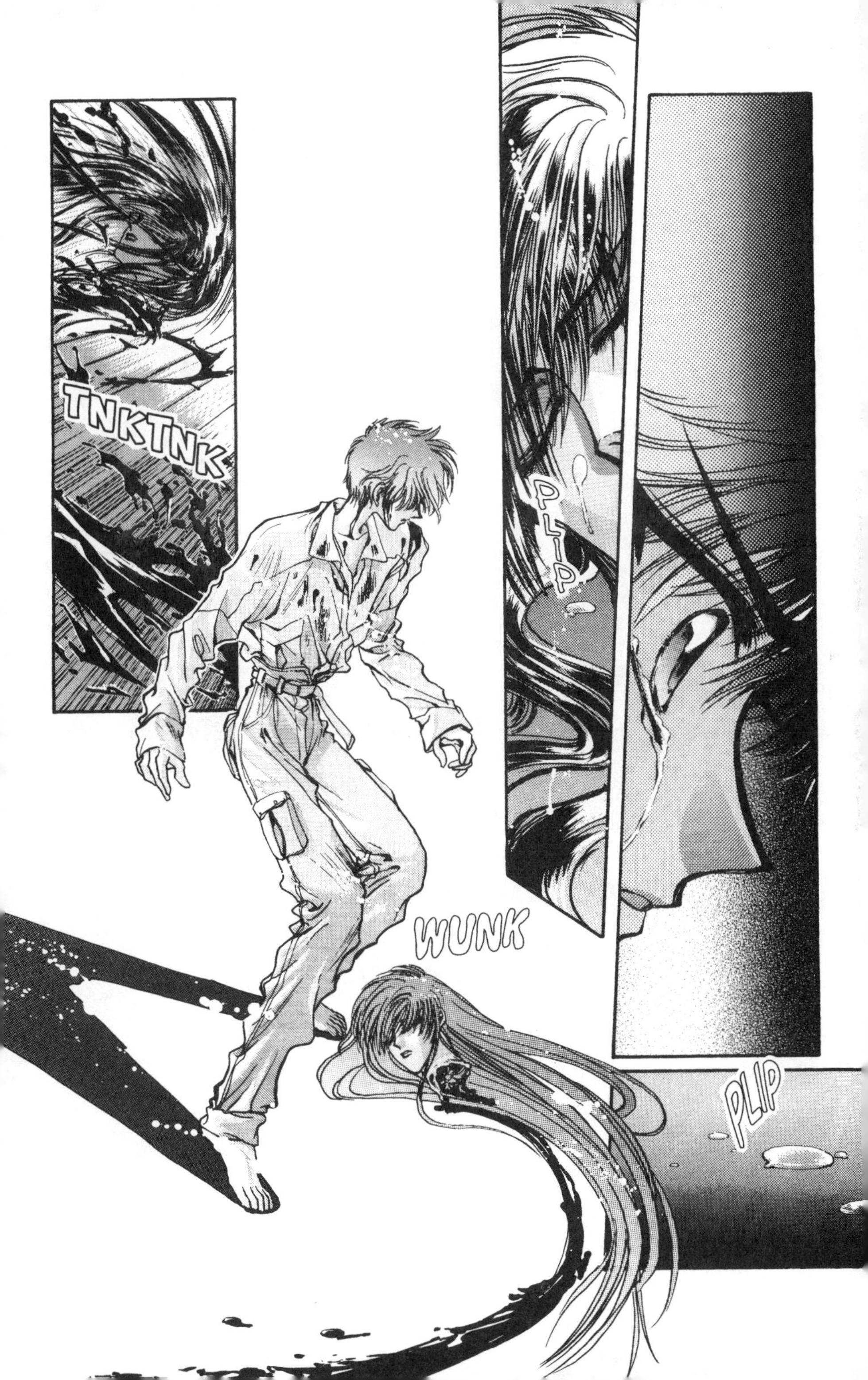
TNKTNK
PLIP
WUNK
PLIP

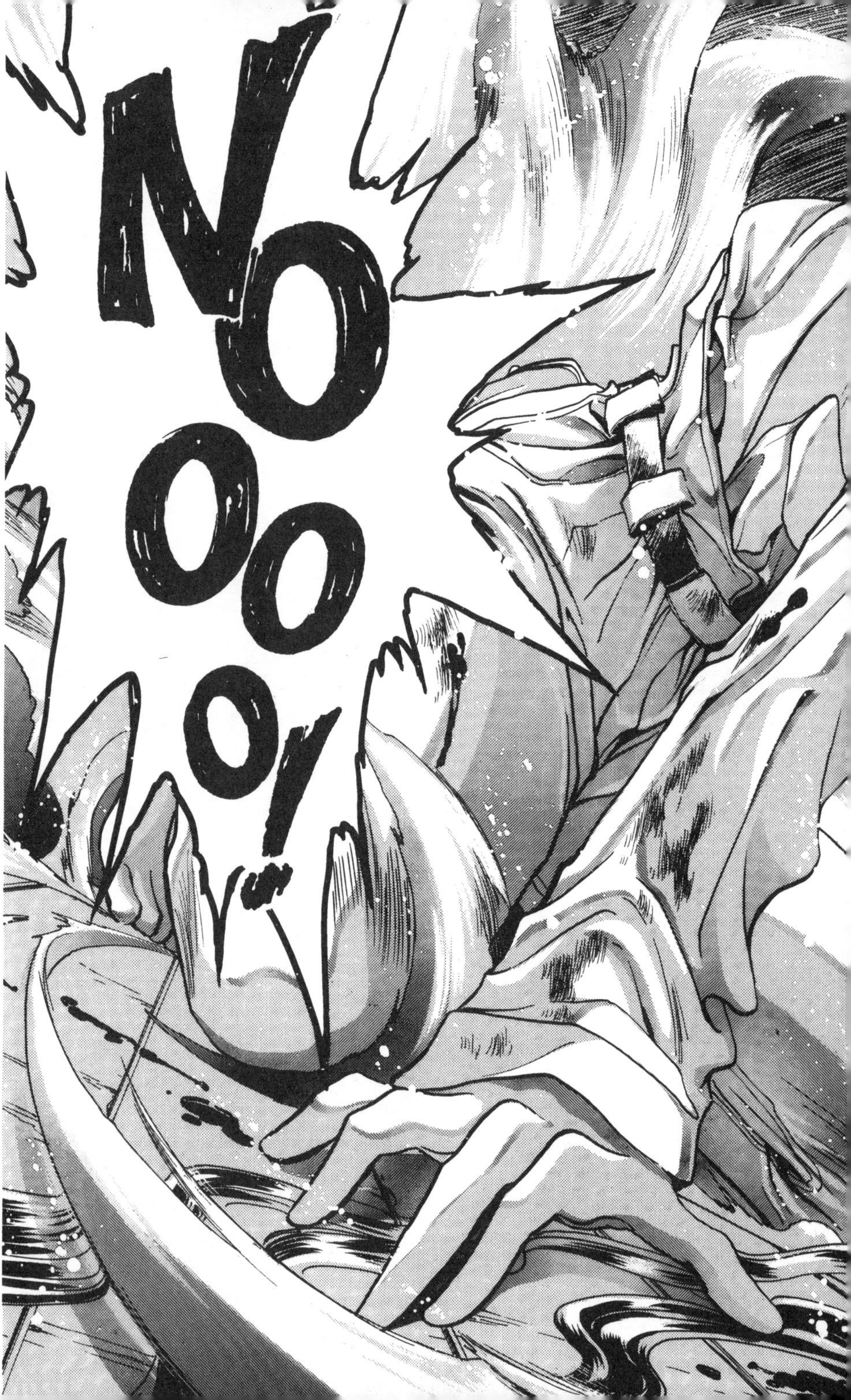
NOOOO!

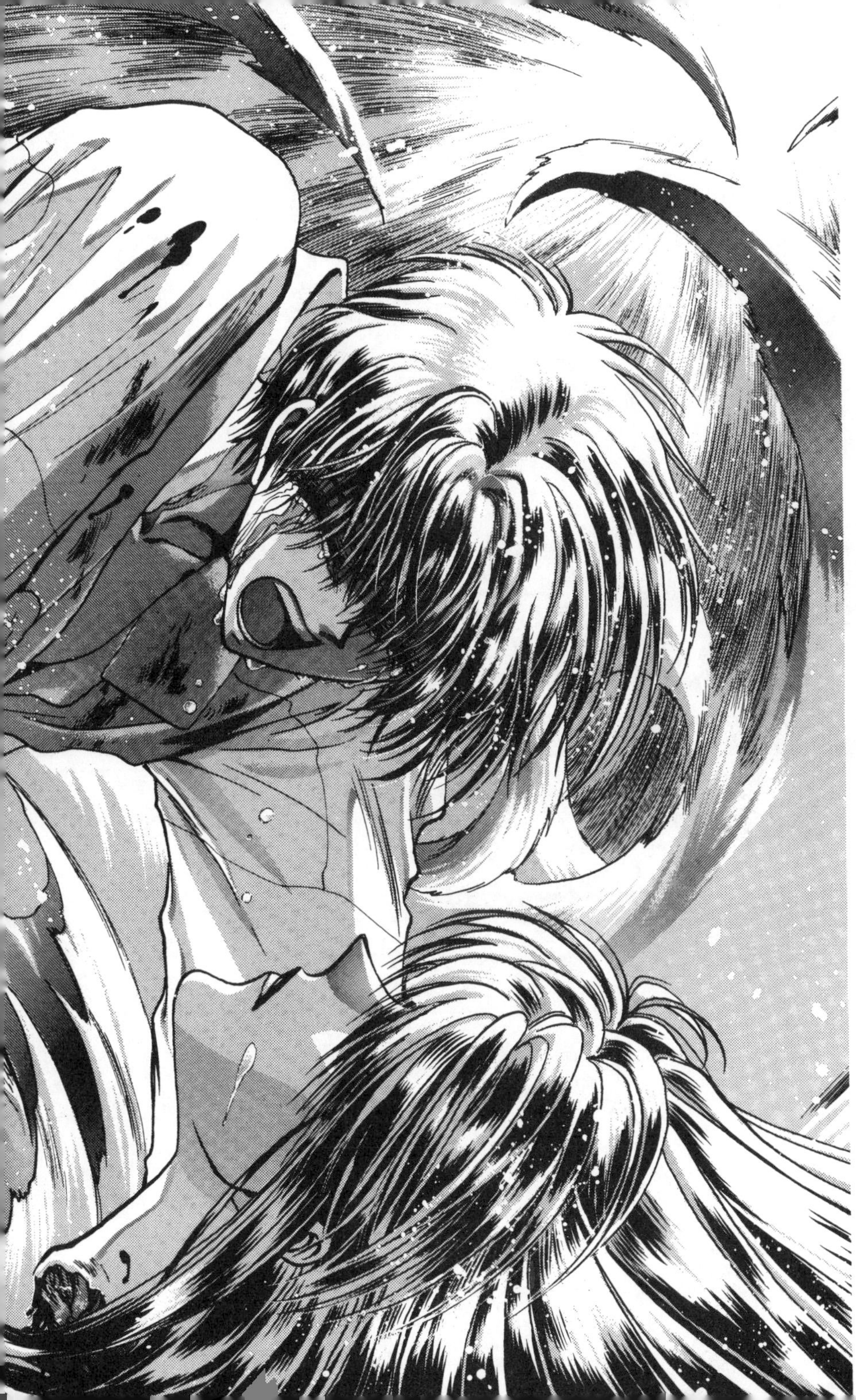

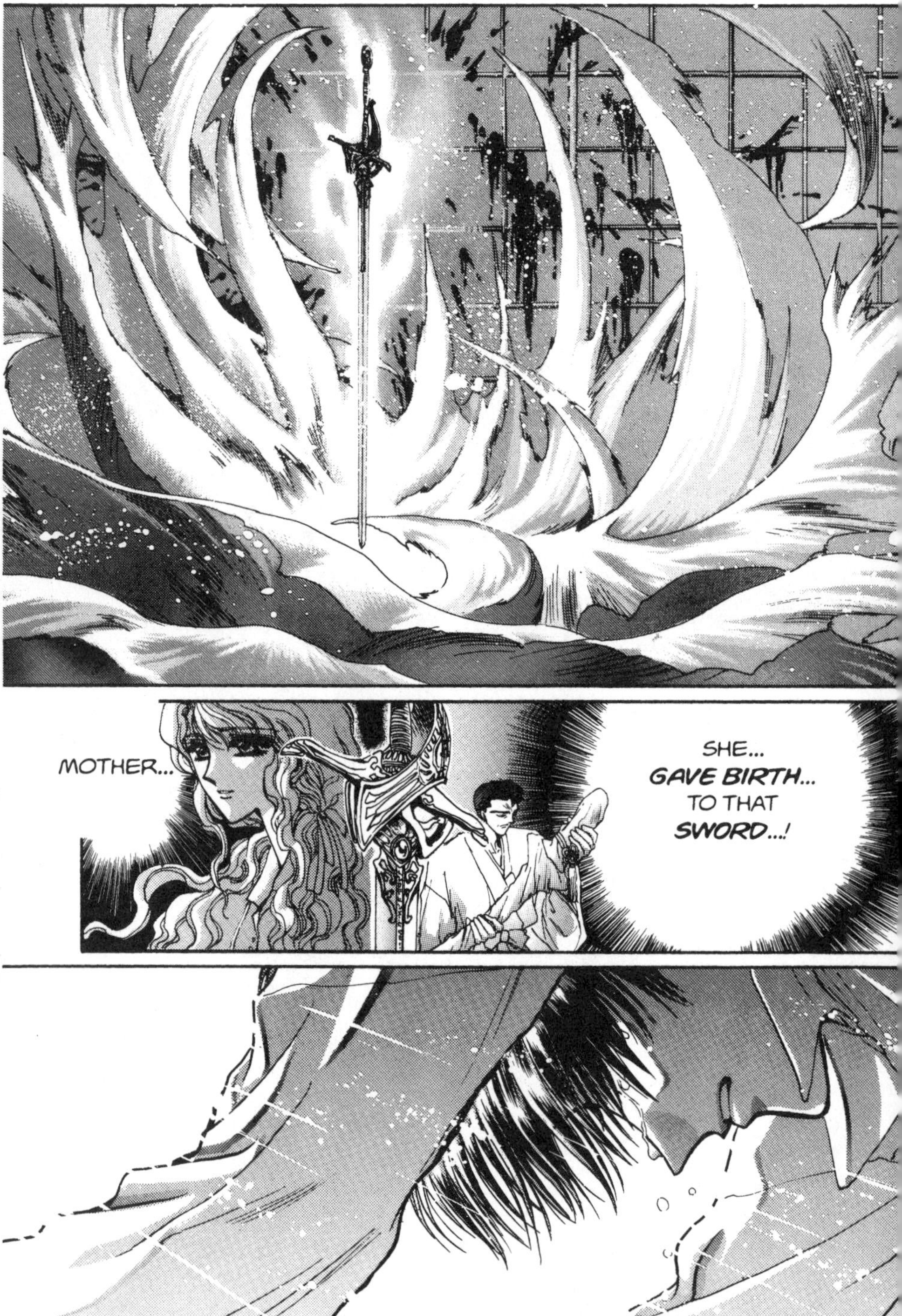
MOTHER...
SHE... GAVE BIRTH... TO THAT SWORD...!

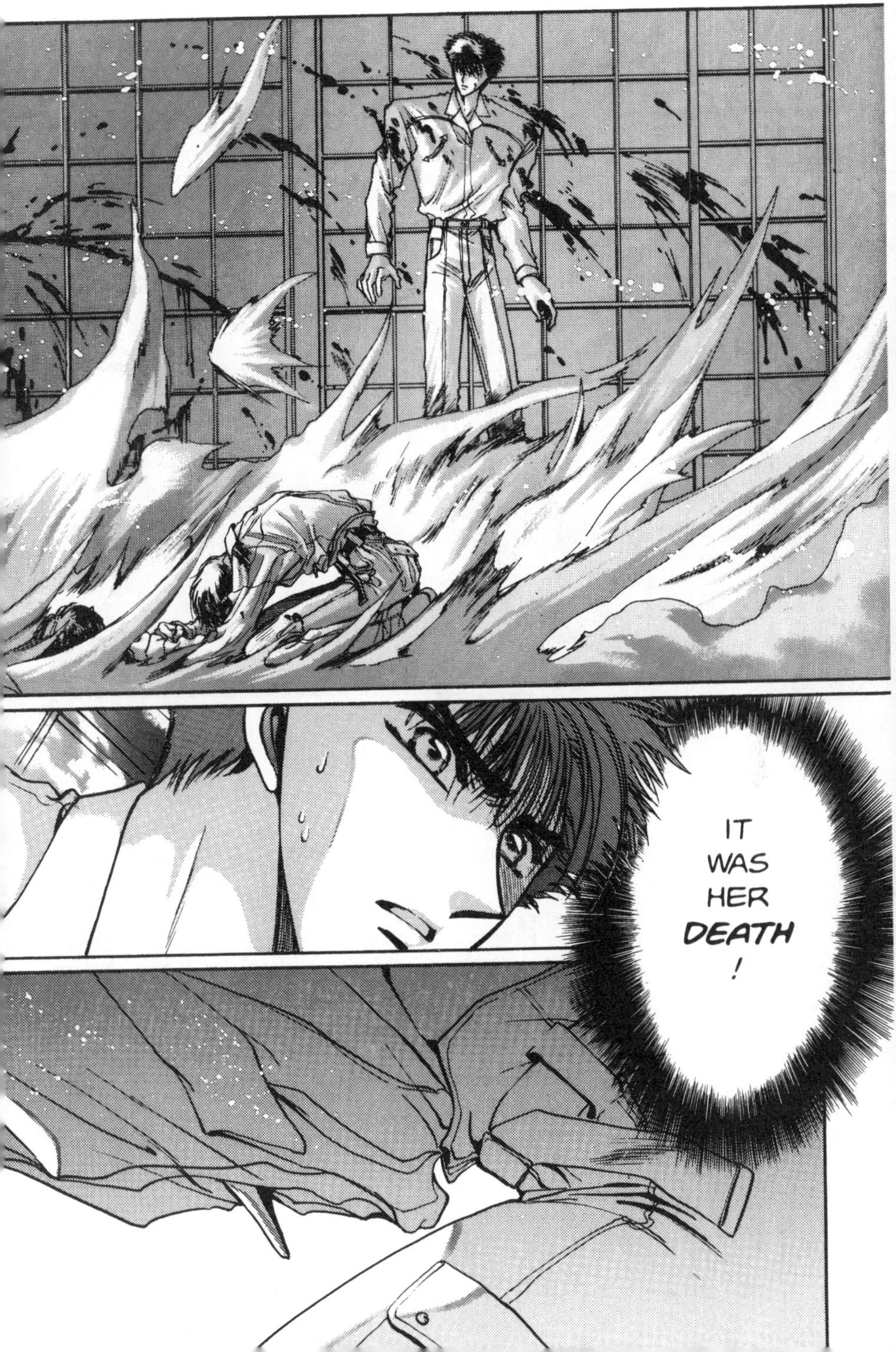
IT WAS HER DEATH!

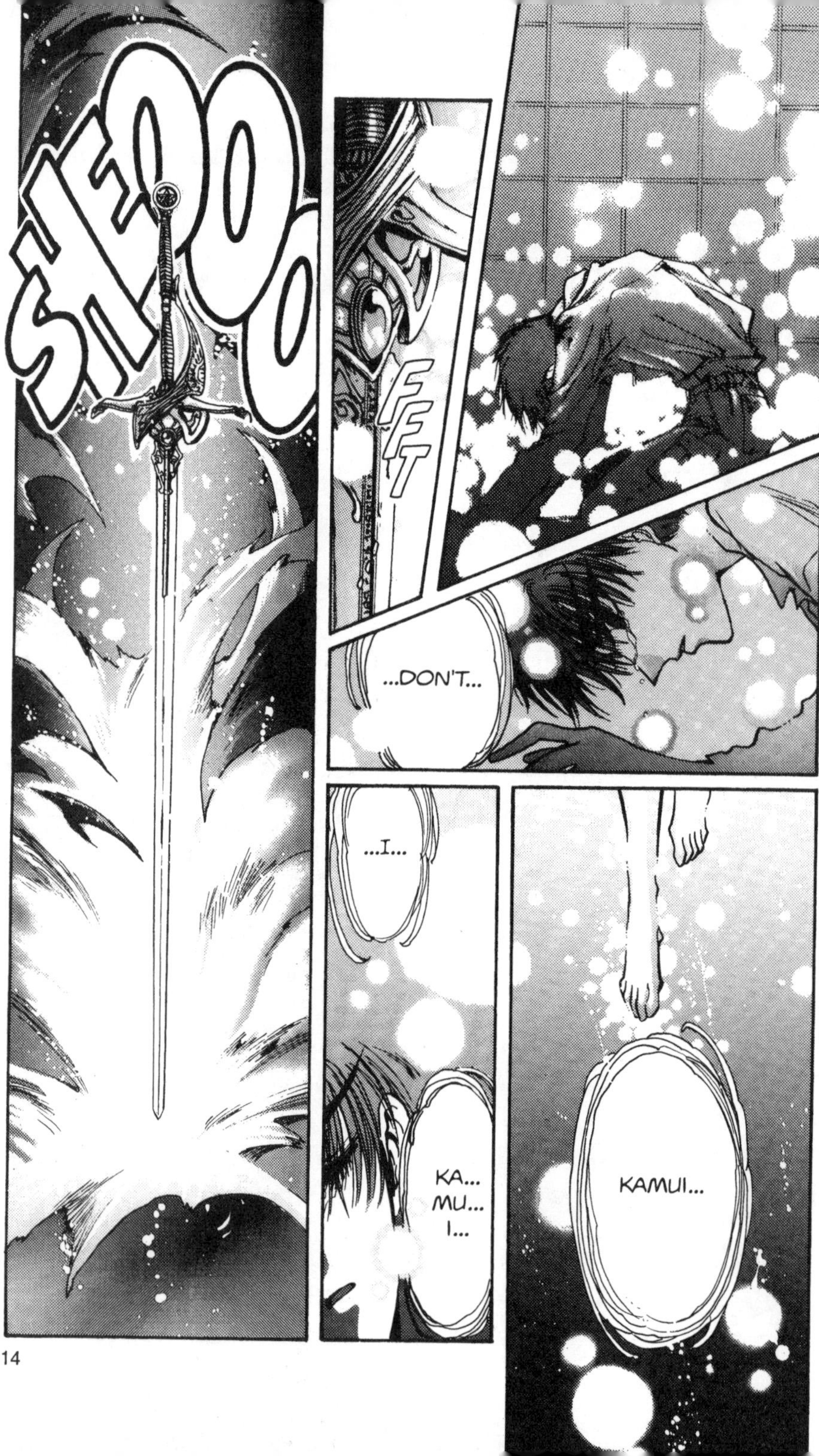
SHOOO
FFT
...DON'T...
...I...
KA...
MU...
I...
KAMUI...

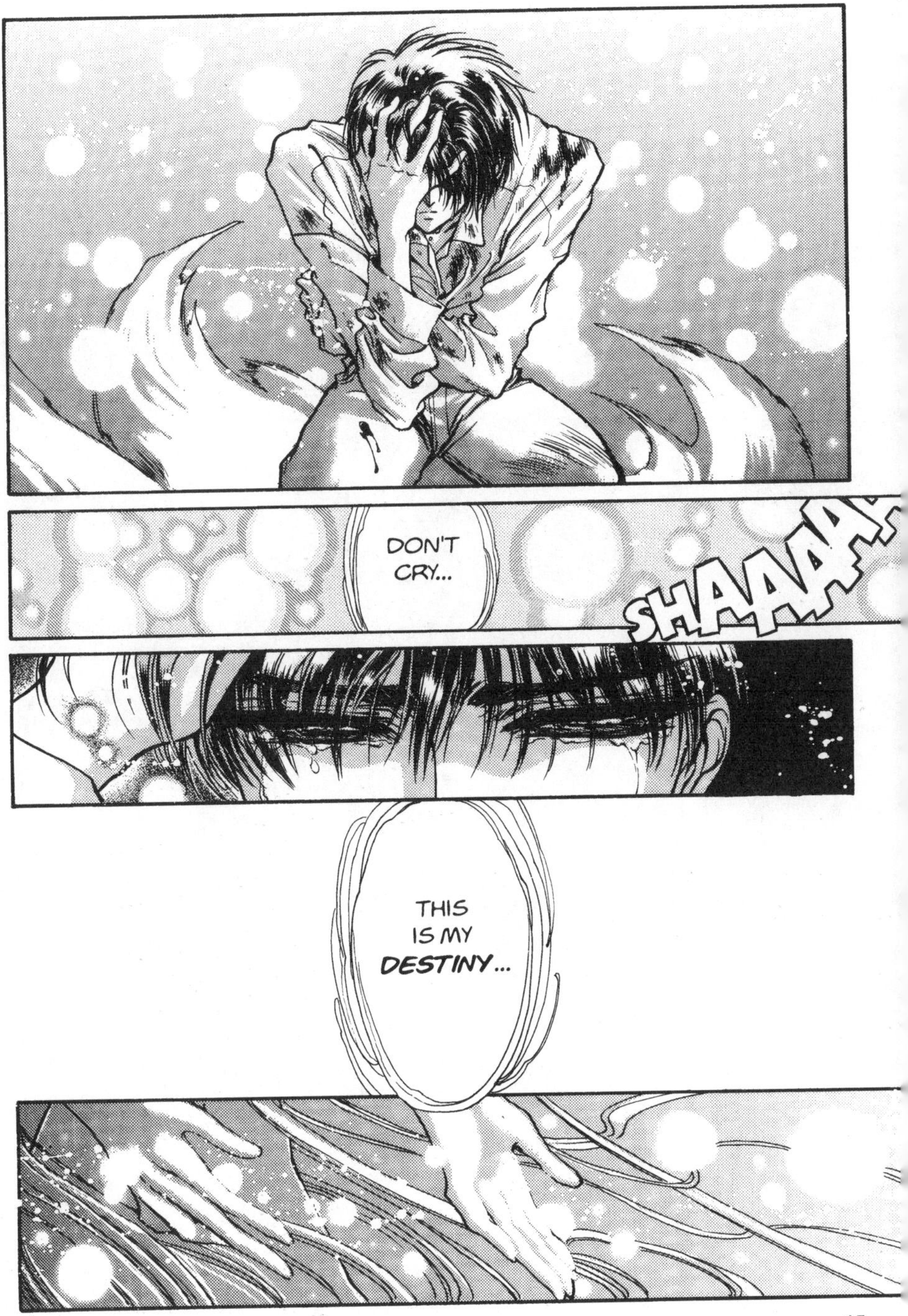
DON'T CRY...
SHAAAA
THIS IS MY DESTINY...

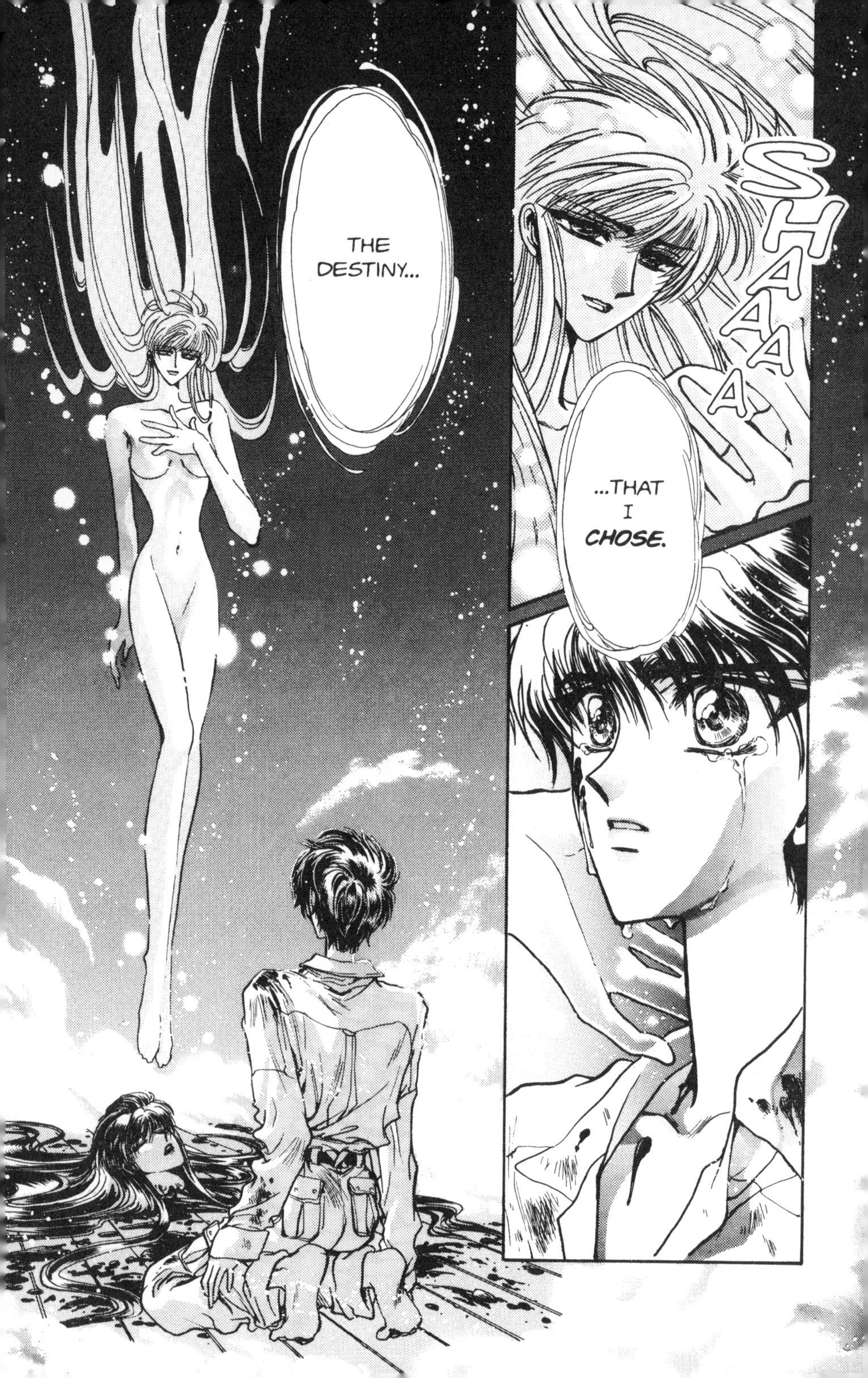
THE DESTINY...
SHAAAA
...THAT I CHOSE.

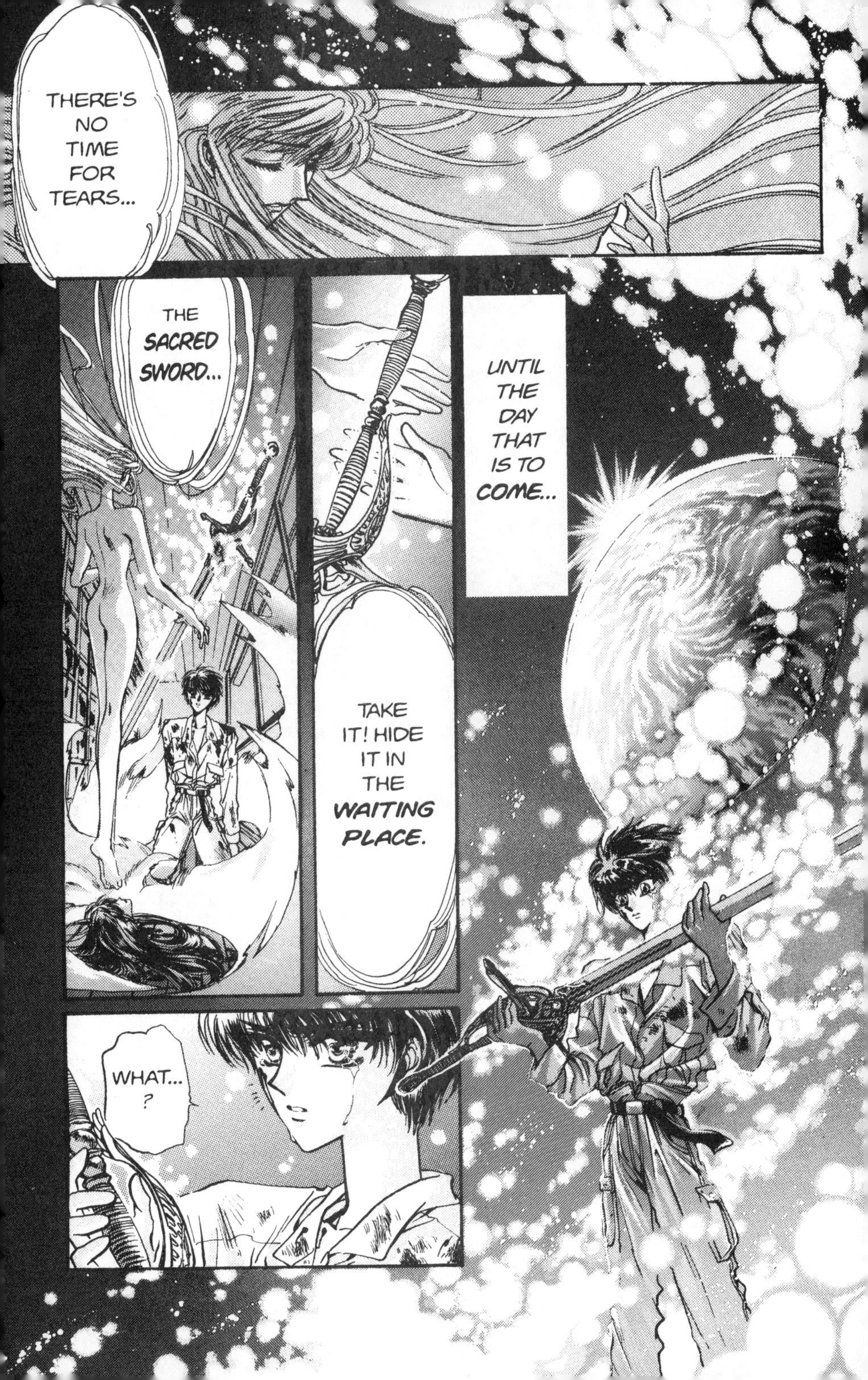
THERE'S NO TIME FOR TEARS...
THE SACRED SWORD...
TAKE IT! HIDE IT IN THE WAITING PLACE.
UNTIL THE DAY THAT IS TO COME...
WHAT... ?

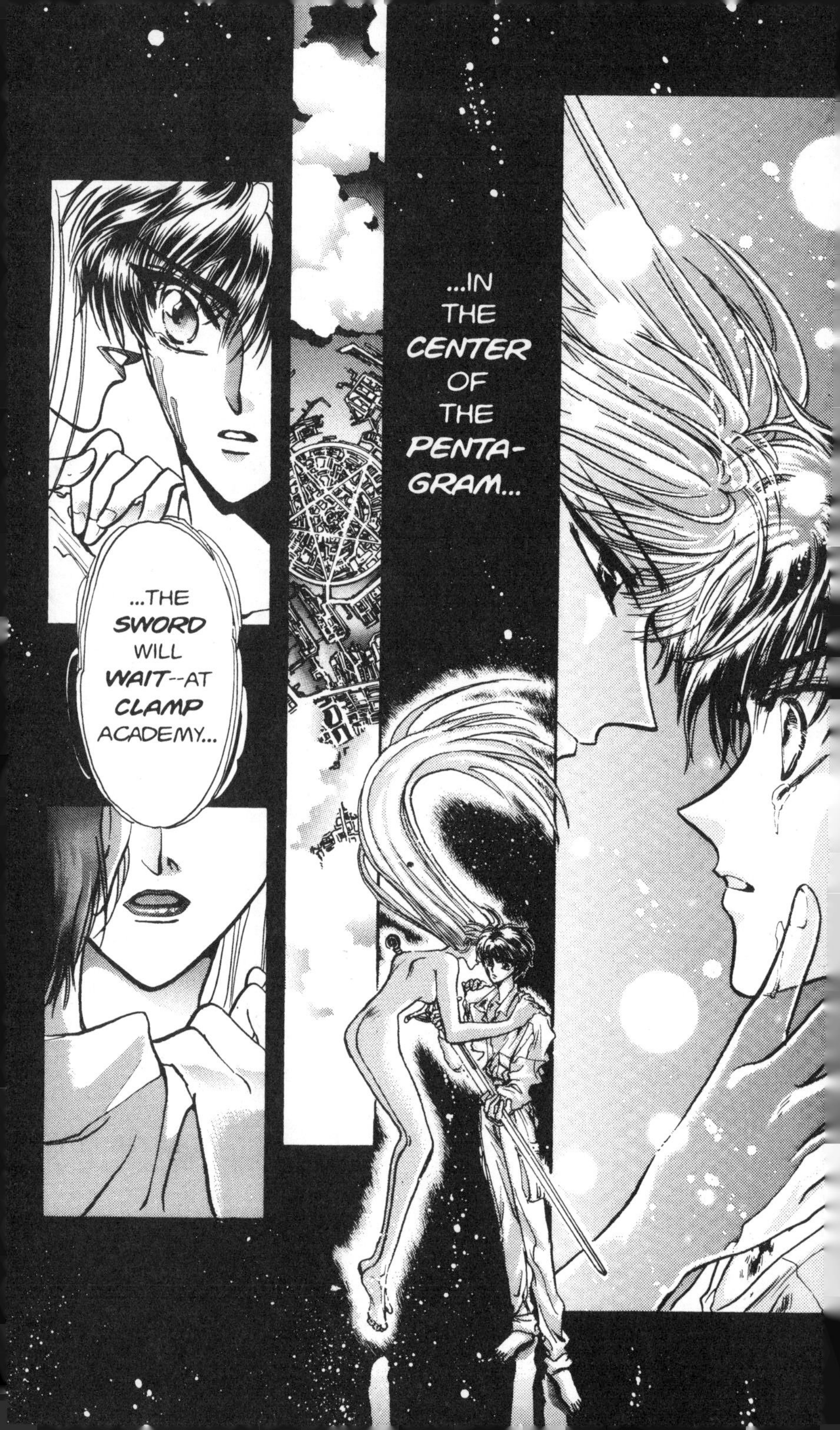
...THE SWORD WILL WAIT--AT CLAMP ACADEMY...
...IN THE CENTER OF THE PENTAGRAM...

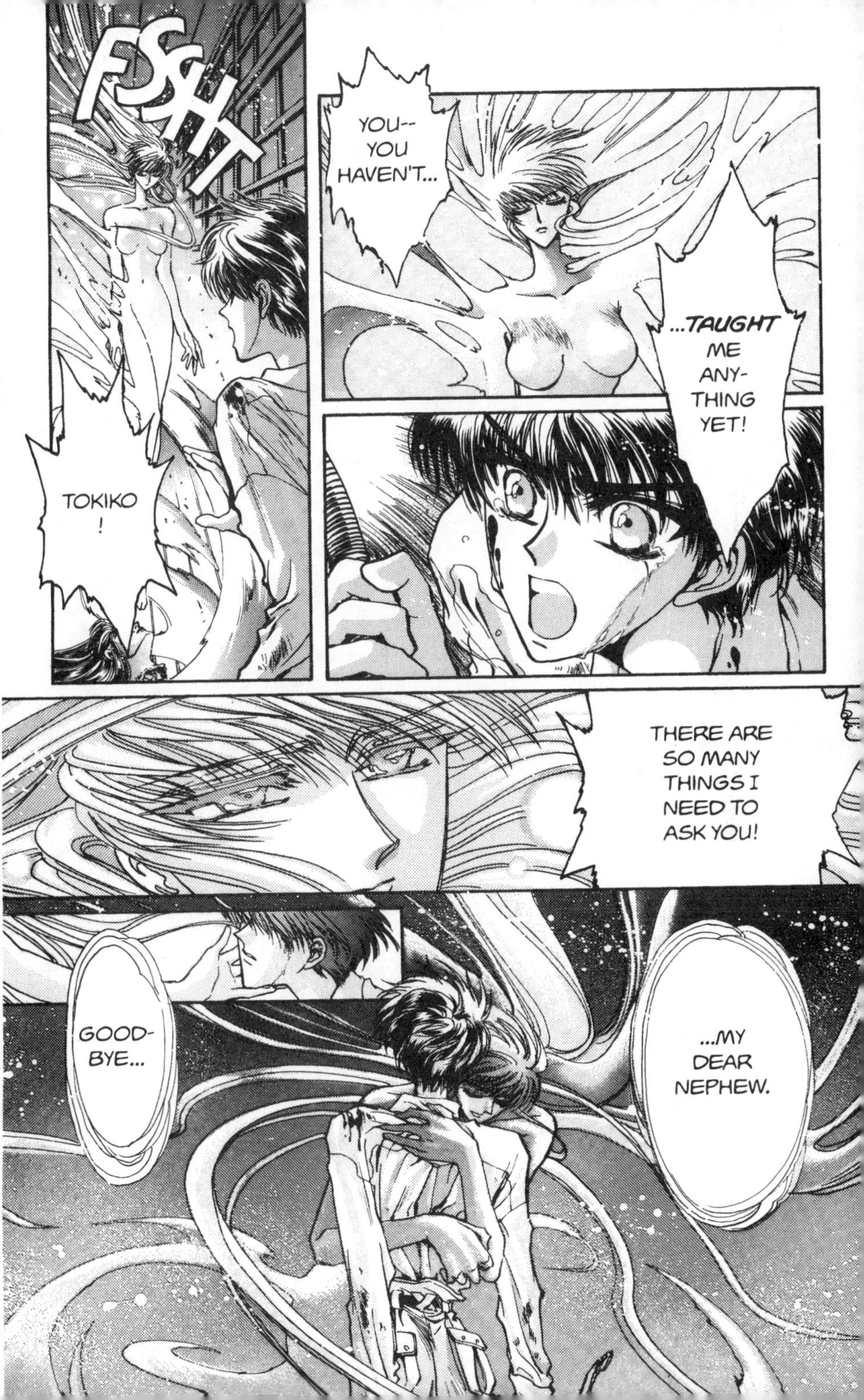
FSHT
TOKIKO!
YOU-- YOU HAVEN'T...
...TAUGHT ME ANYTHING YET!
THERE ARE SO MANY THINGS I NEED TO ASK YOU!
GOOD-BYE...
...MY DEAR NEPHEW.

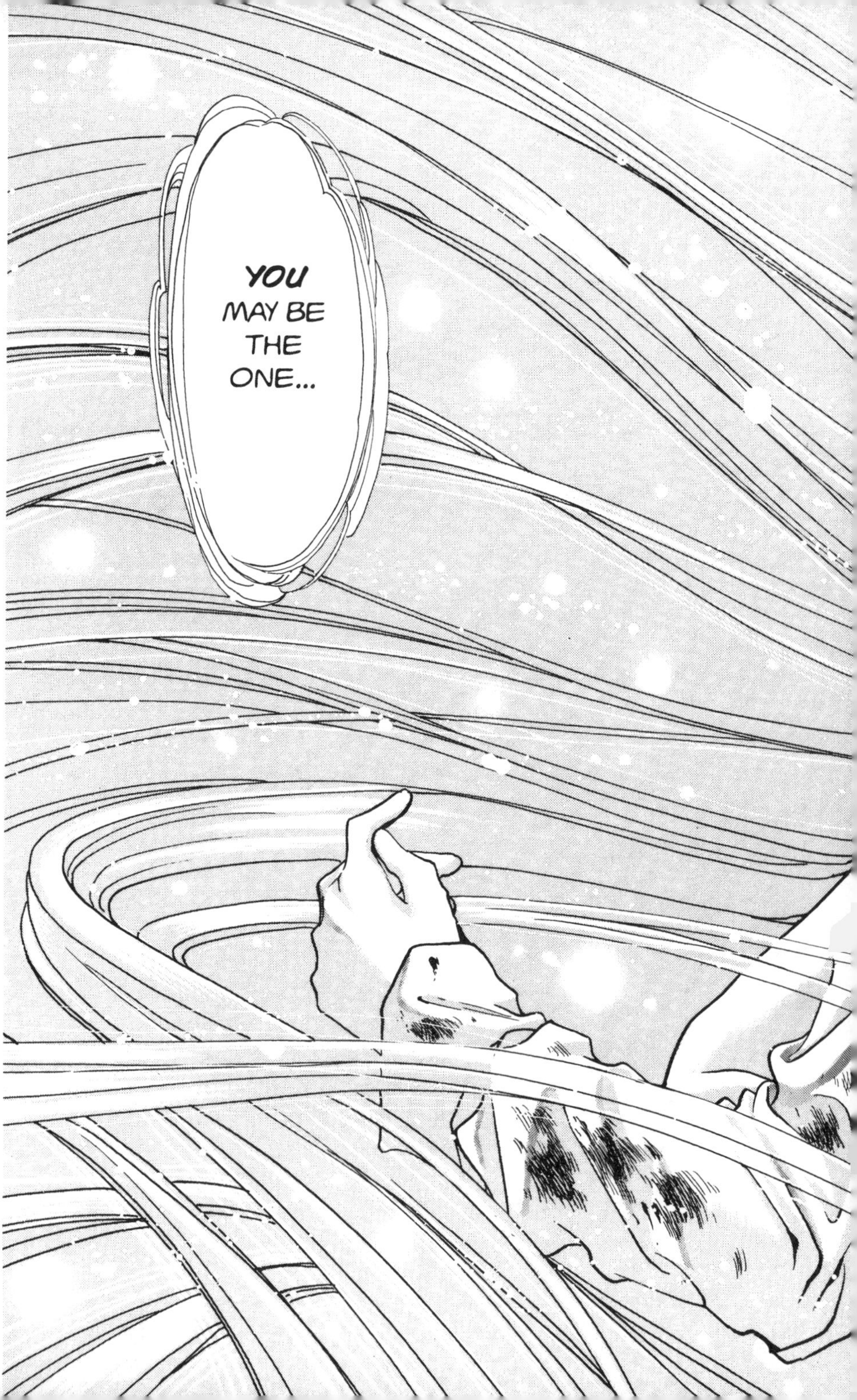
YOU MAY BE THE ONE...

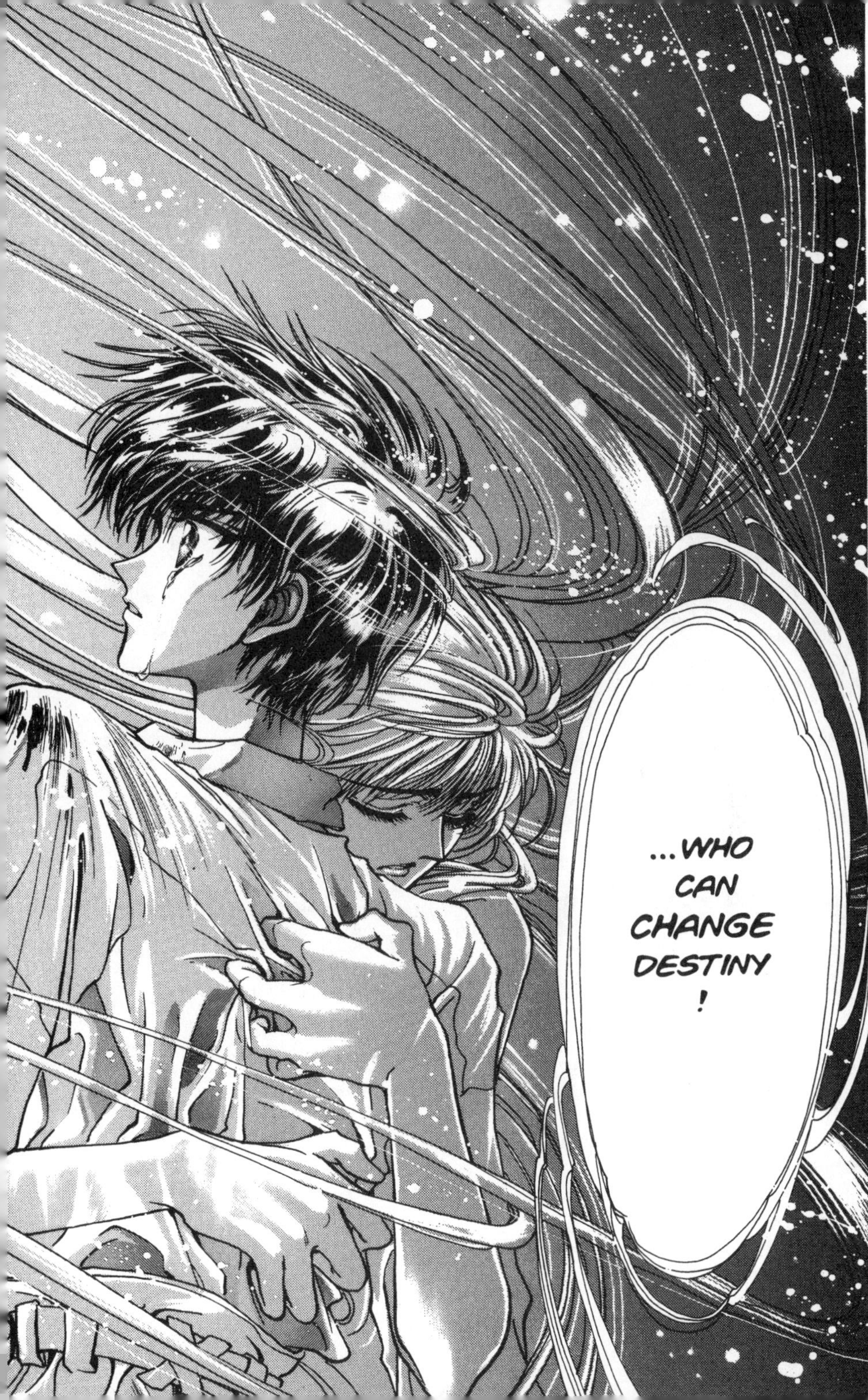
...WHO CAN CHANGE DESTINY !

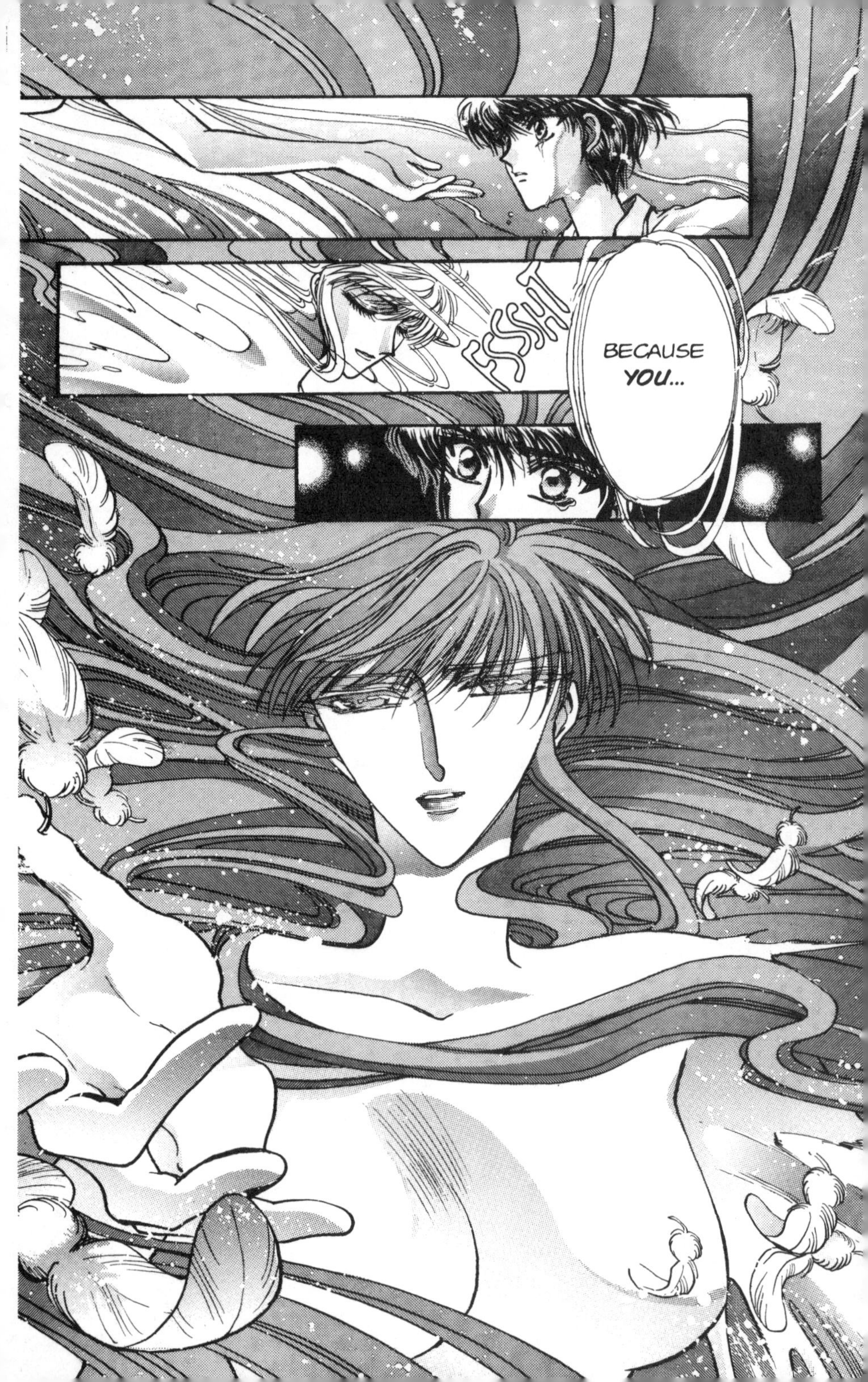
FSSHT
BECAUSE YOU...

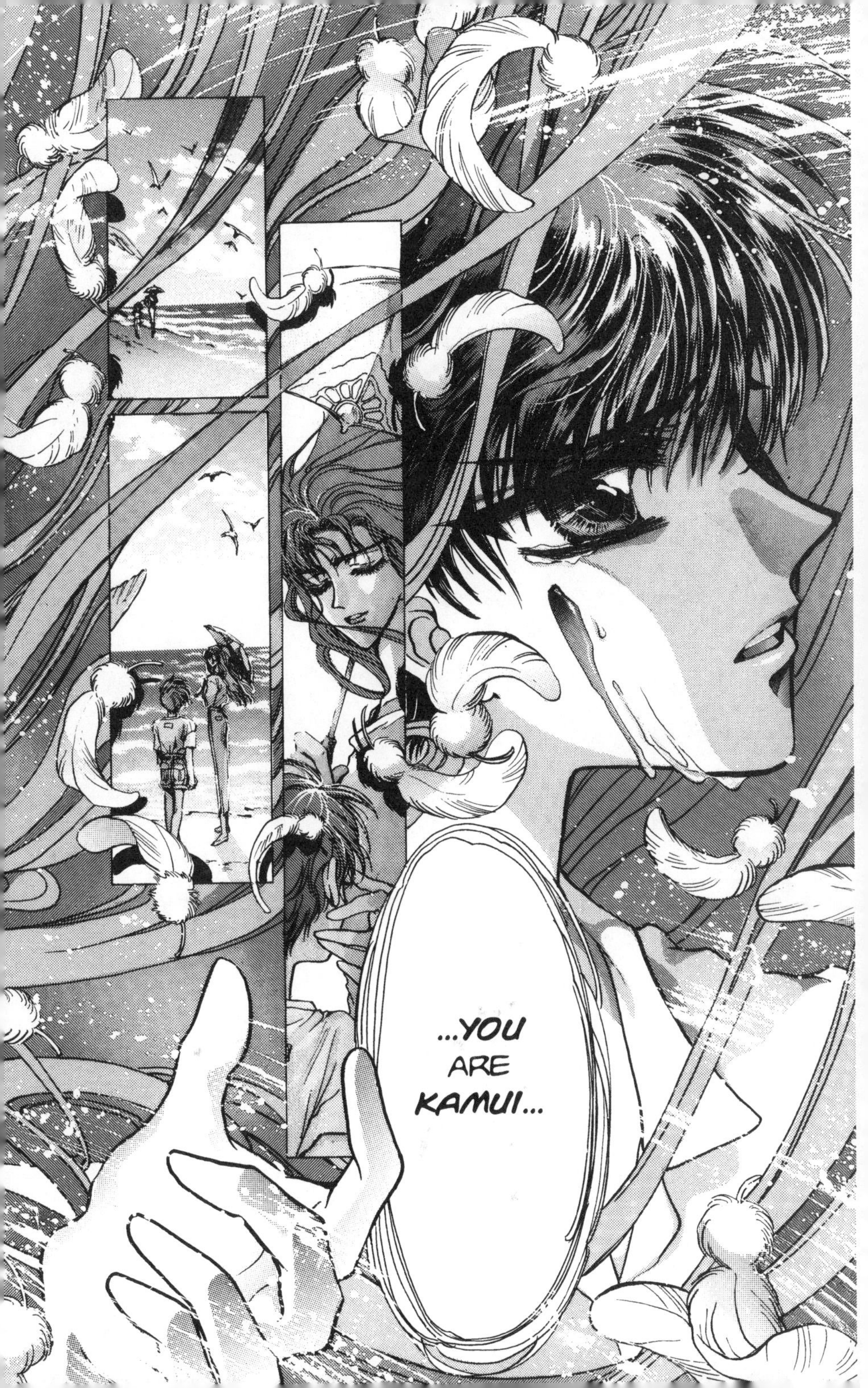
...YOU ARE KAMUI...

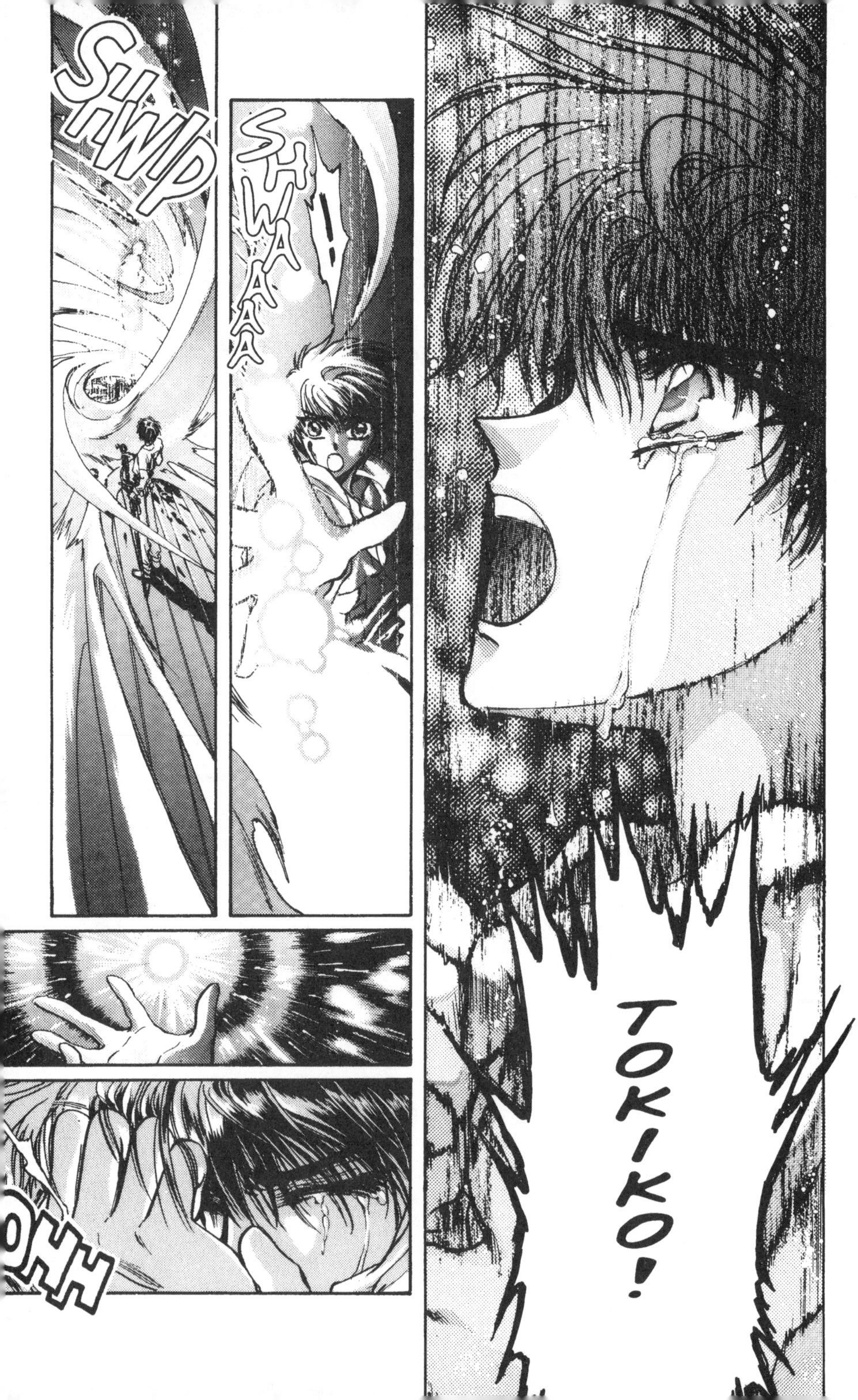
SHWIP
SHWAAAAA
!
OHH
TOKIKO!

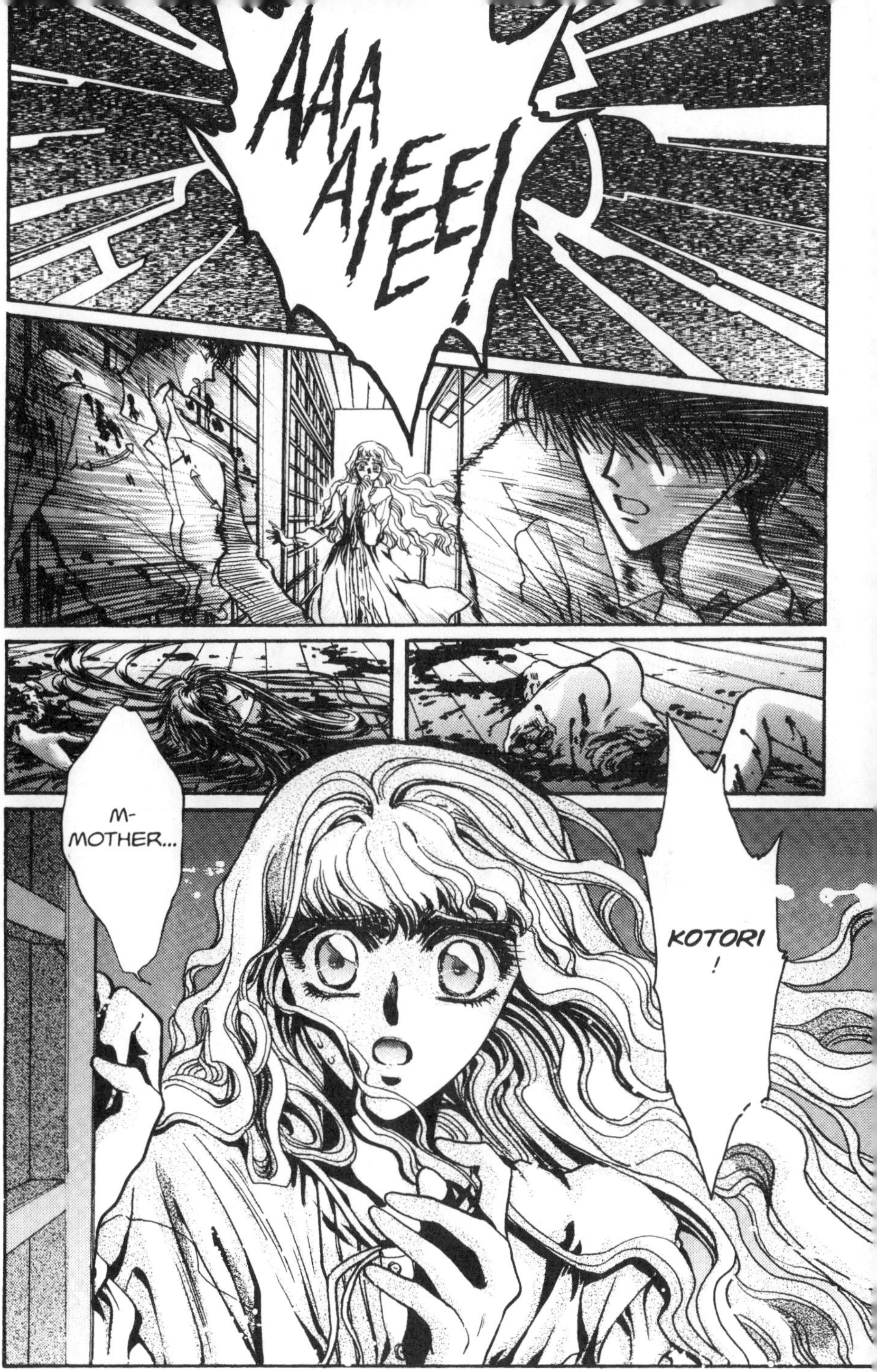
AAAAIEEEE!
M-MOTHER...
KOTORI!

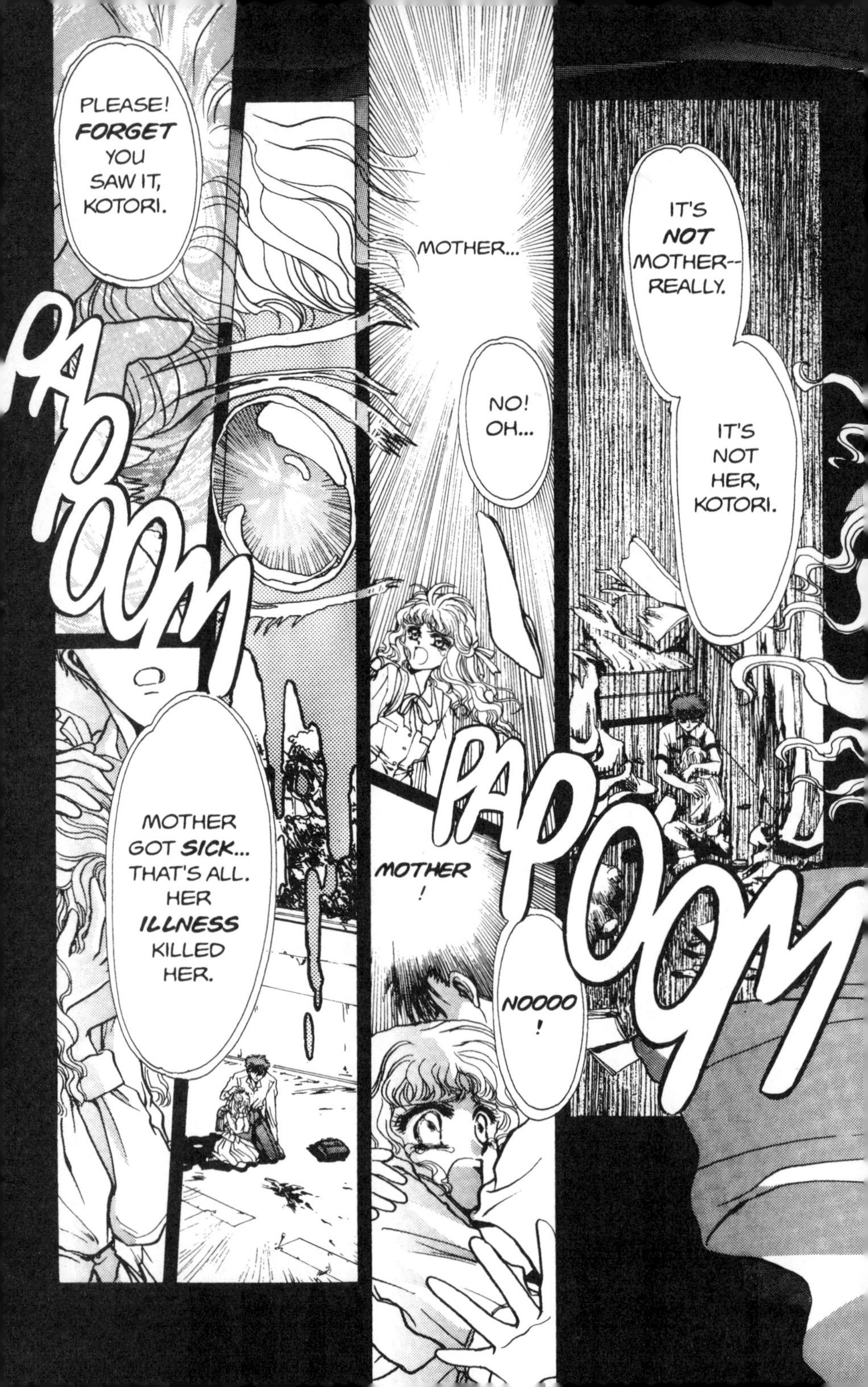
PLEASE! FORGET YOU SAW IT, KOTORI.
PAPOOM
MOTHER GOT SICK... THAT'S ALL. HER ILLNESS KILLED HER.
MOTHER...
NO! OH...
PAPOOM
MOTHER!
NOOOO!
IT'S NOT MOTHER--REALLY.
IT'S NOT HER, KOTORI.

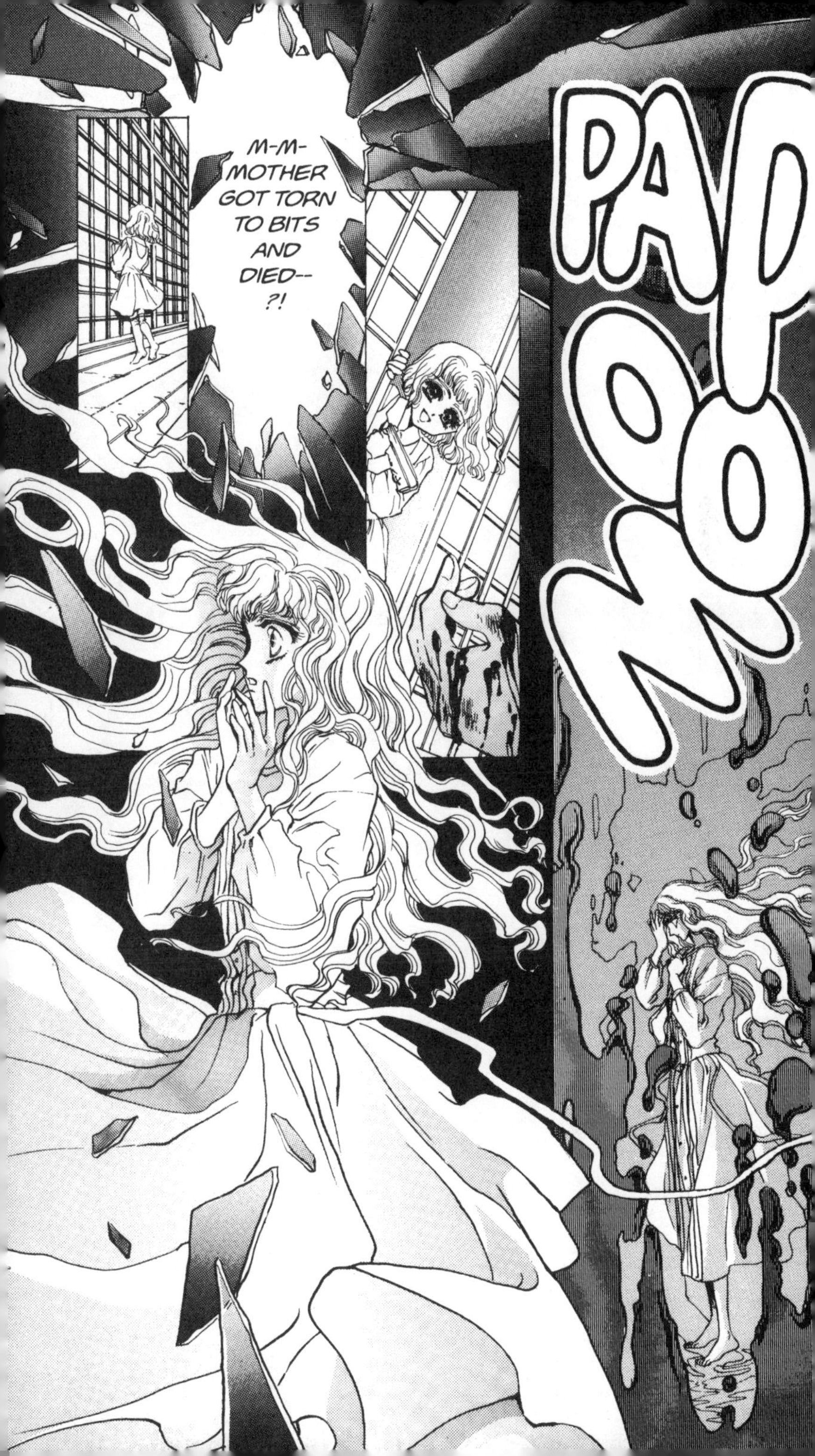
M-M-MOTHER GOT TORN TO BITS AND DIED--?!

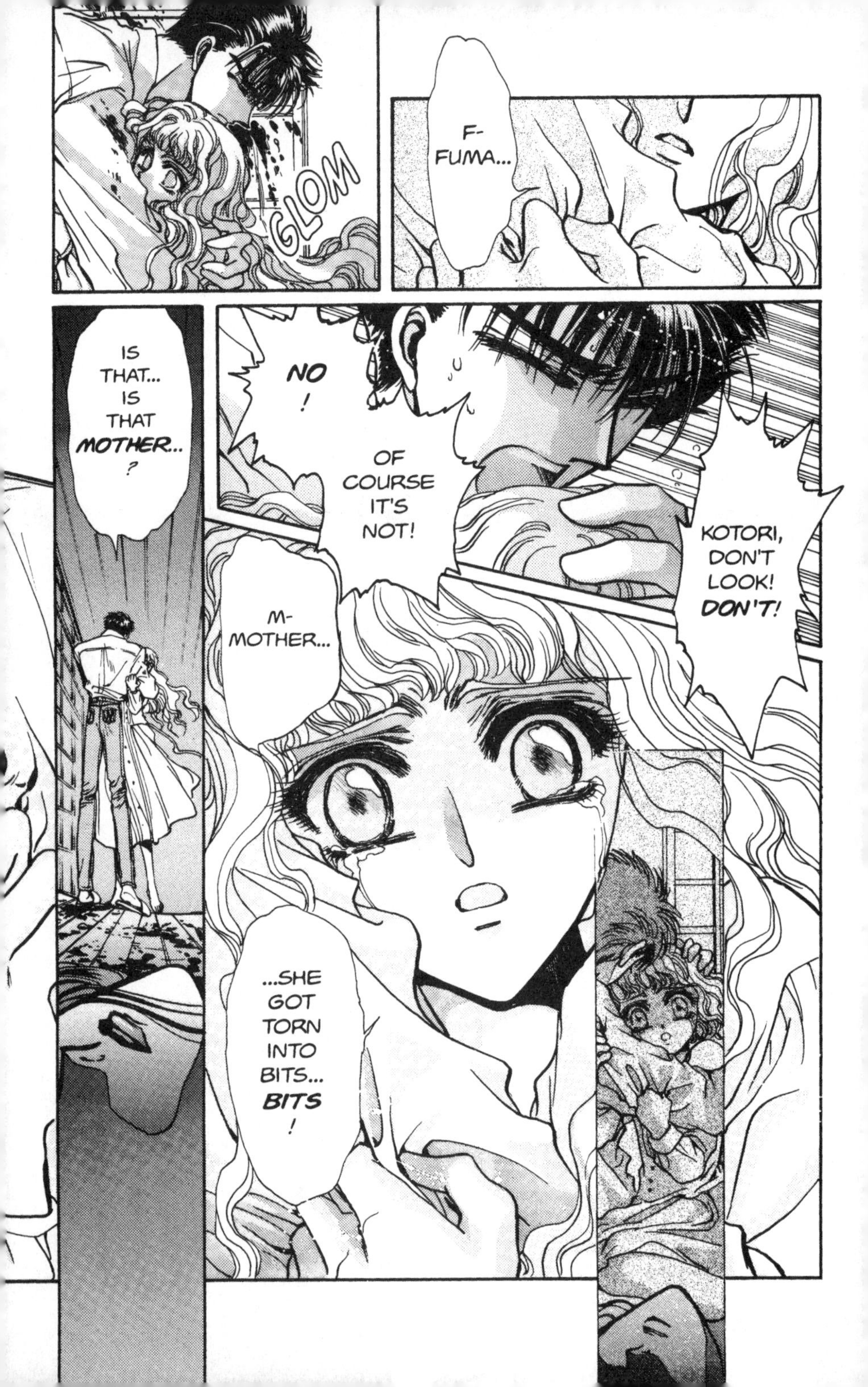
GLOM
F- FUMA...
IS THAT... IS THAT MOTHER...?
NO!
OF COURSE IT'S NOT!
KOTORI, DON'T LOOK! DON'T!
M- MOTHER...
...SHE GOT TORN INTO BITS... BITS!

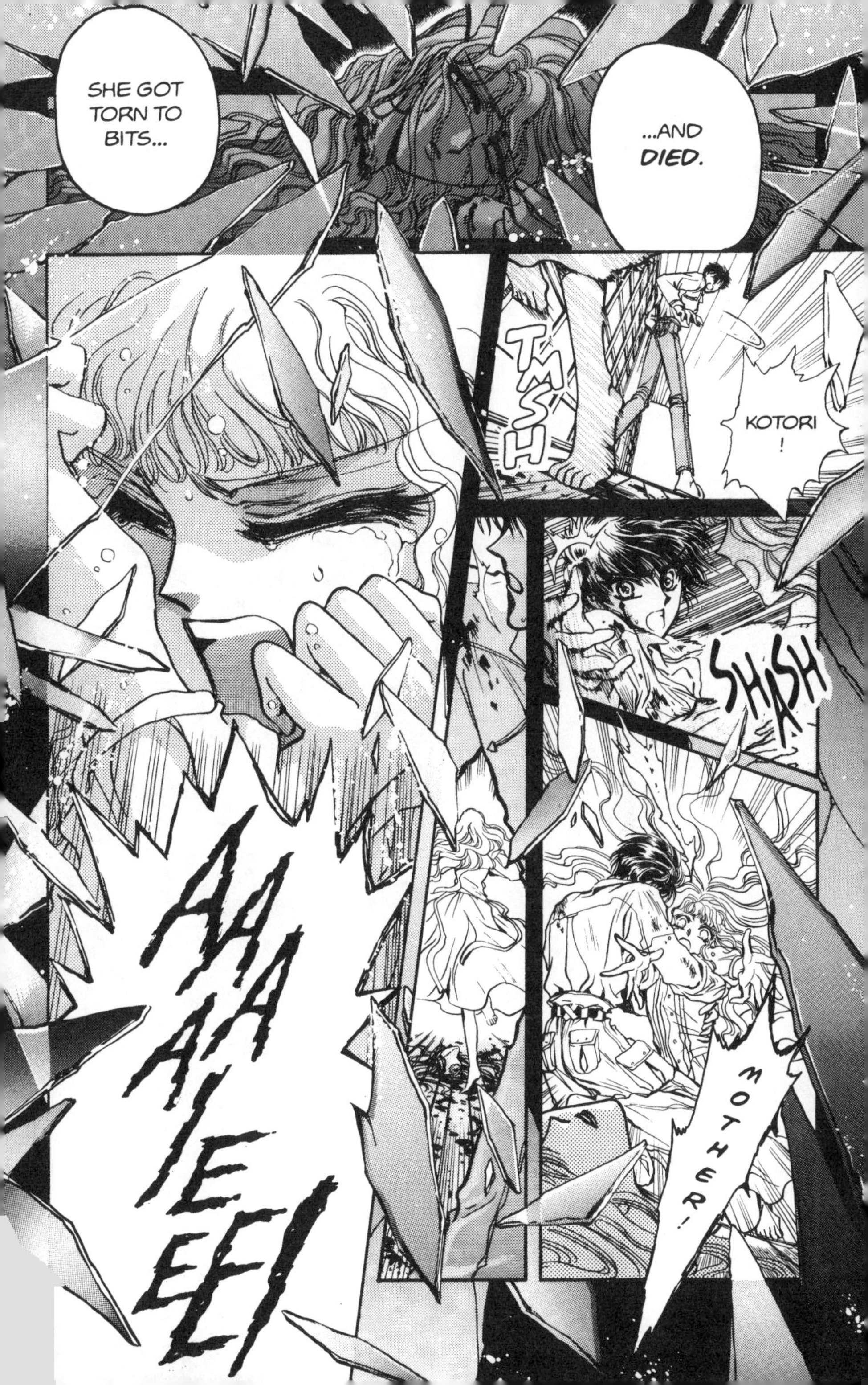
SHE GOT TORN TO BITS...
...AND DIED.
AAAAIIEEEE!
TMSH
KOTORI!
SHASH
MOTHER!

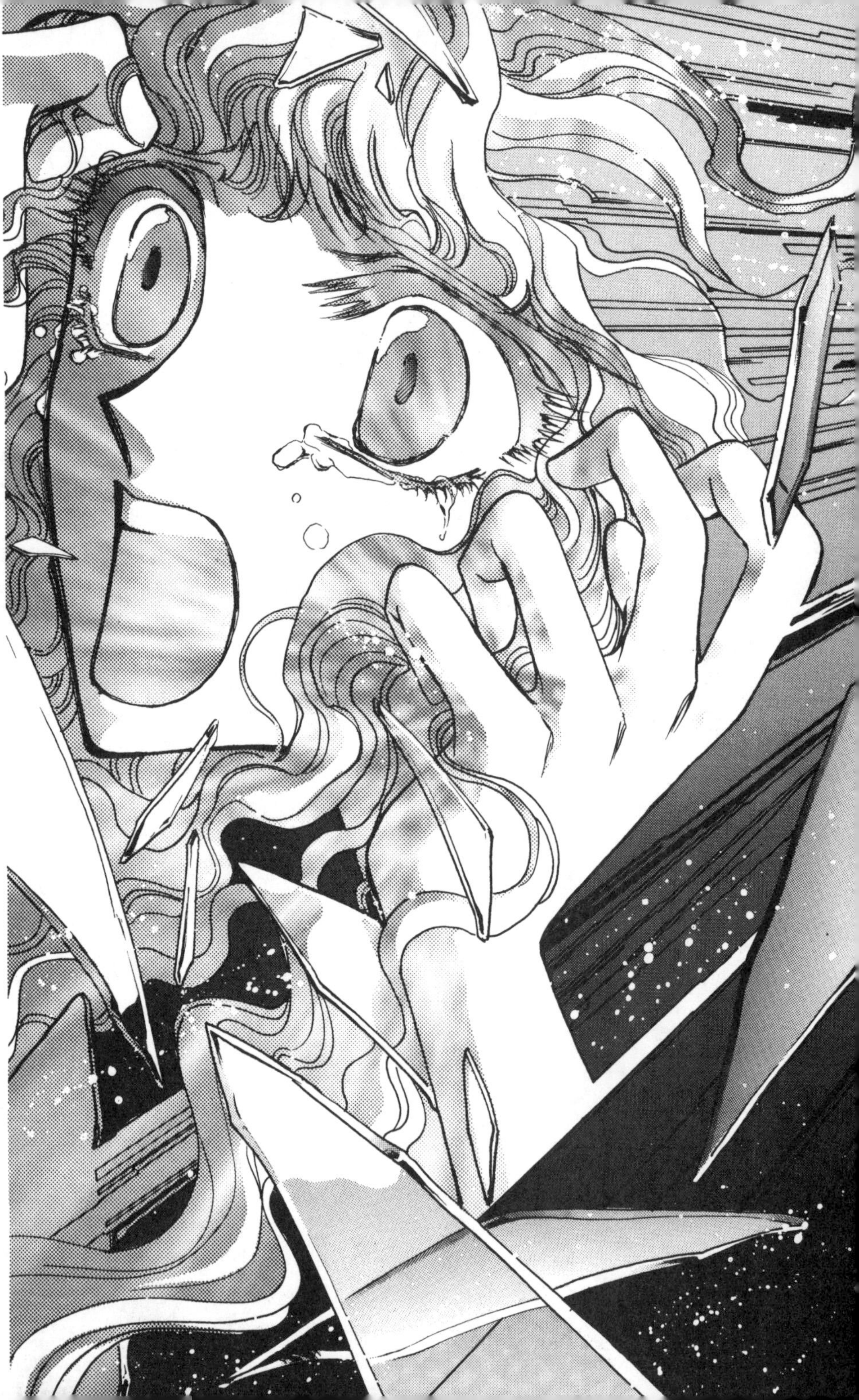

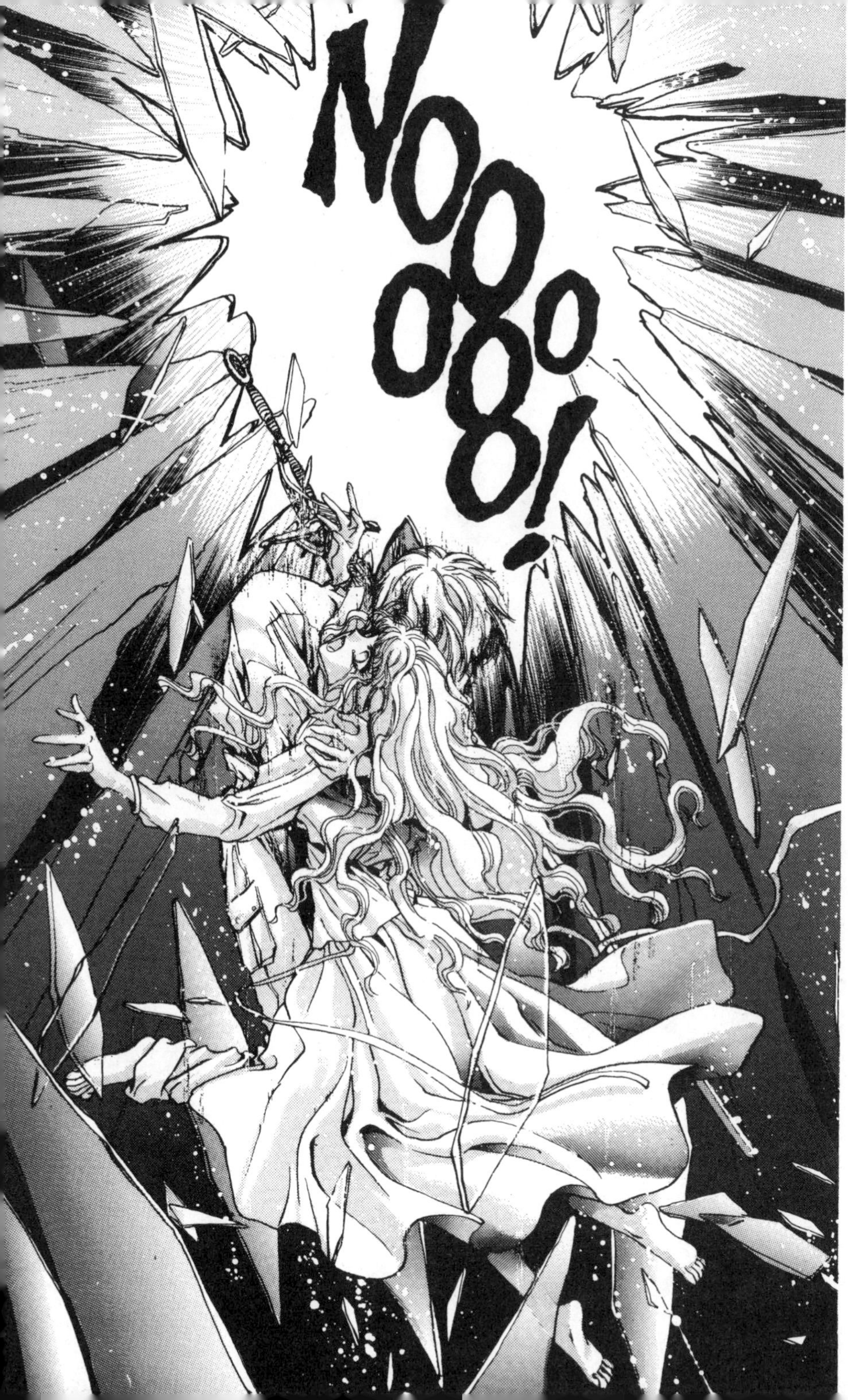
NOOOOOO!

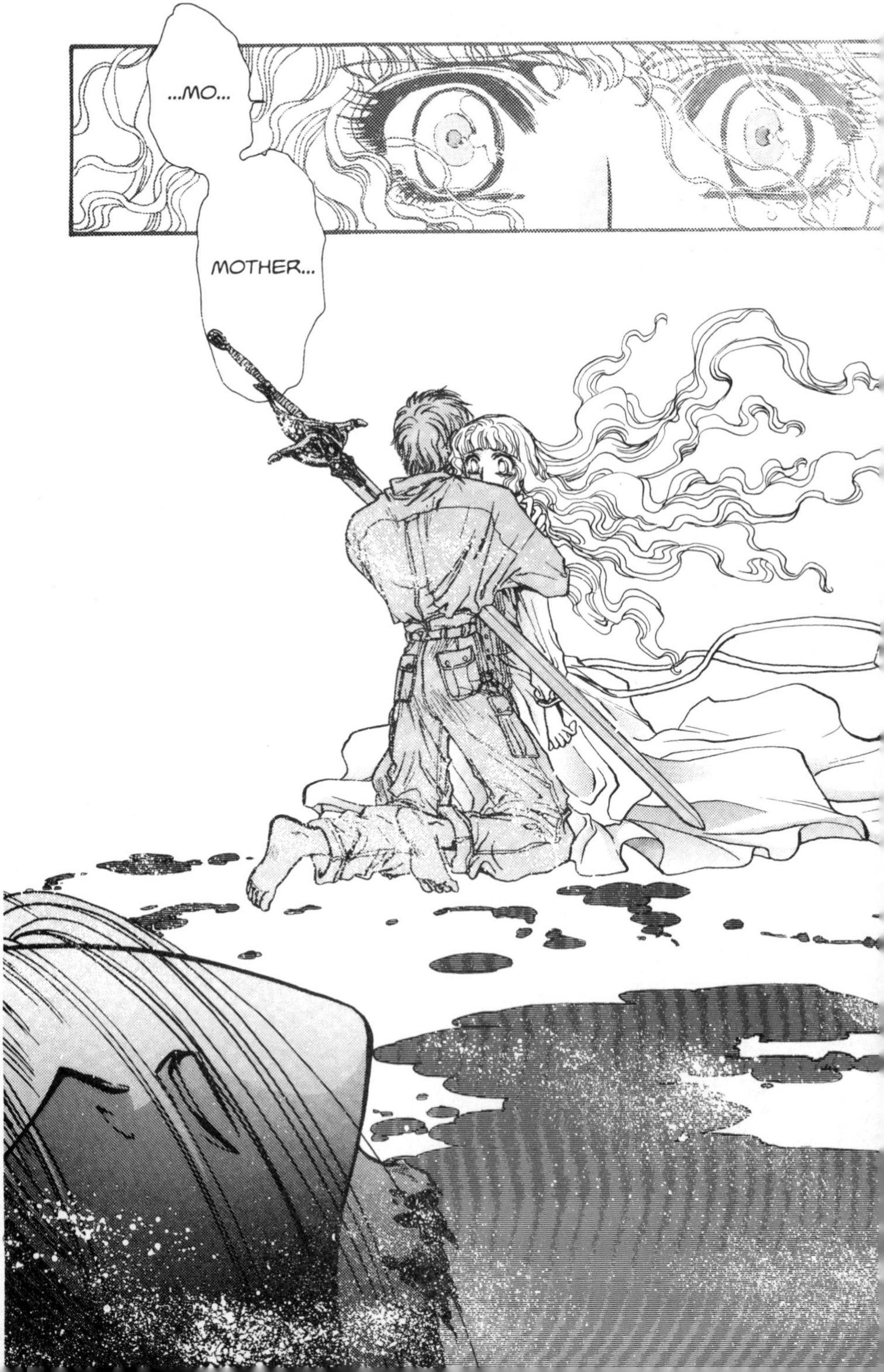
...MO...
MOTHER...

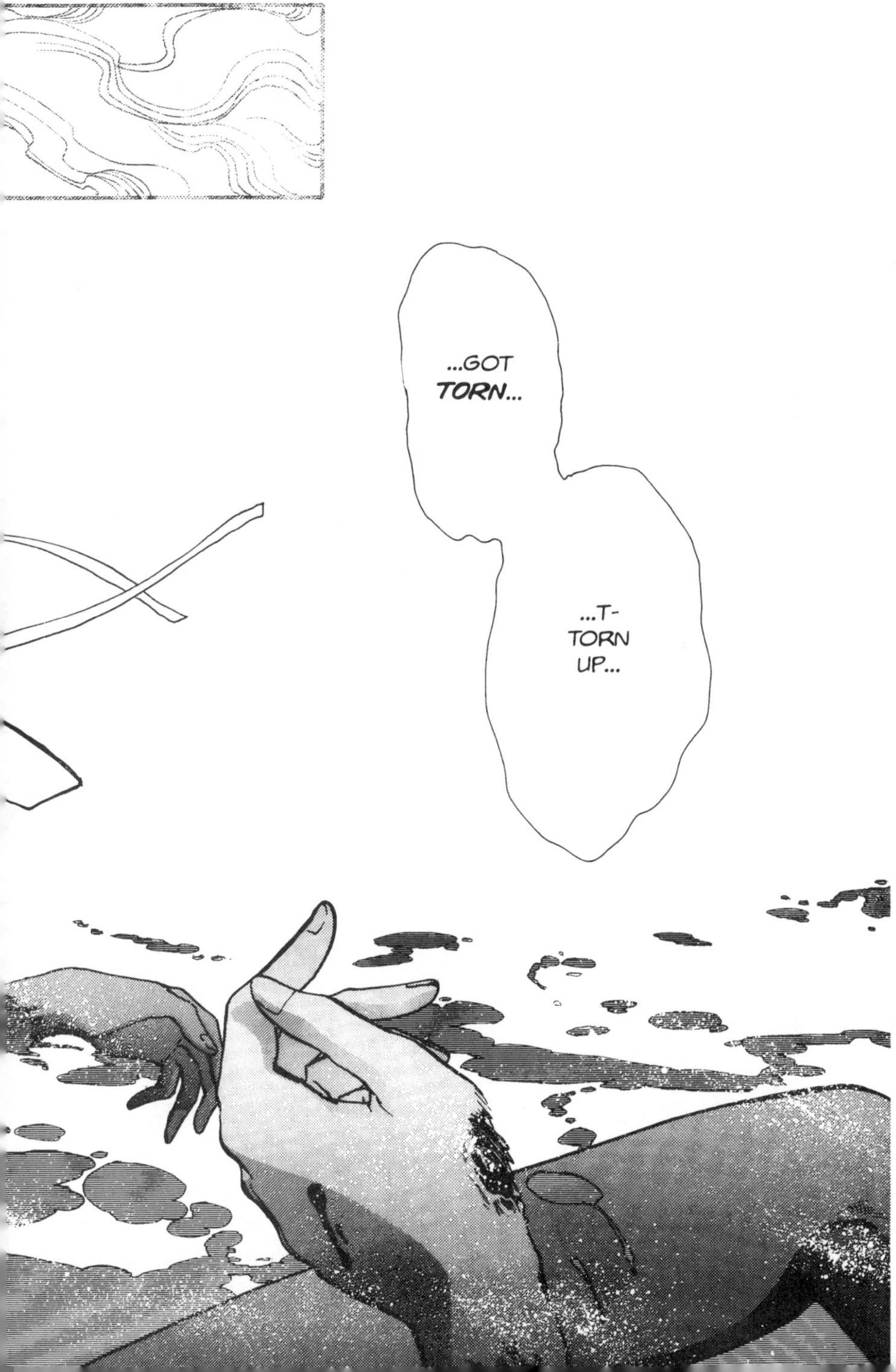
...GOT TORN...
...T-TORN UP...

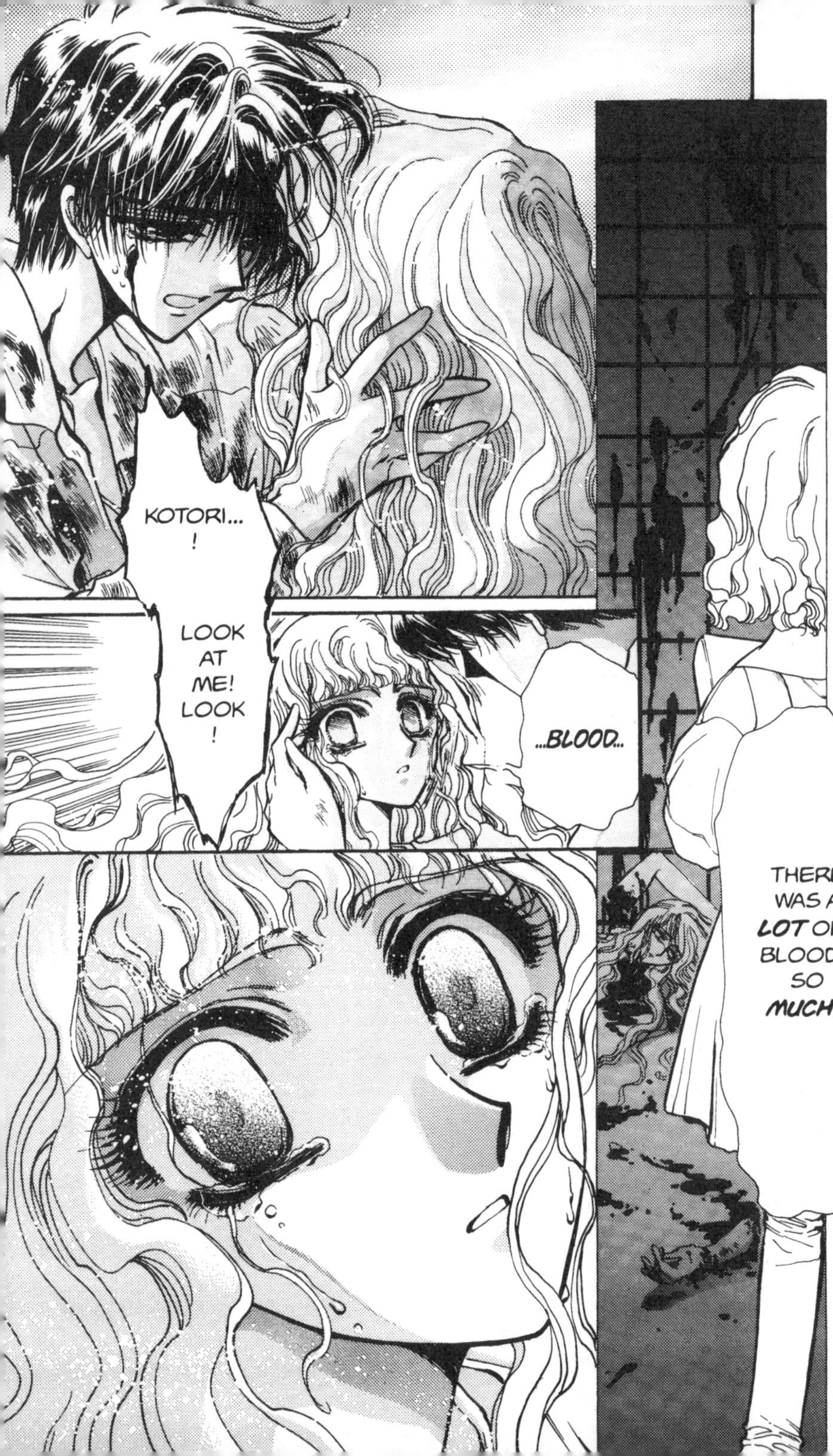
KOTORI... !
LOOK AT ME! LOOK !
...BLOOD...
THERE WAS A LOT OF... BLOOD... SO MUCH...

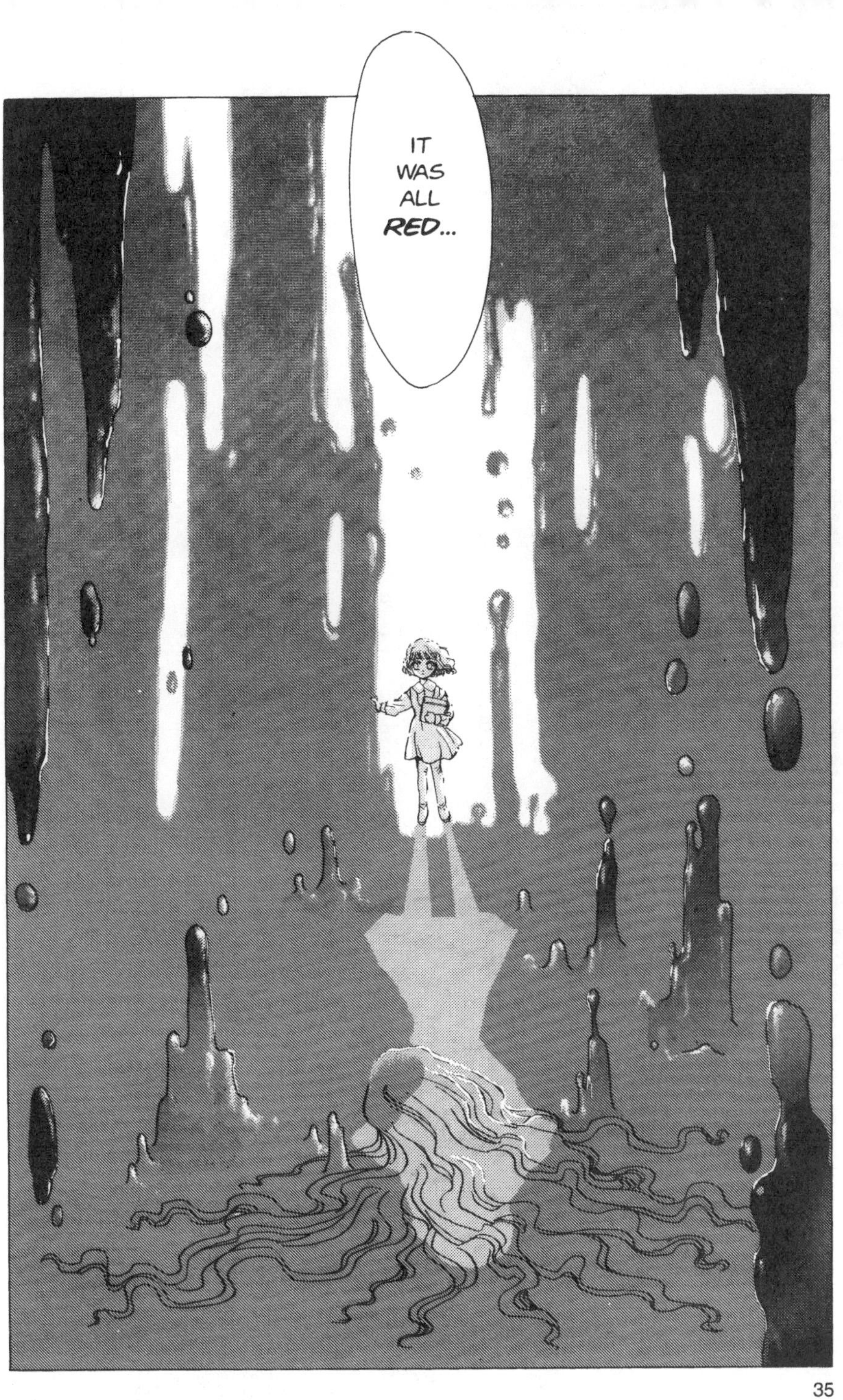
IT WAS ALL RED...

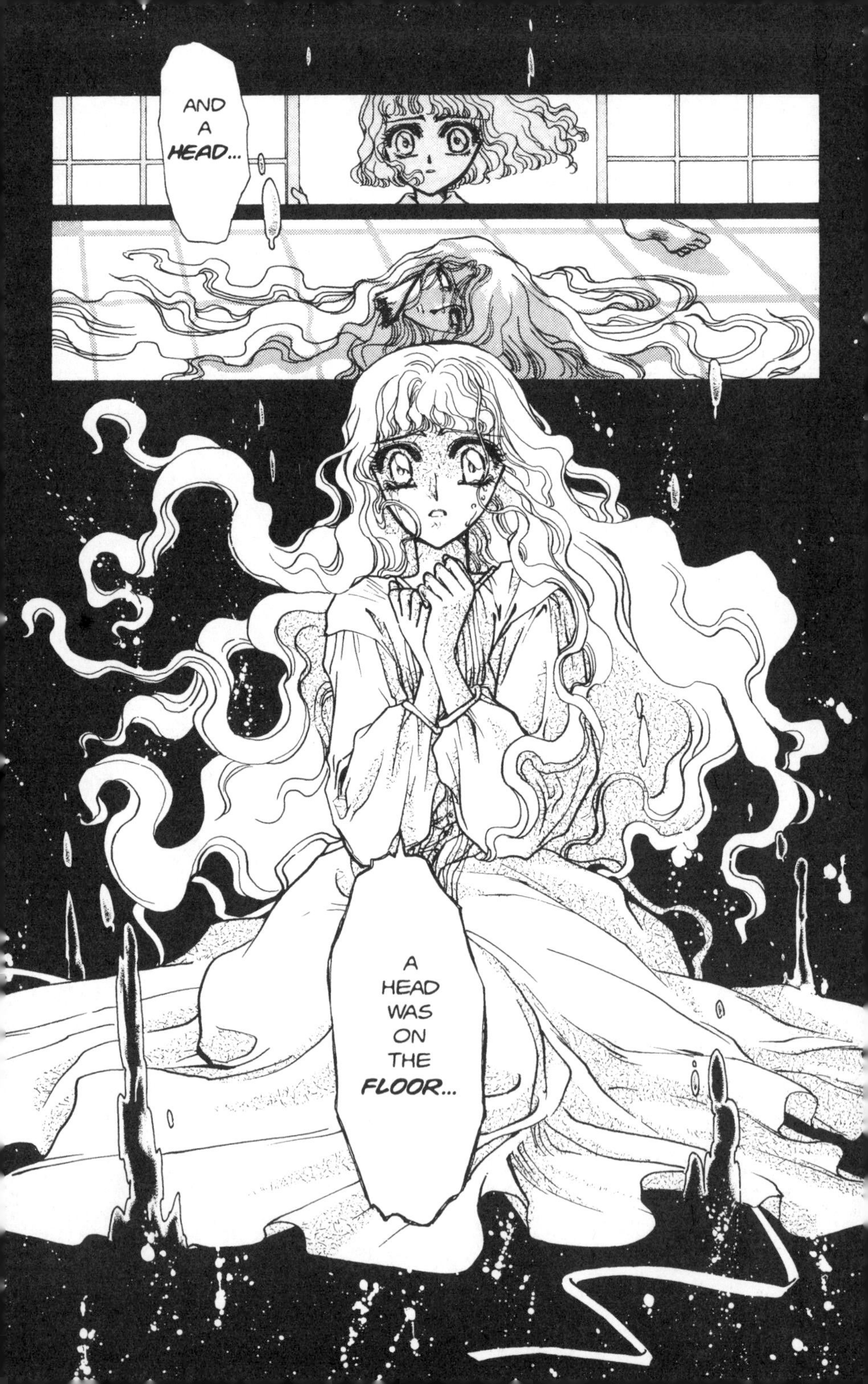
AND A HEAD...
A HEAD WAS ON THE FLOOR...

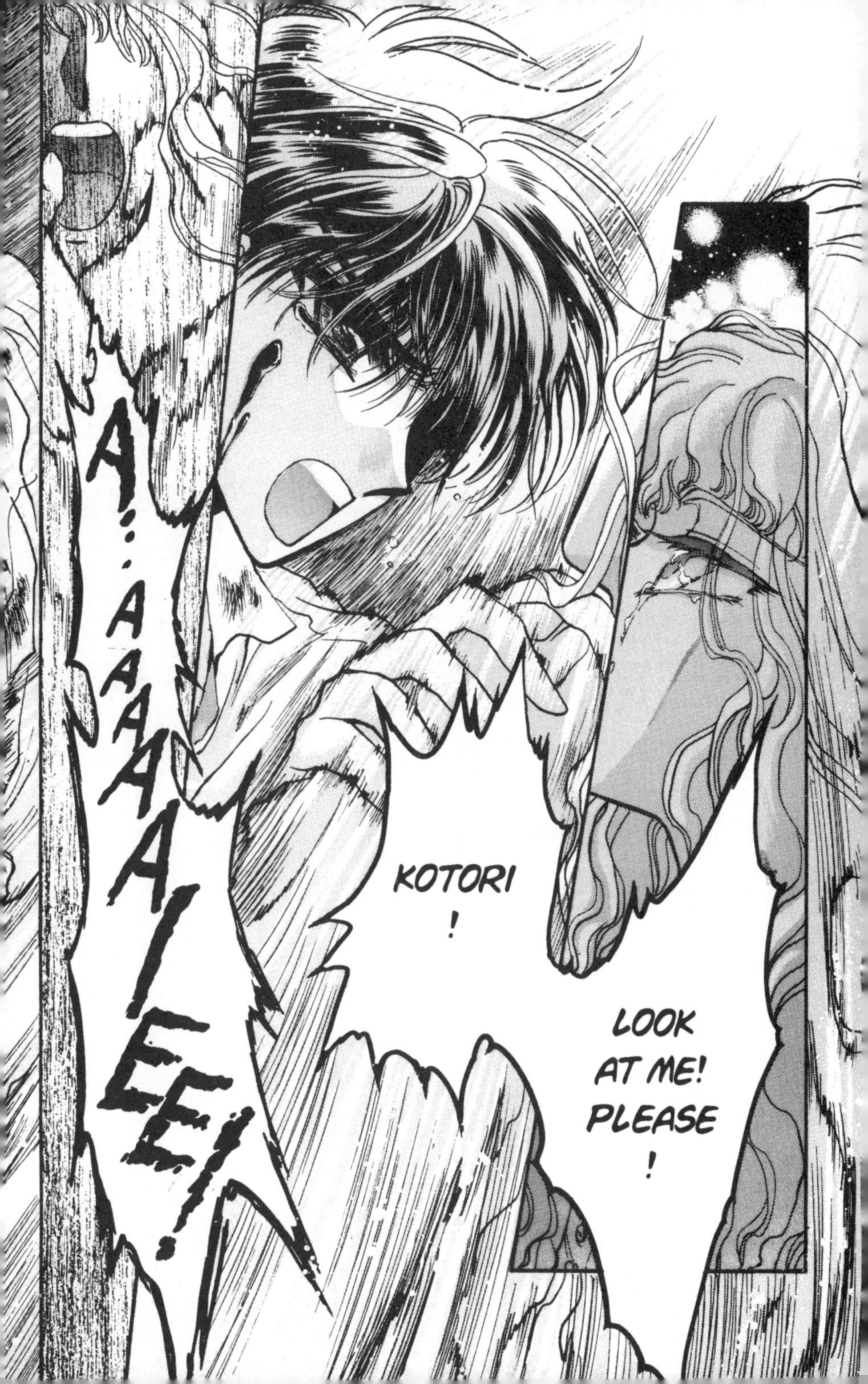
AAAAAAIIEEE!!
KOTORI!
LOOK AT ME! PLEASE!

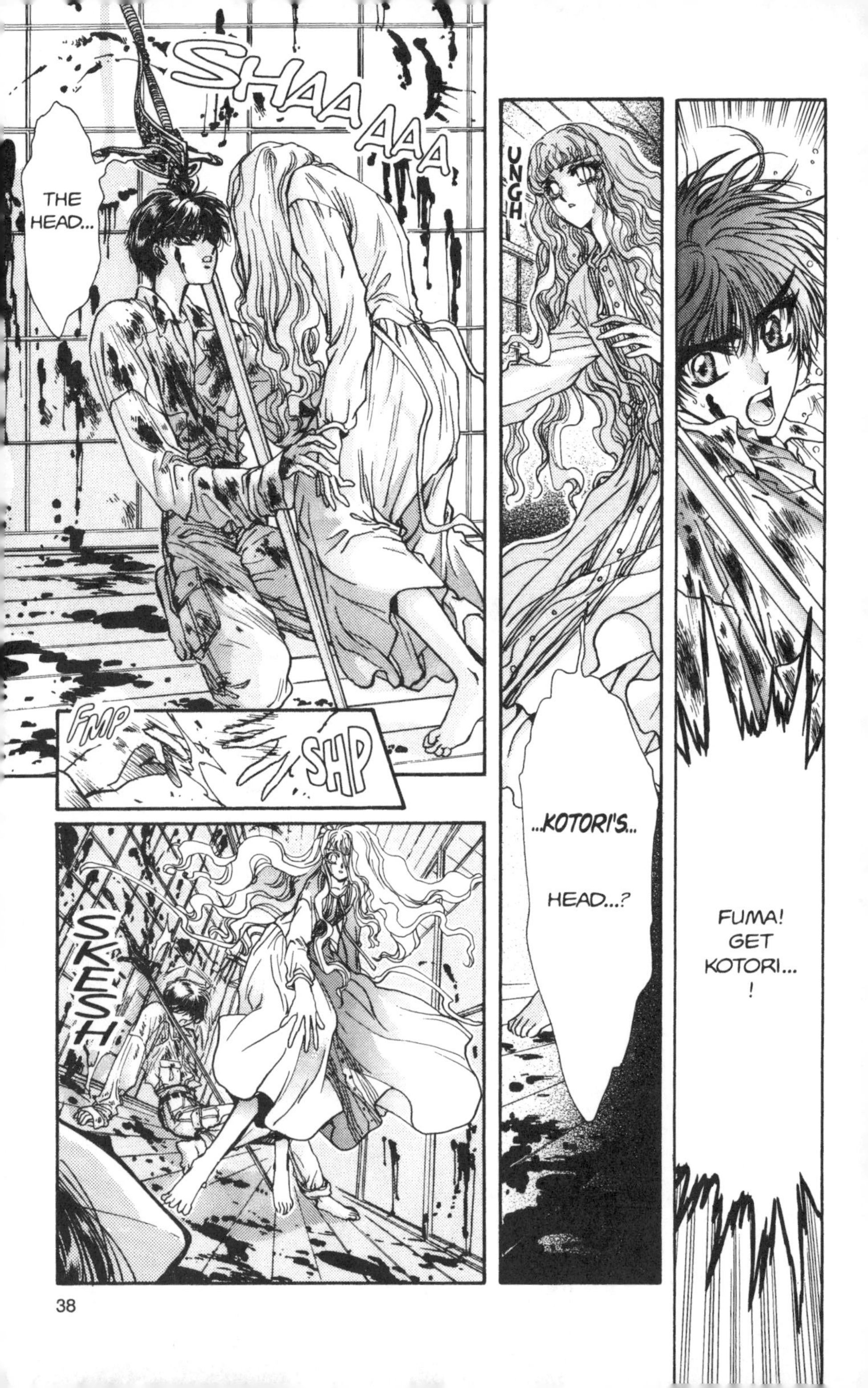
SHAAAAAA
THE HEAD...
FMP
SHP
SKESH
UNGH
...KOTORI'S...
HEAD...?
FUMA! GET KOTORI... !

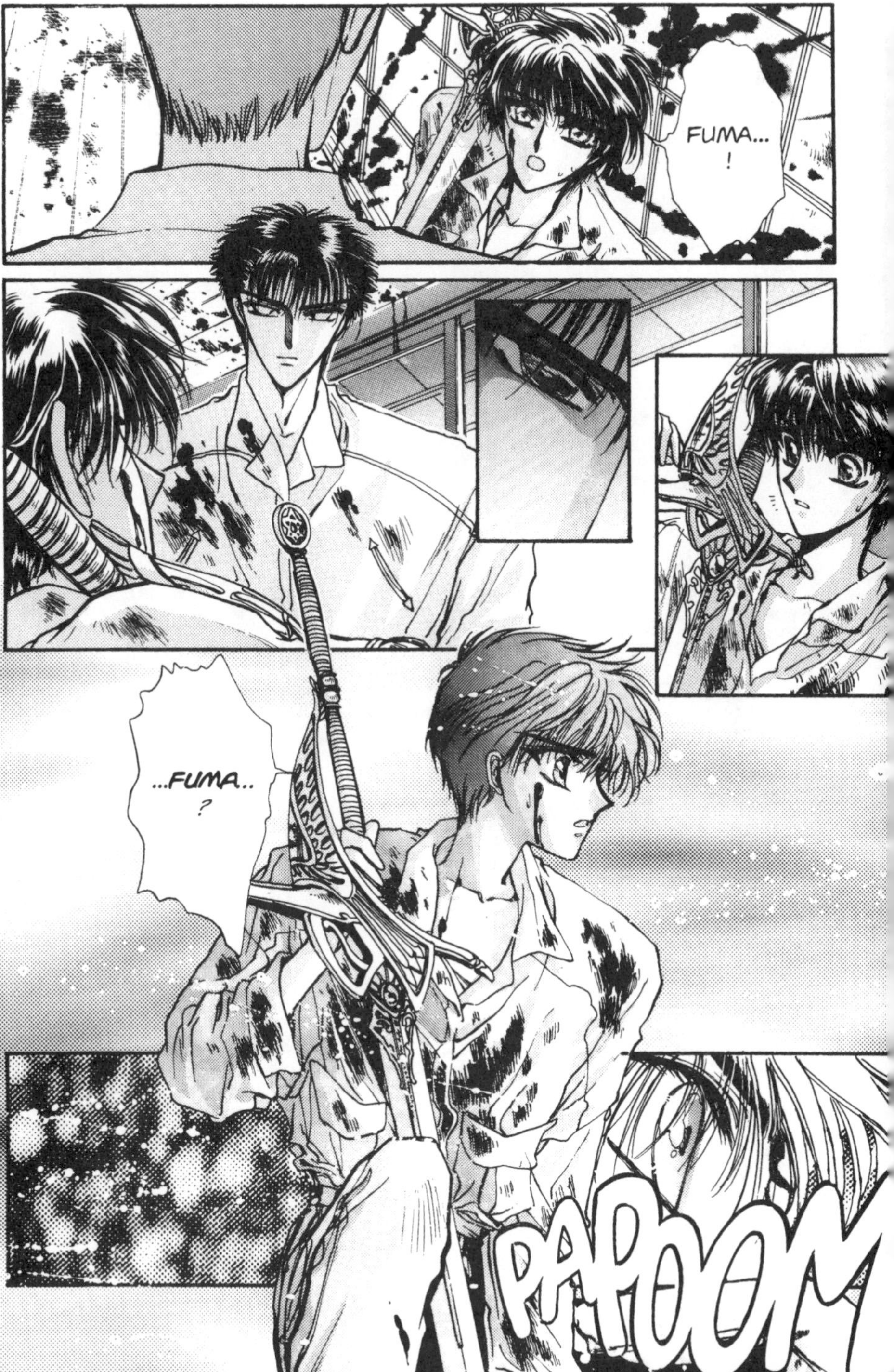
FUMA... !
...FUMA... ?
PAPOOM

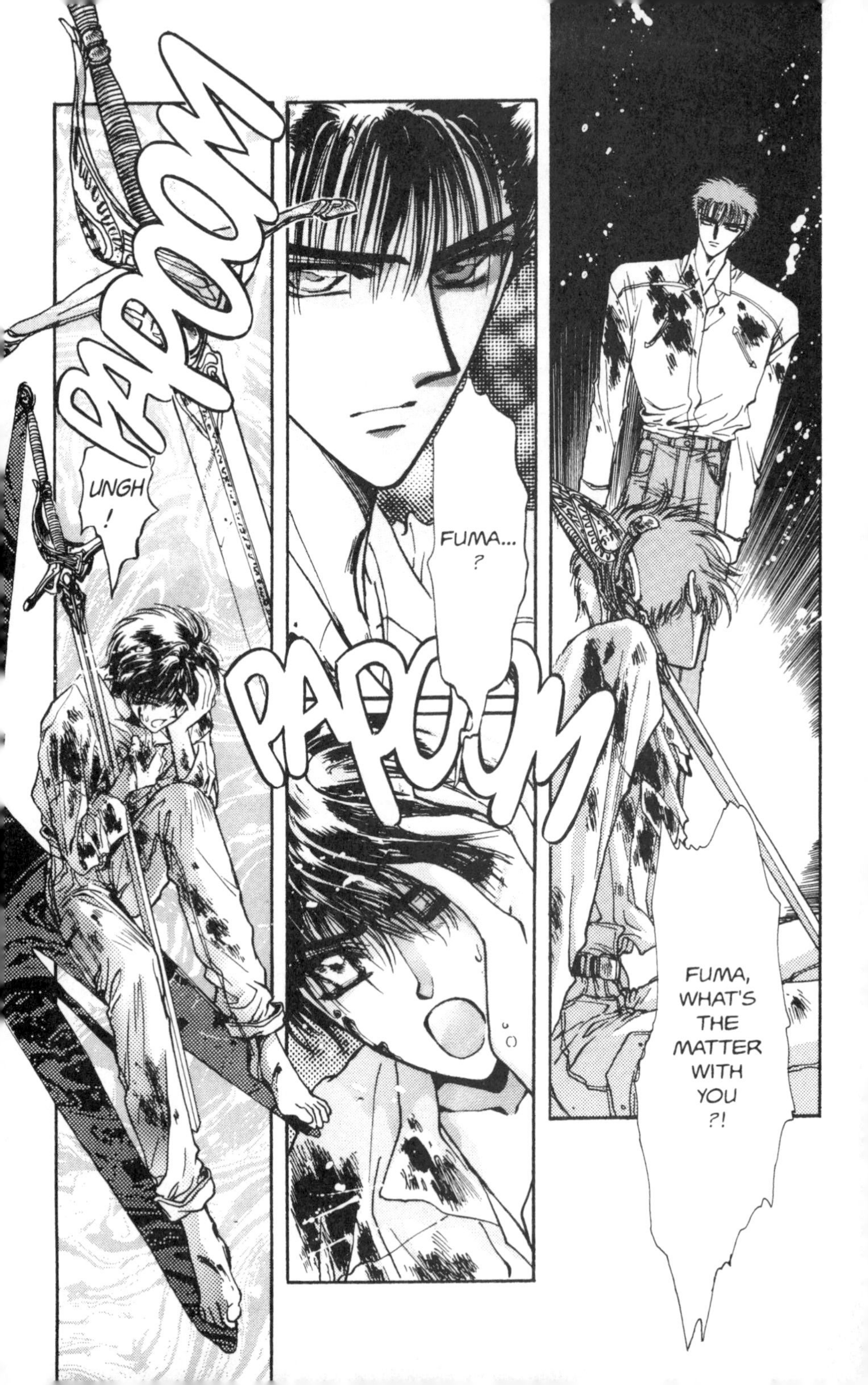
PAPOOM
UNGH!
FUMA...?
PAPOOM
FUMA, WHAT'S THE MATTER WITH YOU?!

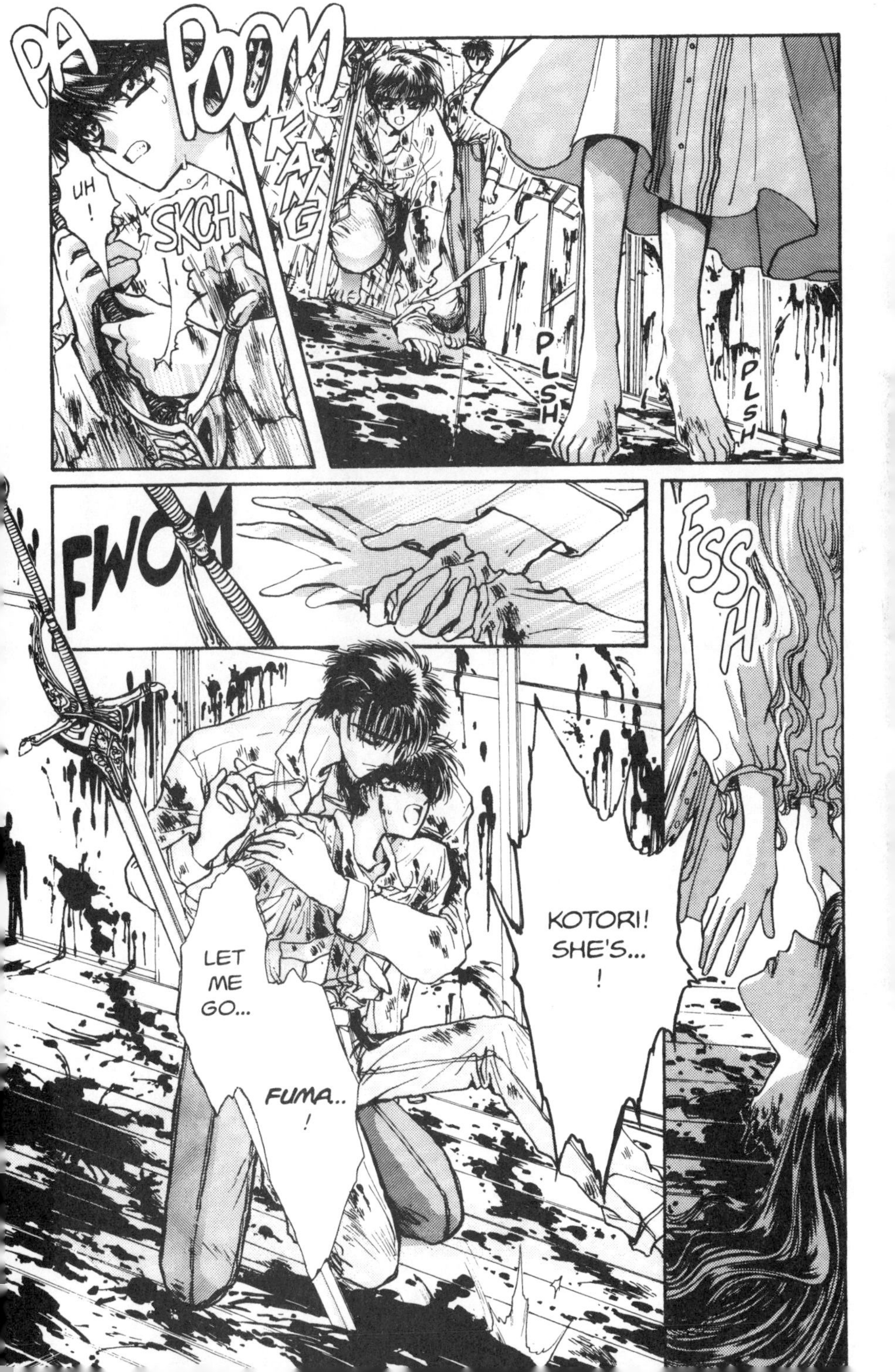
PA POOM
UH!
SKCH
KANG
PLSH
PLSH
FWOM
FSSH
LET ME GO...
FUMA...!
KOTORI! SHE'S...!

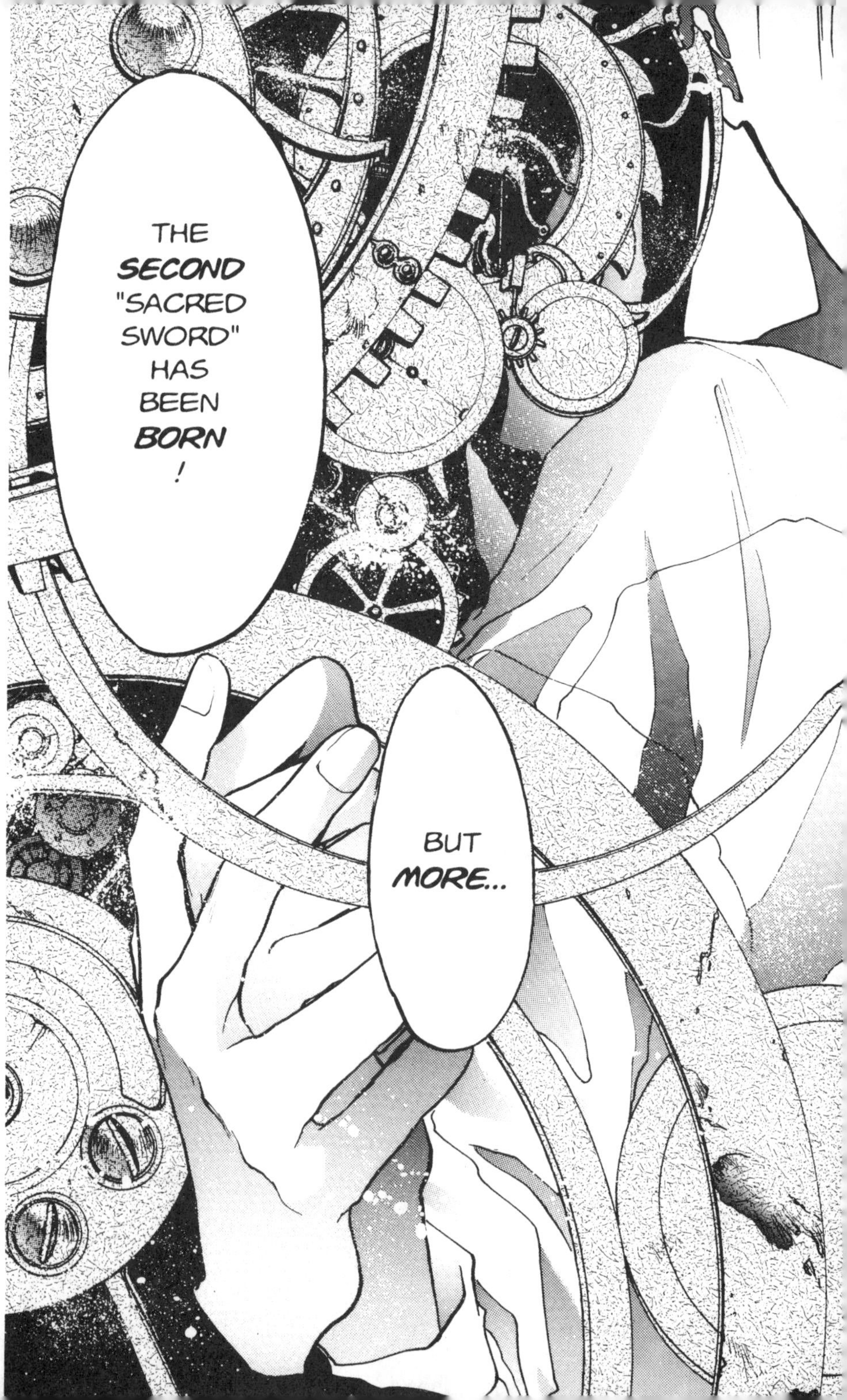
THE **SECOND** "SACRED SWORD" HAS BEEN **BORN** !
BUT **MORE...**

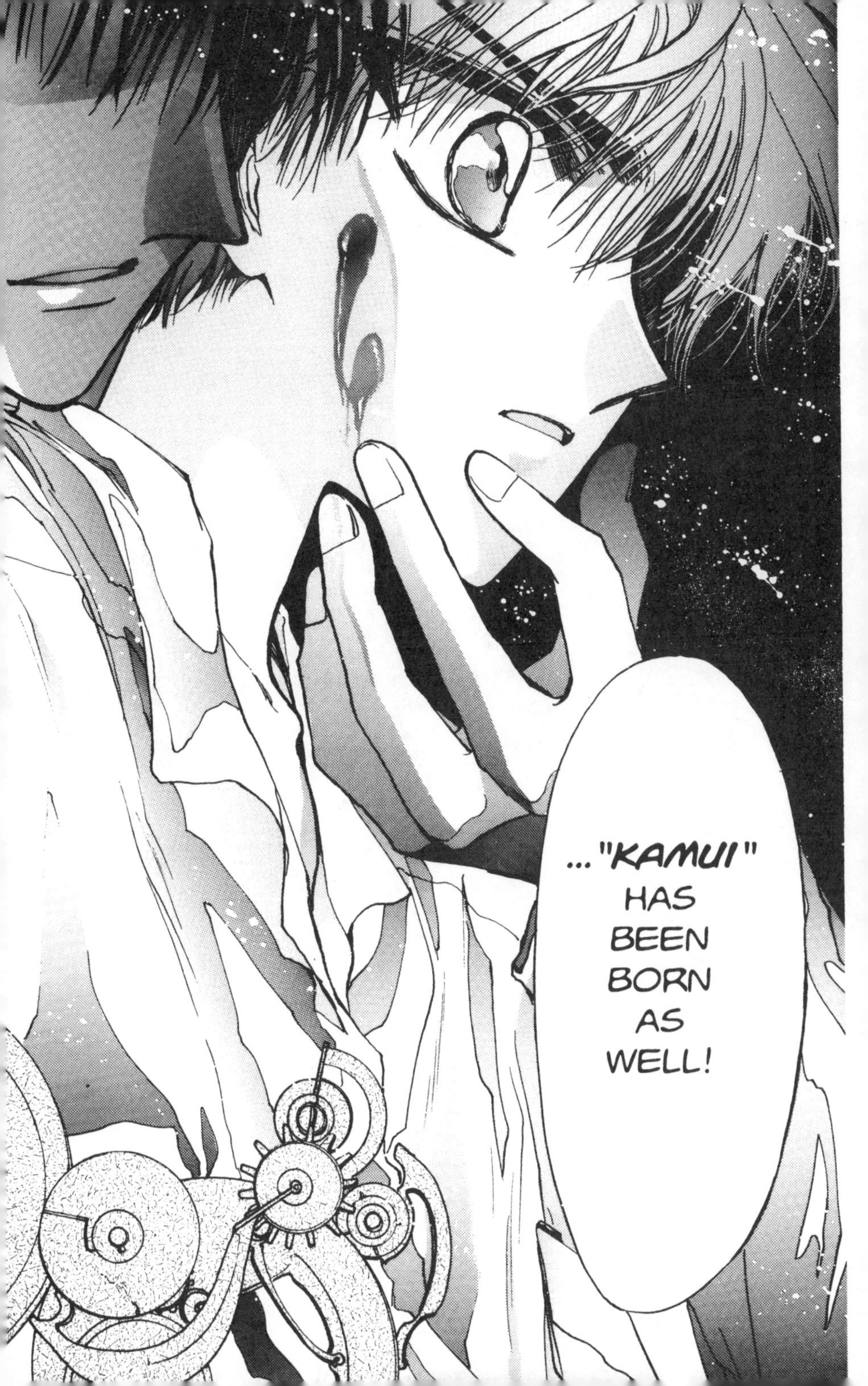
..."KAMUI" HAS BEEN BORN AS WELL!

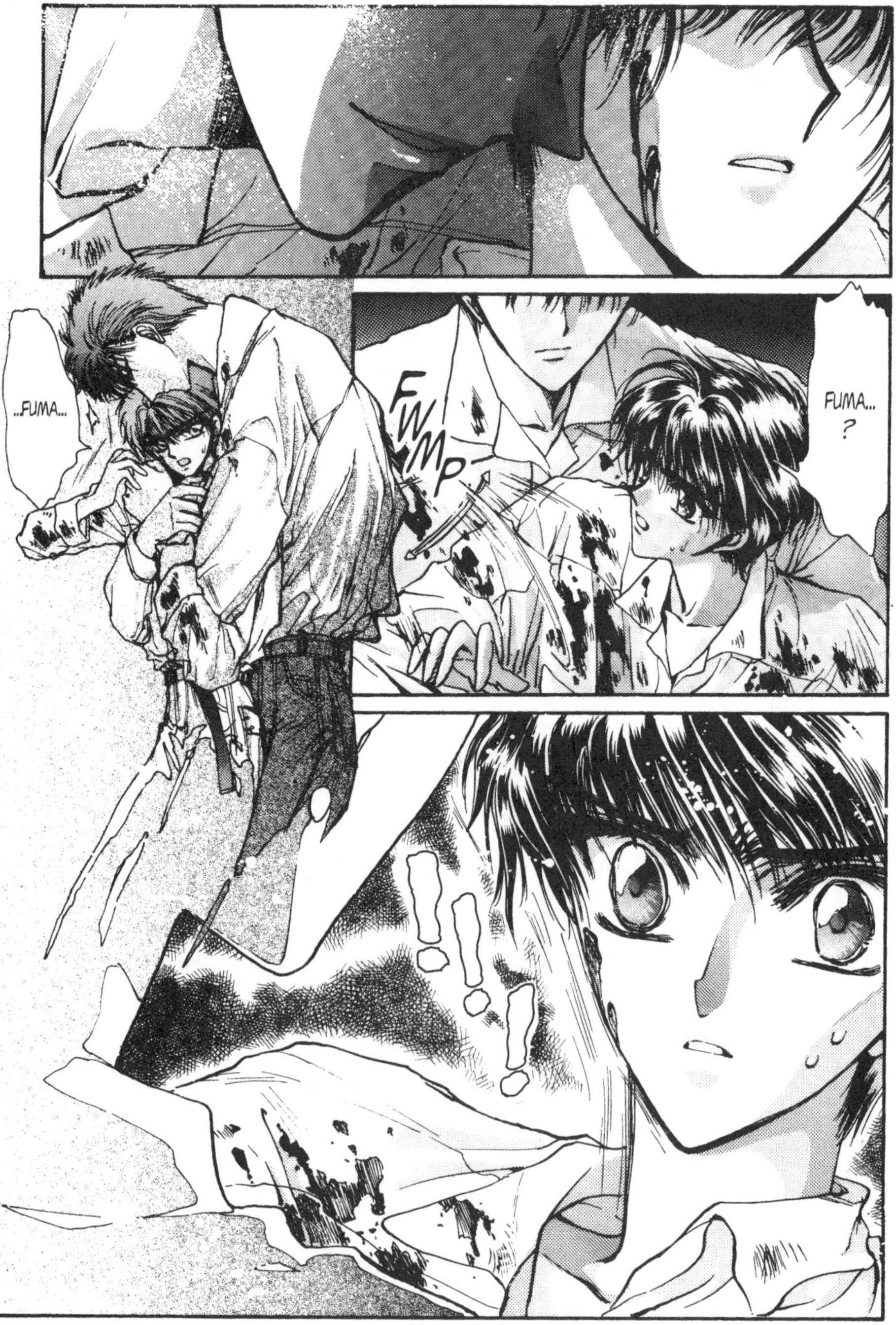
..FUMA...
FWMP
FUMA... ?

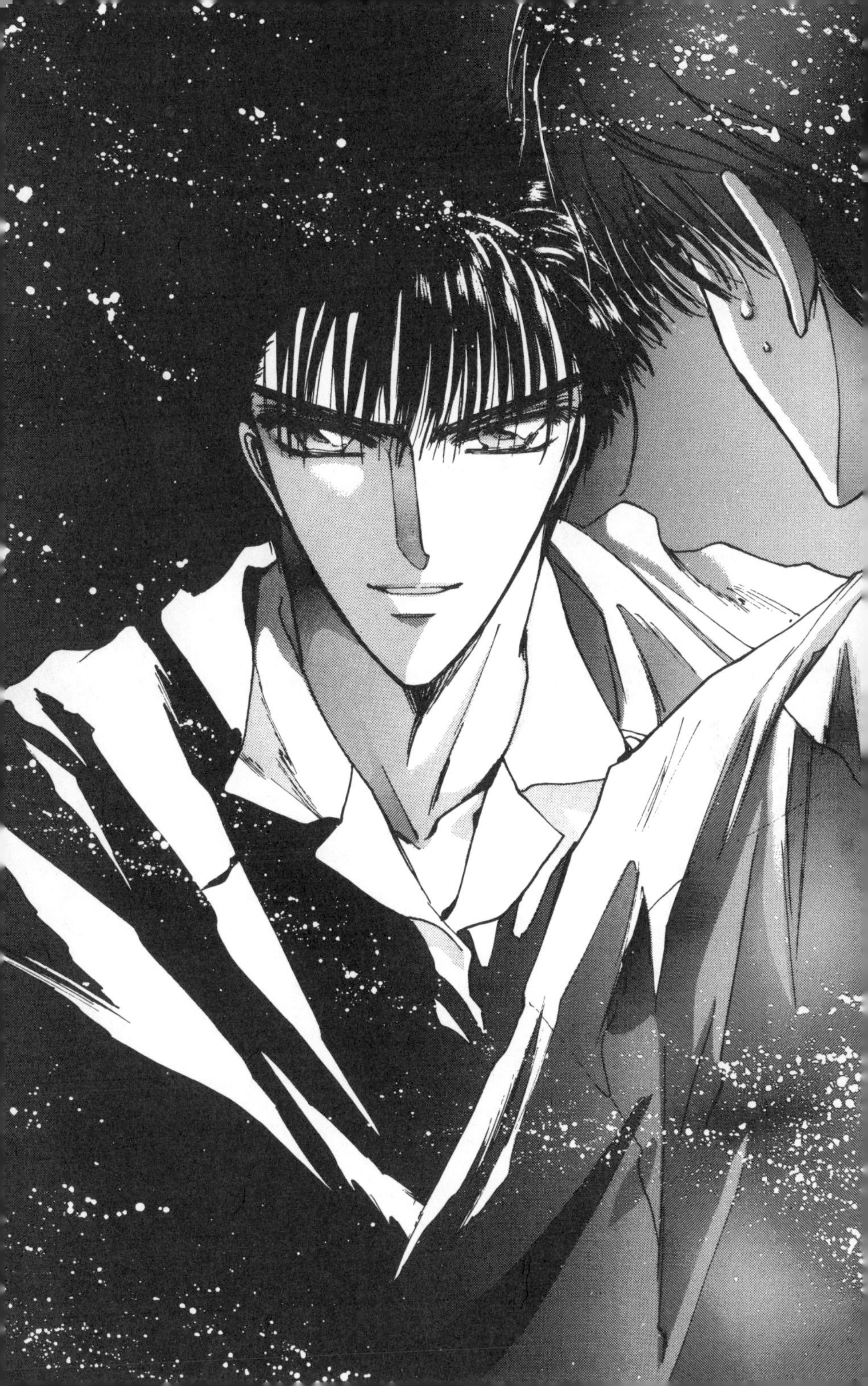

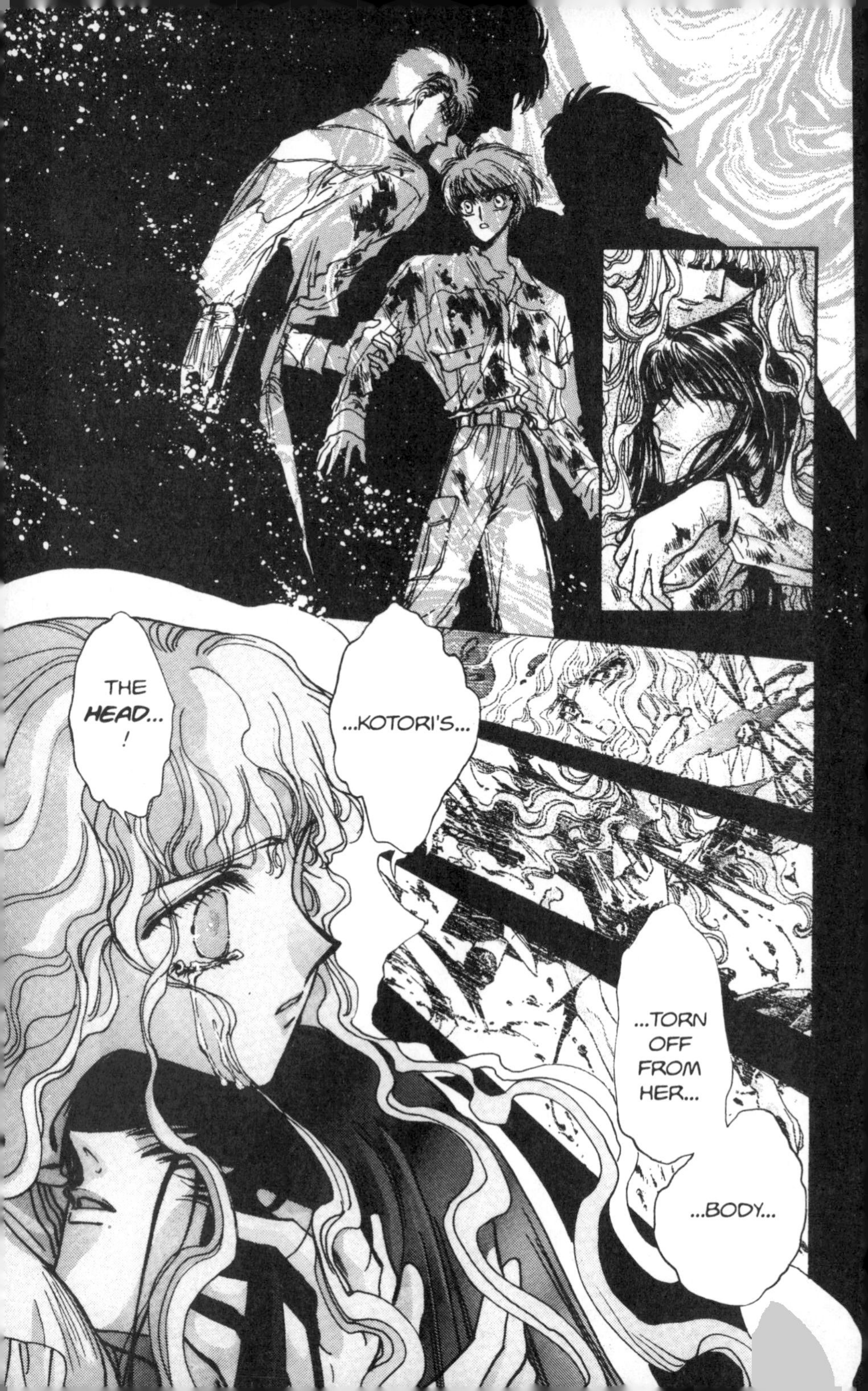
THE HEAD... !
...KOTORI'S...
...TORN OFF FROM HER...
...BODY...

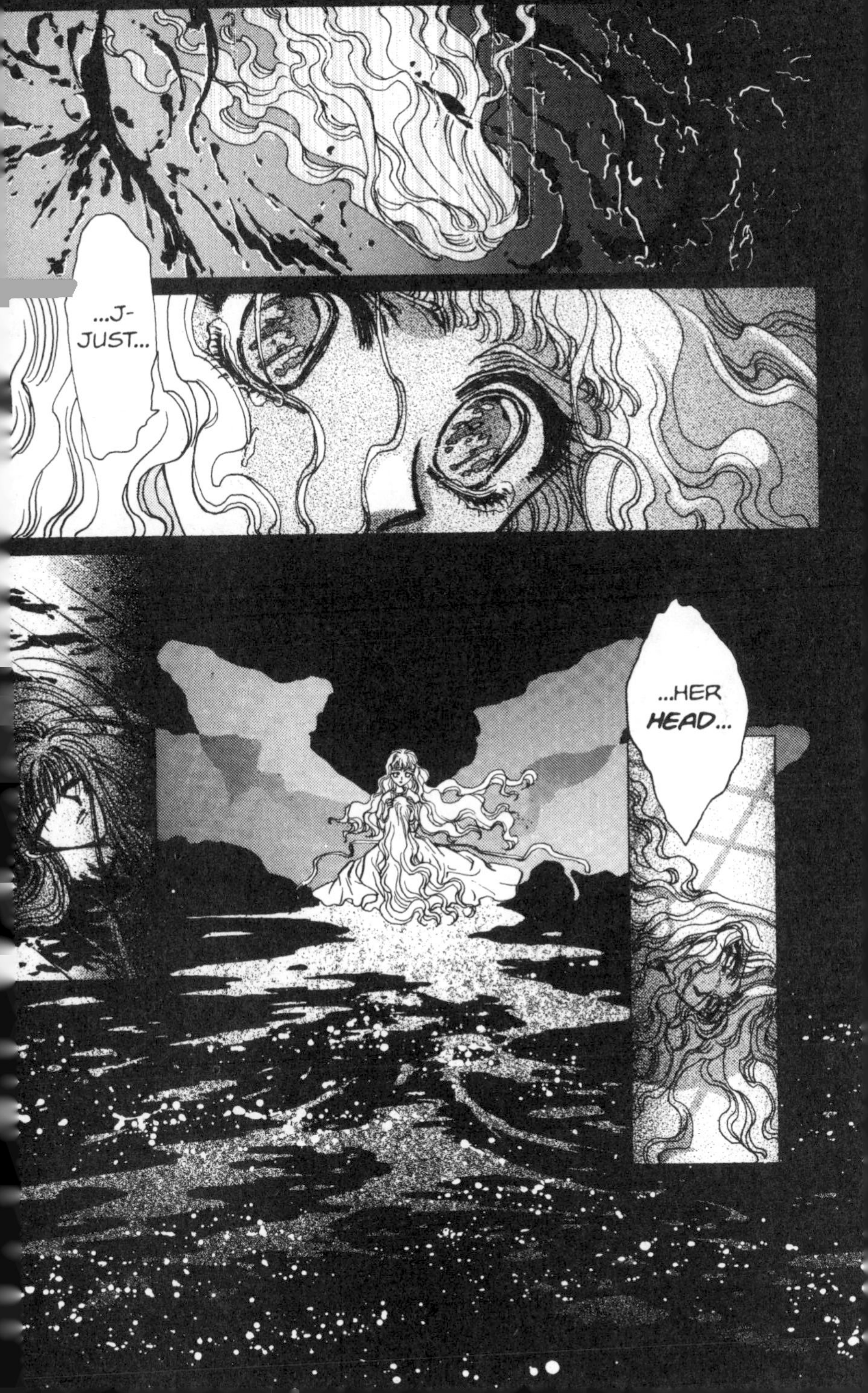
...J-
JUST...
...HER
HEAD...

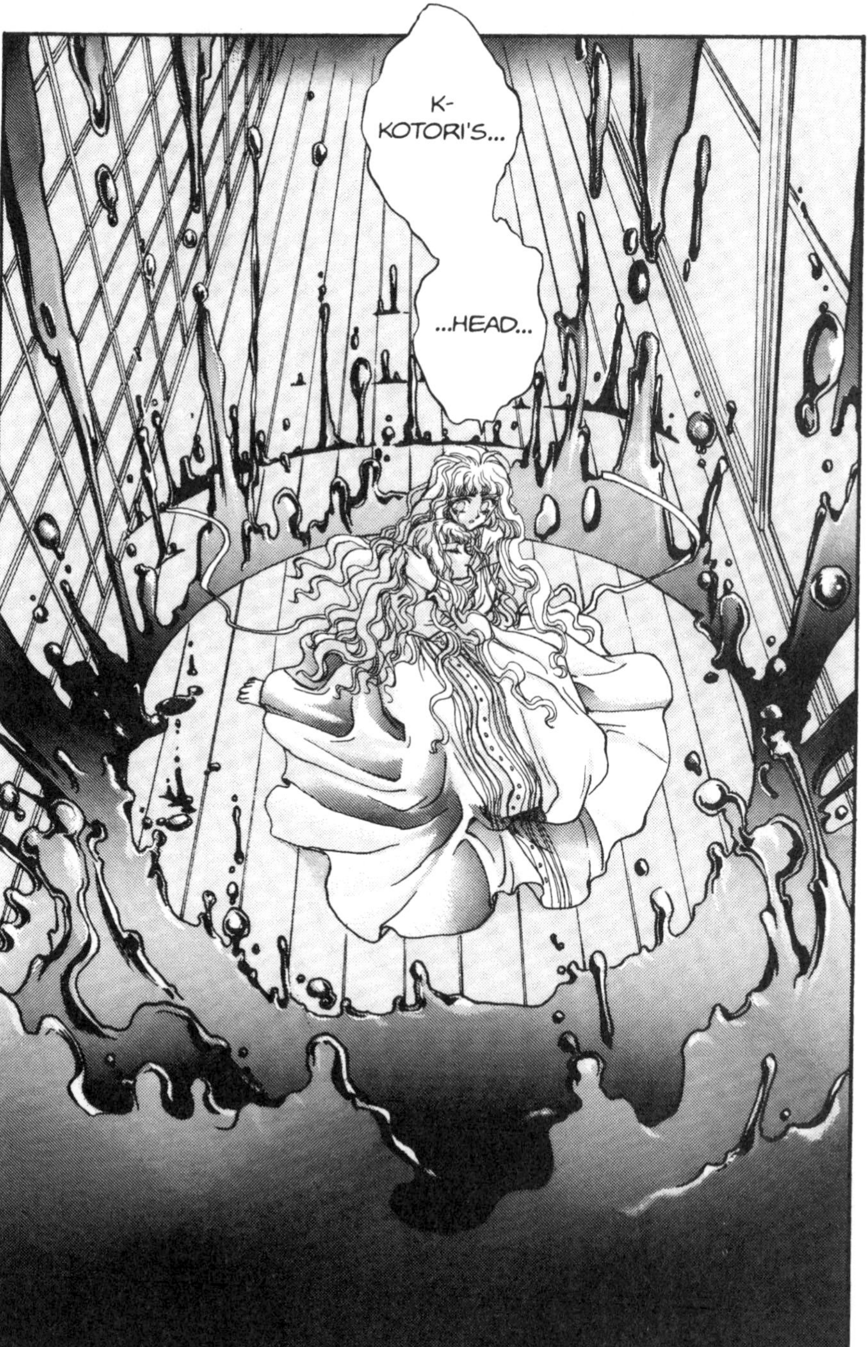
K-
KOTORI'S...
...HEAD...

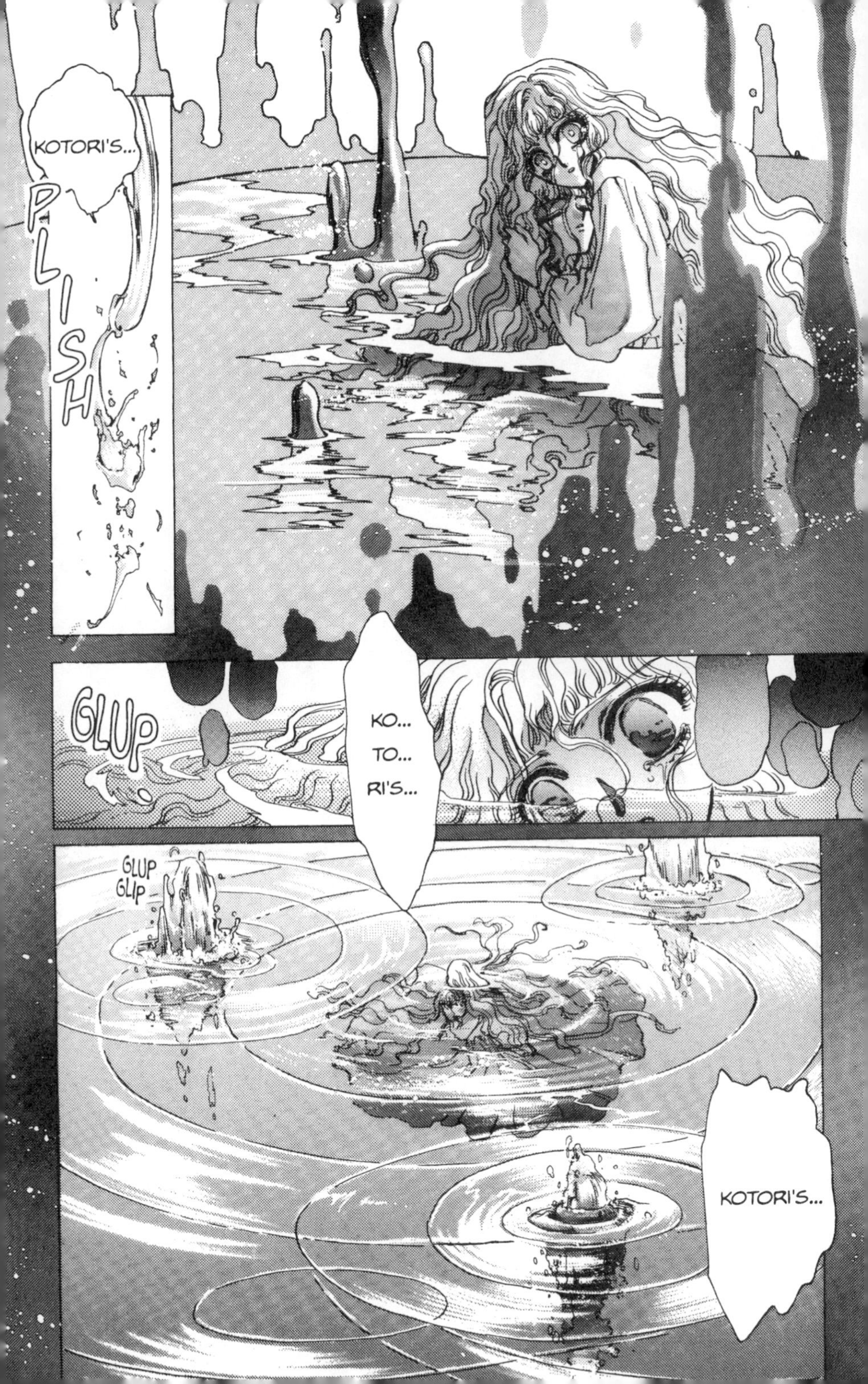
KOTORI'S...
PLISH
GLUP
KO... TO... RI'S...
GLUP GLIP
KOTORI'S...

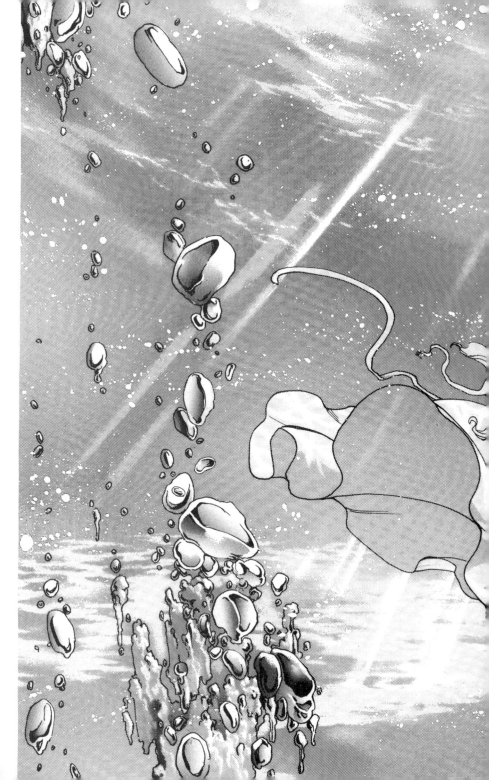

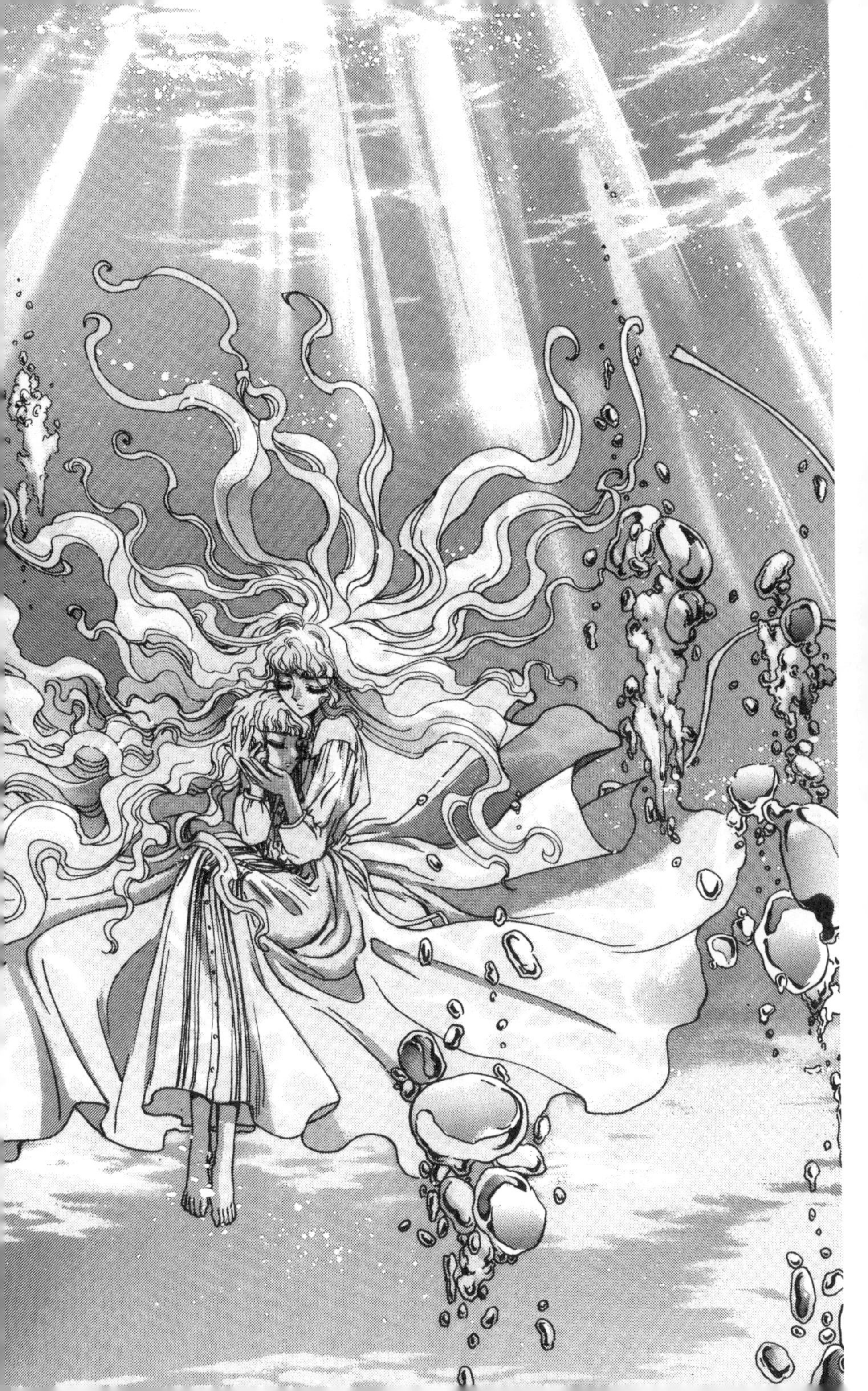

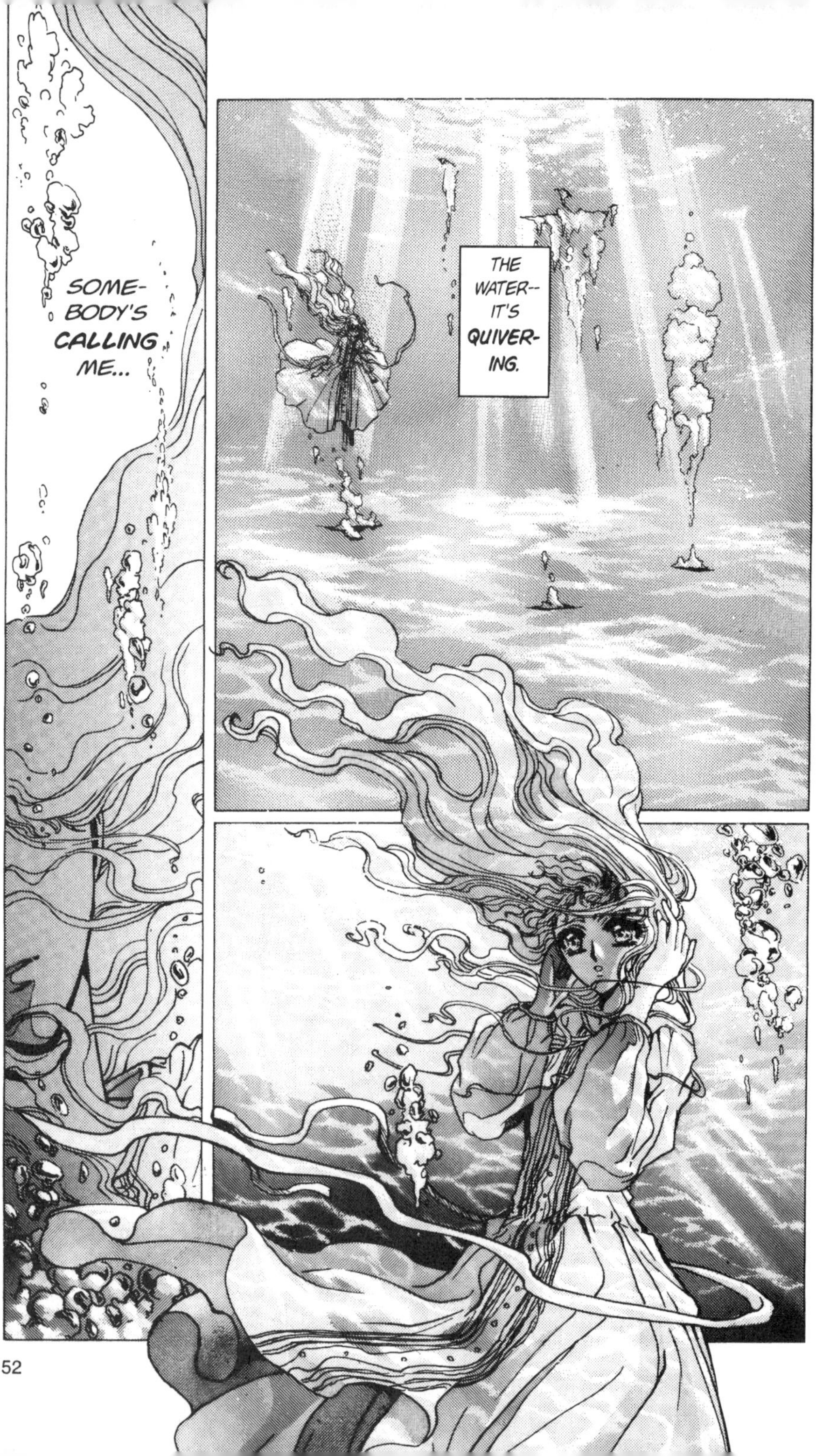
SOME-
BODY'S
CALLING
ME...
THE
WATER--
IT'S
QUIVER-
ING.

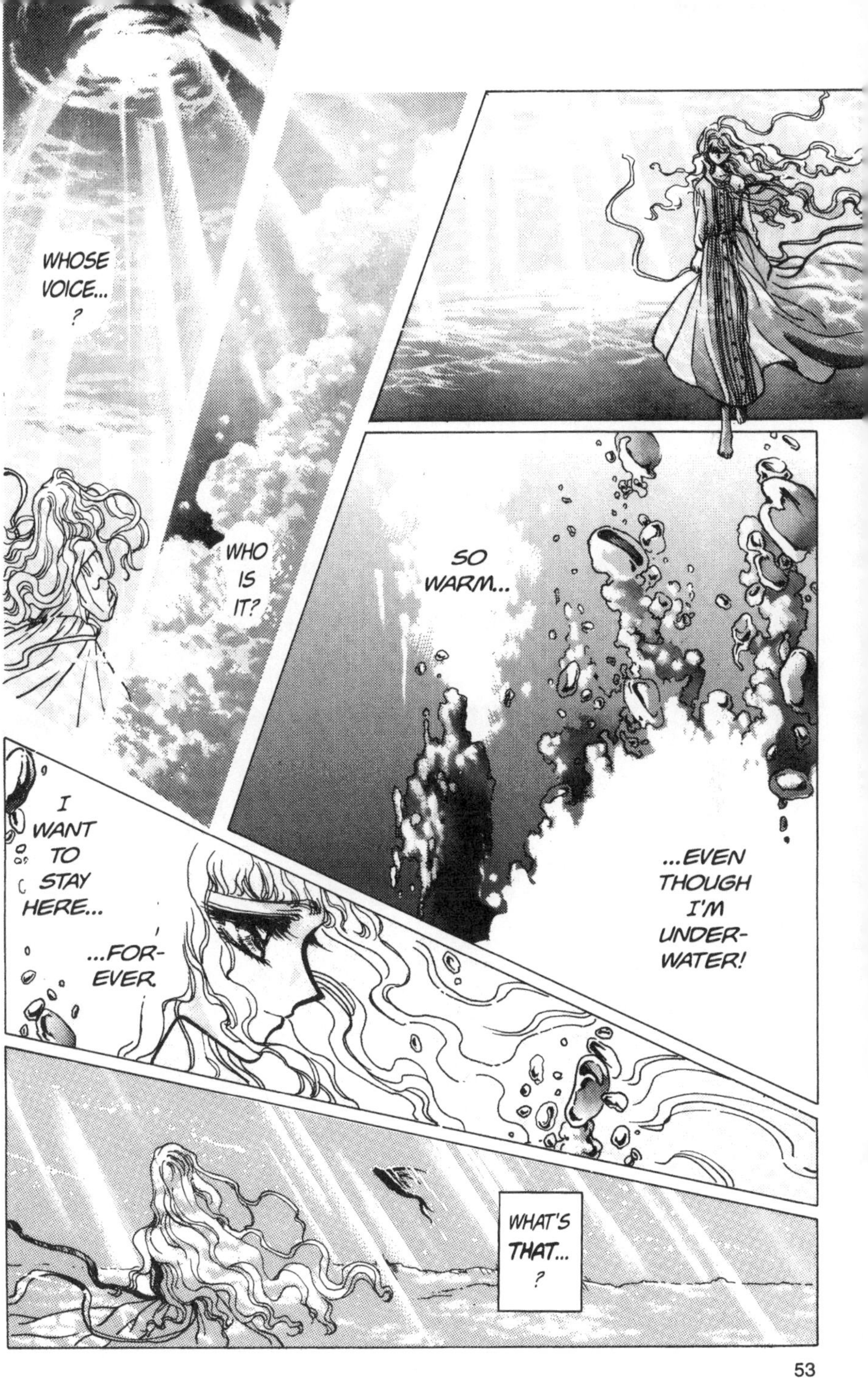
WHOSE VOICE... ?
WHO IS IT?
SO WARM...
...EVEN THOUGH I'M UNDER-WATER!
I WANT TO STAY HERE...
...FOR-EVER.
WHAT'S THAT... ?

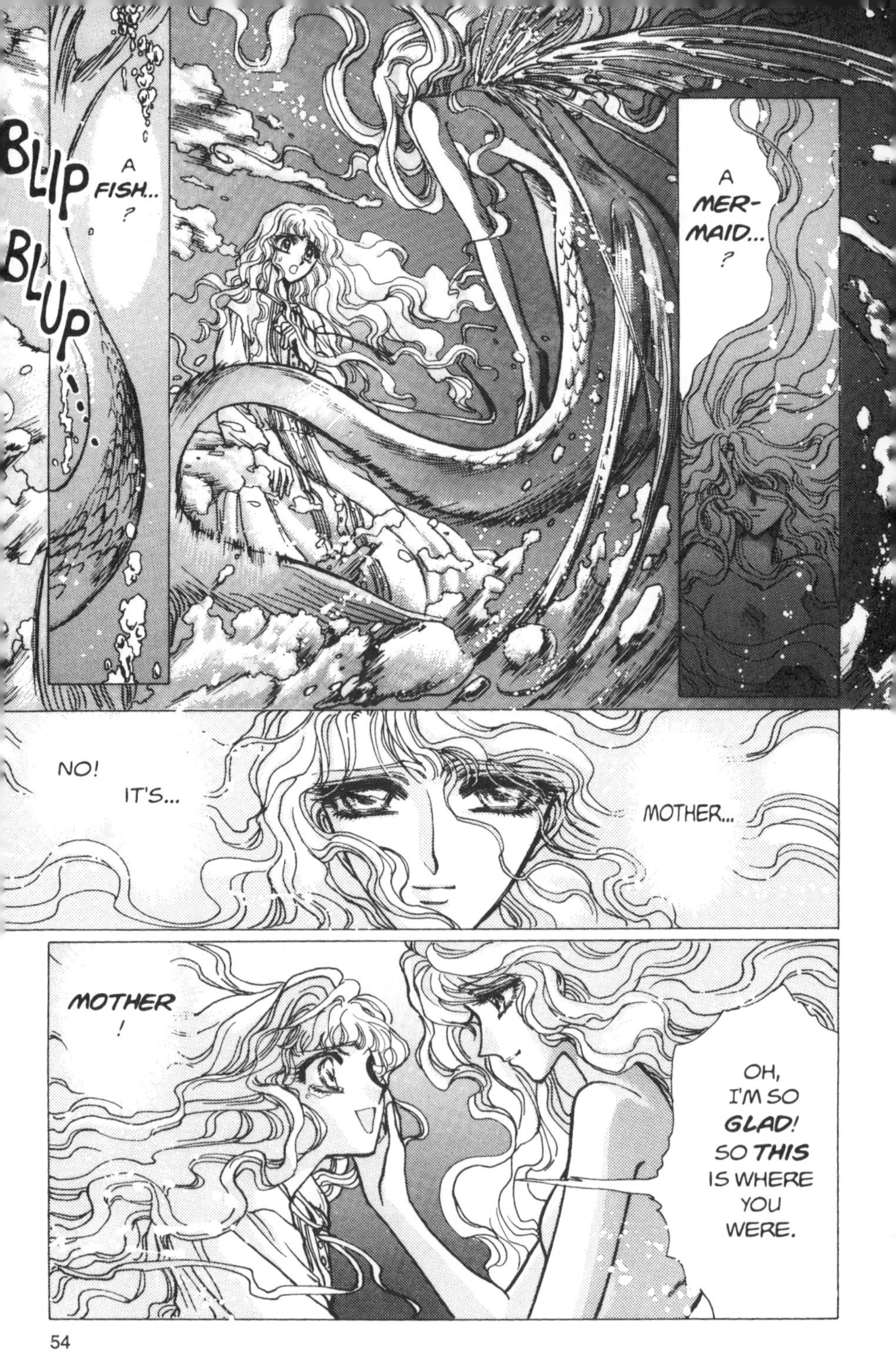
BLIP
BLUP
A FISH...?
A MERMAID...?
NO!
IT'S...
MOTHER...
MOTHER!
OH, I'M SO GLAD! SO THIS IS WHERE YOU WERE.

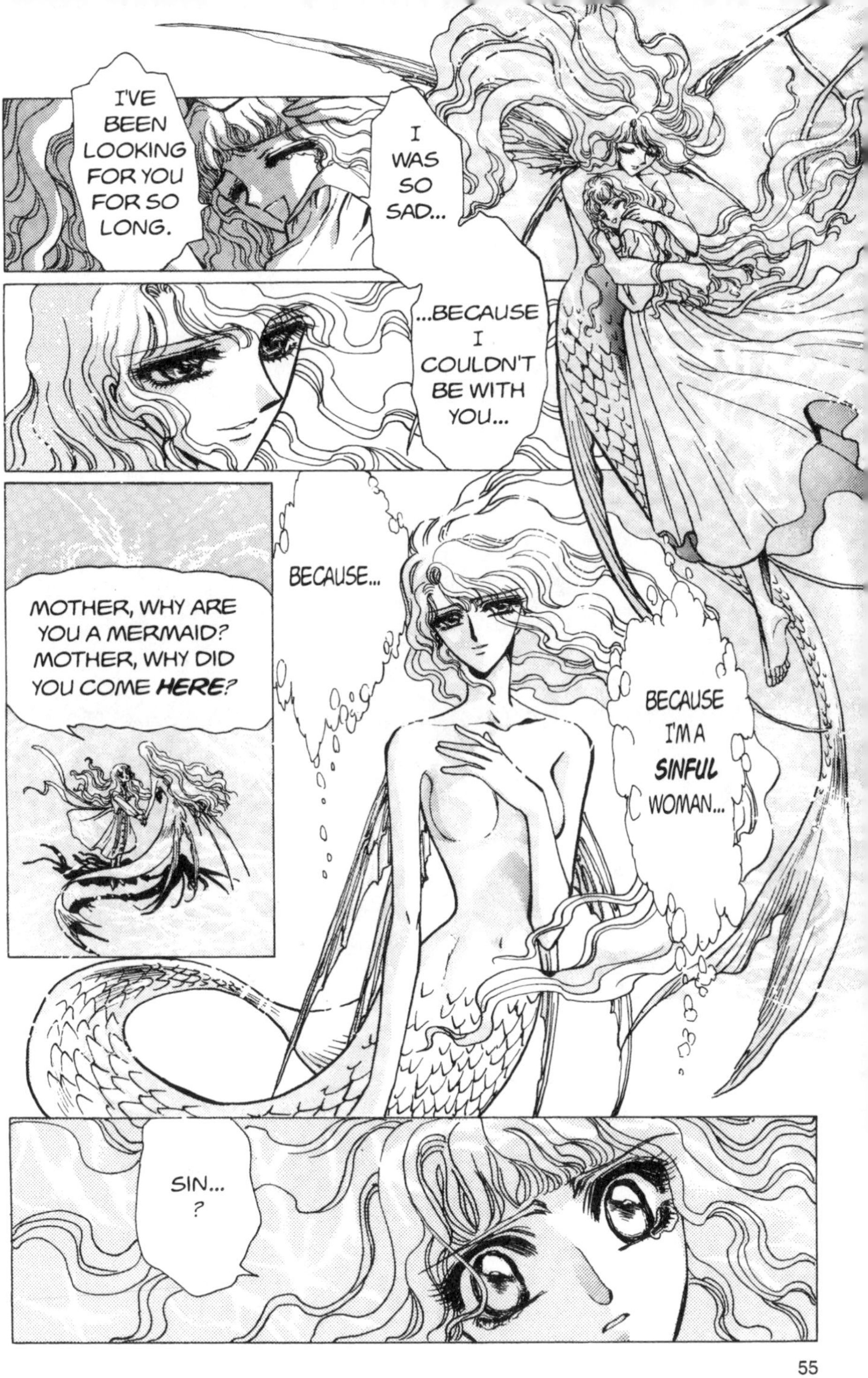

I'VE BEEN LOOKING FOR YOU FOR SO LONG.
I WAS SO SAD...
...BECAUSE I COULDN'T BE WITH YOU...
MOTHER, WHY ARE YOU A MERMAID? MOTHER, WHY DID YOU COME ***HERE***?
BECAUSE...
BECAUSE I'M A ***SINFUL*** WOMAN...
SIN... ?

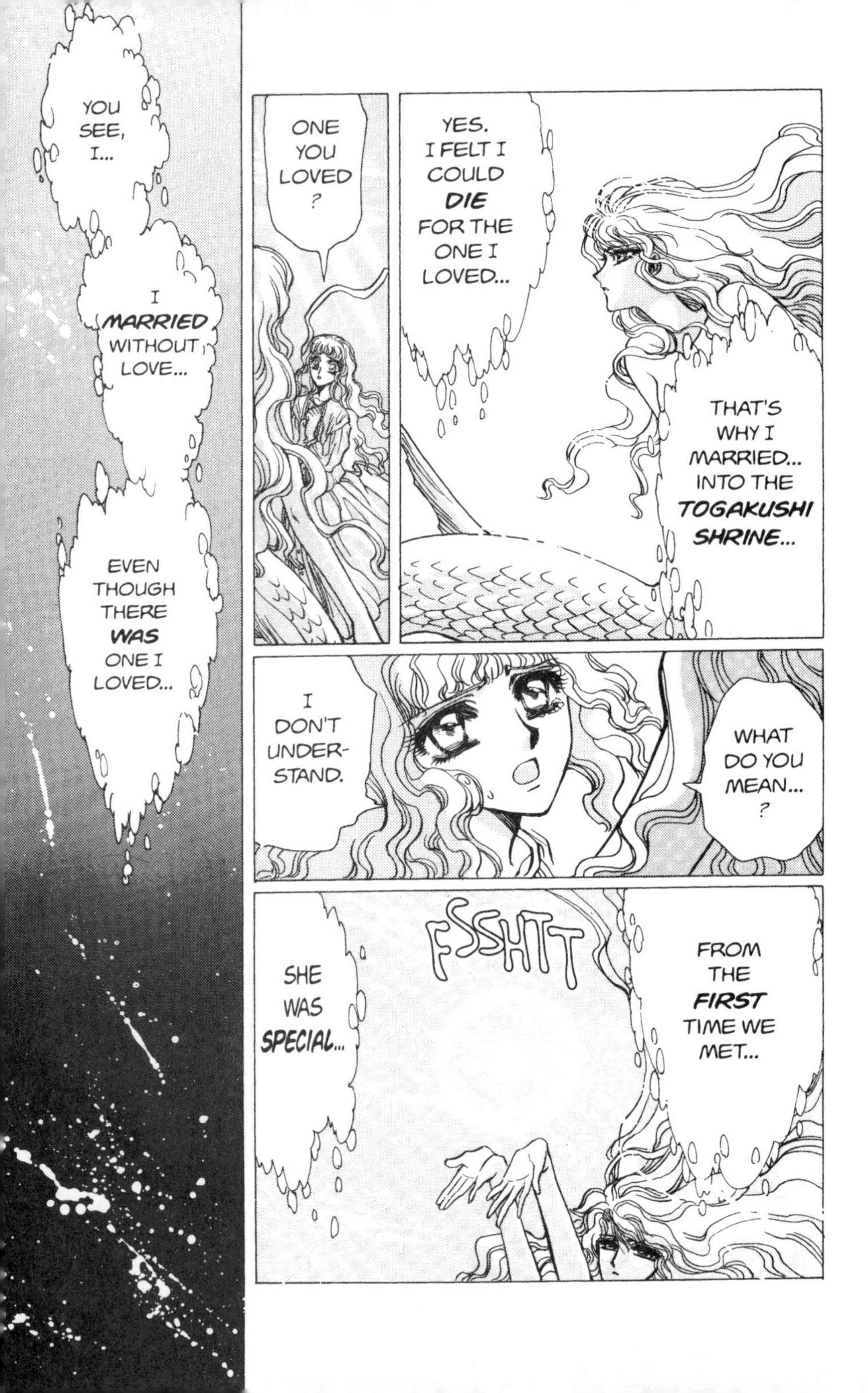
YOU SEE, I...
I MARRIED WITHOUT LOVE...
EVEN THOUGH THERE WAS ONE I LOVED...
ONE YOU LOVED ?
YES. I FELT I COULD DIE FOR THE ONE I LOVED...
THAT'S WHY I MARRIED... INTO THE TOGAKUSHI SHRINE...
I DON'T UNDER-STAND.
WHAT DO YOU MEAN... ?
SHE WAS SPECIAL...
FSSHTT
FROM THE FIRST TIME WE MET...

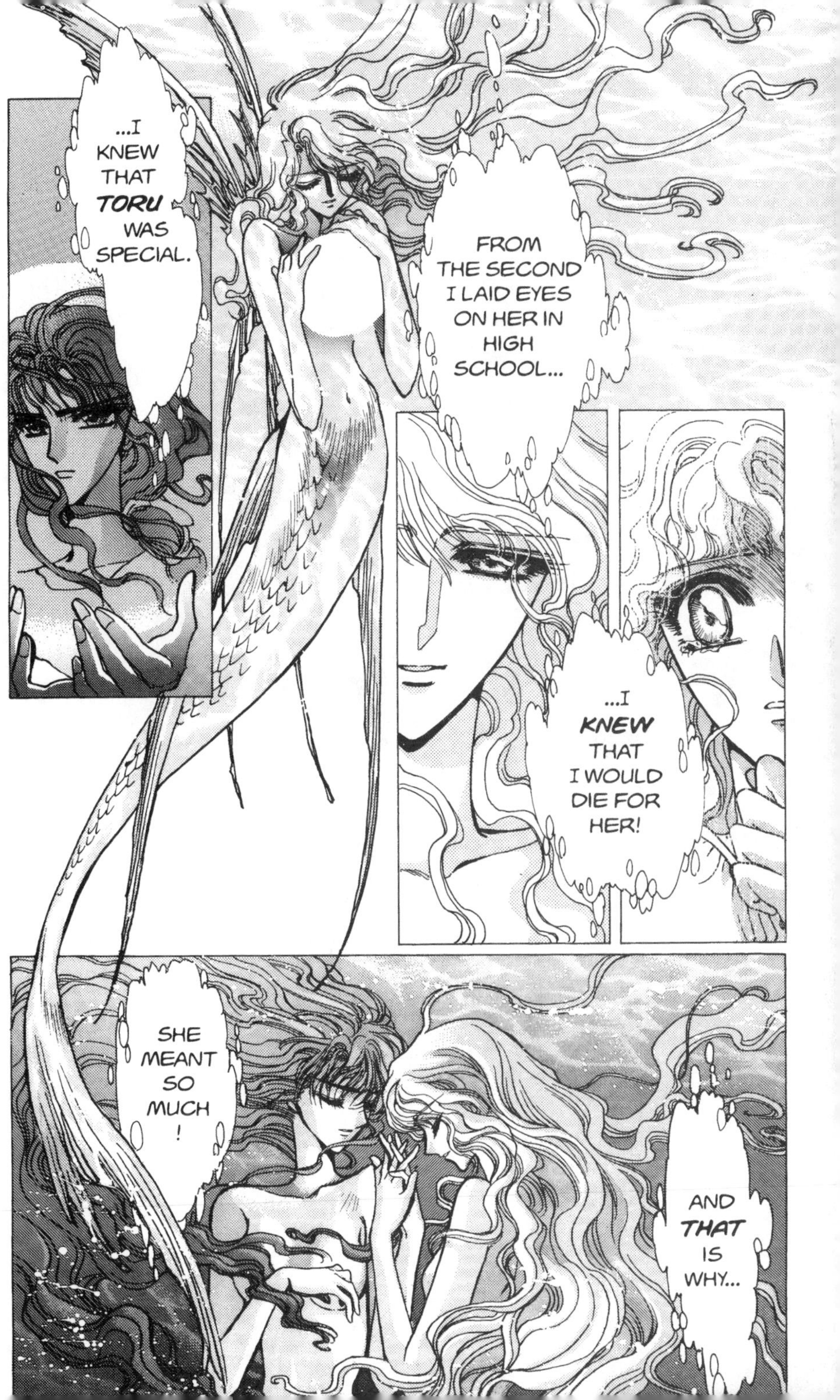
...I KNEW THAT TORU WAS SPECIAL.
FROM THE SECOND I LAID EYES ON HER IN HIGH SCHOOL...
...I KNEW THAT I WOULD DIE FOR HER!
SHE MEANT SO MUCH!
AND THAT IS WHY...

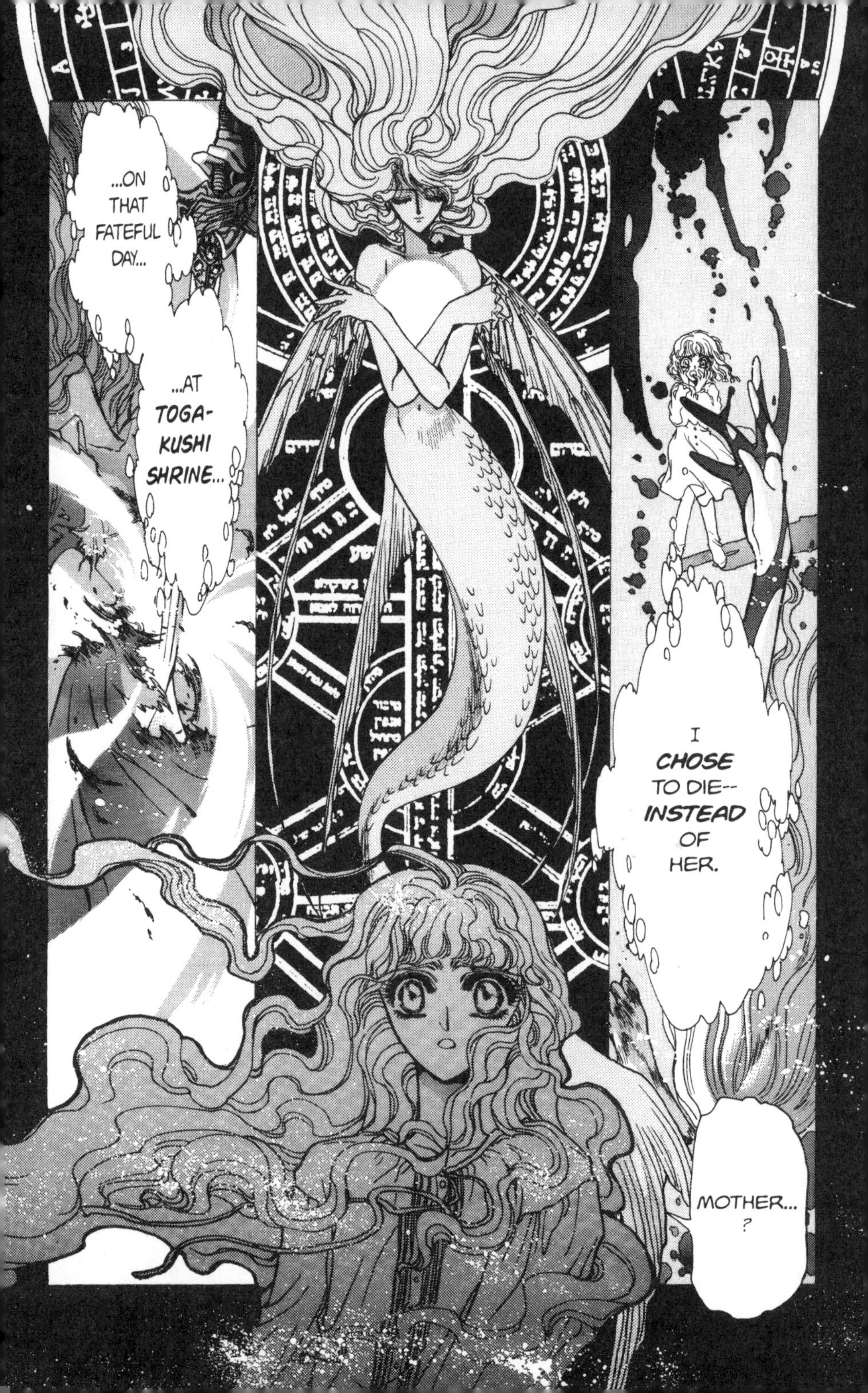
...ON THAT FATEFUL DAY...
...AT TOGA-KUSHI SHRINE...
I CHOSE TO DIE-- INSTEAD OF HER.
MOTHER...?

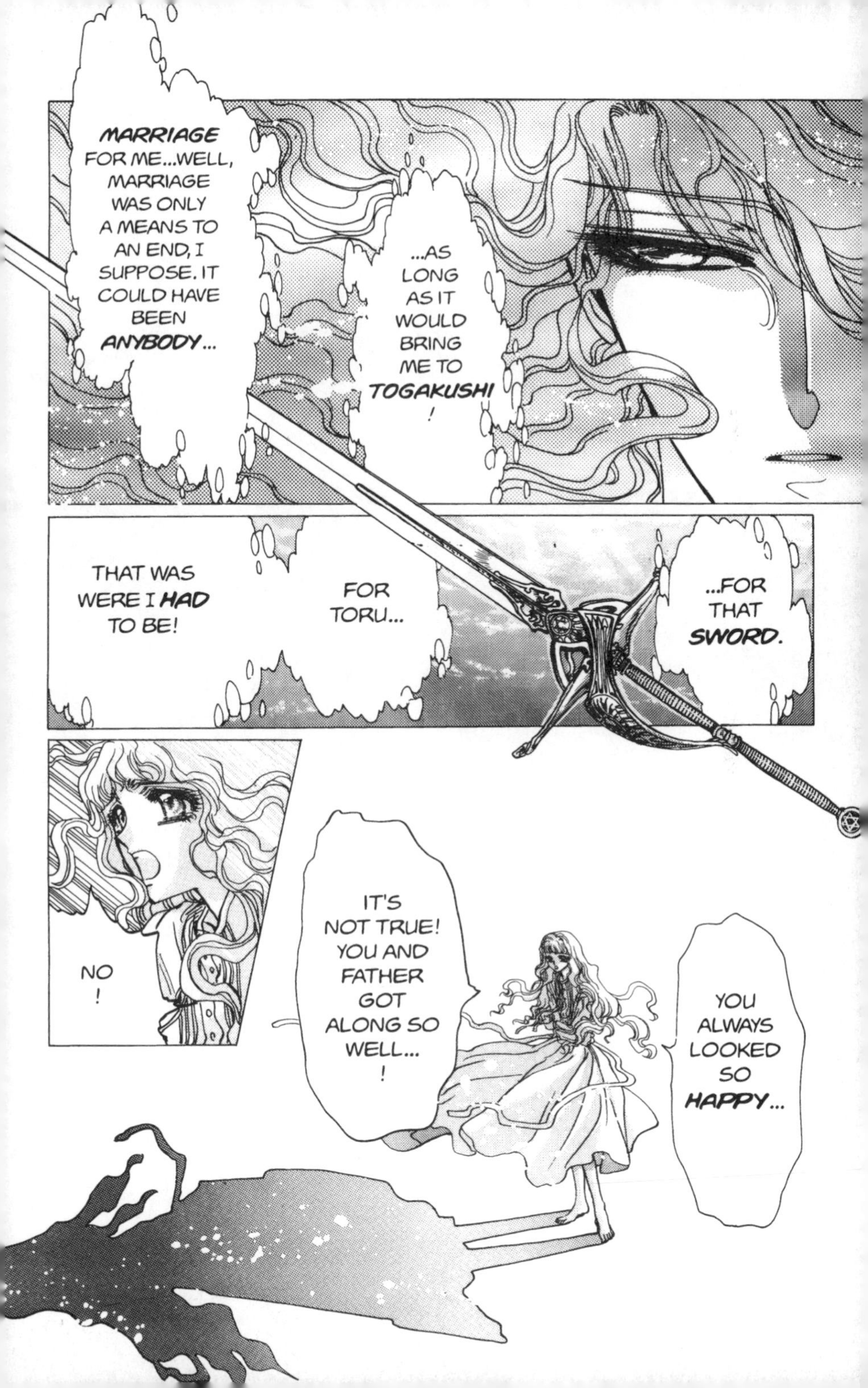
MARRIAGE FOR ME...WELL, MARRIAGE WAS ONLY A MEANS TO AN END, I SUPPOSE. IT COULD HAVE BEEN ANYBODY...
...AS LONG AS IT WOULD BRING ME TO TOGAKUSHI!
THAT WAS WERE I HAD TO BE!
FOR TORU...
...FOR THAT SWORD.
NO!
IT'S NOT TRUE! YOU AND FATHER GOT ALONG SO WELL...!
YOU ALWAYS LOOKED SO HAPPY...

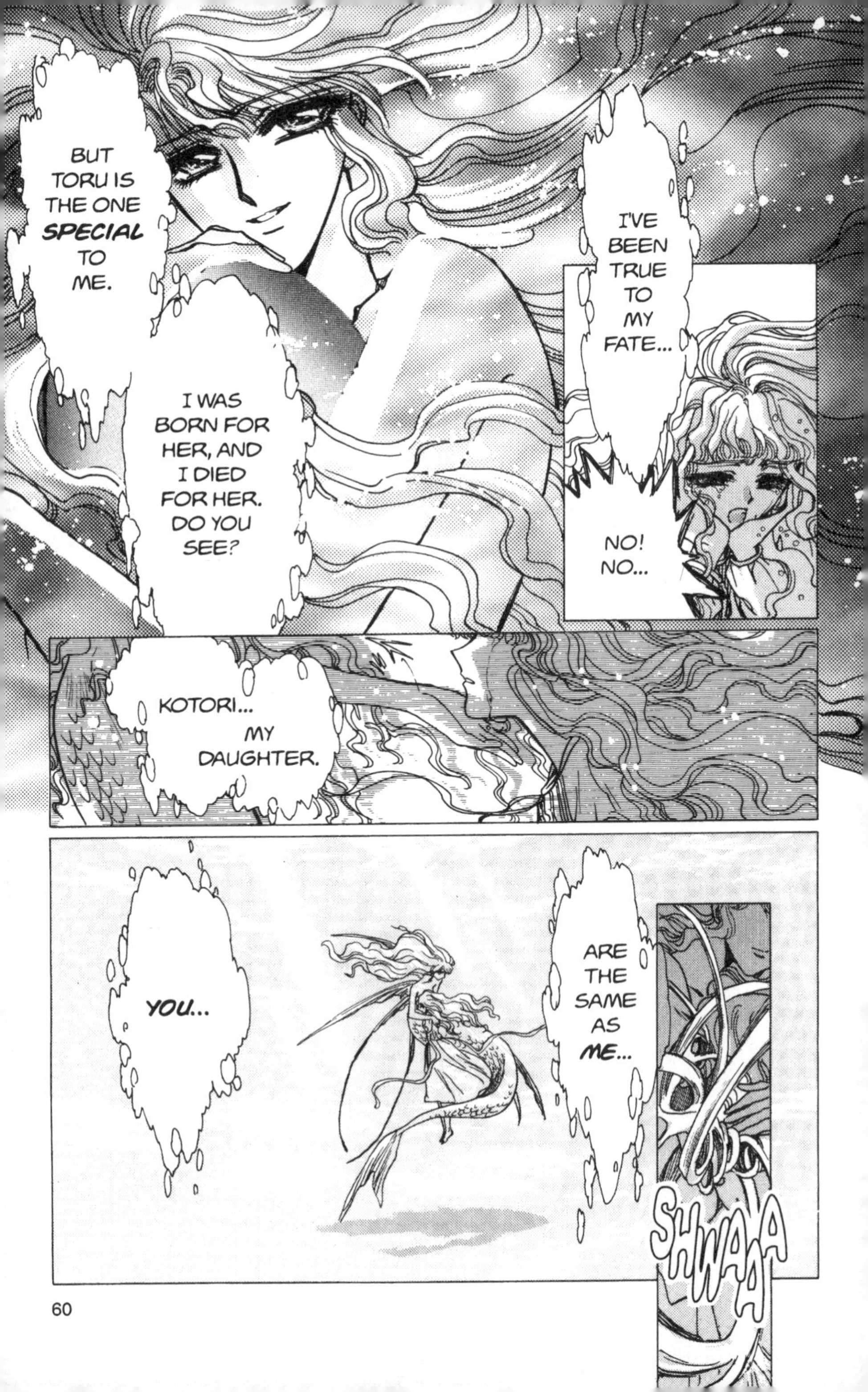
BUT TORU IS THE ONE **SPECIAL** TO ME.
I WAS BORN FOR HER, AND I DIED FOR HER. DO YOU SEE?
I'VE BEEN TRUE TO MY FATE...
NO! NO...
KOTORI... MY DAUGHTER.
YOU...
ARE THE SAME AS **ME...**
SHWAAA

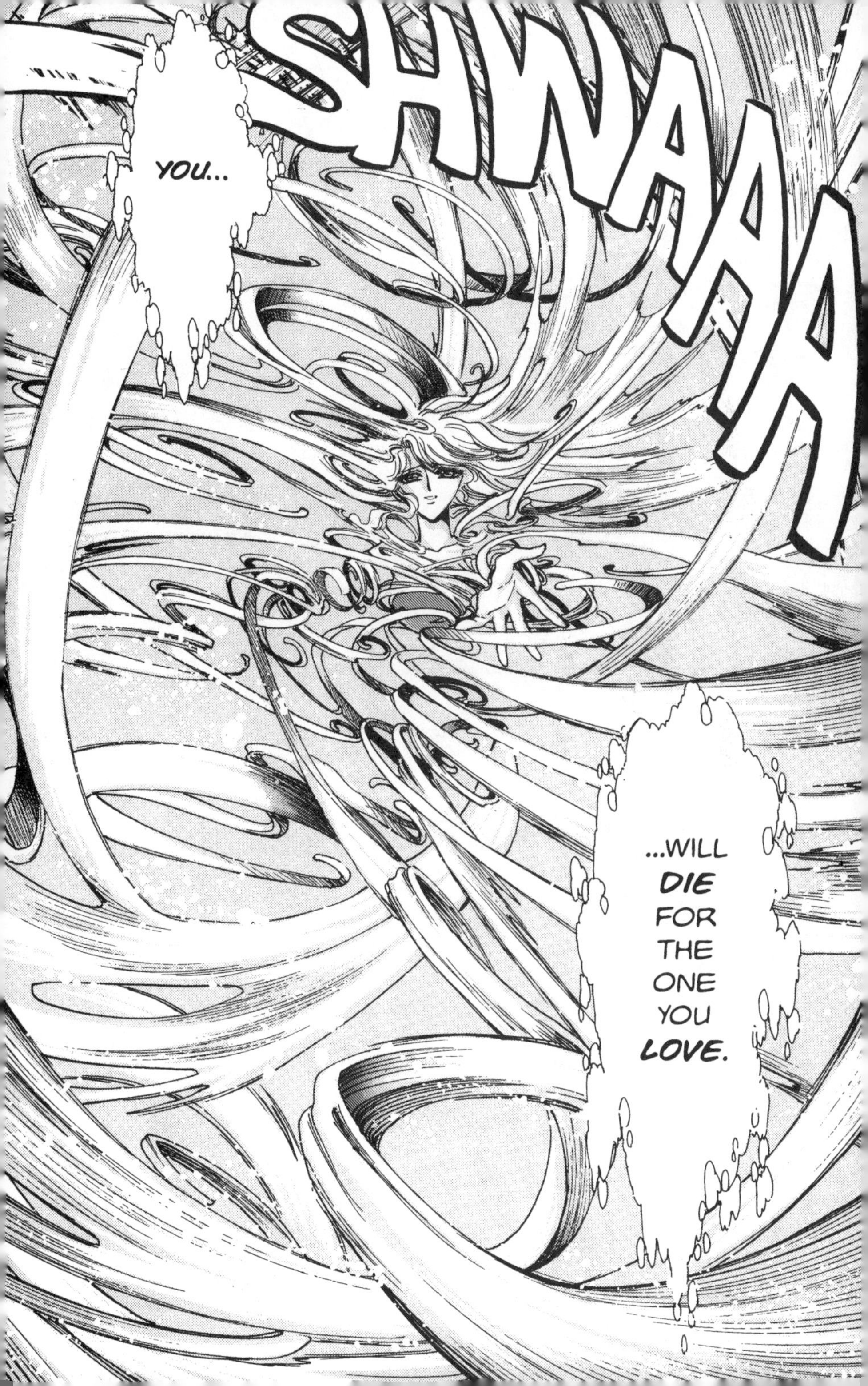
SHWAAAA
YOU...
...WILL DIE FOR THE ONE YOU LOVE.

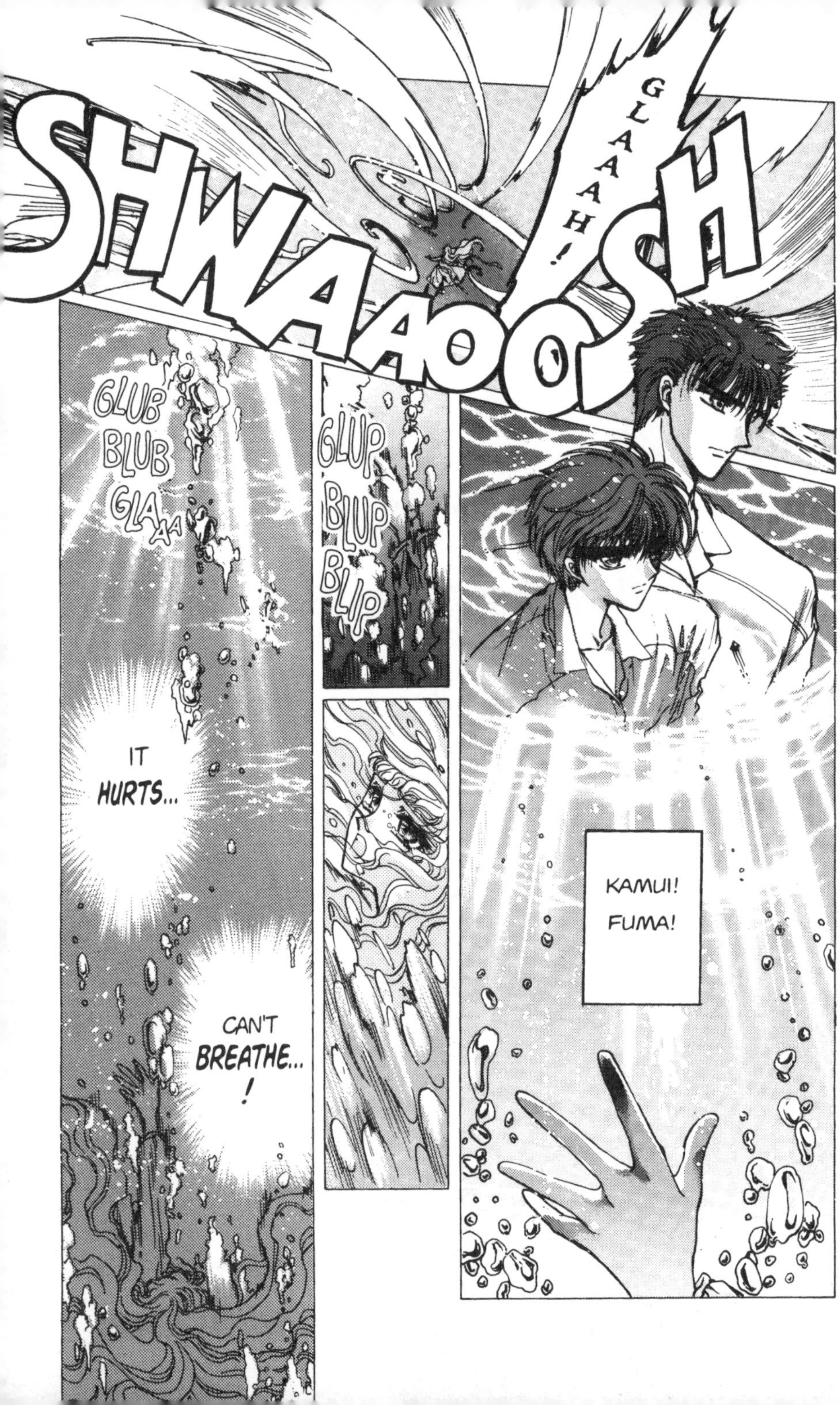
SHWAAOOSH
GLAAAH!
GLUB BLUB GLAAA
IT HURTS...
CAN'T BREATHE... !
GLUP BLUP BLIP
KAMUI! FUMA!

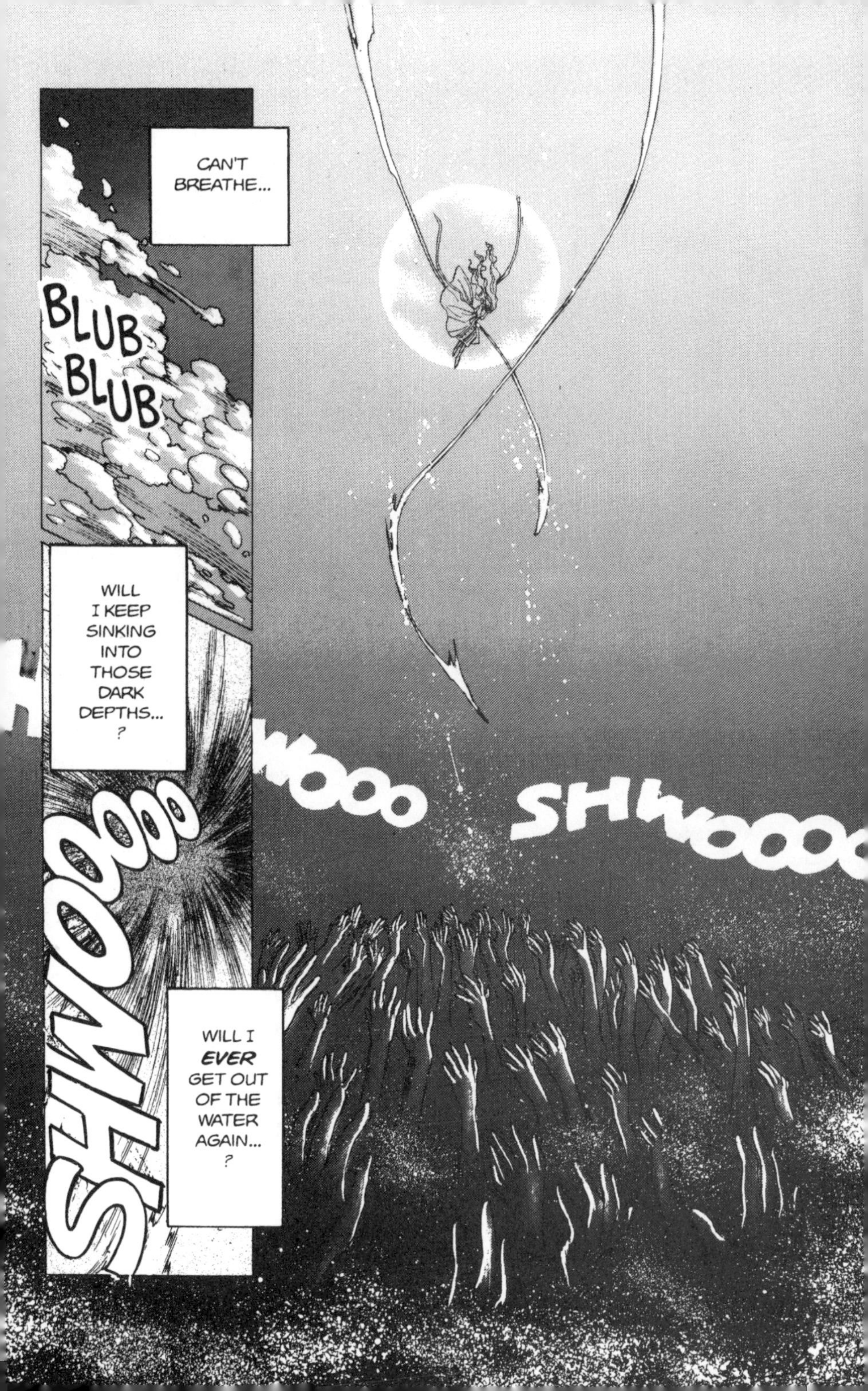
CAN'T BREATHE...
BLUB BLUB
WILL I KEEP SINKING INTO THOSE DARK DEPTHS...?
SHWOOOOO
WOOO
SHWOOOO
WILL I *EVER* GET OUT OF THE WATER AGAIN...?

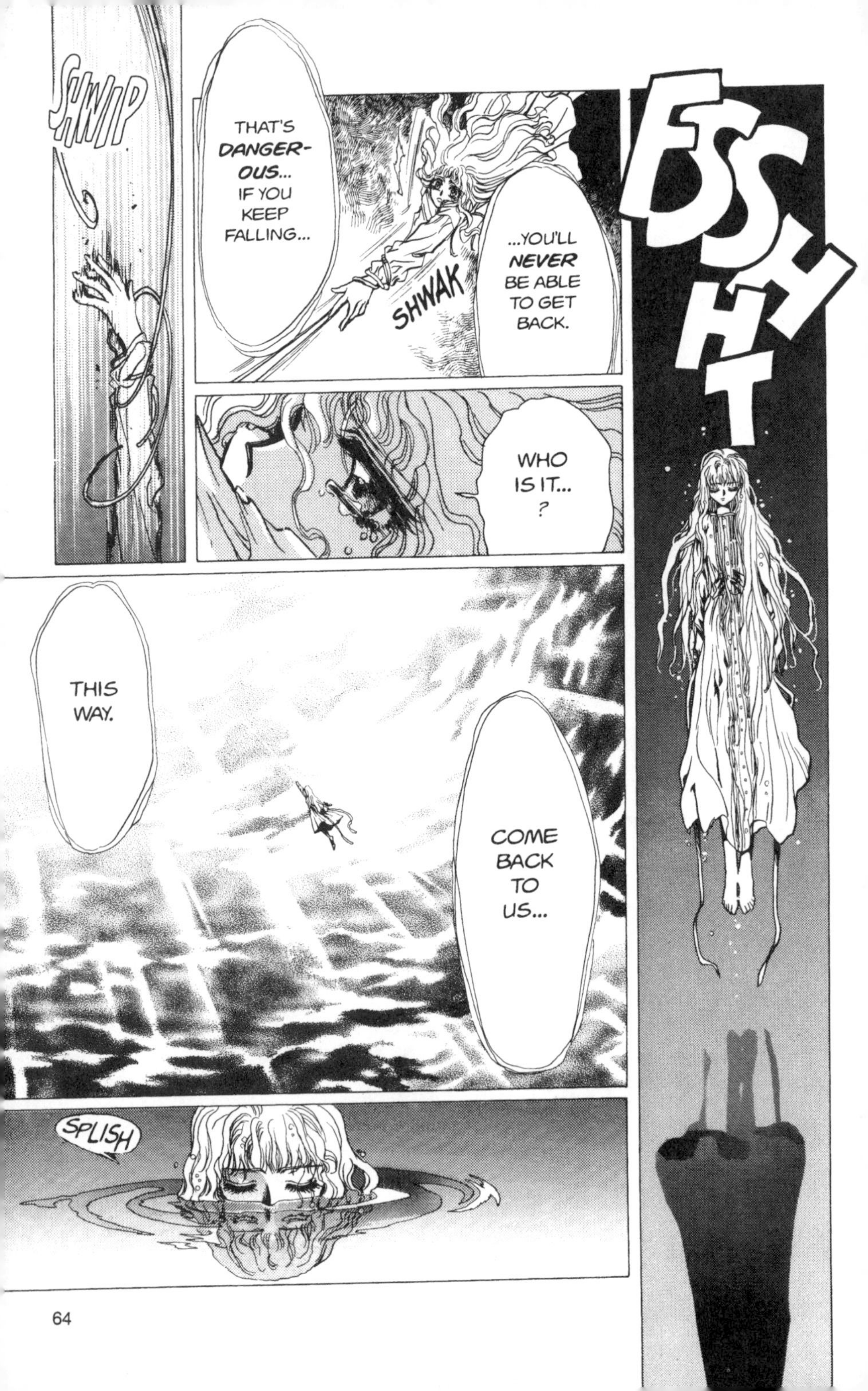
SHWIP
THAT'S **DANGER-OUS...** IF YOU KEEP FALLING...
SHWAK
...YOU'LL **NEVER** BE ABLE TO GET BACK.
WHO IS IT... ?
THIS WAY.
COME BACK TO US...
SPLISH
FSSHHT

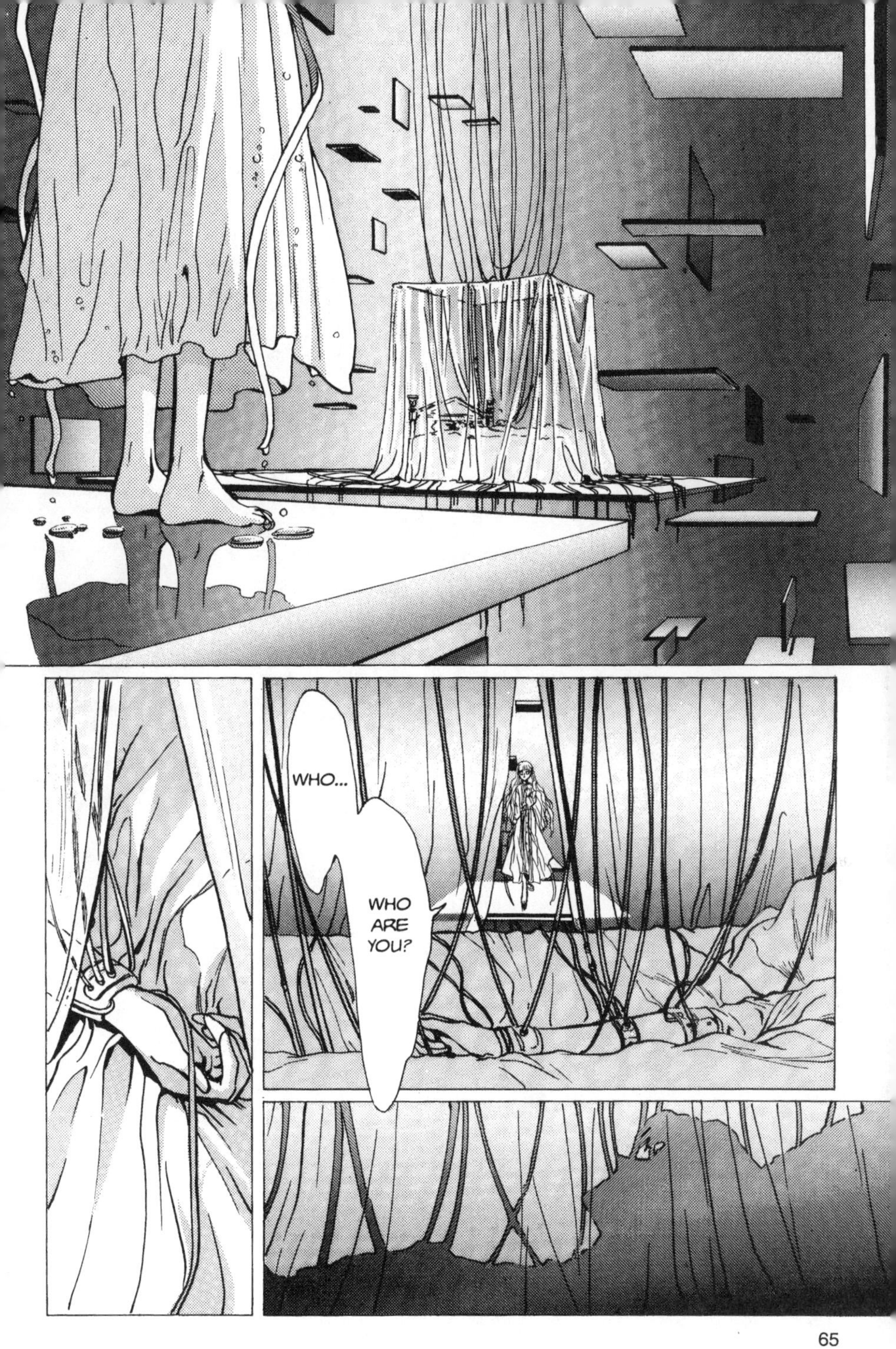
WHO...
WHO ARE YOU?

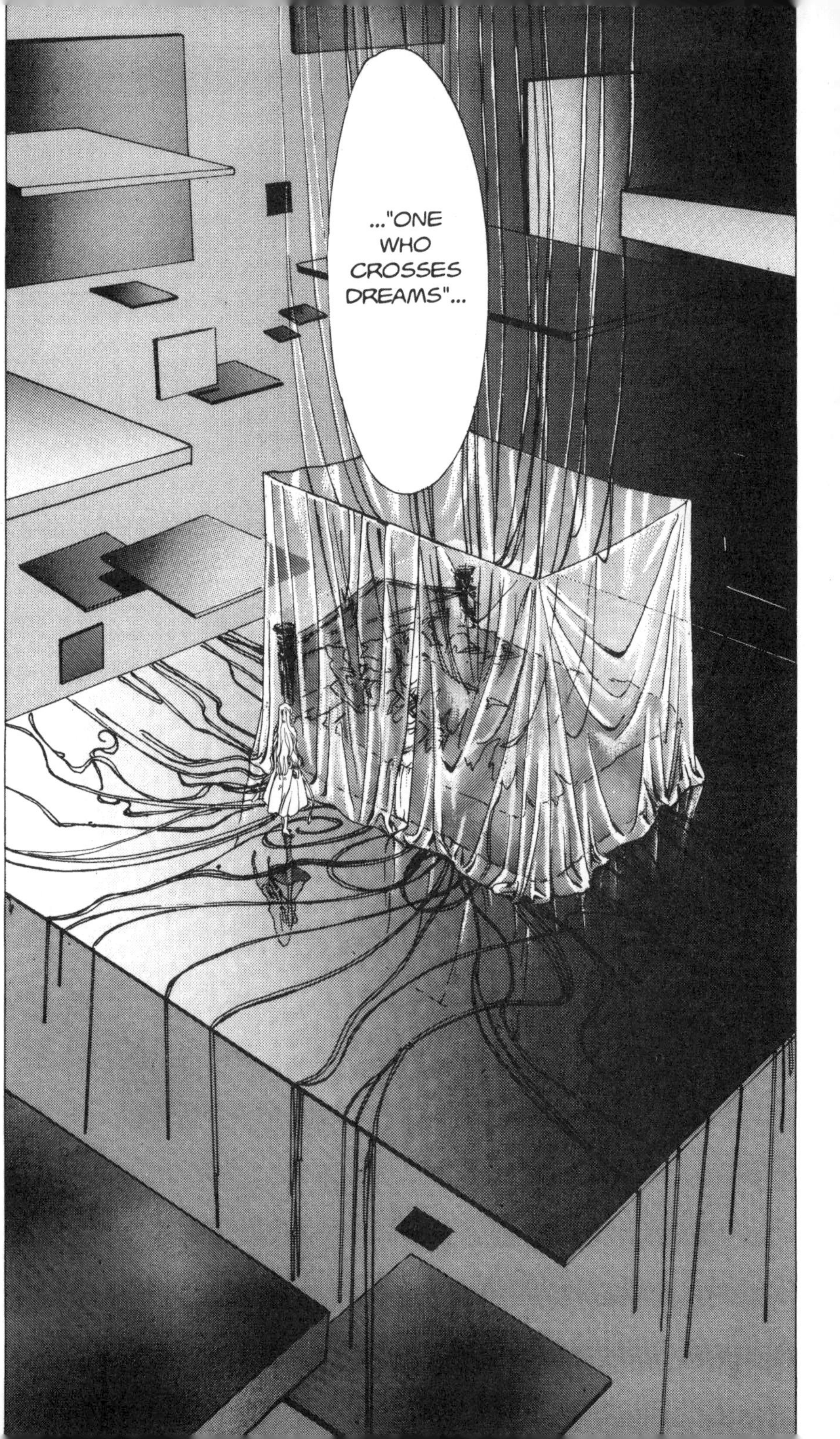
..."ONE WHO CROSSES DREAMS"...

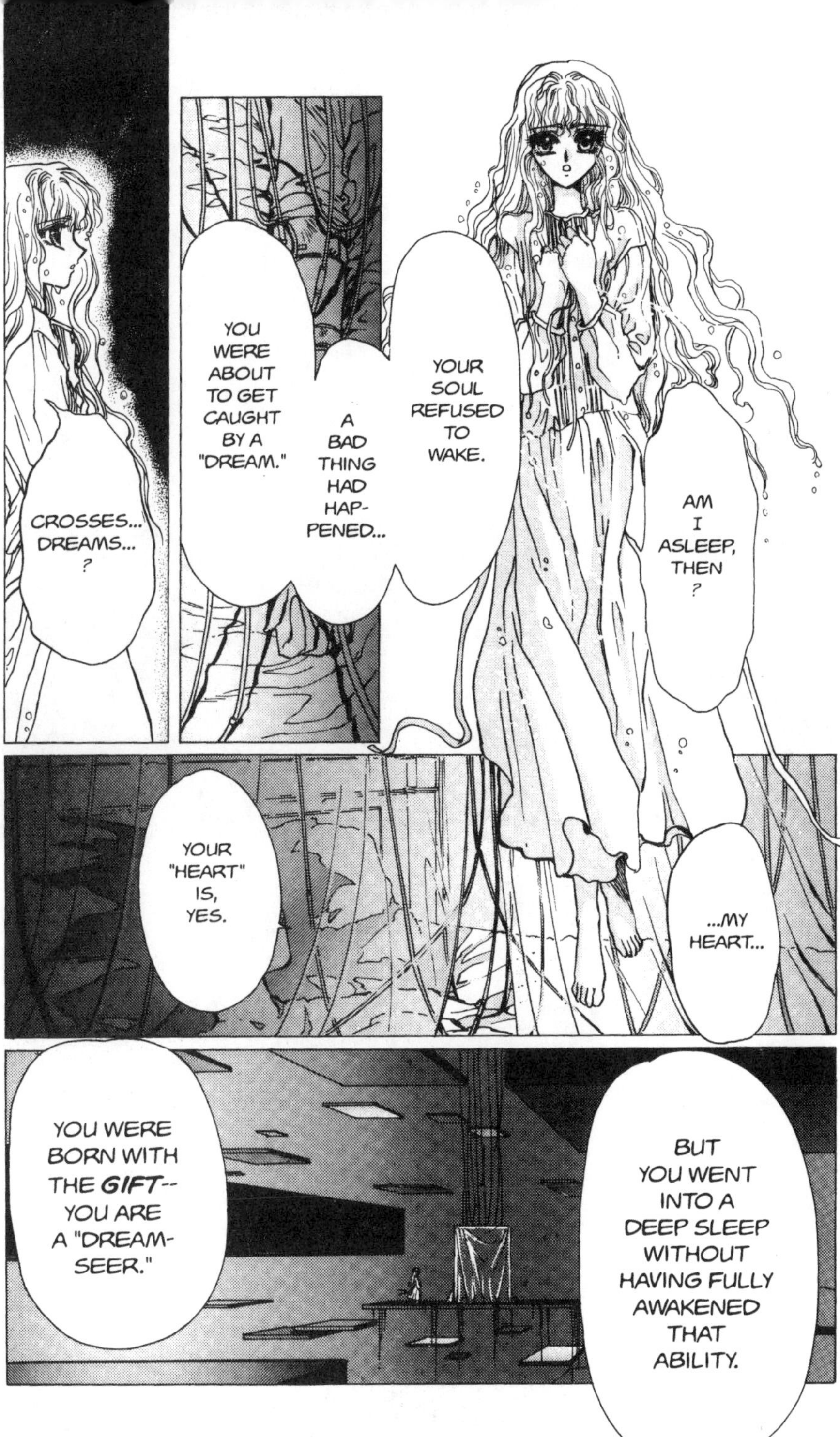
CROSSES... DREAMS...?
YOU WERE ABOUT TO GET CAUGHT BY A "DREAM."
A BAD THING HAD HAP-PENED...
YOUR SOUL REFUSED TO WAKE.
AM I ASLEEP, THEN?
YOUR "HEART" IS, YES.
...MY HEART...
YOU WERE BORN WITH THE GIFT-- YOU ARE A "DREAM-SEER."
BUT YOU WENT INTO A DEEP SLEEP WITHOUT HAVING FULLY AWAKENED THAT ABILITY.

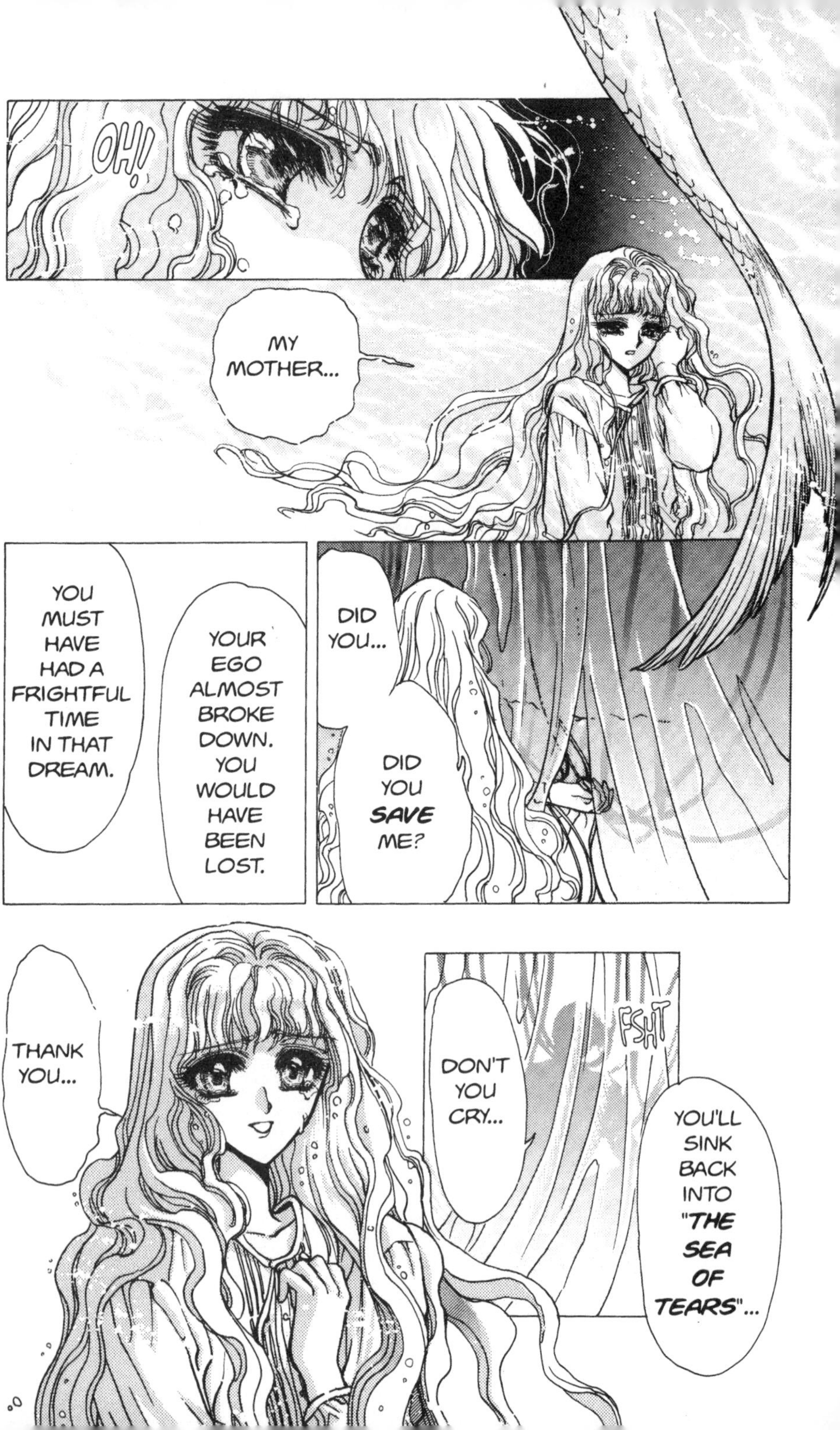
OH!
MY MOTHER...
YOU MUST HAVE HAD A FRIGHTFUL TIME IN THAT DREAM.
YOUR EGO ALMOST BROKE DOWN. YOU WOULD HAVE BEEN LOST.
DID YOU...
DID YOU **SAVE** ME?
THANK YOU...
DON'T YOU CRY...
FSHT
YOU'LL SINK BACK INTO "**THE SEA OF TEARS**"...

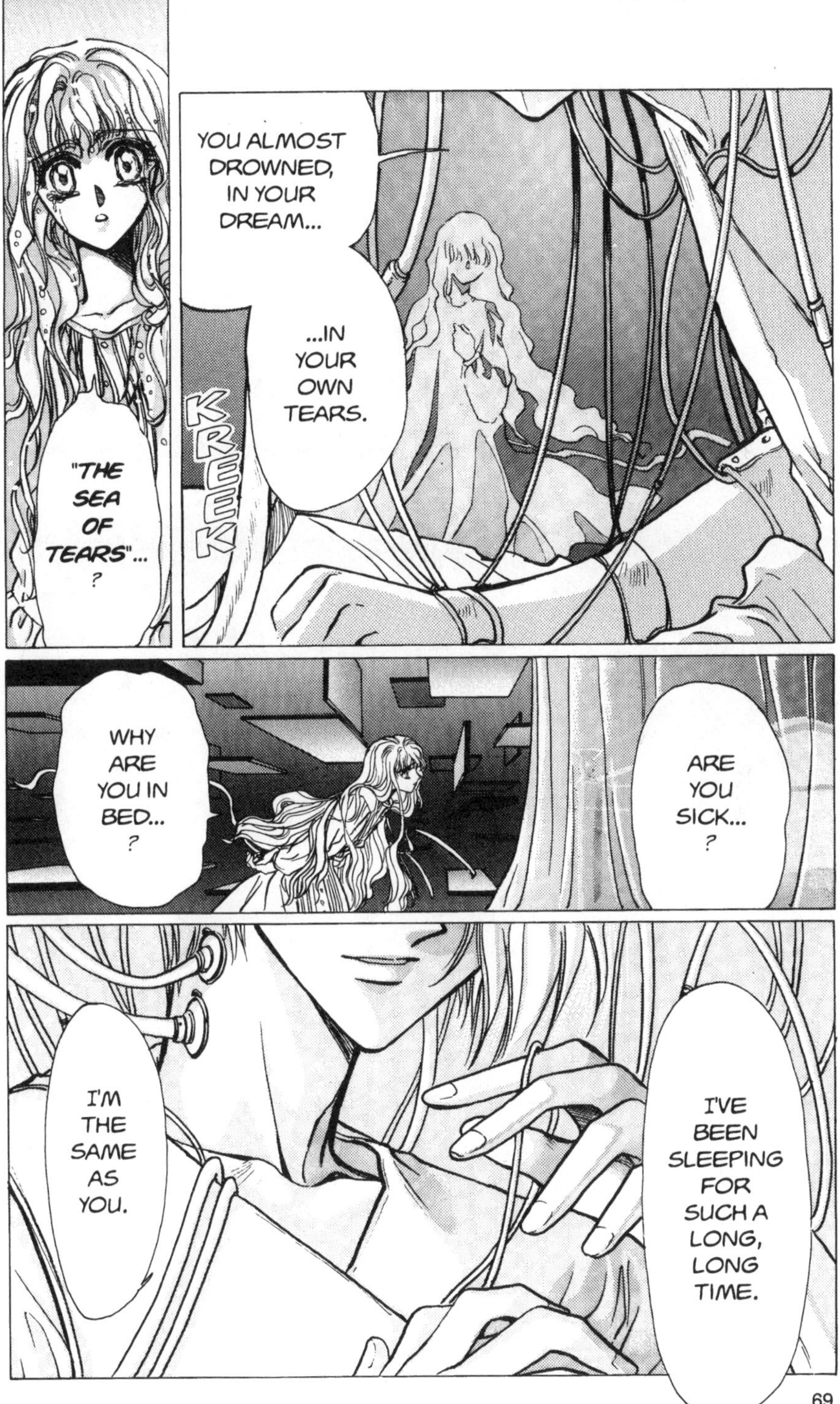
YOU ALMOST DROWNED, IN YOUR DREAM...
...IN YOUR OWN TEARS.
KREEK
"THE SEA OF TEARS"...?
ARE YOU SICK...?
WHY ARE YOU IN BED...?
I'VE BEEN SLEEPING FOR SUCH A LONG, LONG TIME.
I'M THE SAME AS YOU.

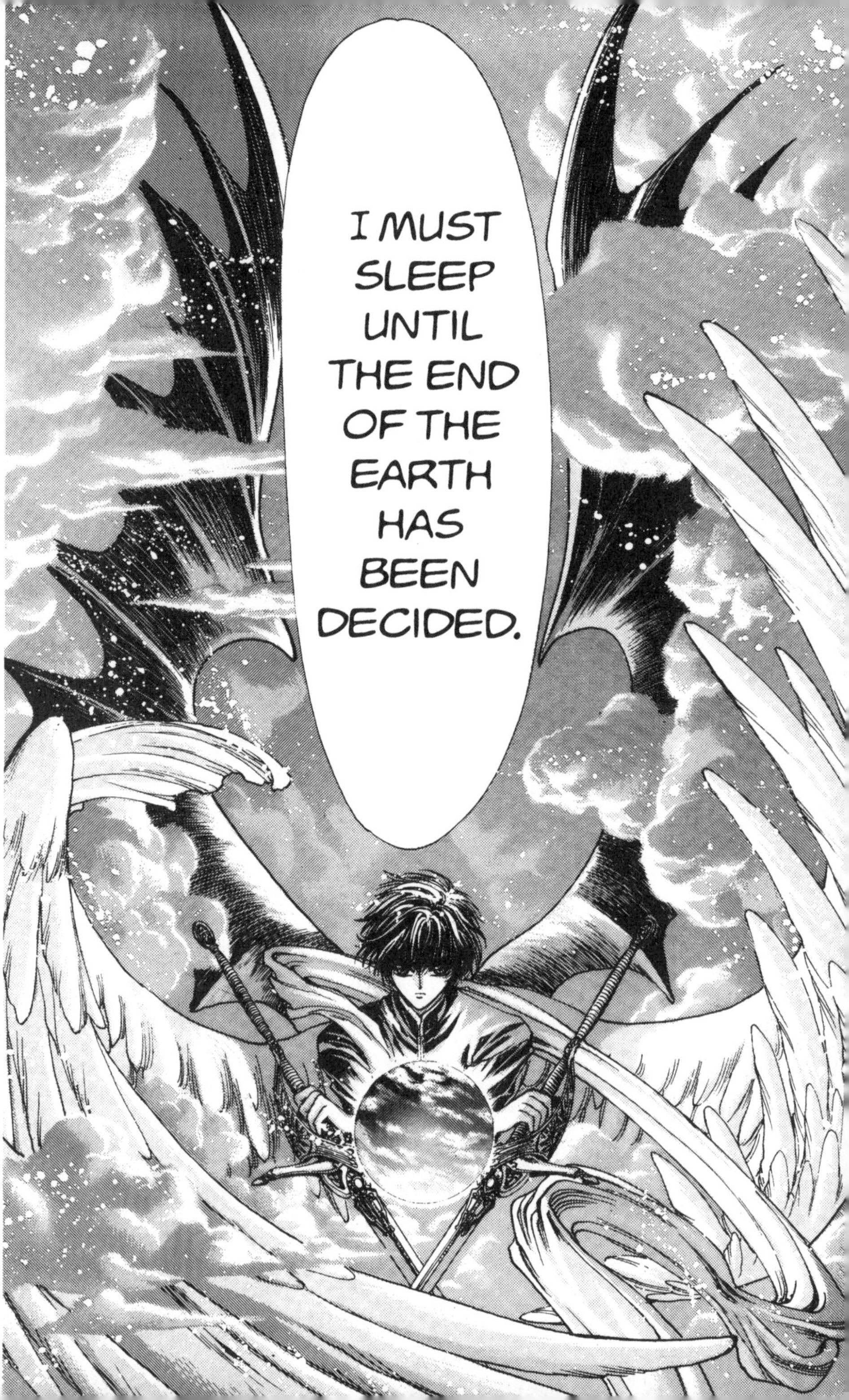
I MUST SLEEP UNTIL THE END OF THE EARTH HAS BEEN DECIDED.

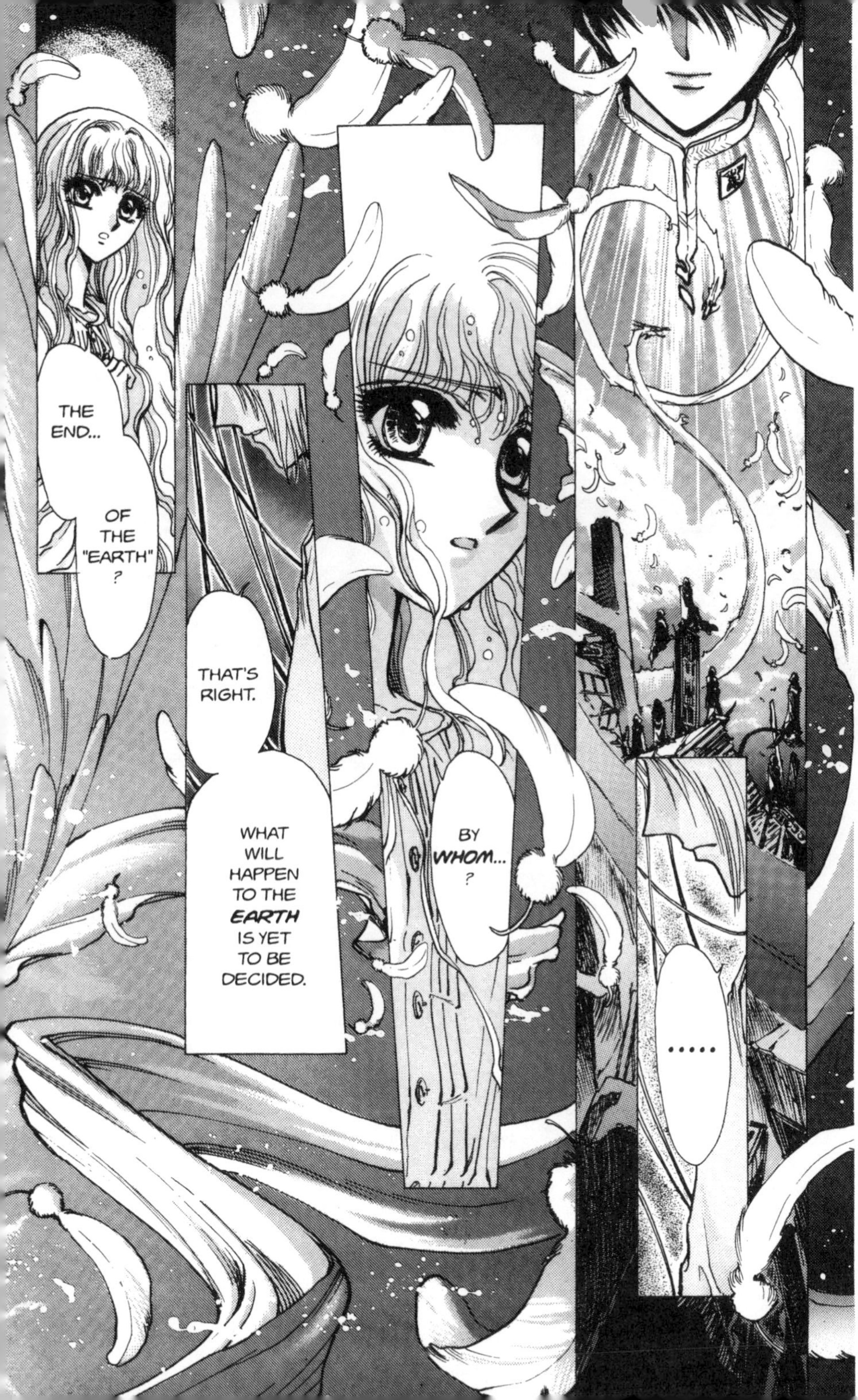
THE END... OF THE "EARTH" ?
THAT'S RIGHT.
WHAT WILL HAPPEN TO THE EARTH IS YET TO BE DECIDED.
BY WHOM...?
.....

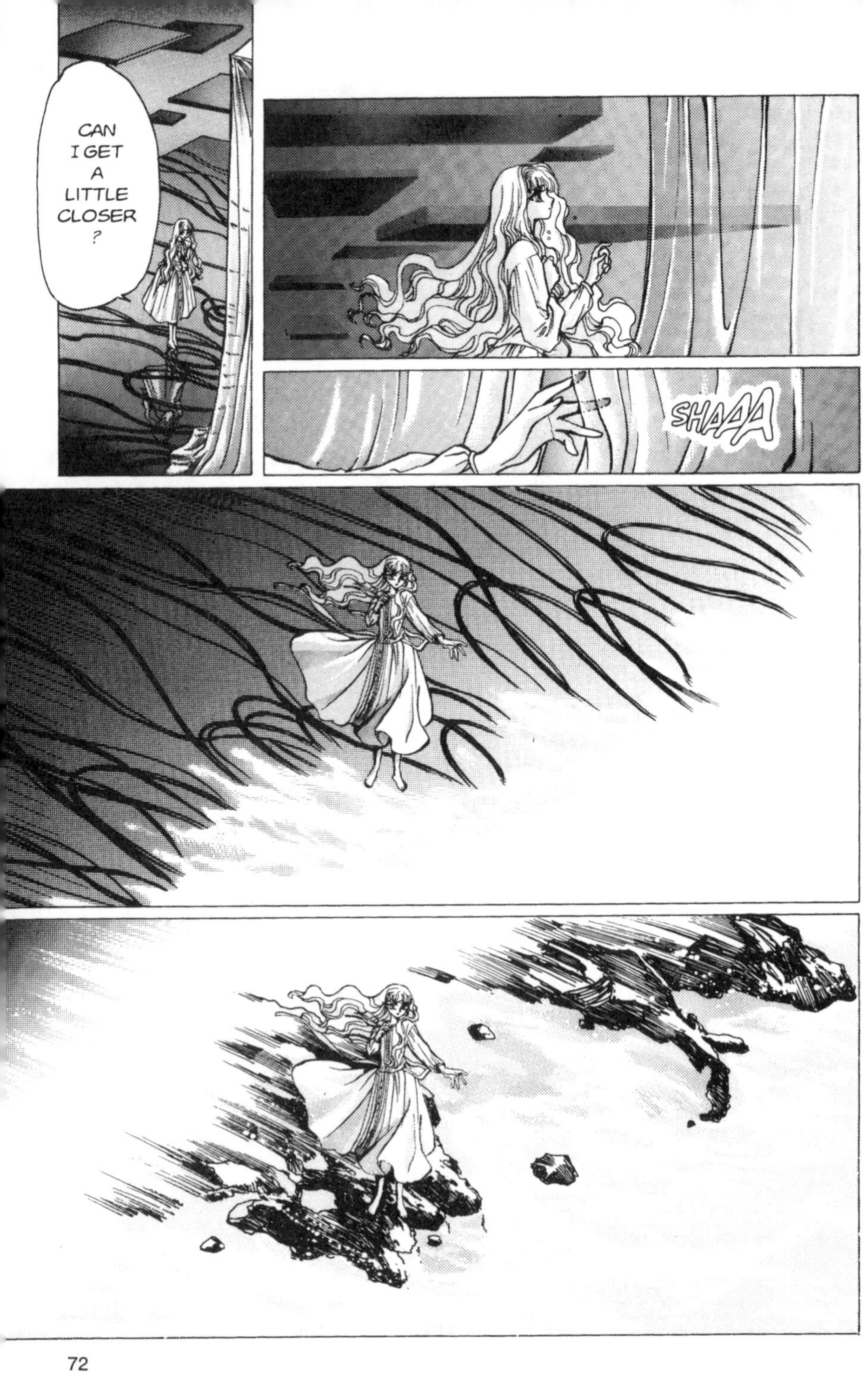
CAN I GET A LITTLE CLOSER ?
SHAAA

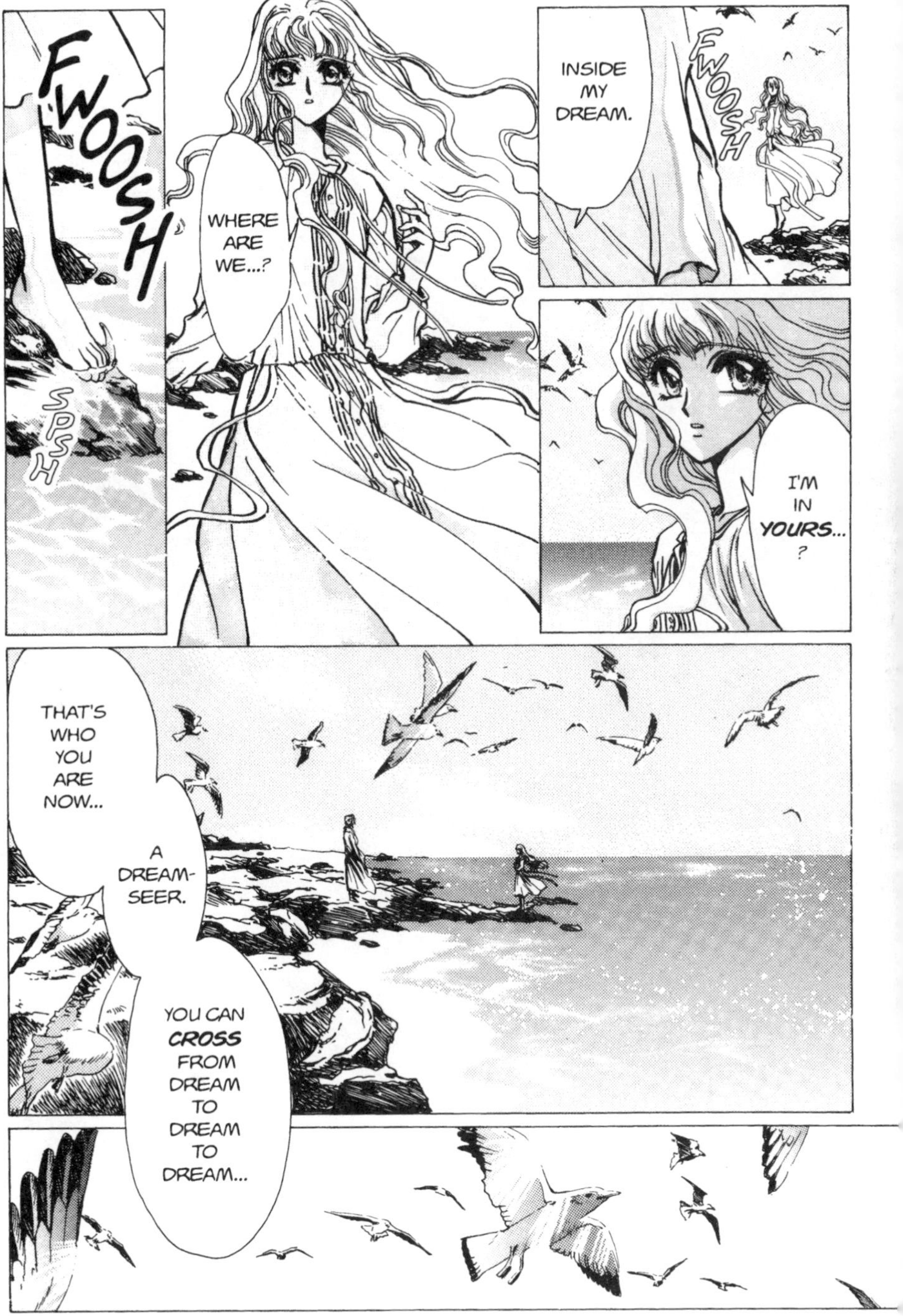
FWOOSH
SPSH
WHERE ARE WE...?
INSIDE MY DREAM.
FWOOSH
I'M IN *YOURS*...?
THAT'S WHO YOU ARE NOW...
A DREAM-SEER.
YOU CAN *CROSS* FROM DREAM TO DREAM TO DREAM...

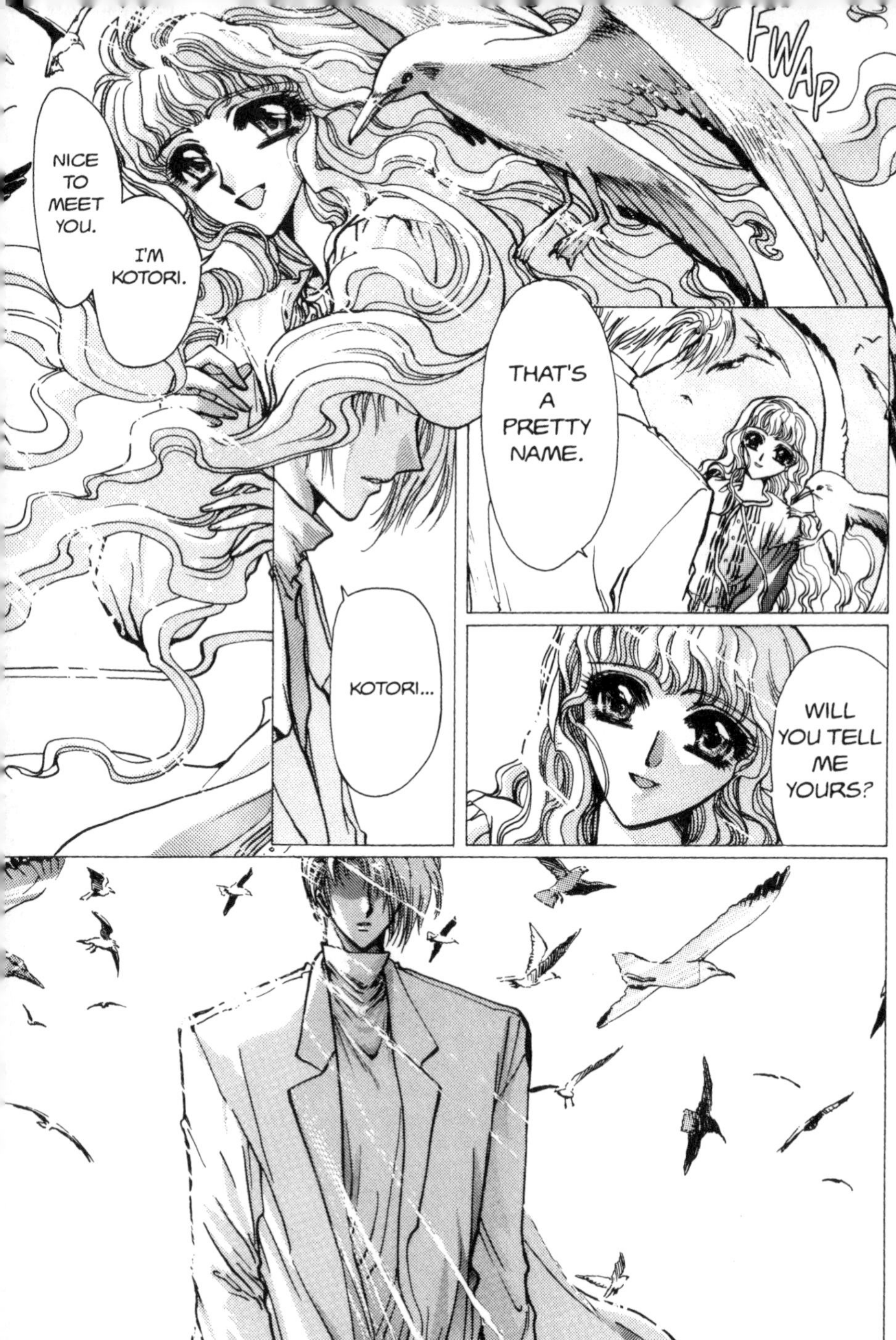
FWAP
NICE TO MEET YOU.
I'M KOTORI.
THAT'S A PRETTY NAME.
KOTORI...
WILL YOU TELL ME YOURS?

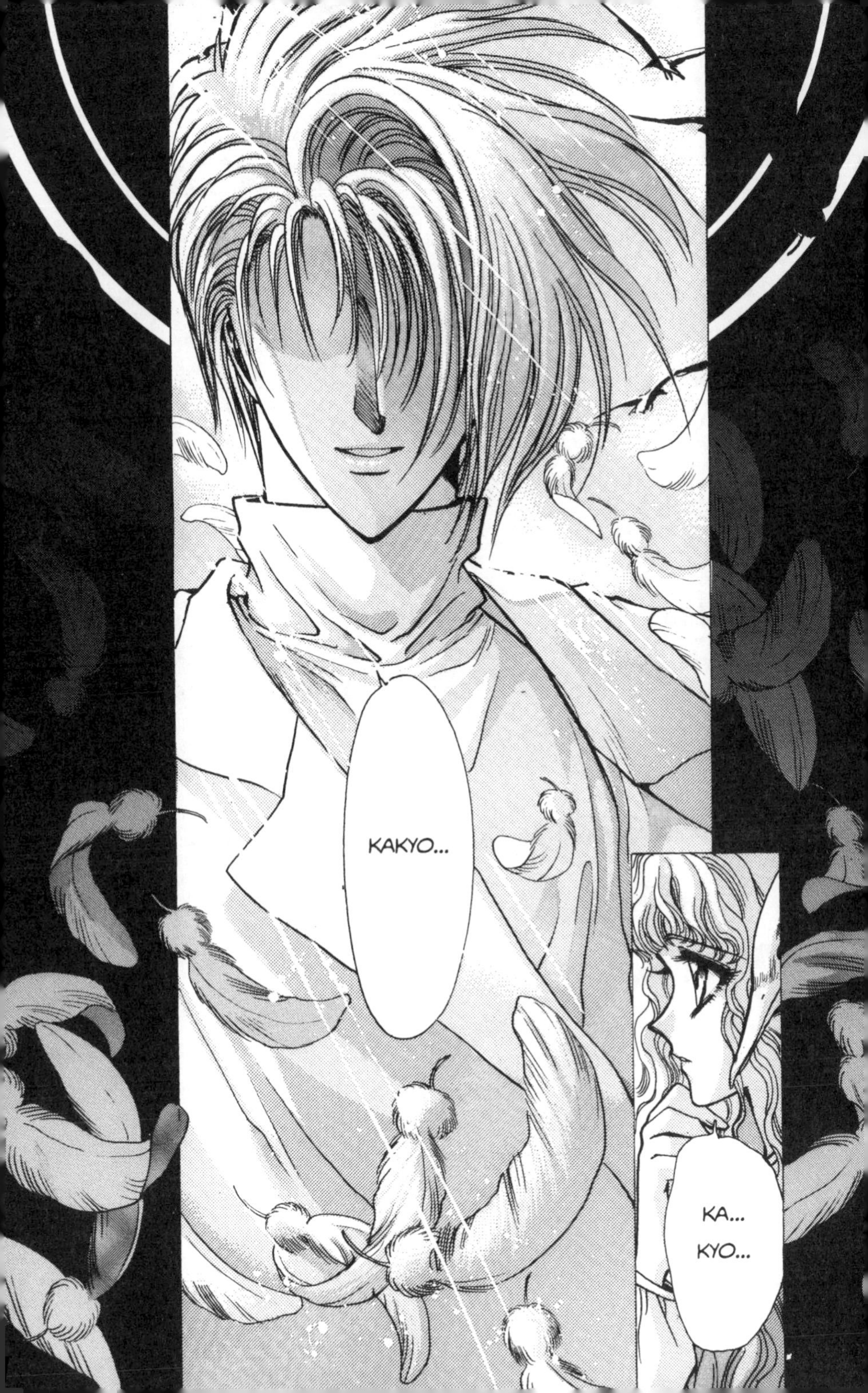
KAKYO...
KA... KYO...

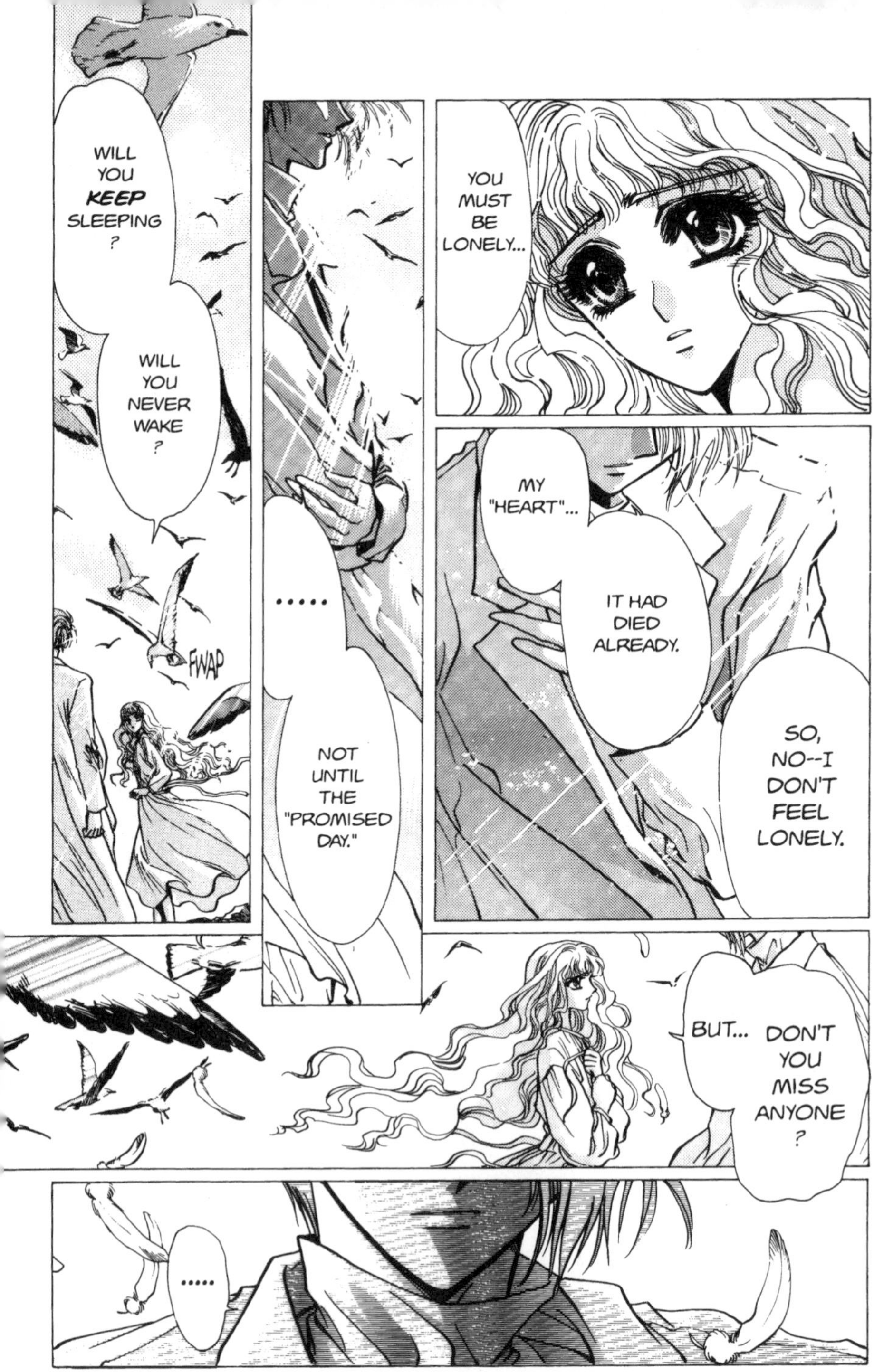
WILL YOU KEEP SLEEPING ?
WILL YOU NEVER WAKE ?
FWAP
.....
NOT UNTIL THE "PROMISED DAY."
YOU MUST BE LONELY...
MY "HEART"...
IT HAD DIED ALREADY.
SO, NO--I DON'T FEEL LONELY.
BUT... DON'T YOU MISS ANYONE ?
.....

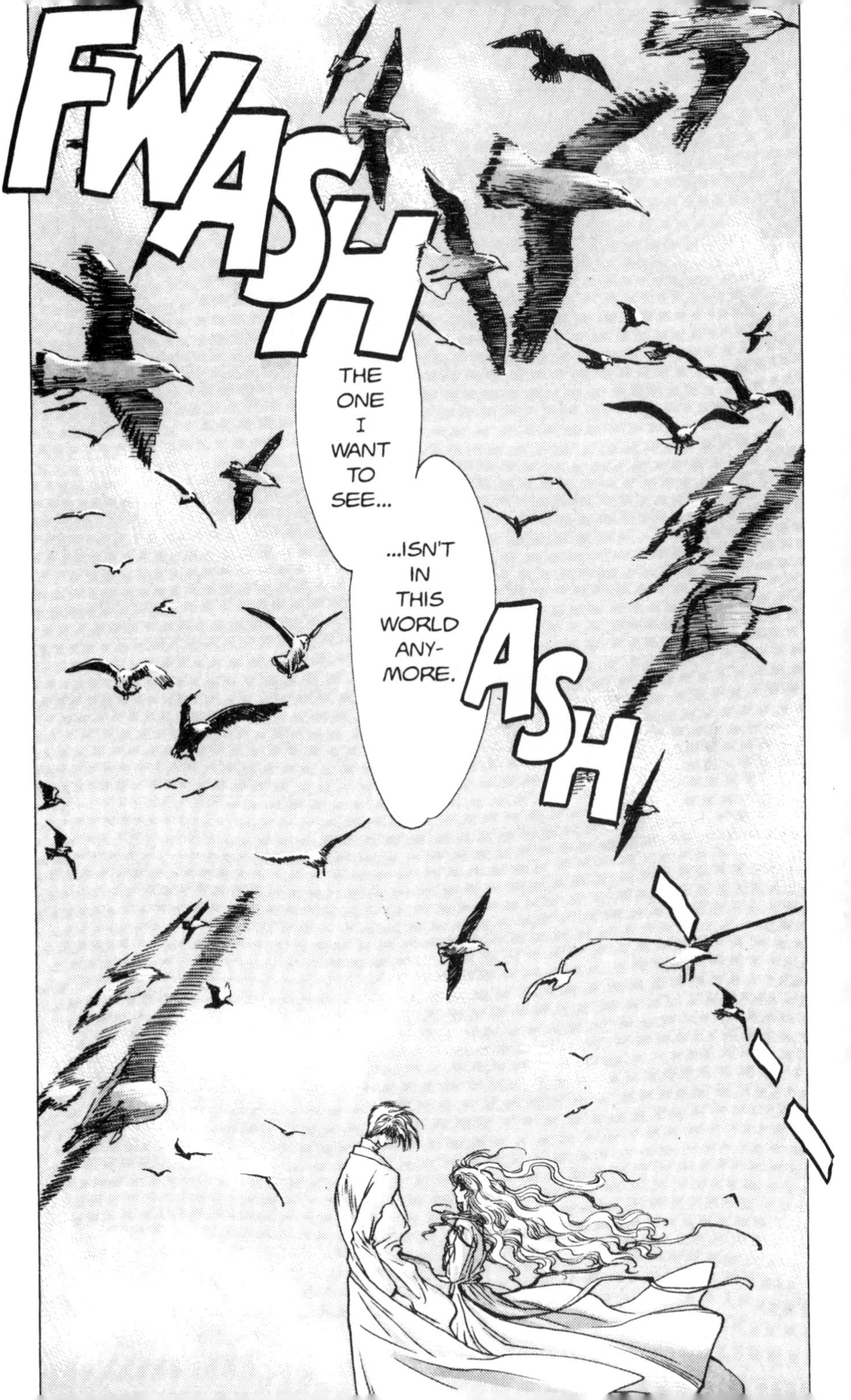
FWASH
THE ONE I WANT TO SEE...
...ISN'T IN THIS WORLD ANY-MORE.
ASH

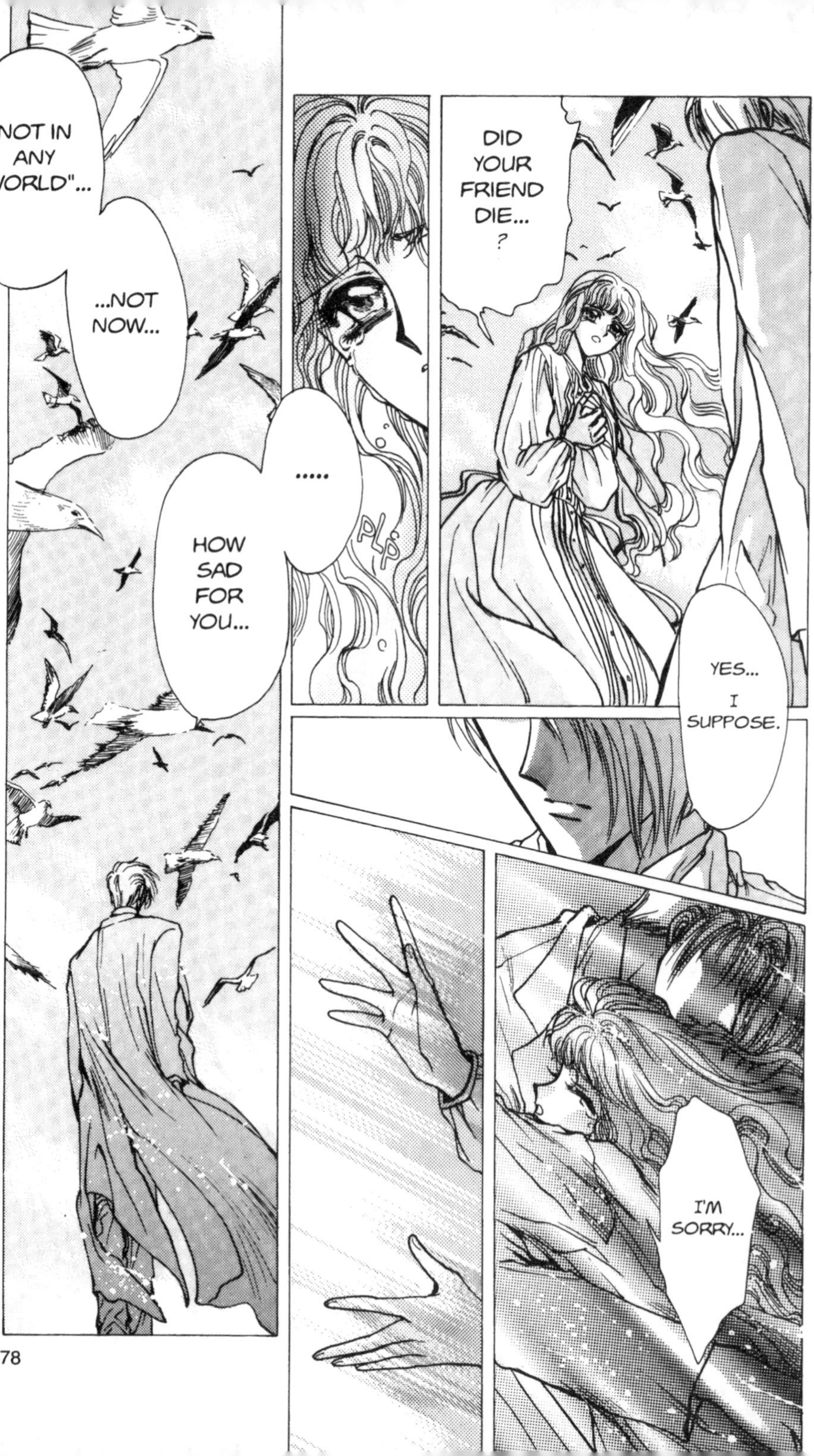
NOT IN ANY "WORLD"...
...NOT NOW...
HOW SAD FOR YOU...
.....
DID YOUR FRIEND DIE...?
YES... I SUPPOSE.
I'M SORRY...

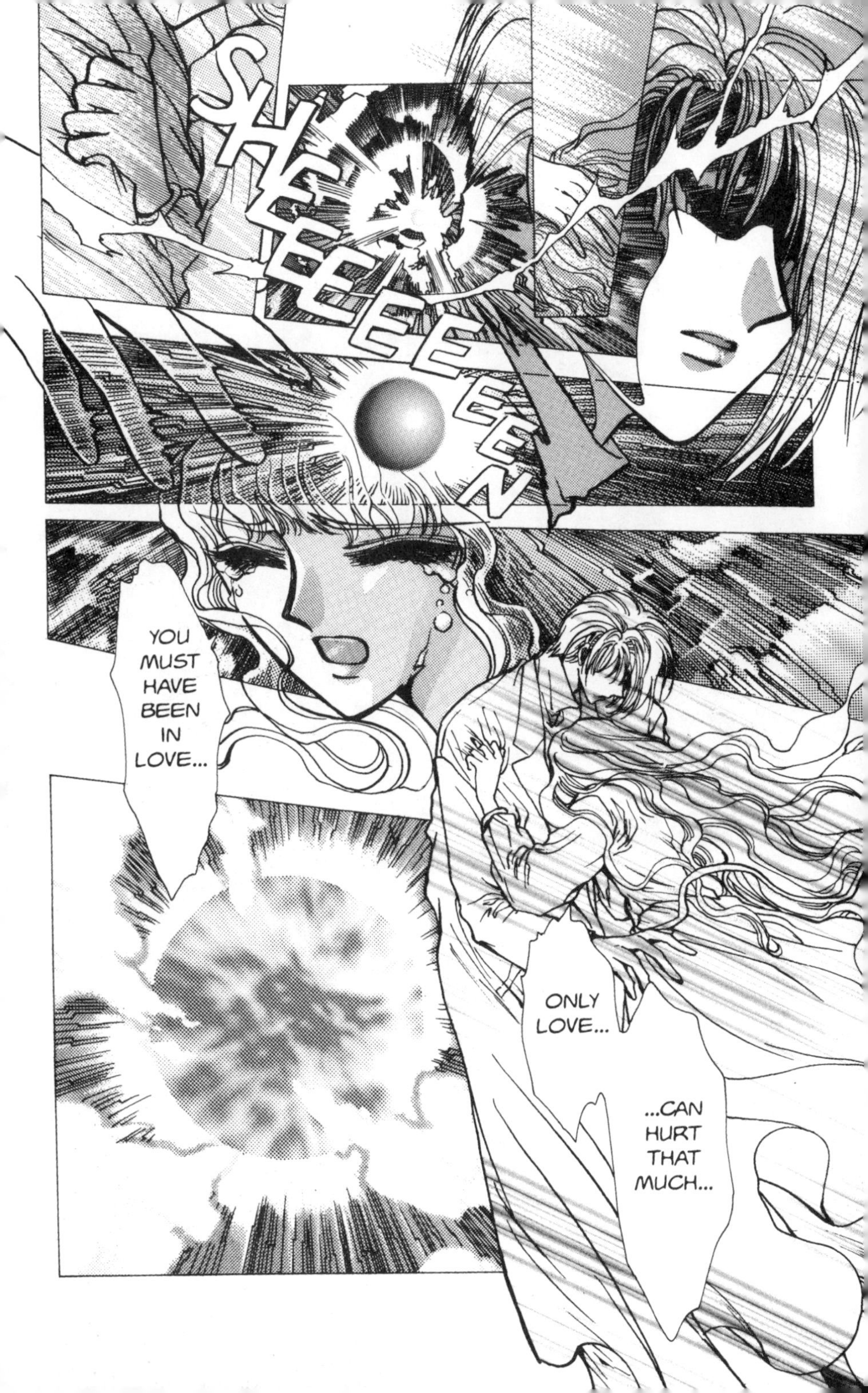
SHEEEEEEEN
YOU MUST HAVE BEEN IN LOVE...
ONLY LOVE...
...CAN HURT THAT MUCH...

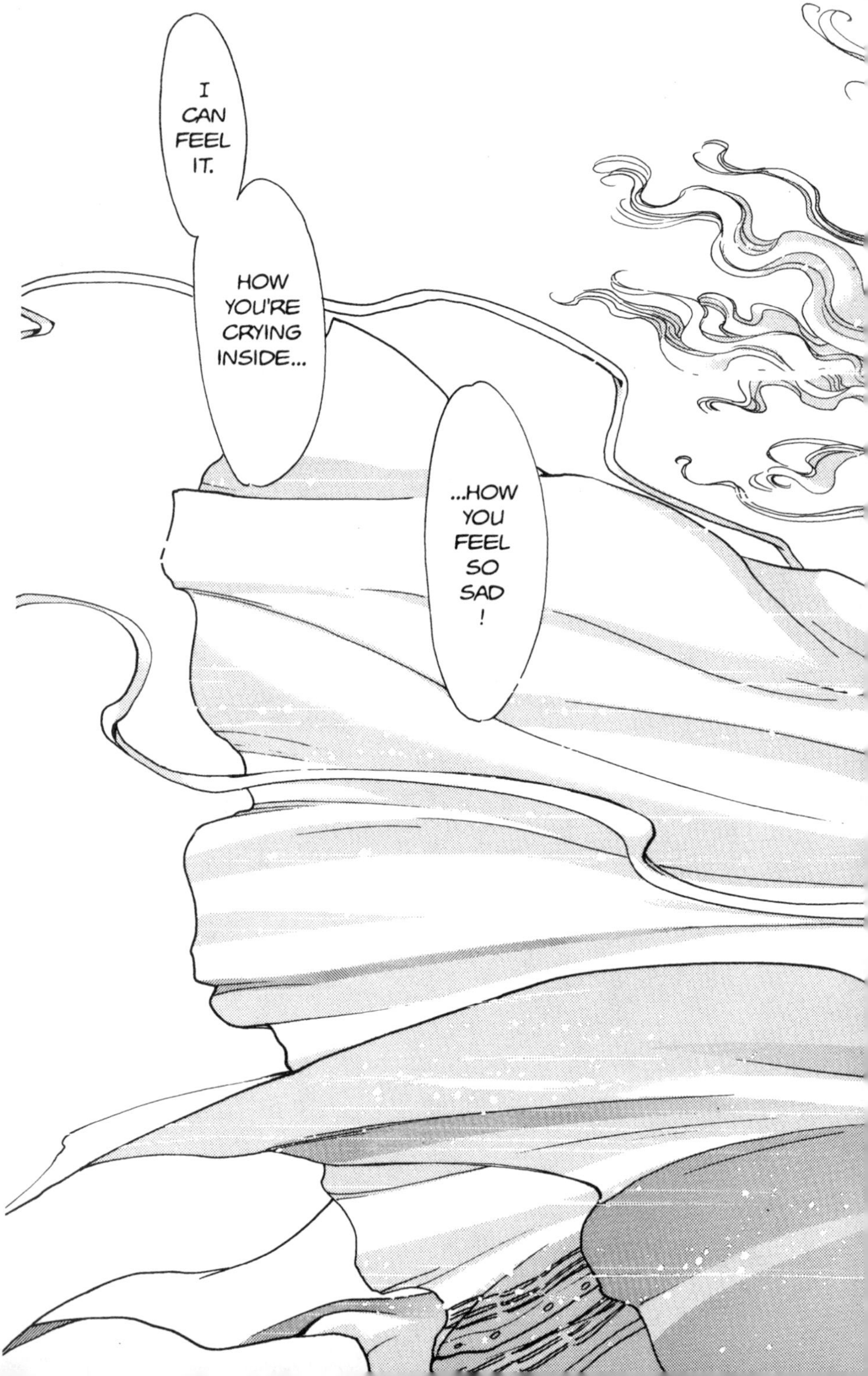
I CAN FEEL IT.
HOW YOU'RE CRYING INSIDE...
...HOW YOU FEEL SO SAD!

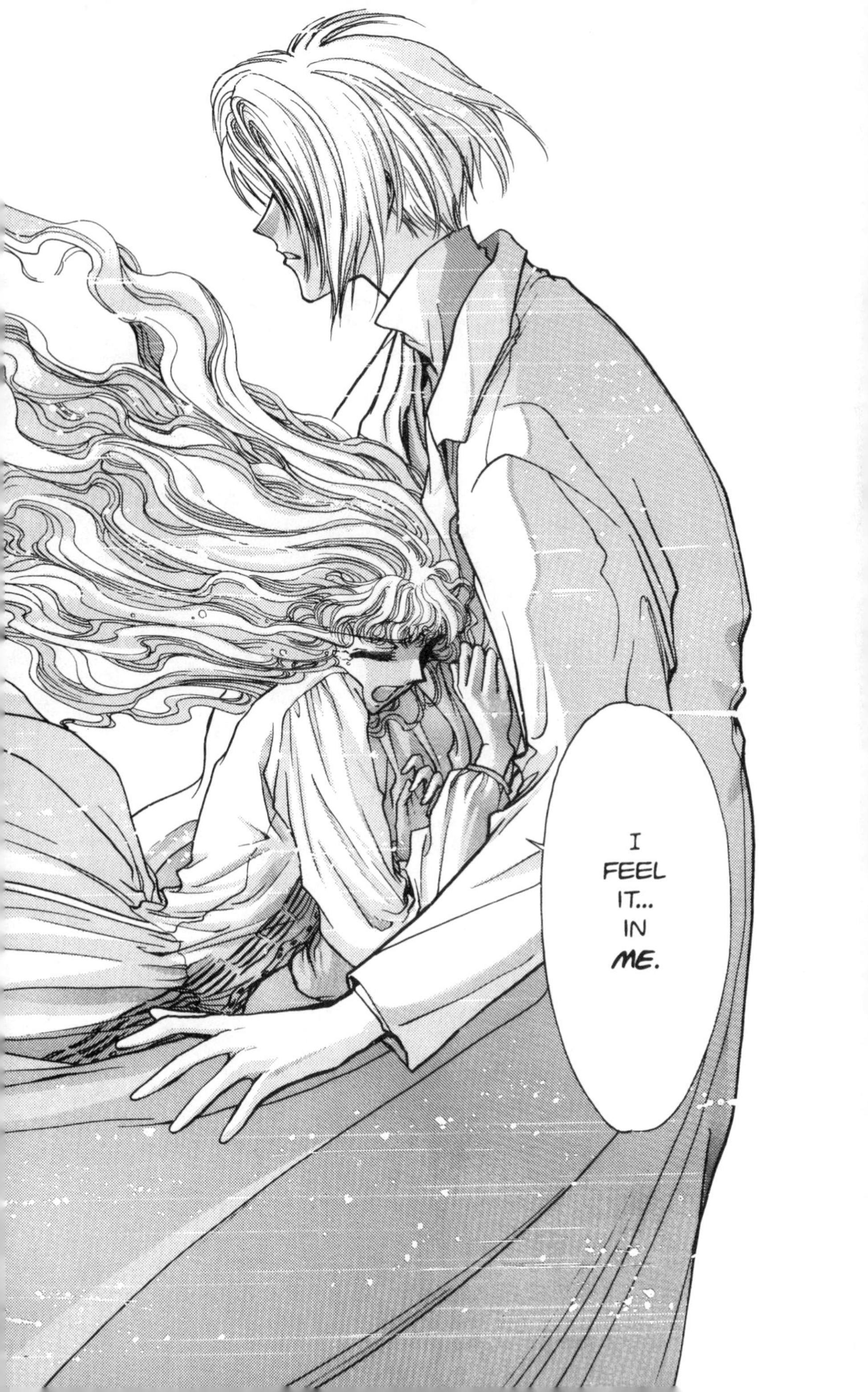
I FEEL IT... IN ME.

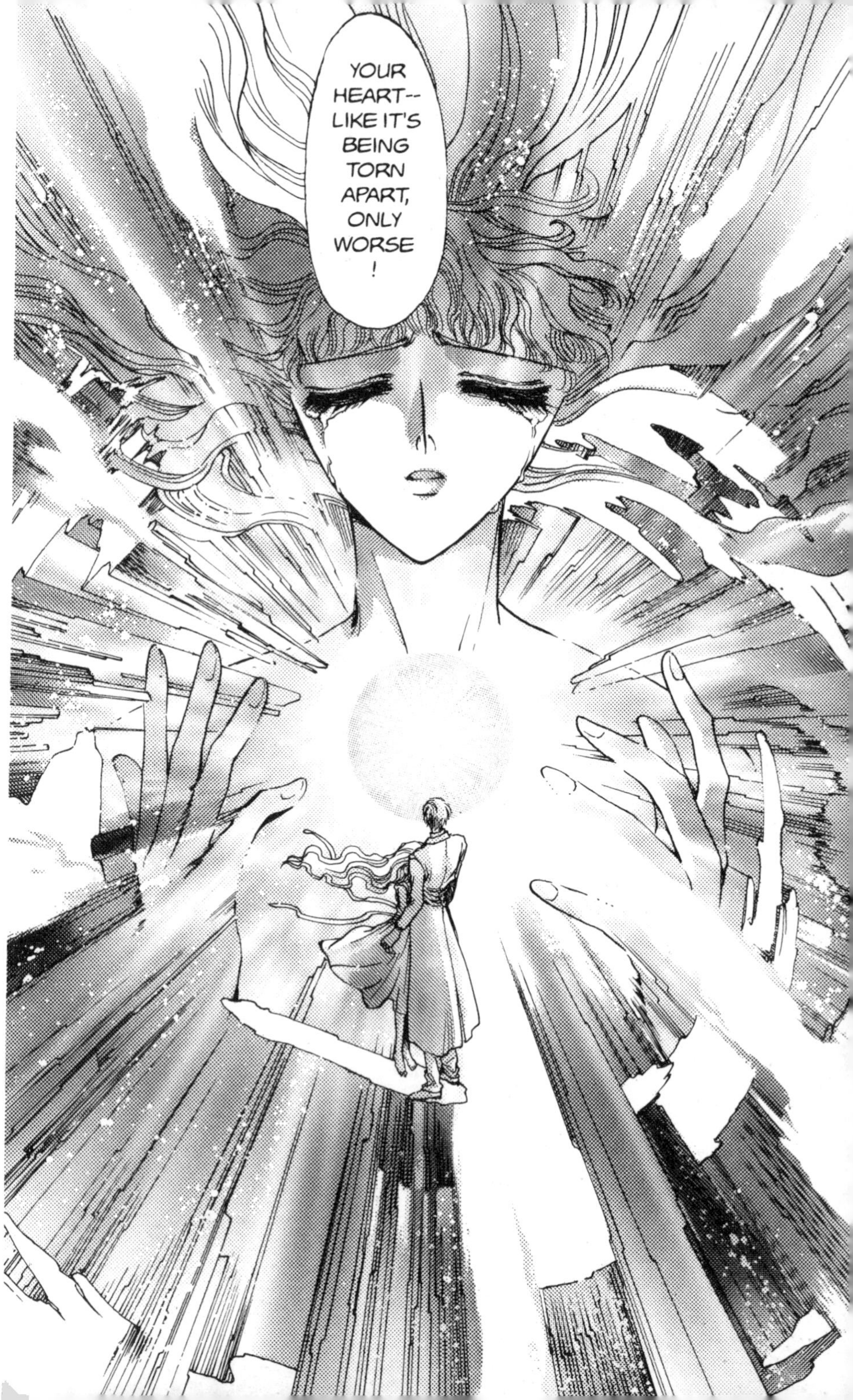
YOUR HEART-- LIKE IT'S BEING TORN APART, ONLY WORSE!

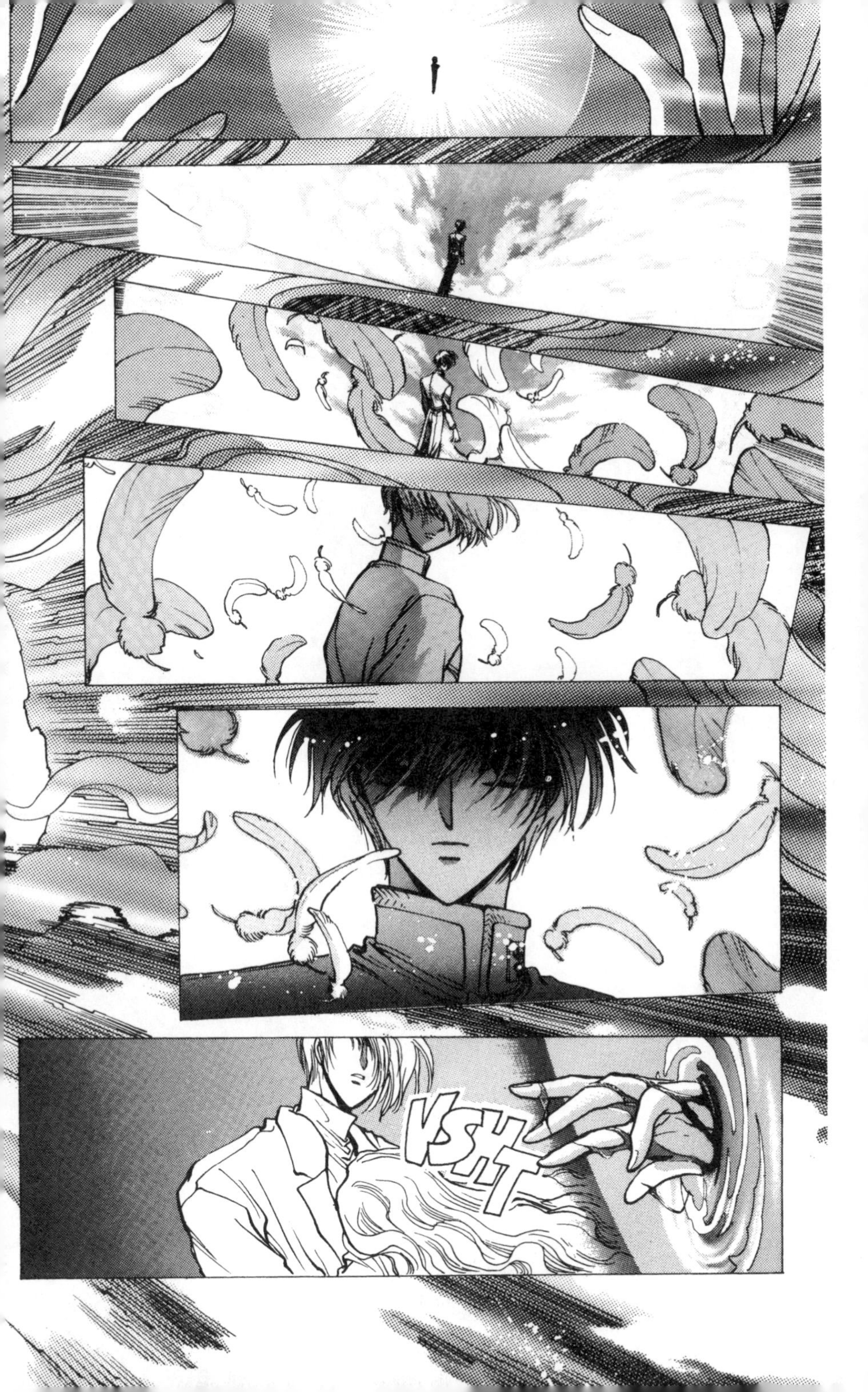
VSHT

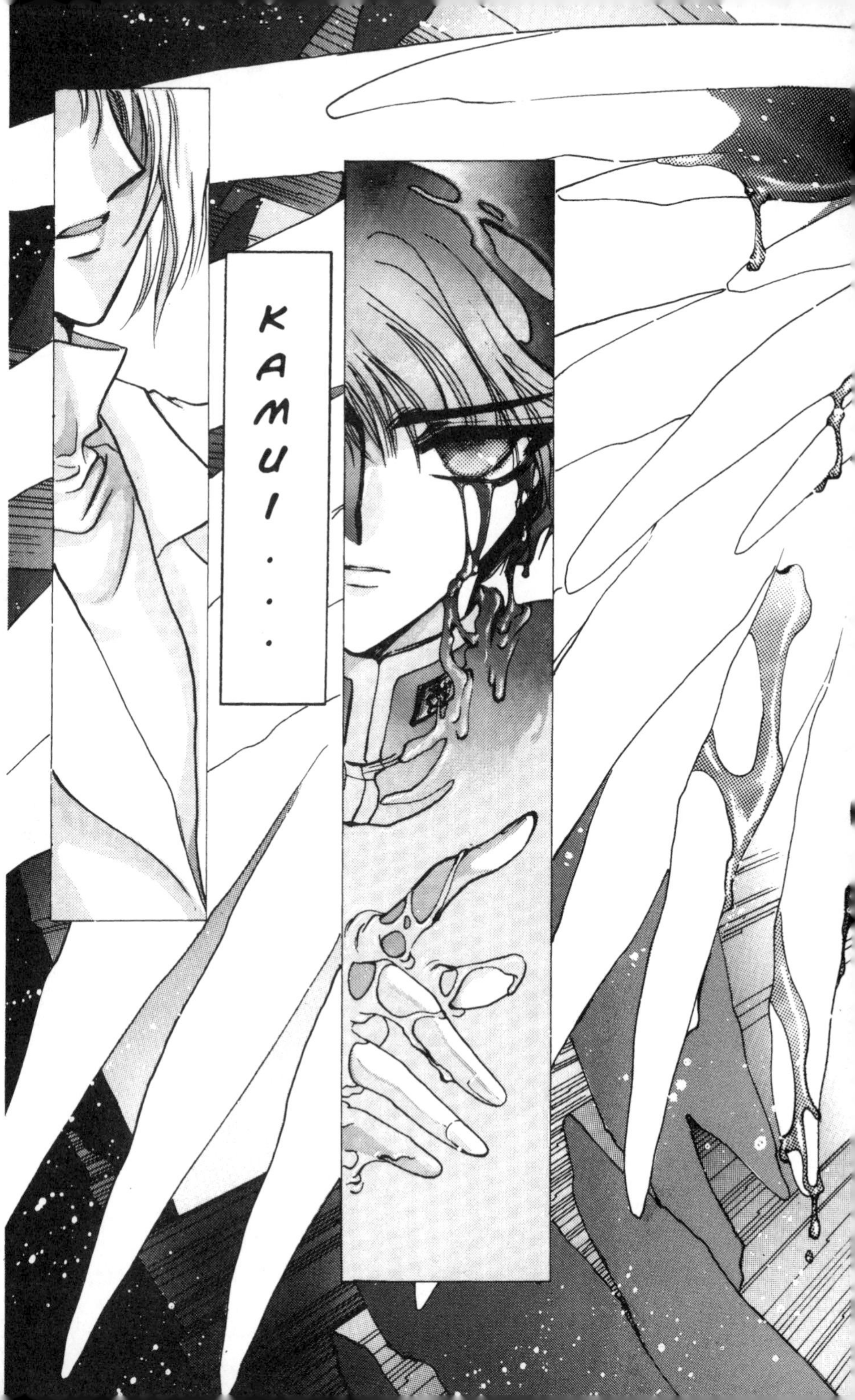
KAMUI . . .

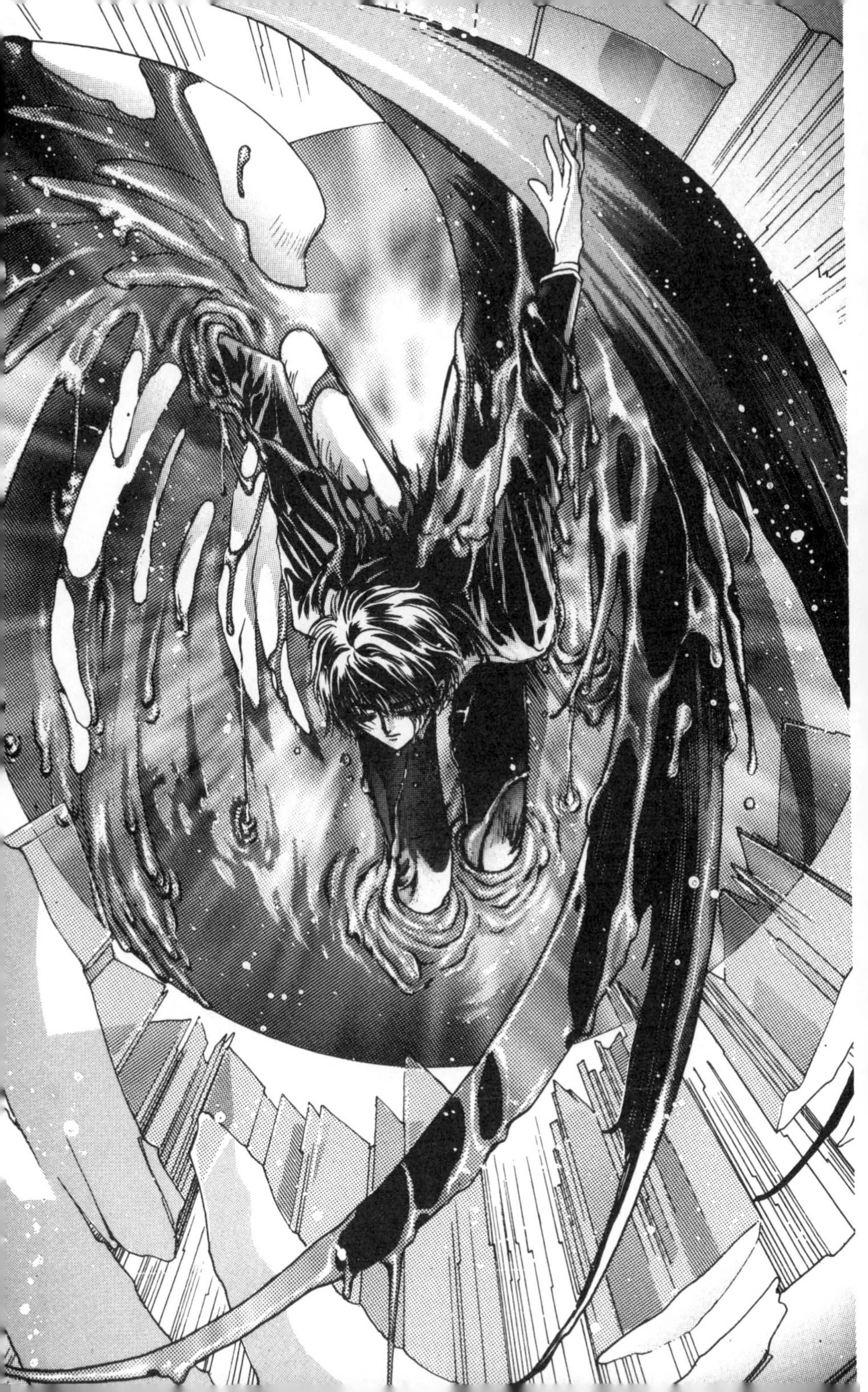

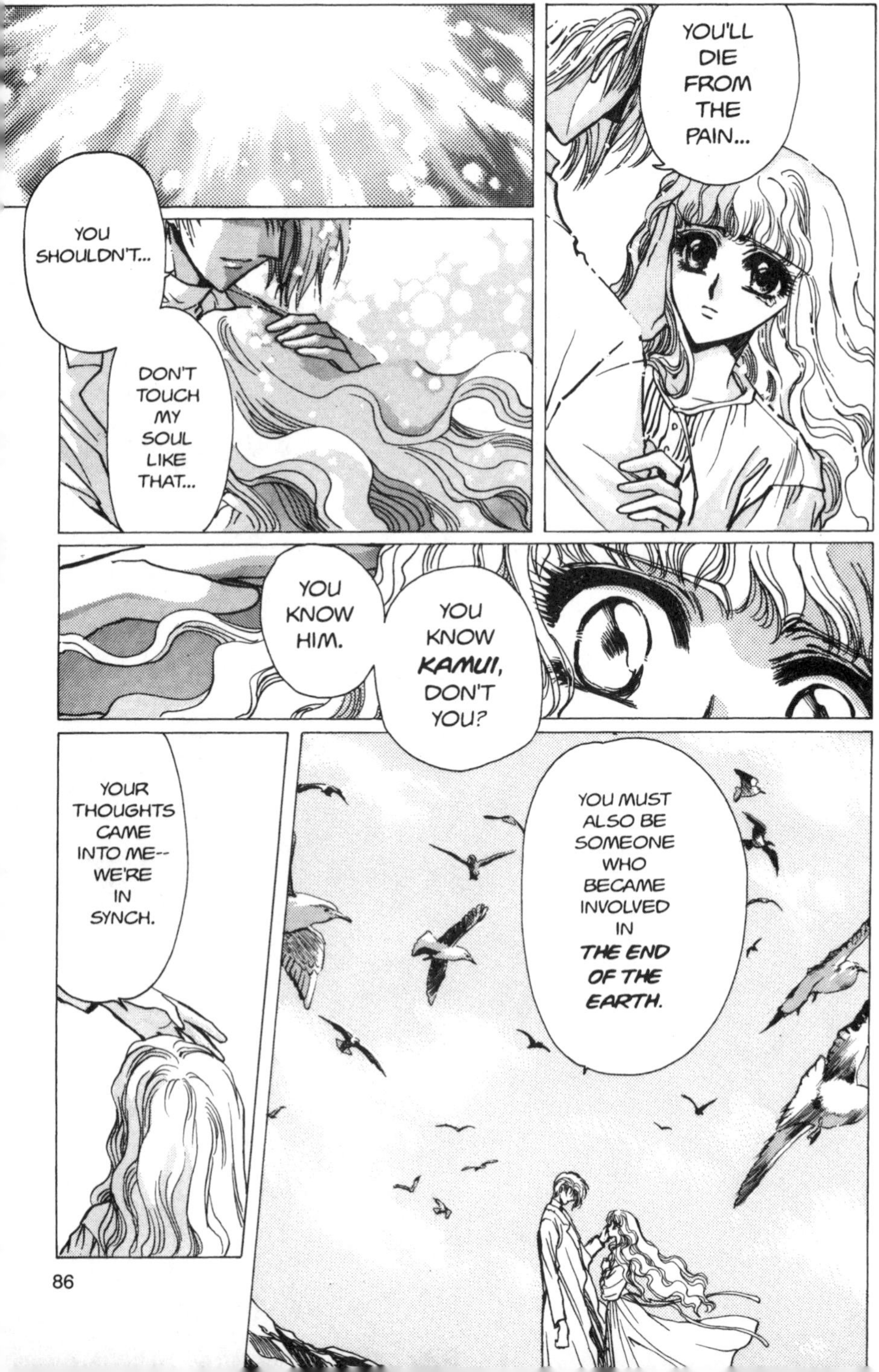
YOU SHOULDN'T...
DON'T TOUCH MY SOUL LIKE THAT...
YOU'LL DIE FROM THE PAIN...
YOU KNOW HIM.
YOU KNOW ***KAMUI***, DON'T YOU?
YOUR THOUGHTS CAME INTO ME-- WE'RE IN SYNCH.
YOU MUST ALSO BE SOMEONE WHO BECAME INVOLVED IN ***THE END OF THE EARTH.***

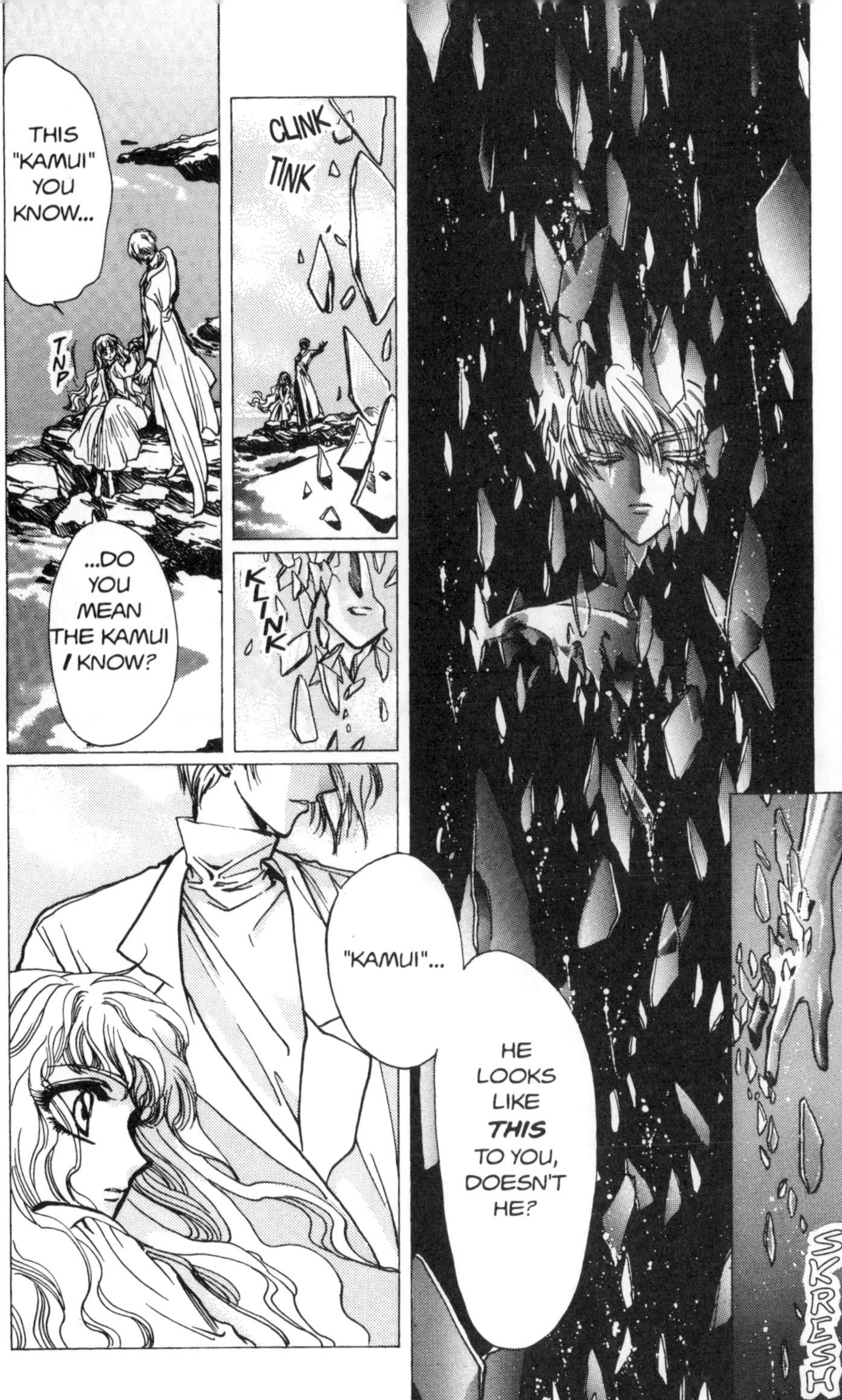

THIS "KAMUI" YOU KNOW...
TNP
...DO YOU MEAN THE KAMUI *I* KNOW?
CLINK
TINK
KLINK
"KAMUI"...
HE LOOKS LIKE ***THIS*** TO YOU, DOESN'T HE?
SKRESH

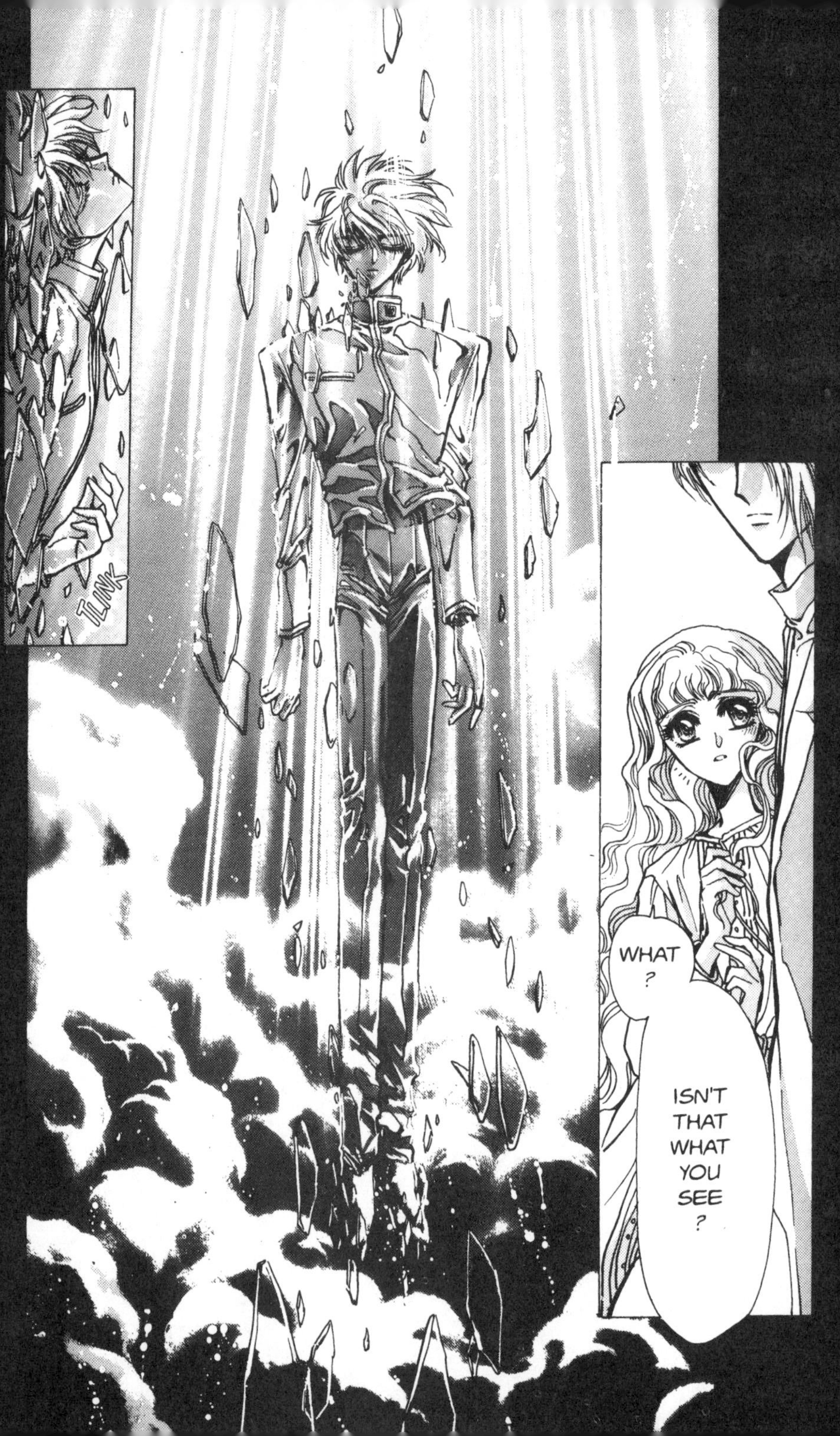
TLINK
WHAT?
ISN'T THAT WHAT YOU SEE?

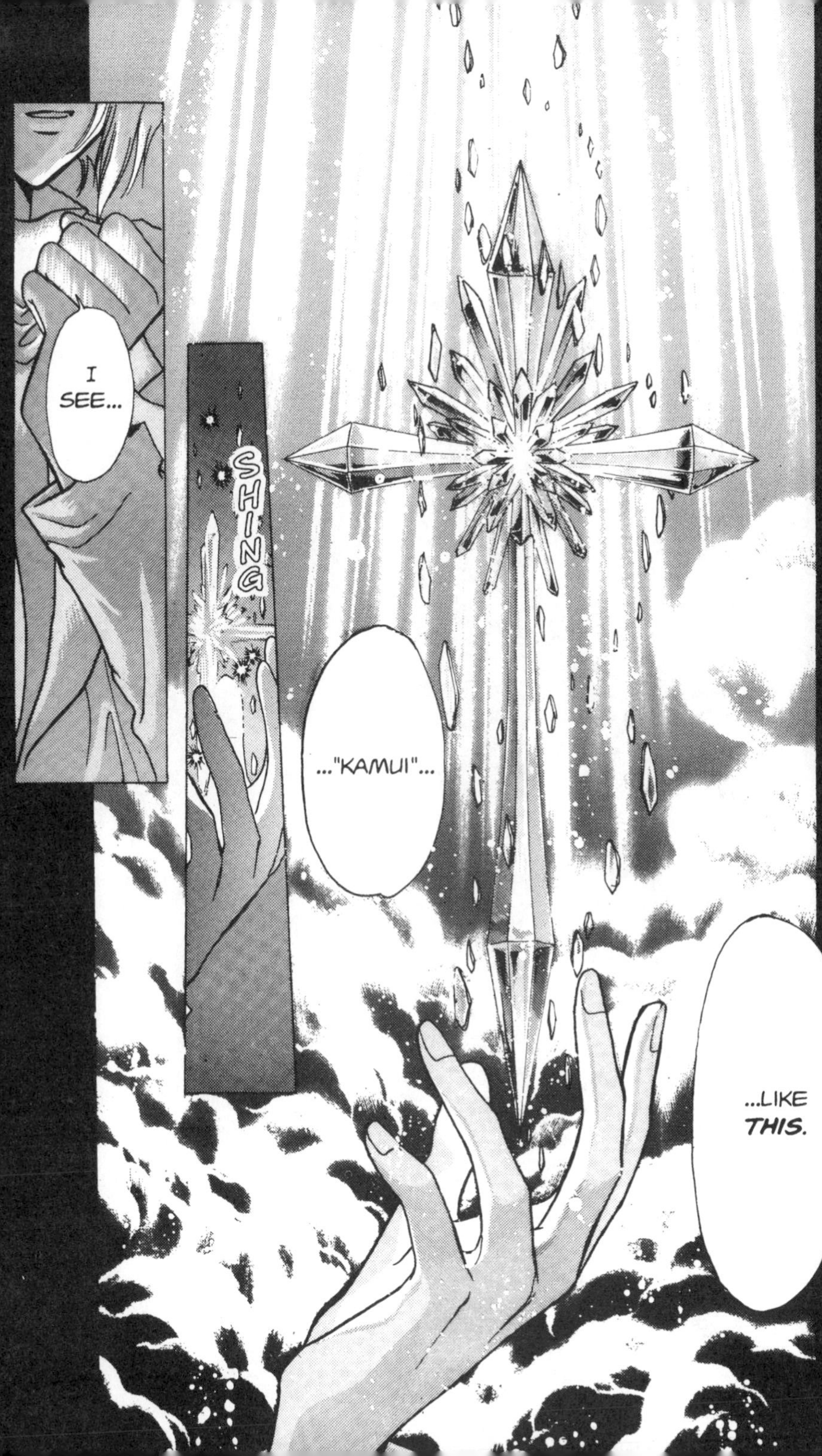
I SEE...
SHING
..."KAMUI"...
...LIKE THIS.

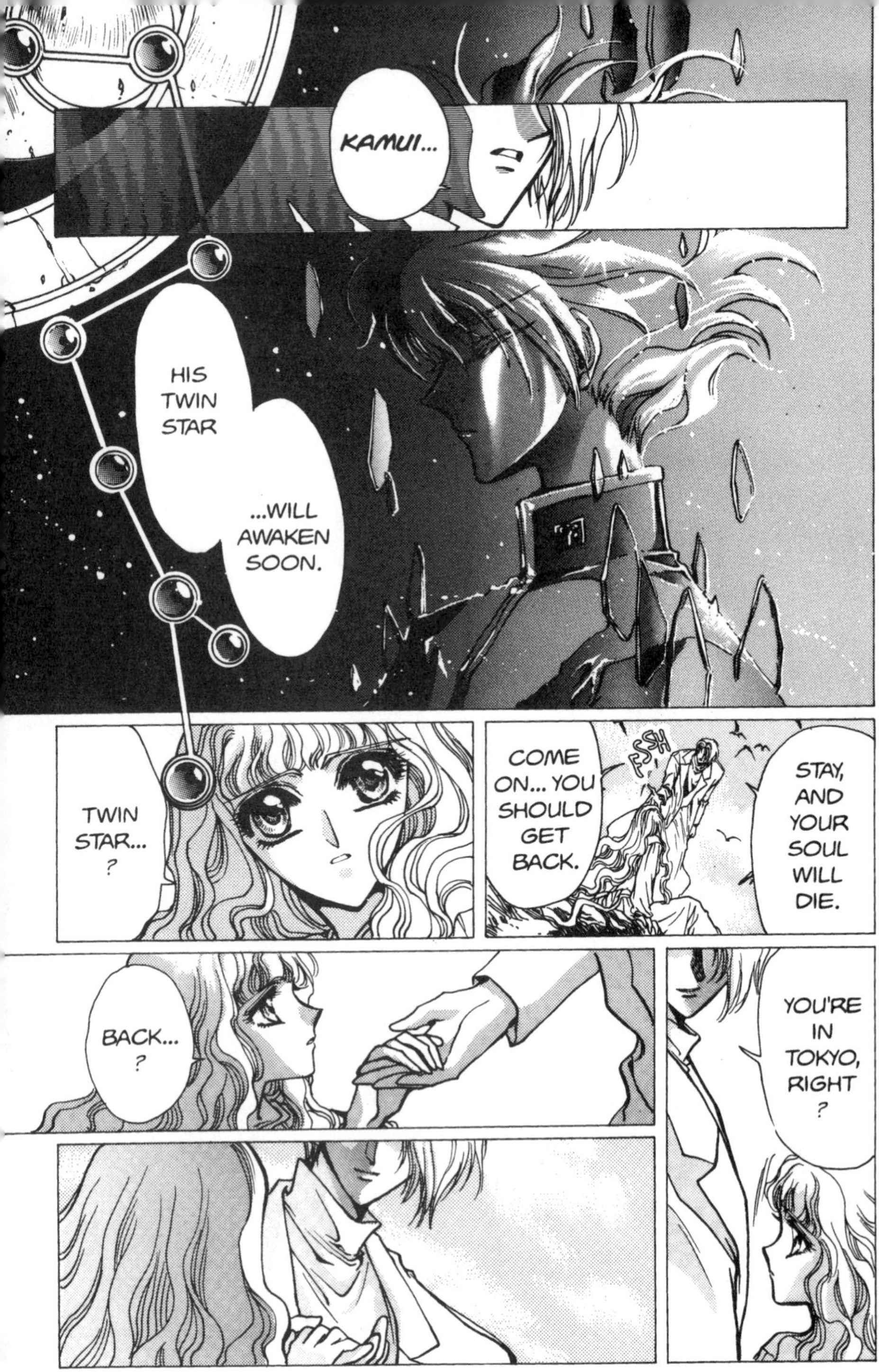
KAMUI...
HIS TWIN STAR
...WILL AWAKEN SOON.
TWIN STAR...?
COME ON... YOU SHOULD GET BACK.
FSSH
STAY, AND YOUR SOUL WILL DIE.
BACK...?
YOU'RE IN TOKYO, RIGHT?

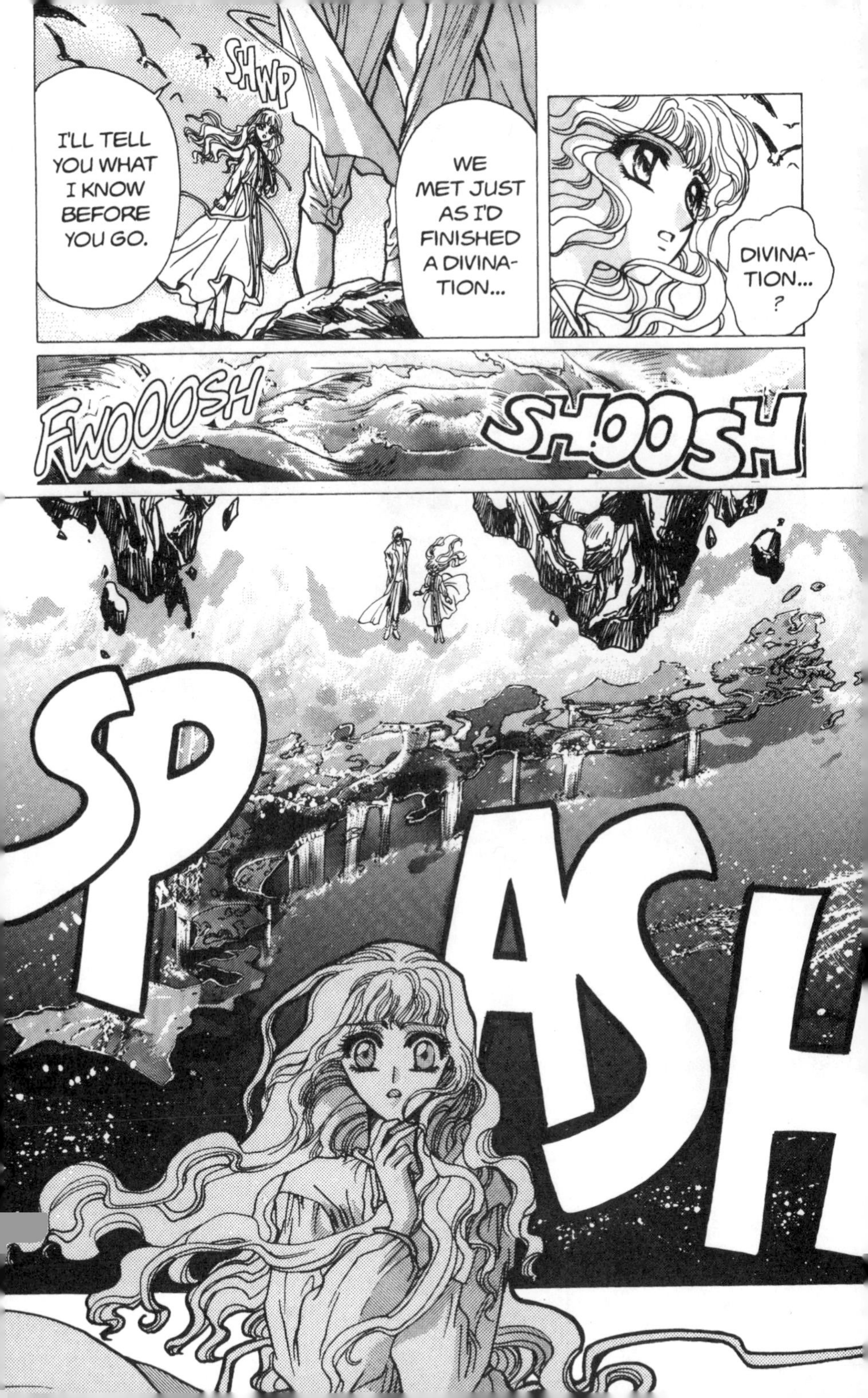
SHWP
I'LL TELL YOU WHAT I KNOW BEFORE YOU GO.
WE MET JUST AS I'D FINISHED A DIVINATION...
DIVINATION...?
FWOOOSH
SHOOSH
SPASH

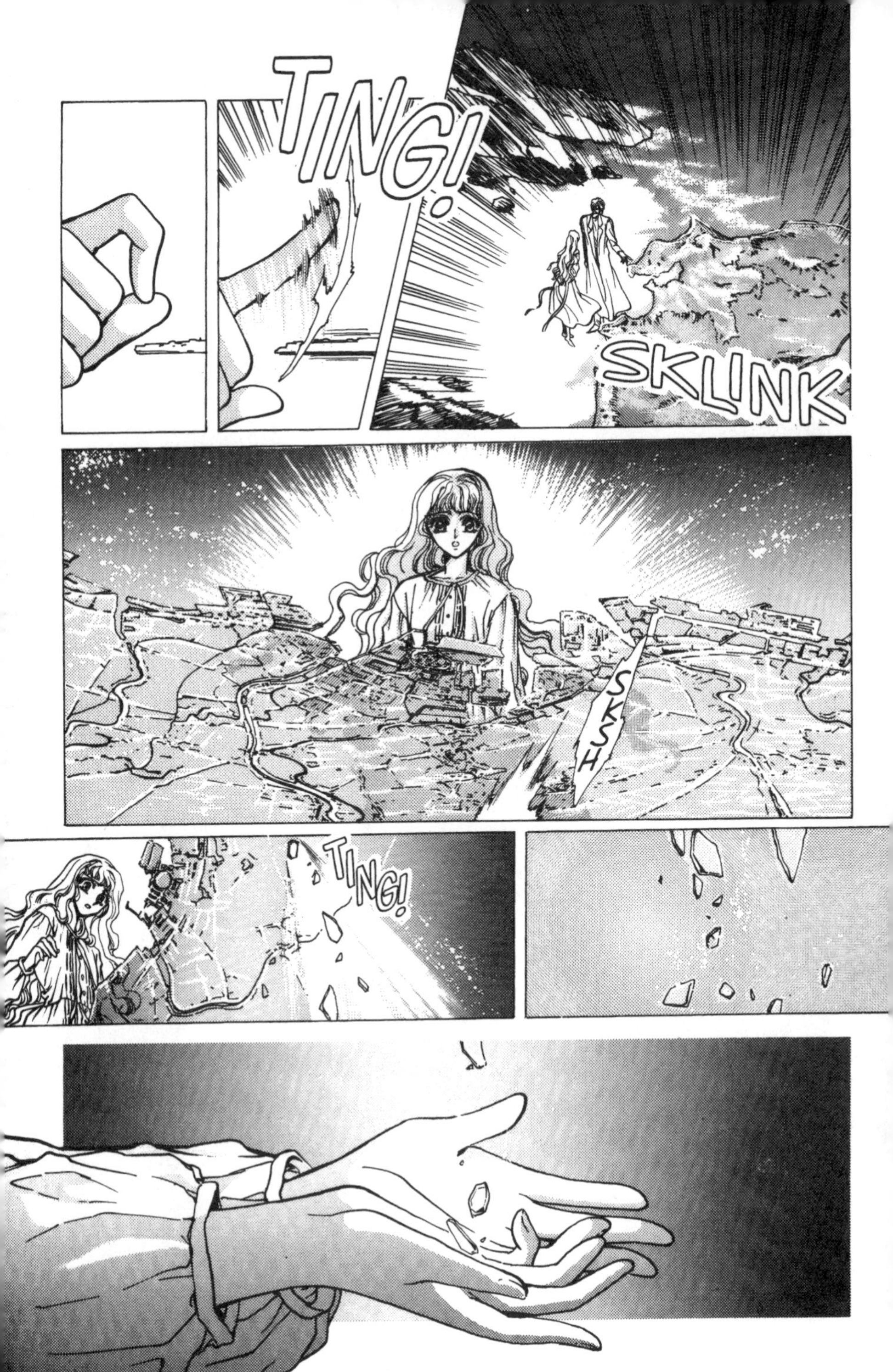
TING!
SKLINK
SKSH
TING!

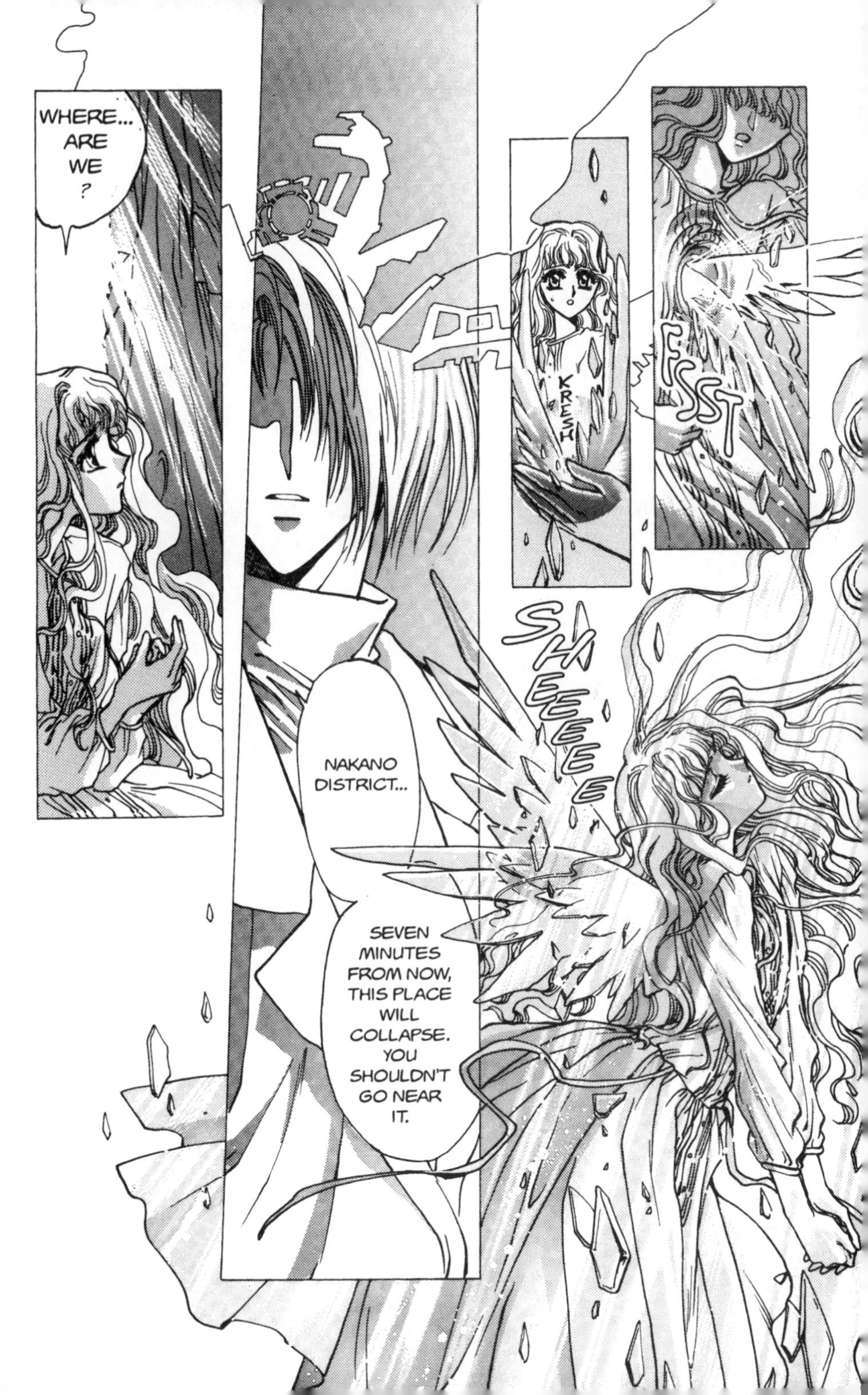
WHERE... ARE WE ?
NAKANO DISTRICT...
SEVEN MINUTES FROM NOW, THIS PLACE WILL COLLAPSE. YOU SHOULDN'T GO NEAR IT.
KRESH
FSSST
SHEEEEEE

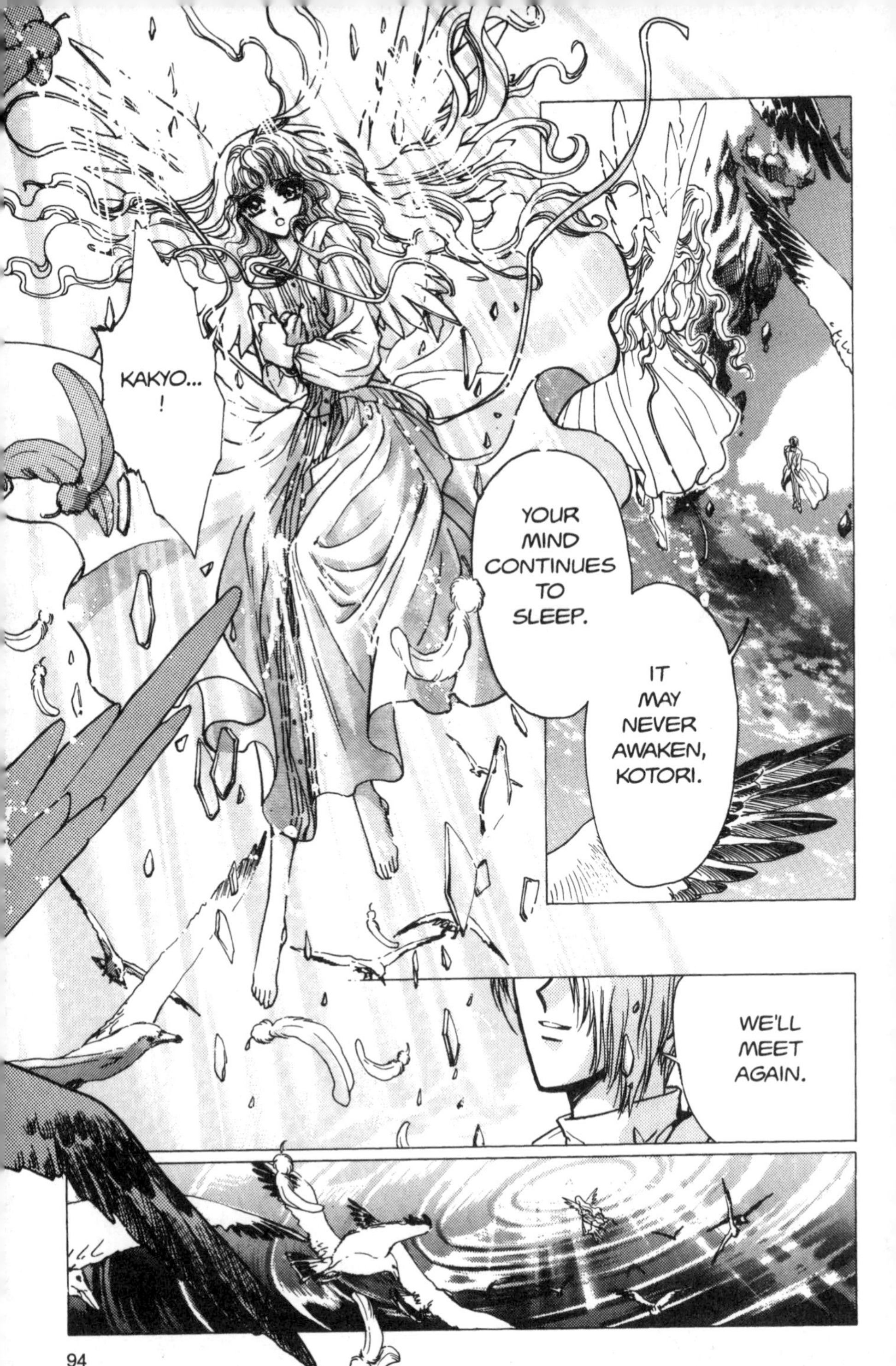
KAKYO... !
YOUR MIND CONTINUES TO SLEEP.
IT MAY NEVER AWAKEN, KOTORI.
WE'LL MEET AGAIN.

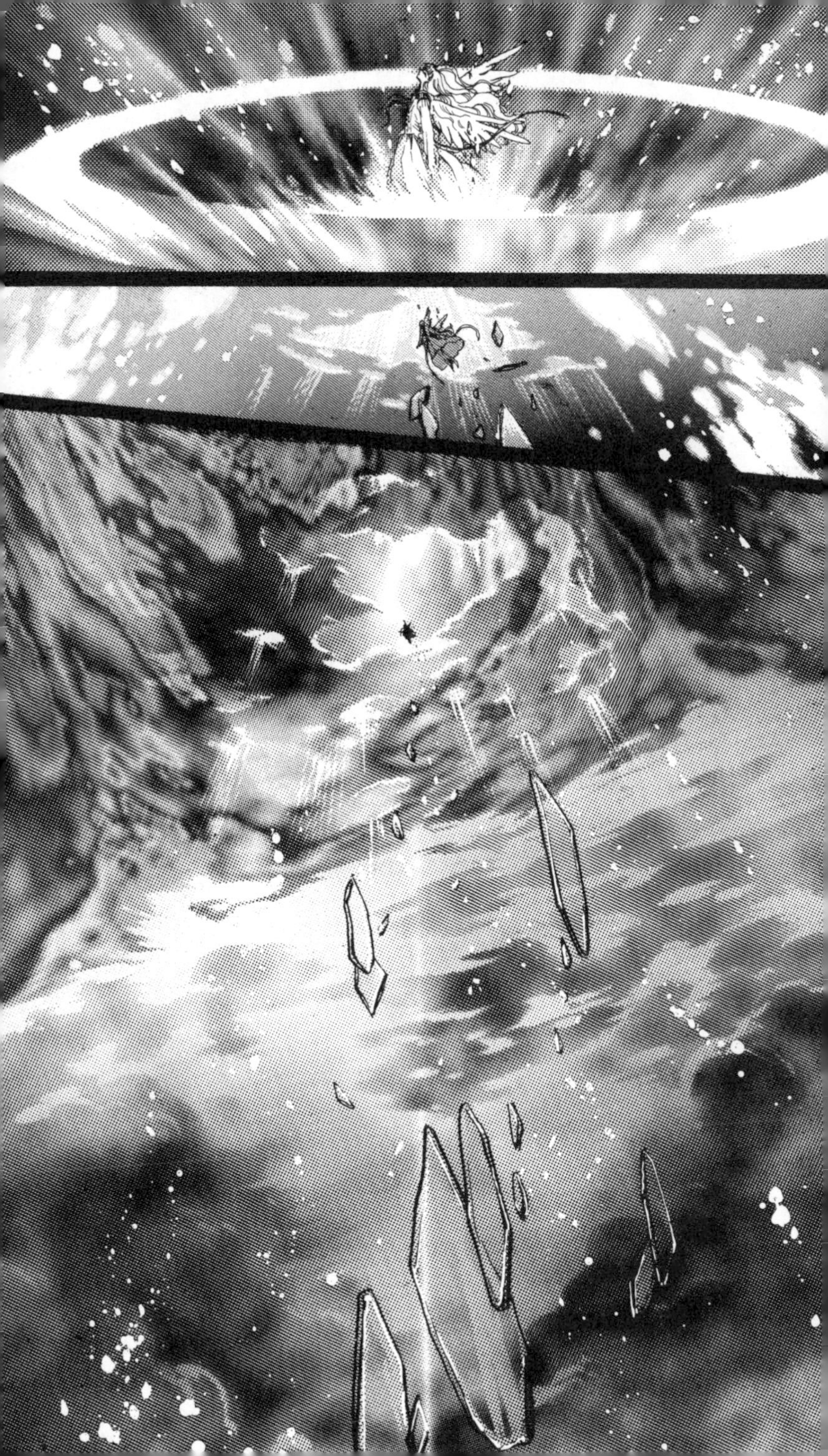

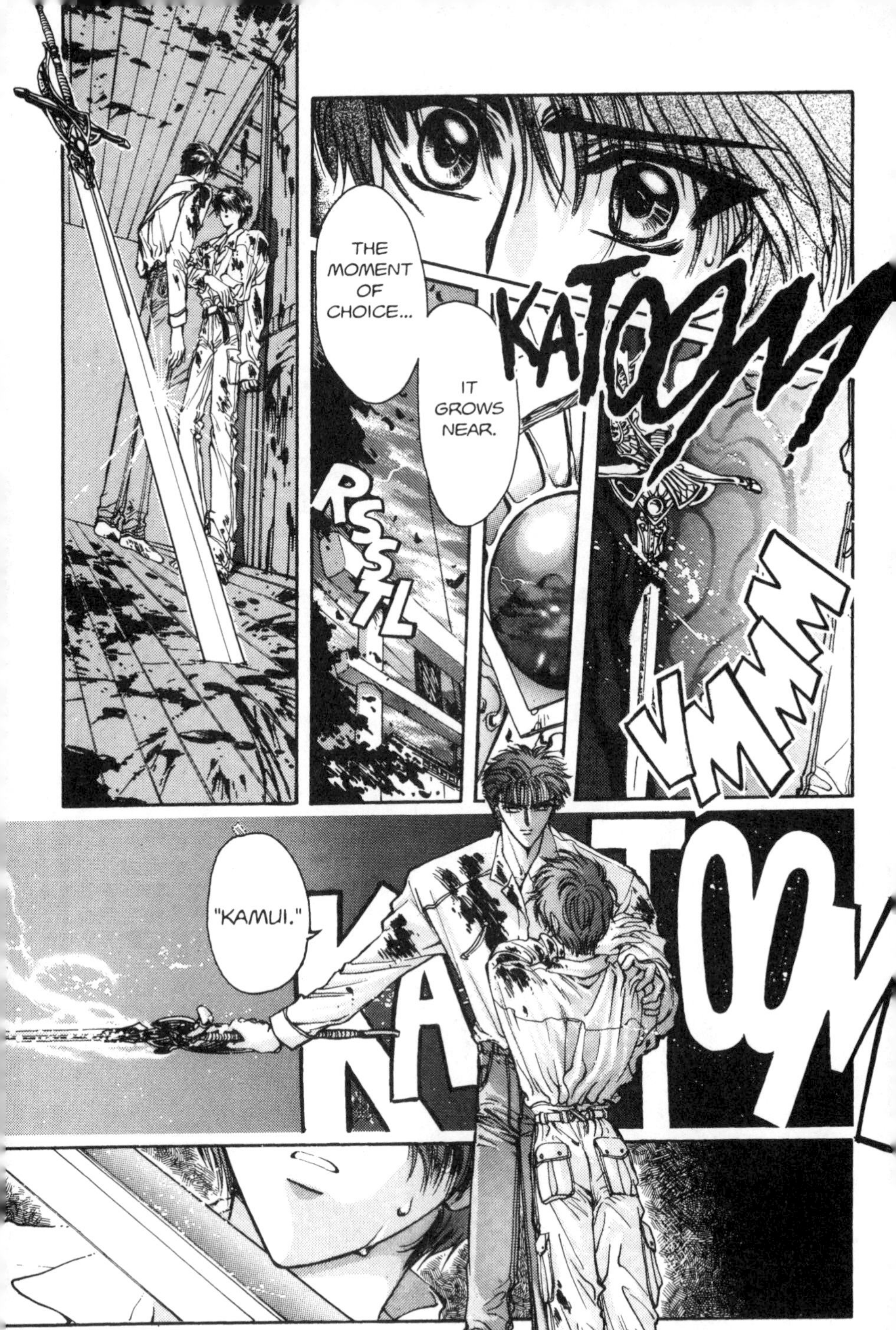
THE MOMENT OF CHOICE...
IT GROWS NEAR.
KATOOM
RSSTL
VMMMM
"KAMUI."
KATOOM

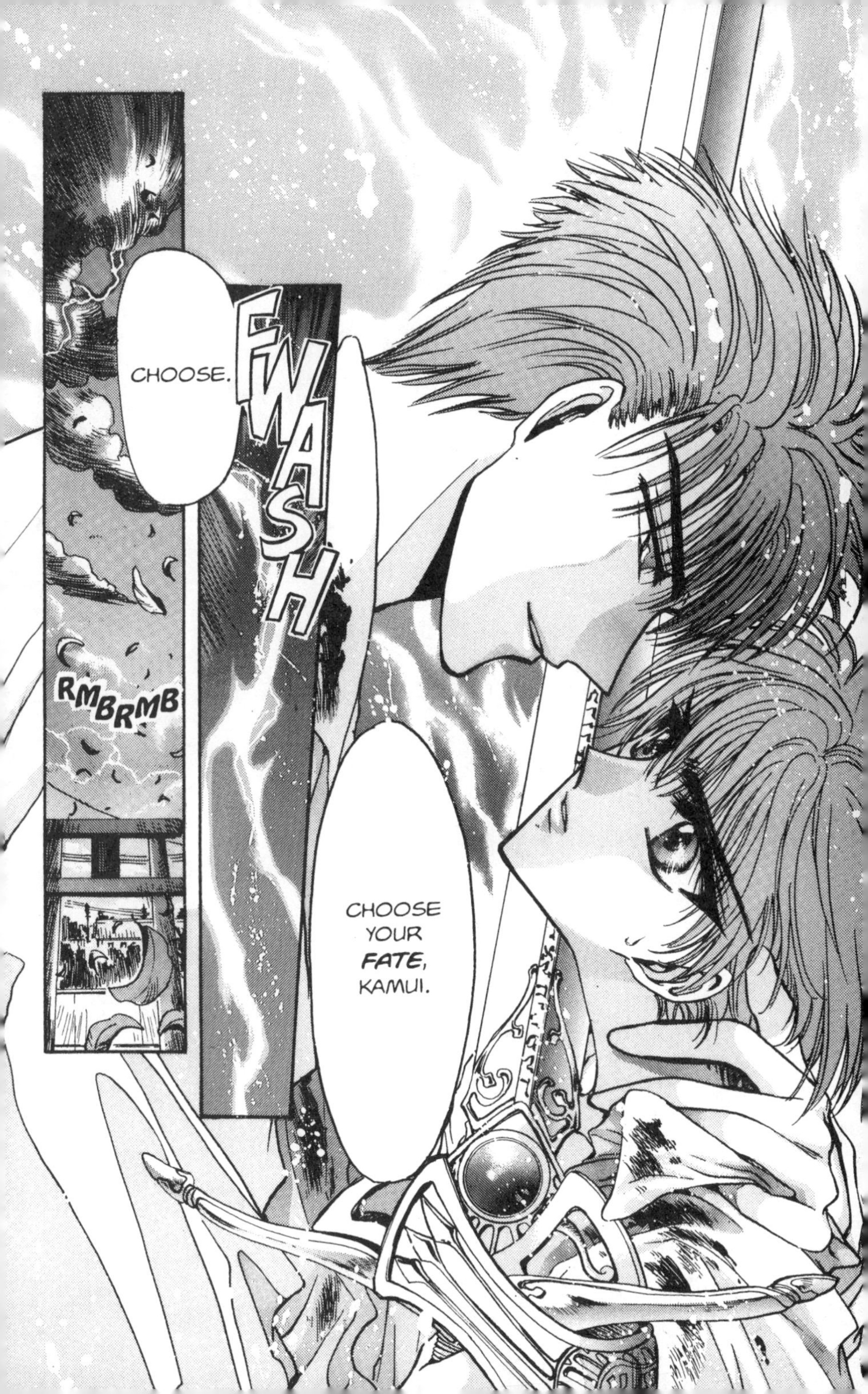
CHOOSE.
RMBRMB
FWASH
CHOOSE YOUR *FATE*, KAMUI.

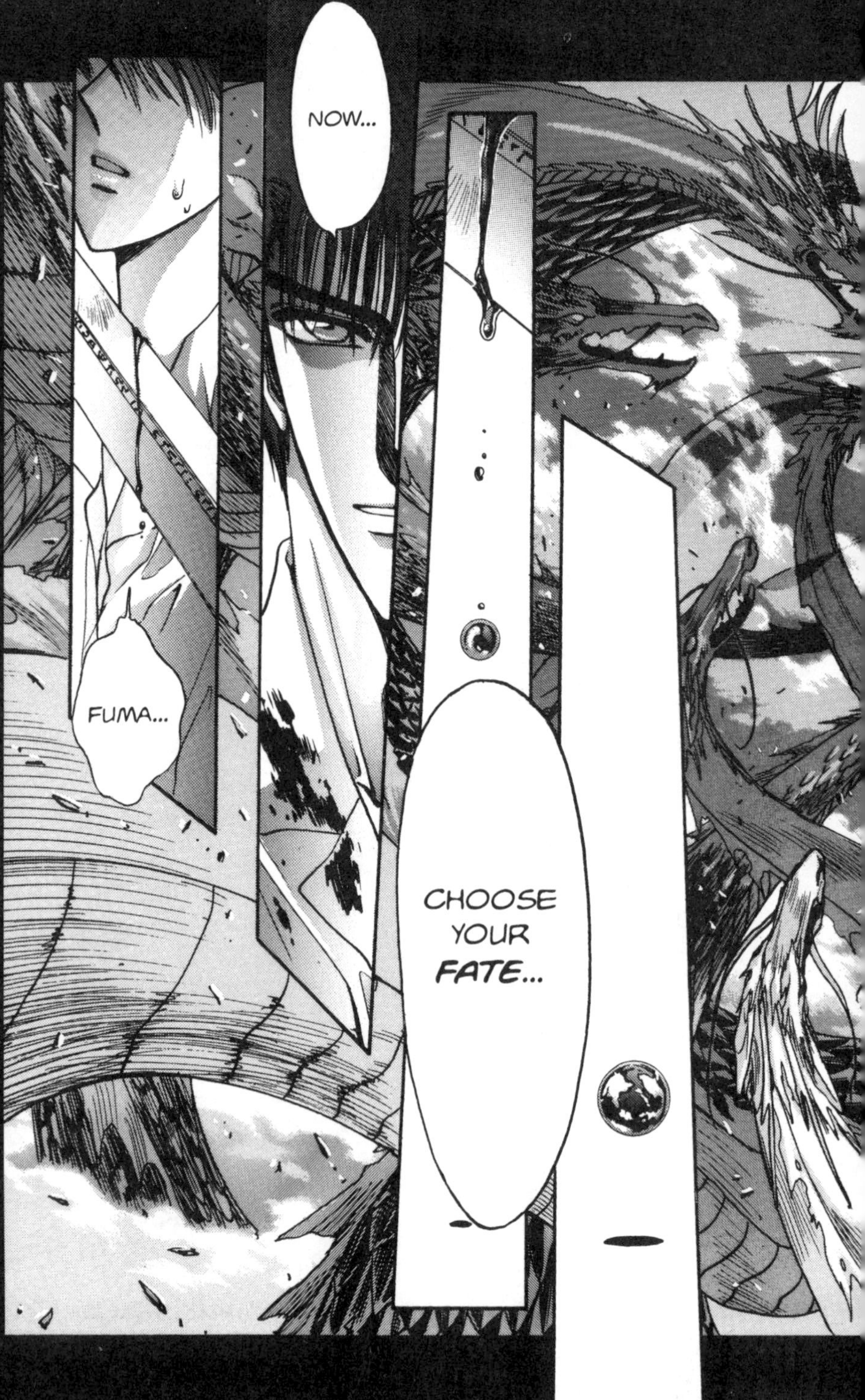
FUMA...
NOW...
CHOOSE YOUR FATE...

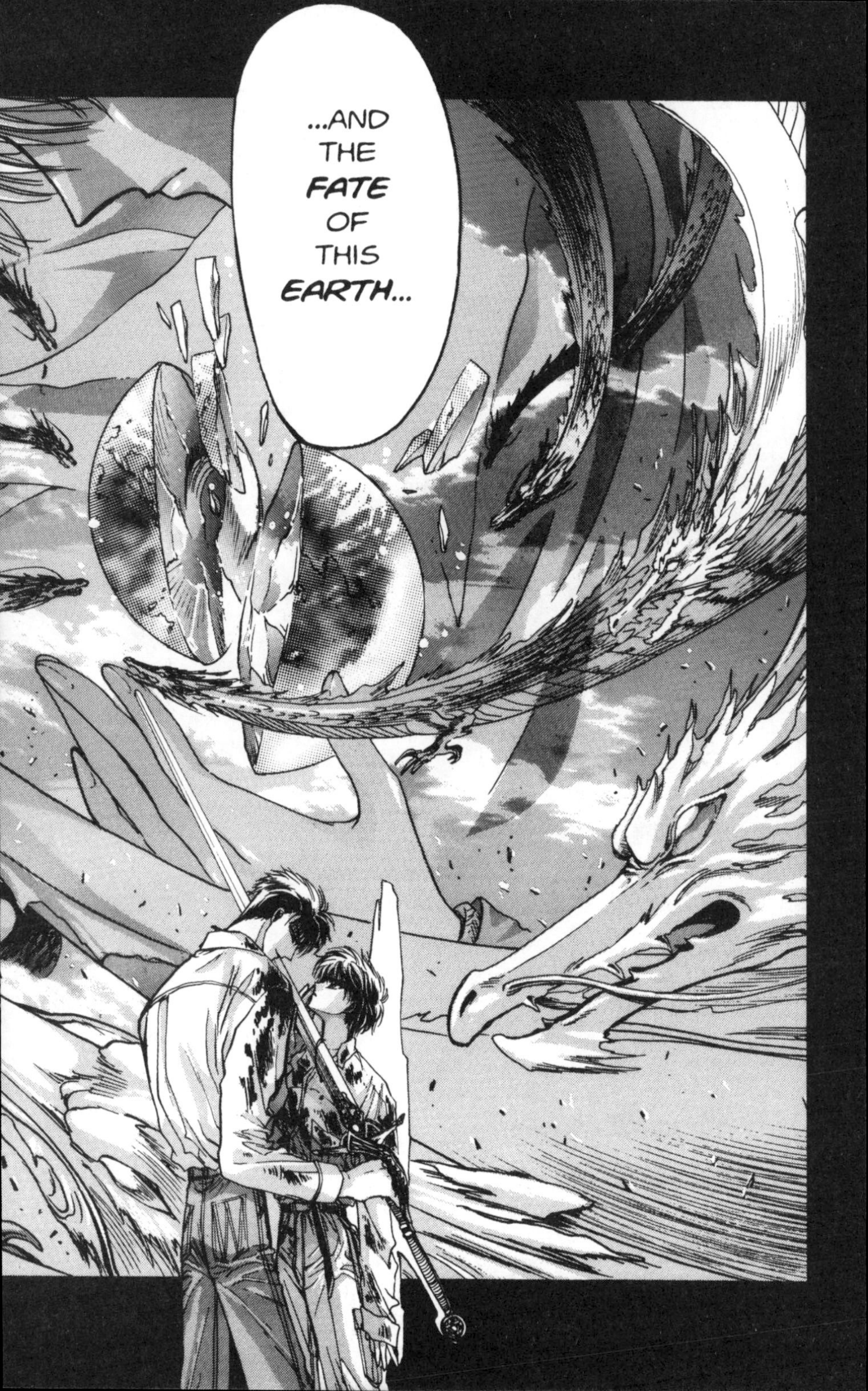
...AND THE *FATE* OF THIS *EARTH*...

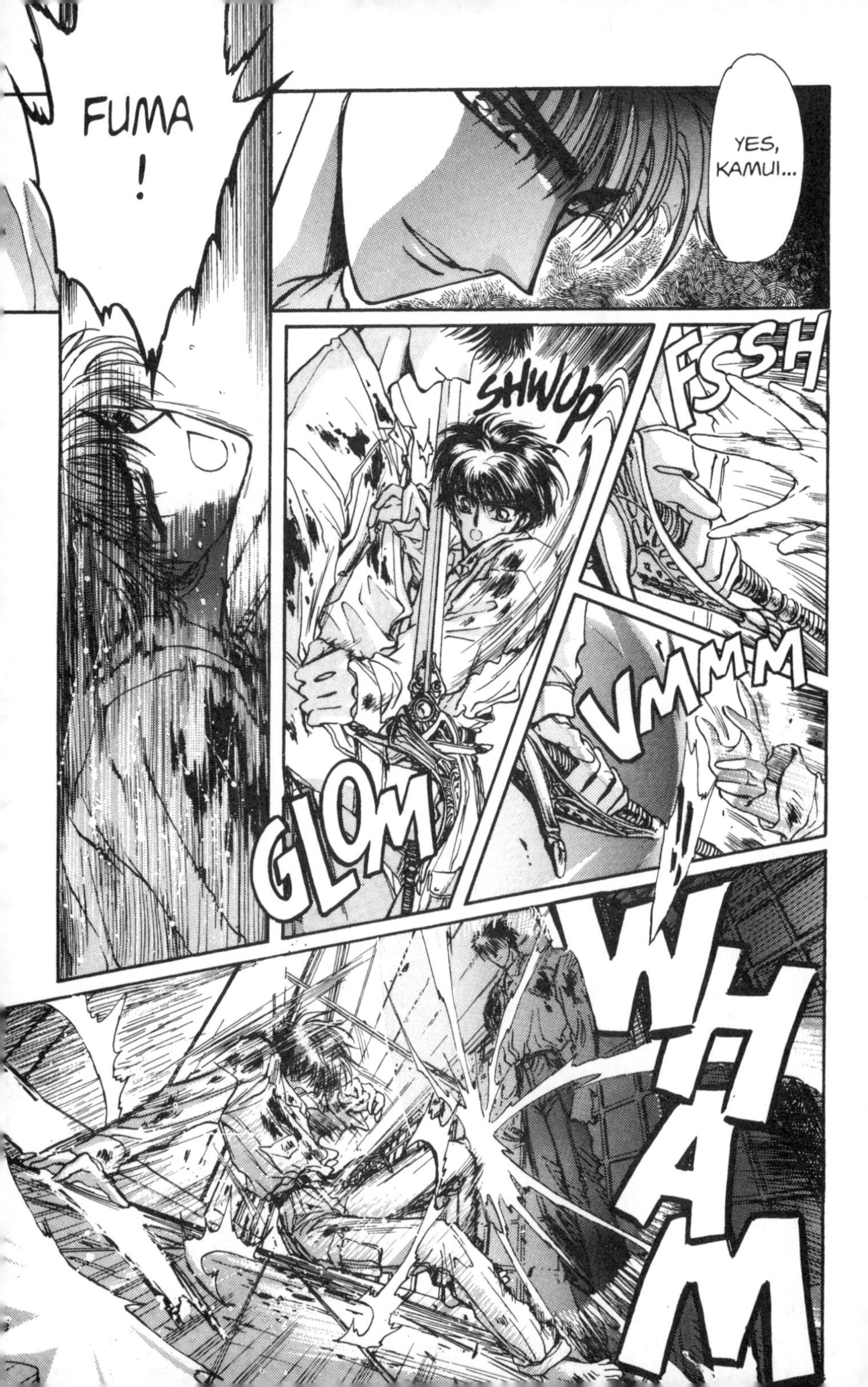
FUMA
!
YES, KAMUI...
SHWUP
FSSH
GLOM
VMMMM
WHAM

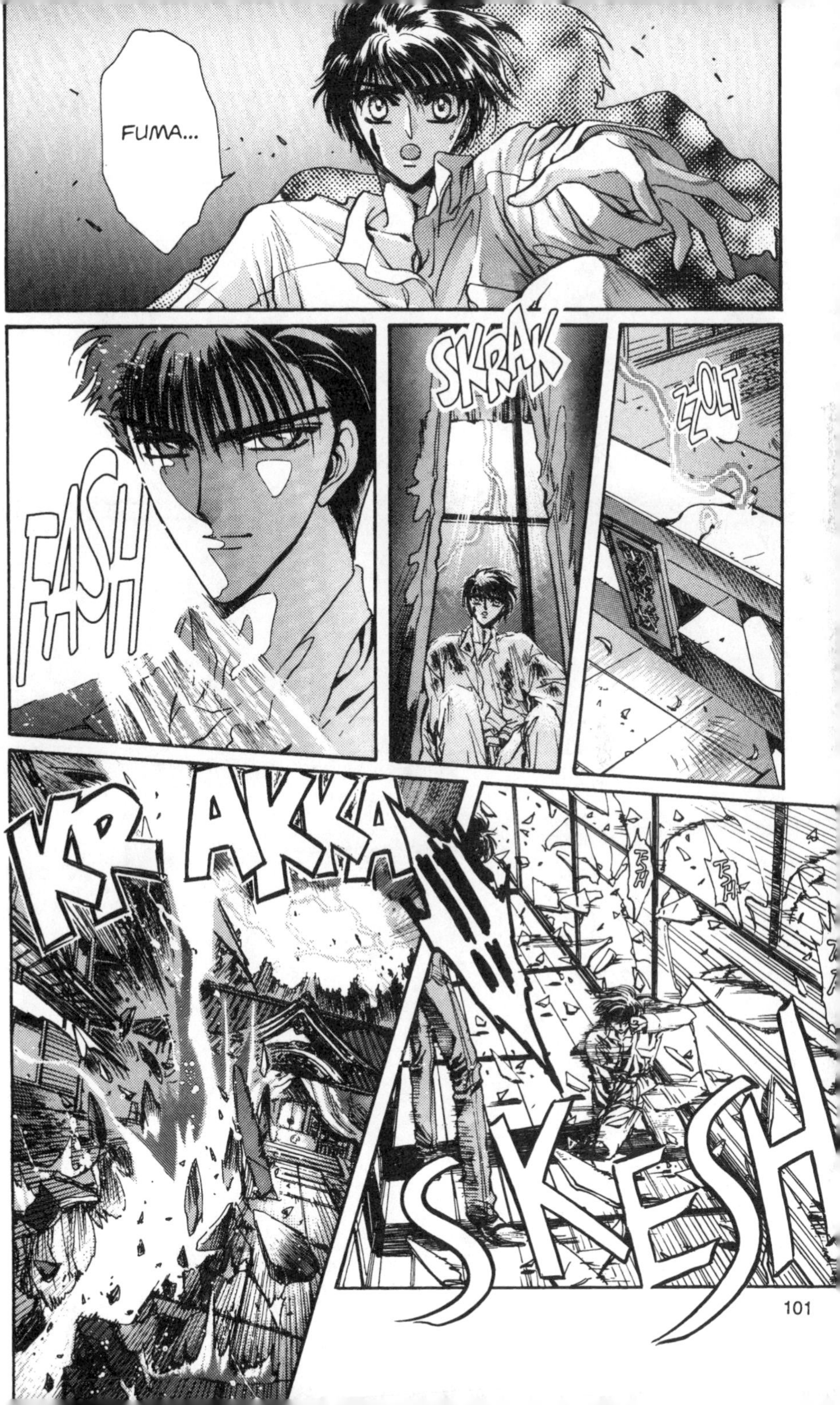
FUMA...
FASH
SKRAK
ZZOLT
KRAKKA
SKESH

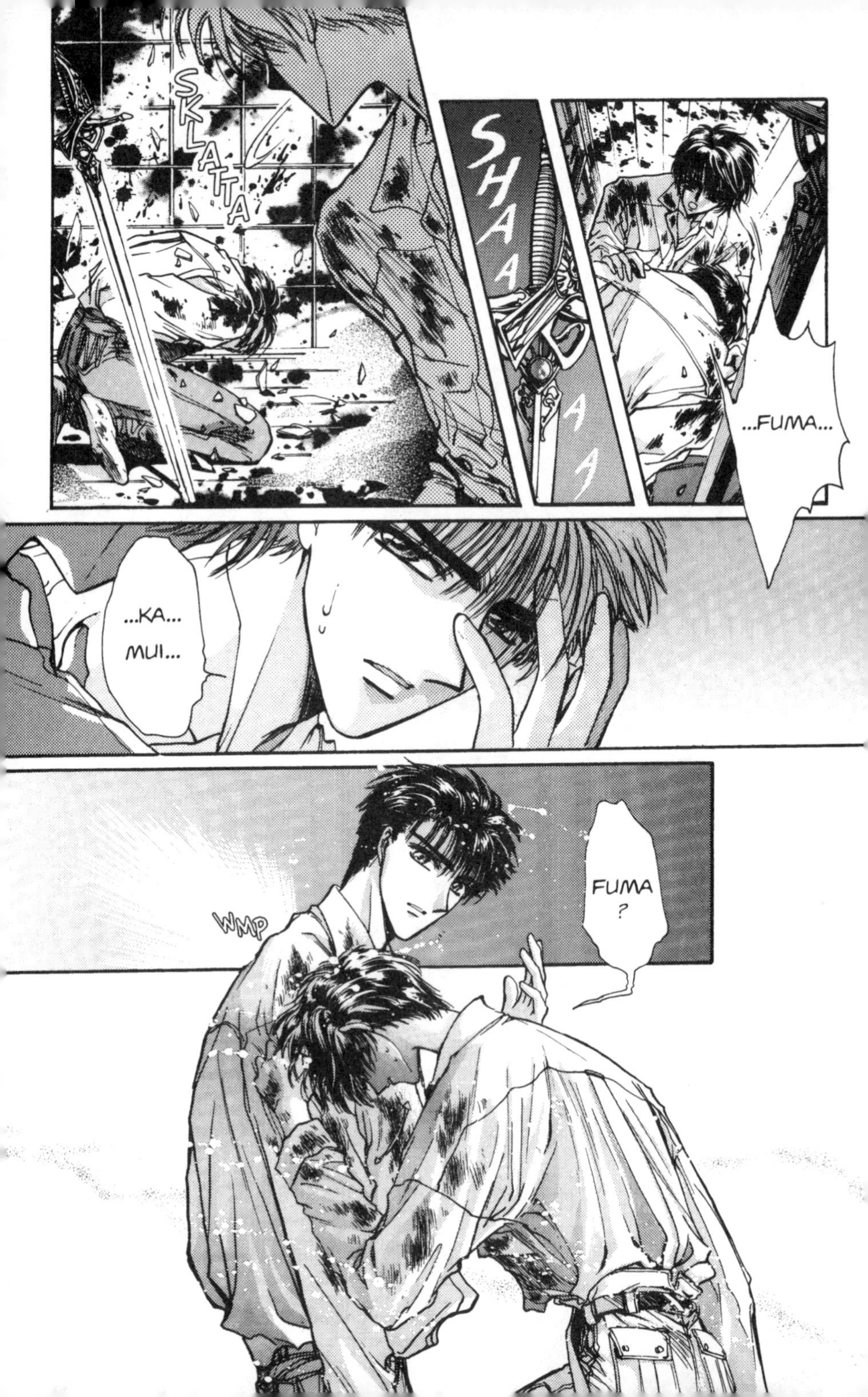
SKLATTA
SHAAAAAA
...FUMA...
...KA...
MUI...
WMP
FUMA
?

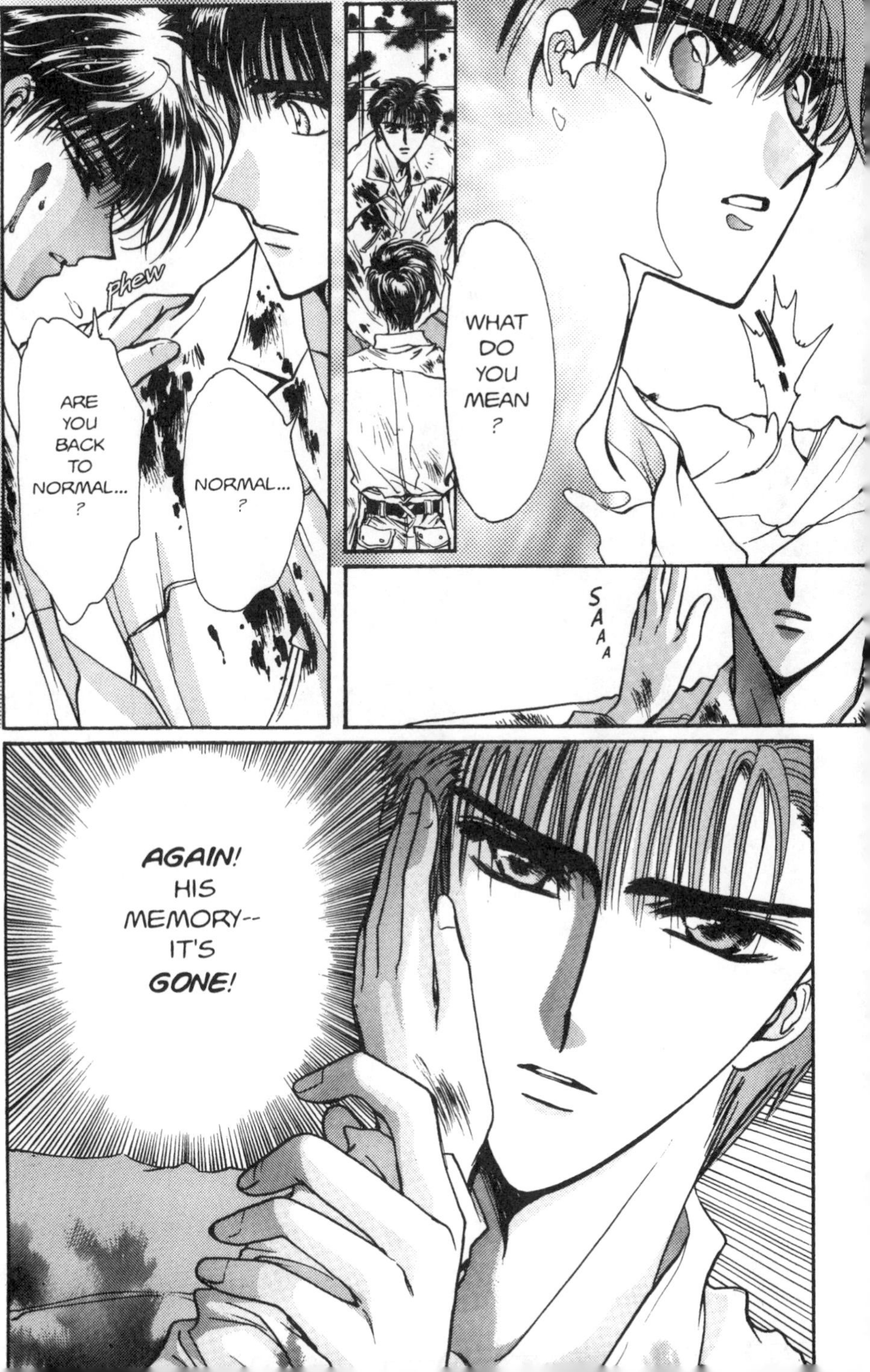
phew
ARE YOU BACK TO NORMAL...?
NORMAL...?
WHAT DO YOU MEAN?
SAAAA
AGAIN! HIS MEMORY-- IT'S GONE!

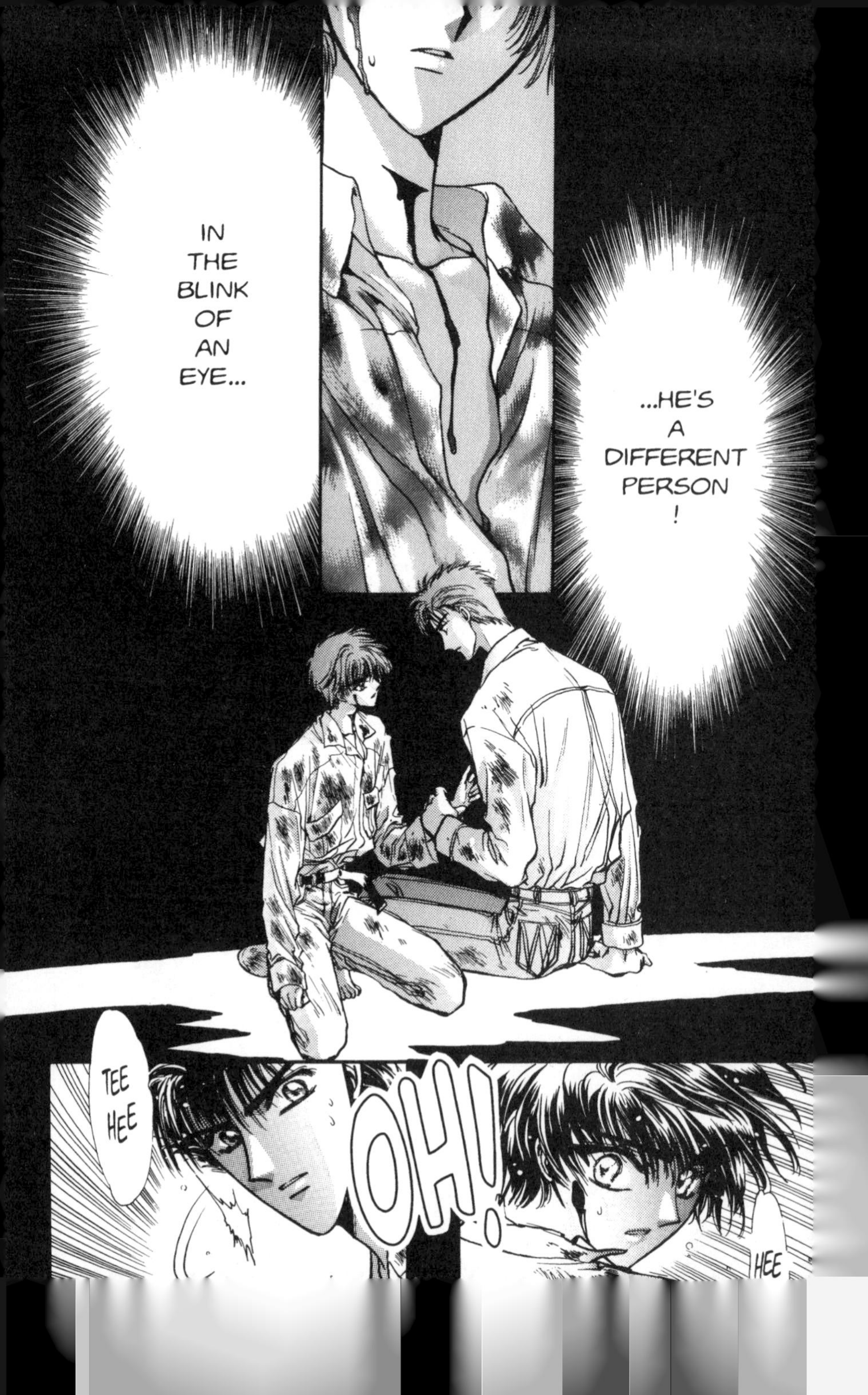
IN THE BLINK OF AN EYE...
...HE'S A DIFFERENT PERSON !
TEE HEE
OH!
HEE

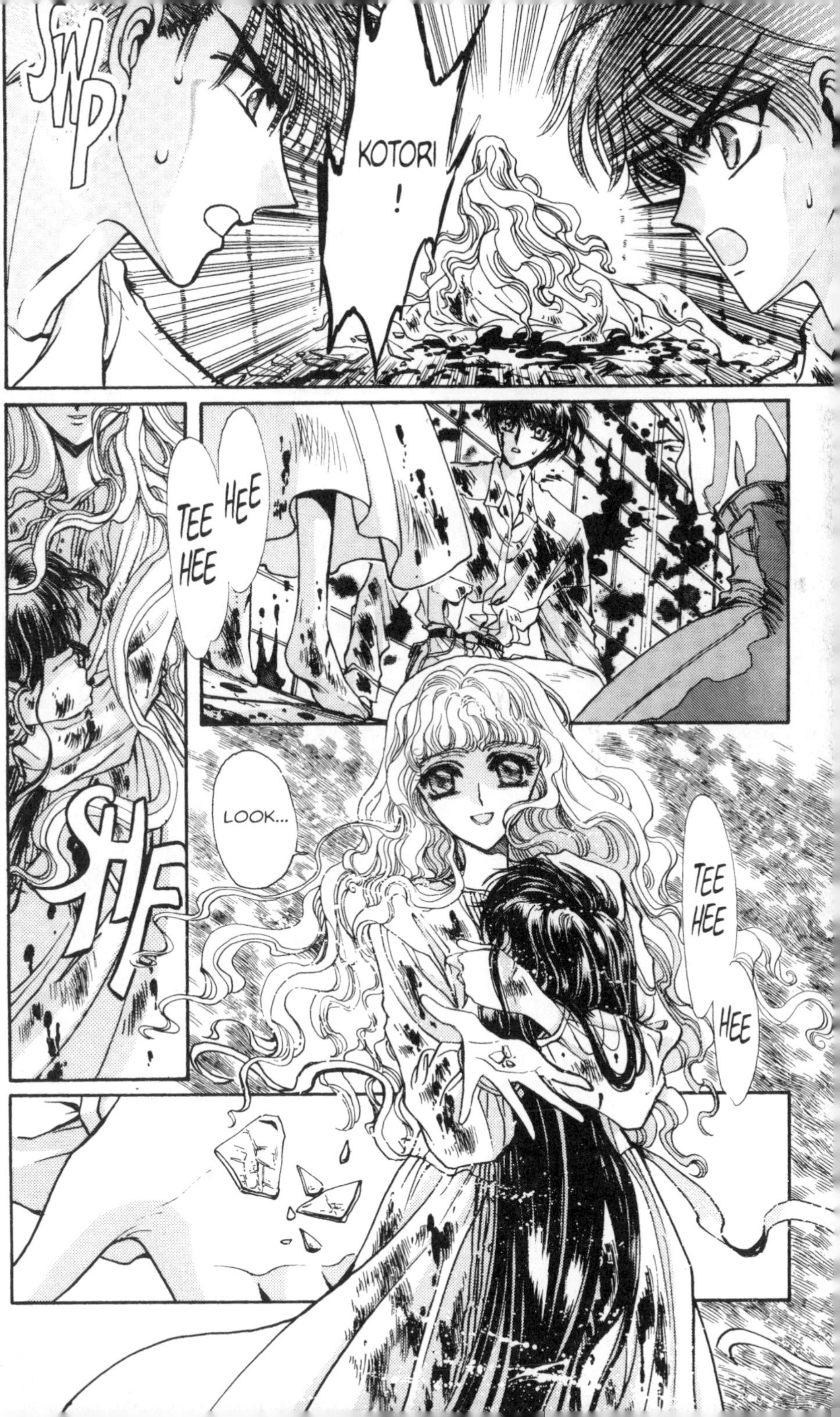
SWIP
KOTORI!
TEE HEE HEE
SHF
LOOK...
TEE HEE HEE

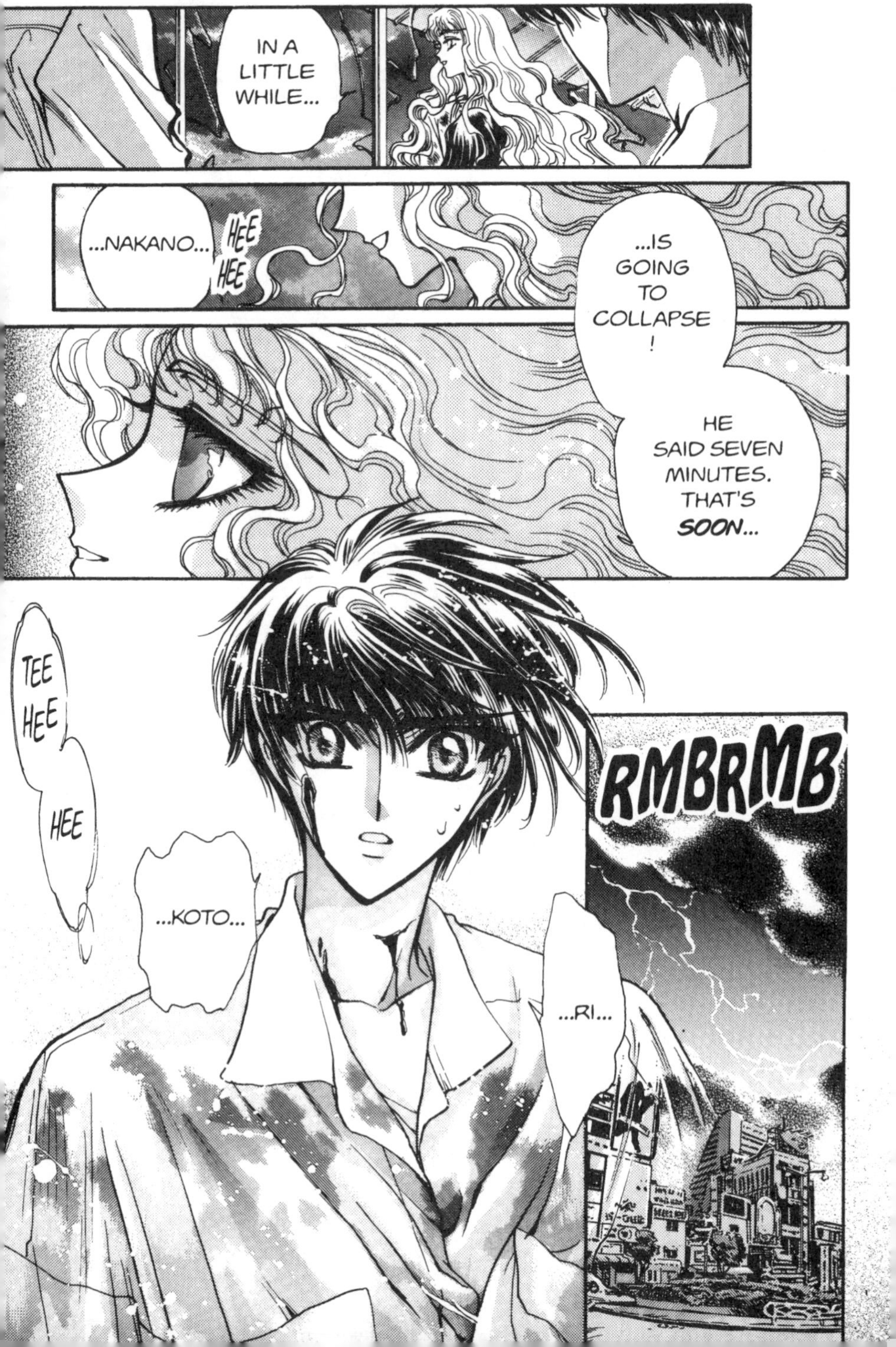
IN A LITTLE WHILE...
...NAKANO...
HEE HEE
...IS GOING TO COLLAPSE!
HE SAID SEVEN MINUTES. THAT'S **SOON**...
TEE HEE
HEE
...KOTO...
...RI...
RMBRMB

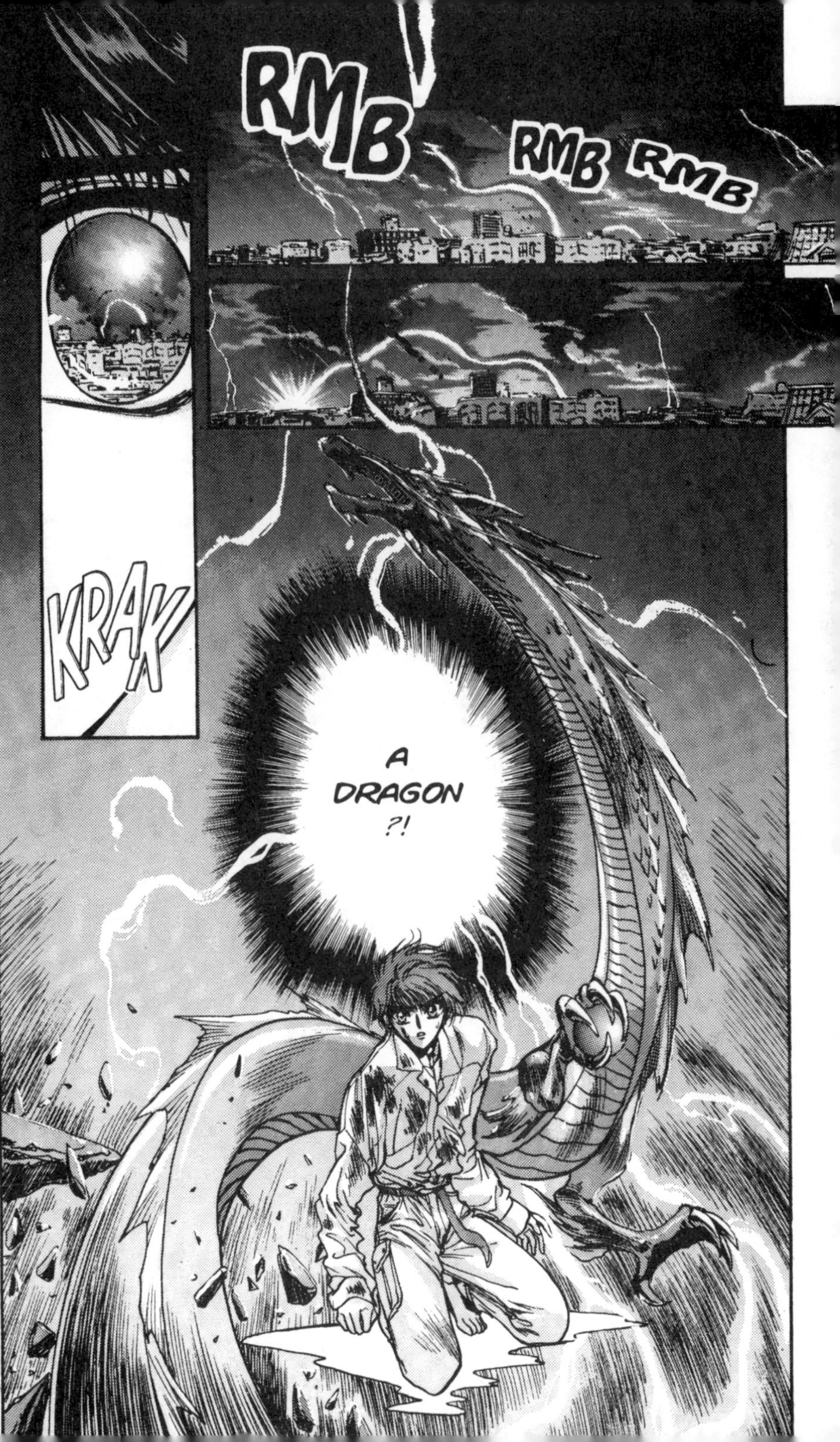
RMB
RMB RMB
KRAK
A DRAGON ?!

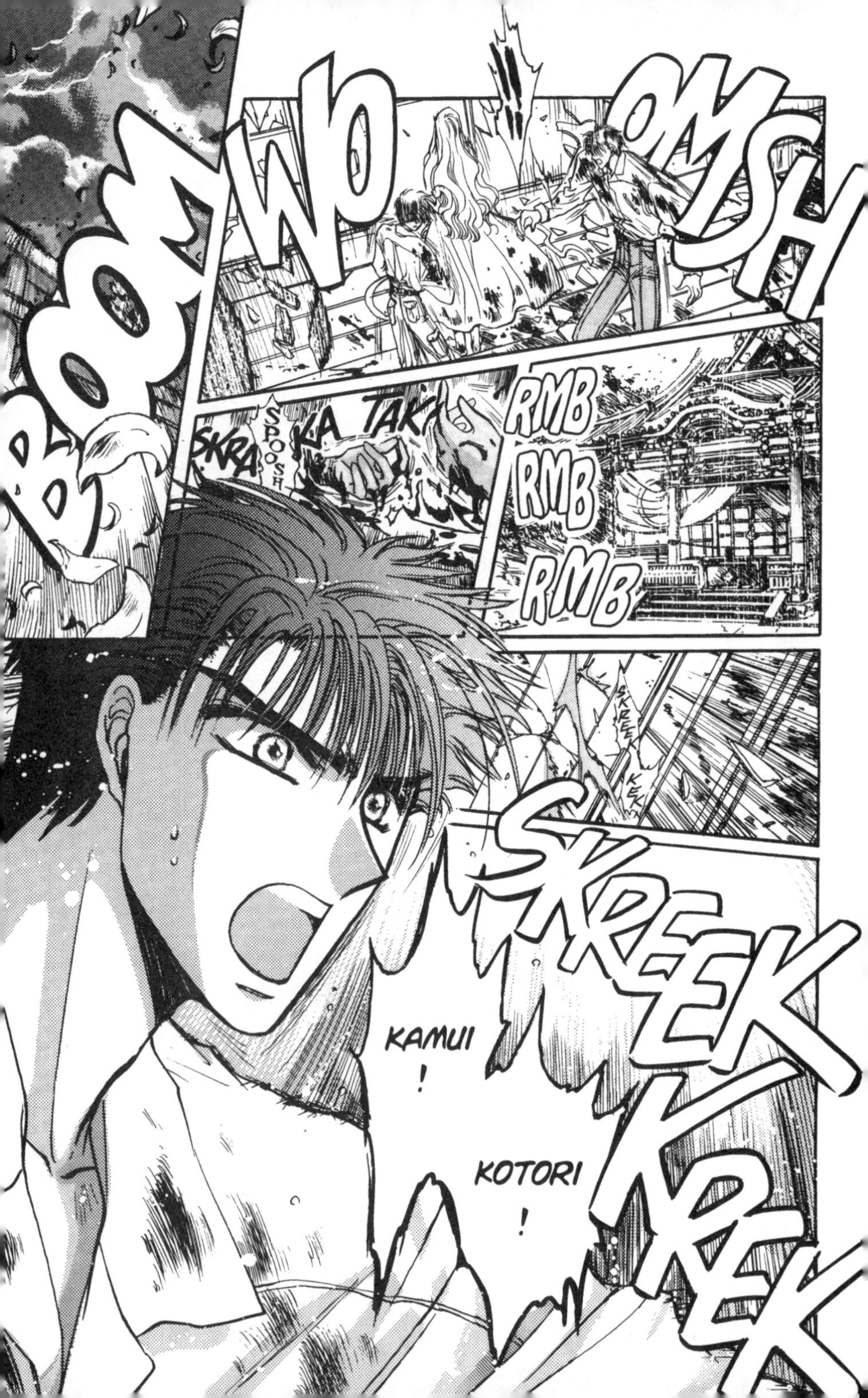
BOOM
WOOMSH
SKRA
SPOOSH
KA TAK
RMB
RMB
RMB
SKREEK KEK
KAMUI!
KOTORI!
SKREEK
KEK

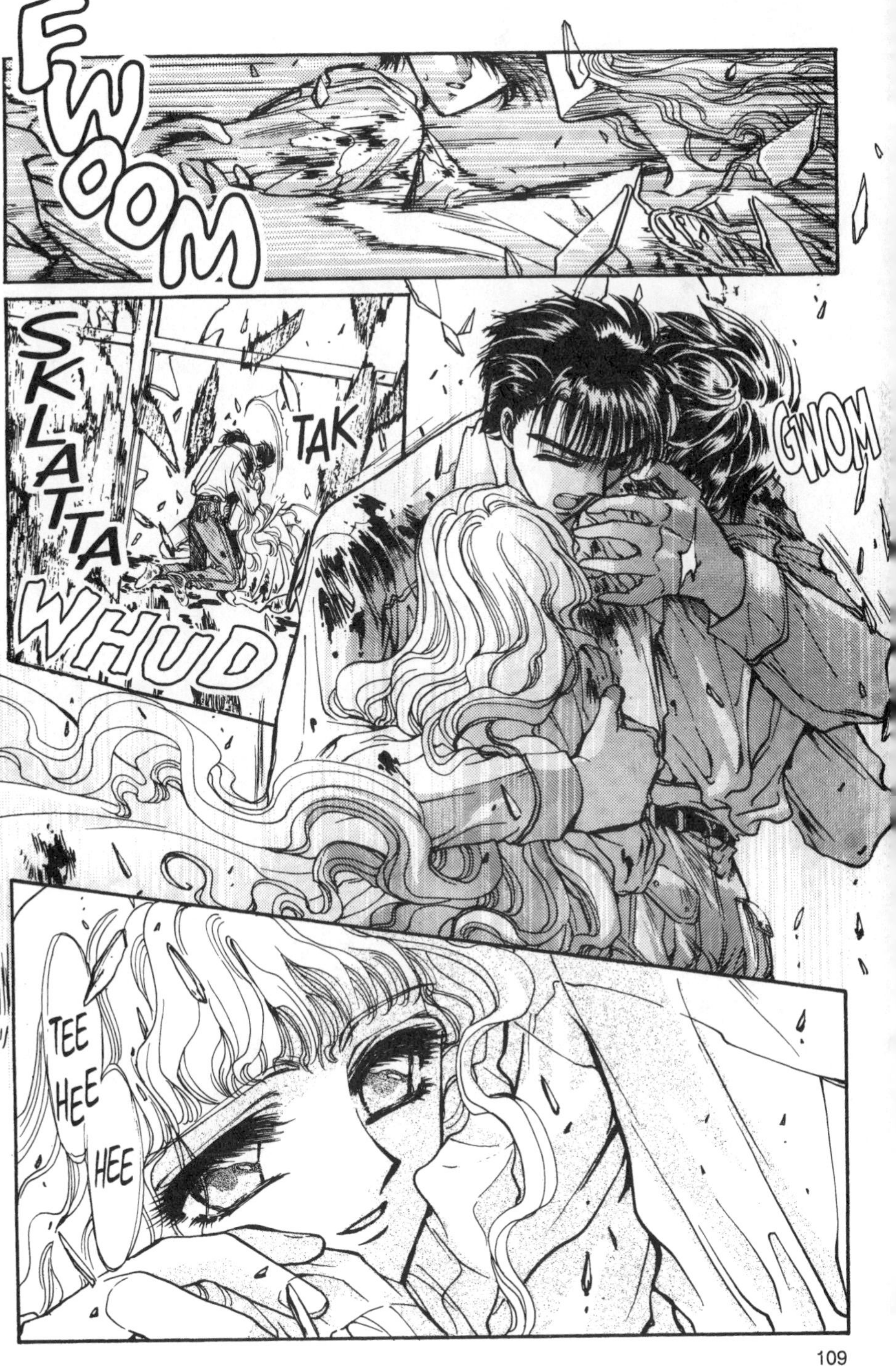
FWOOM
SKLATTA
TAK
WHUD
GNOM
TEE HEE HEE

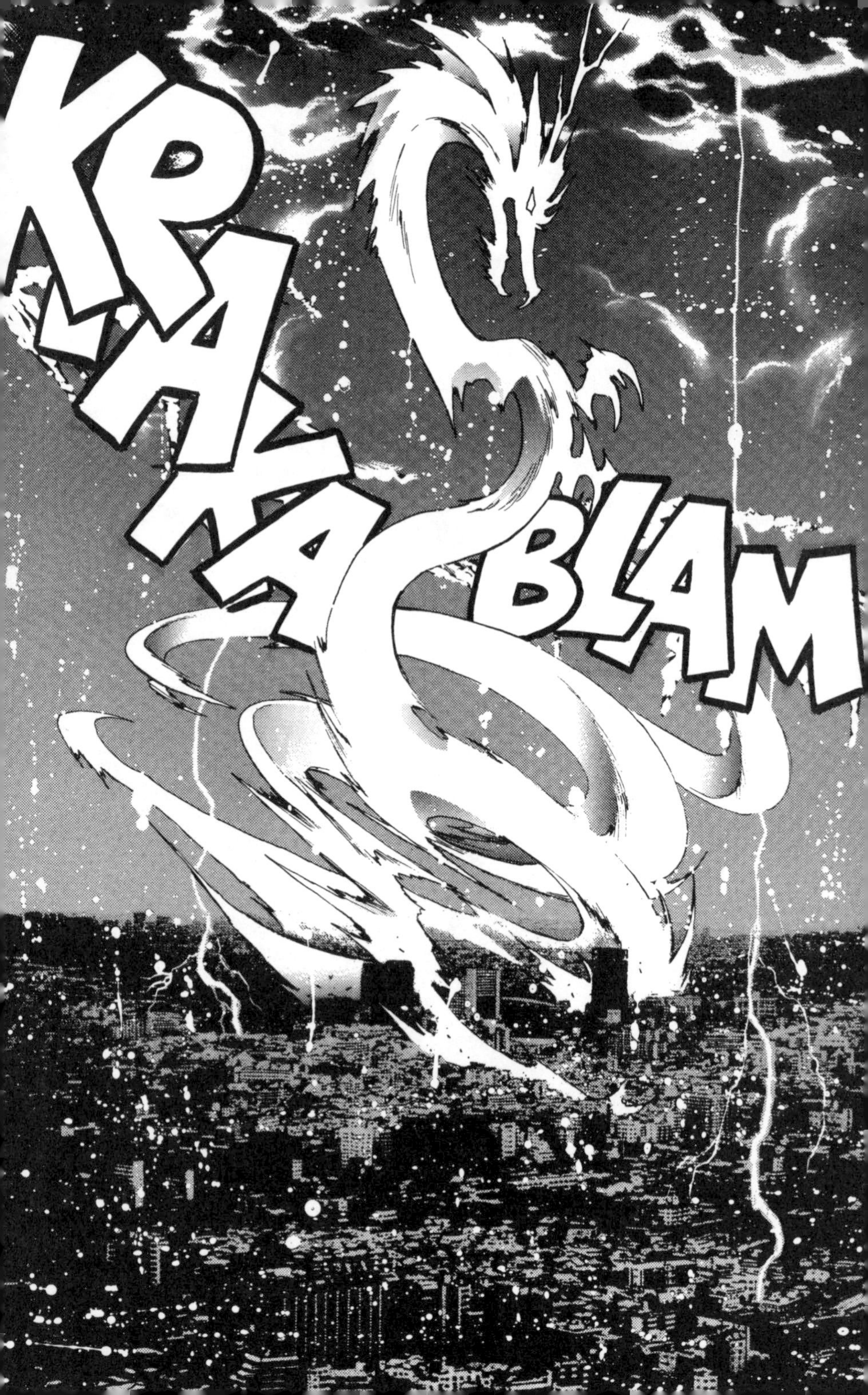
KRAKA BLAM

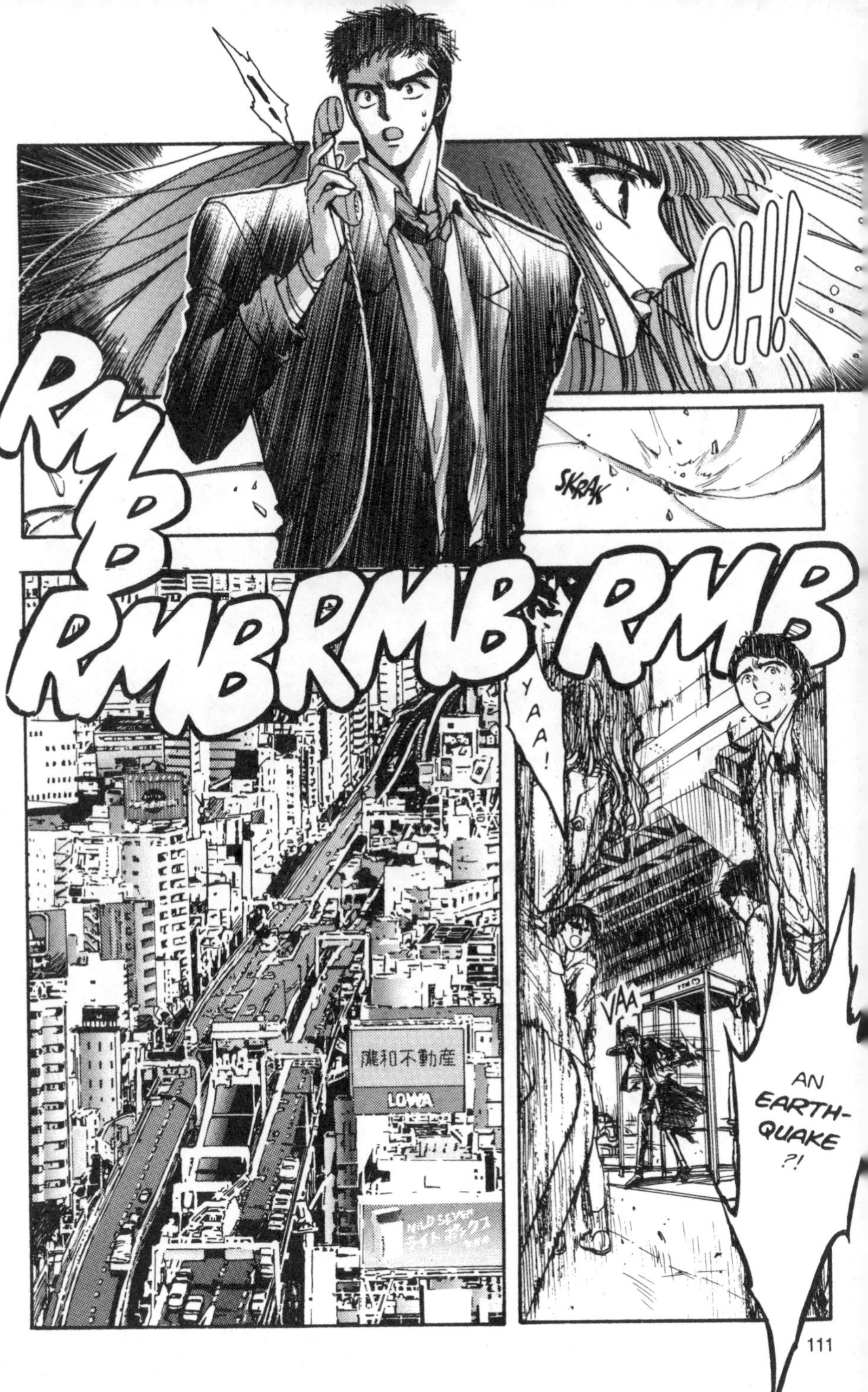
OH!
SKRAK
RMB
RMBRMBRMB RMB
YAA!
VAA
AN EARTH-QUAKE?!

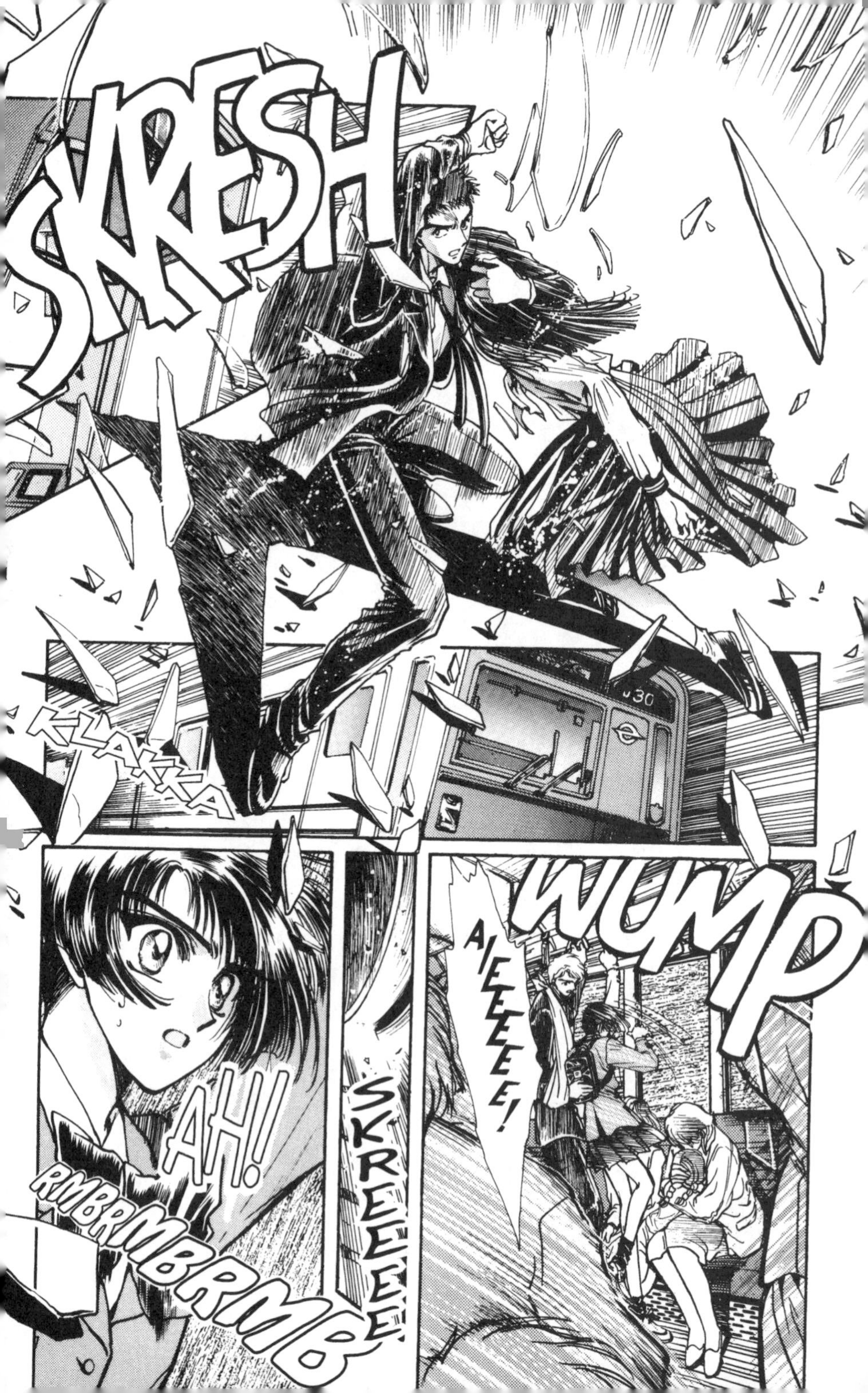
SKRESH
KLAKKA
AH!
RMBRMBRMB
SKREEEEE
WUMP
AIEEEEE!

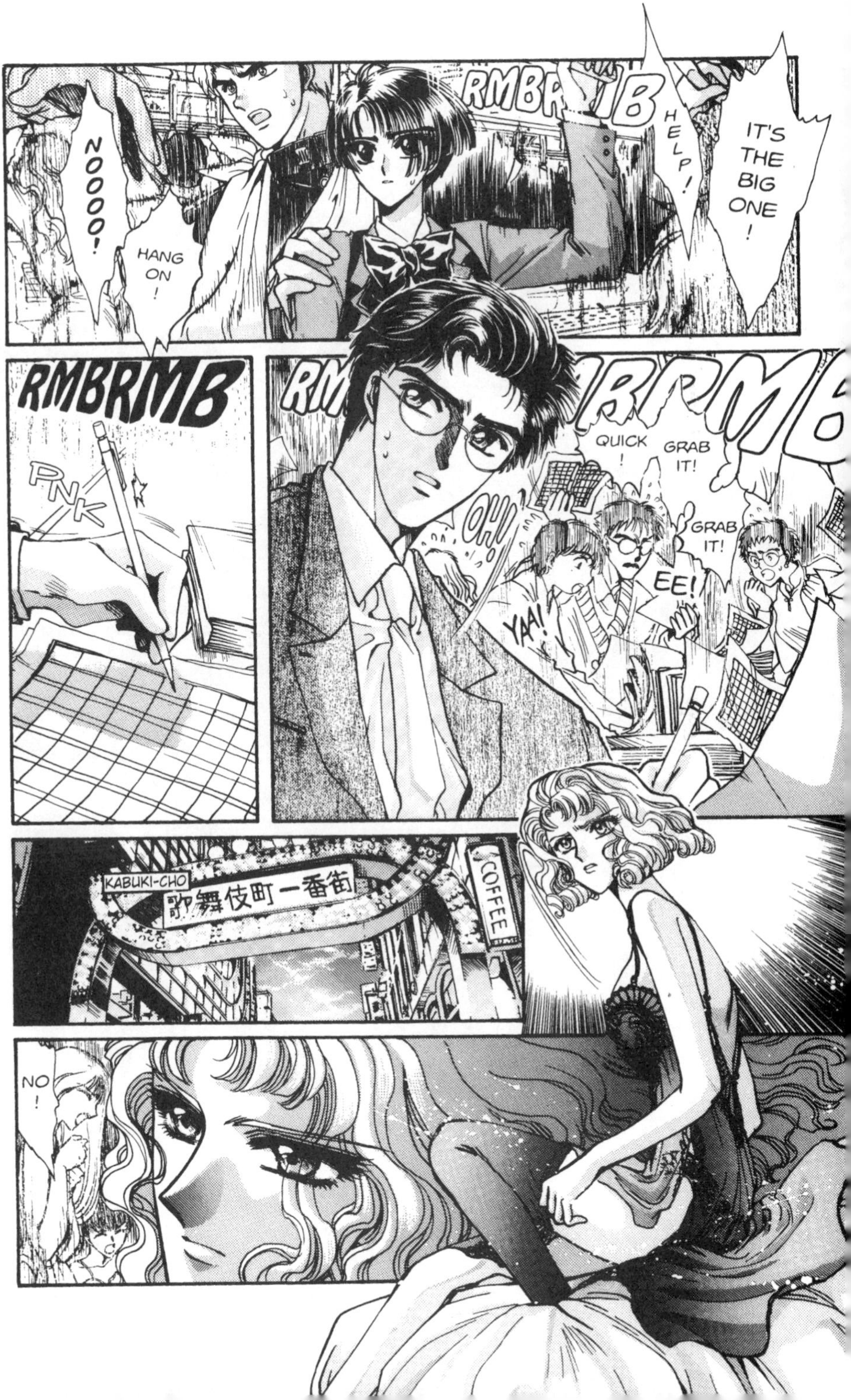
NOOOOO!
HANG ON!
HELP!
IT'S THE BIG ONE!
RMBRMB
PNK
OH!
QUICK!
GRAB IT!
GRAB IT!
EE!
YAA!
KABUKI-CHO
歌舞伎町一番街
COFFEE
NO!

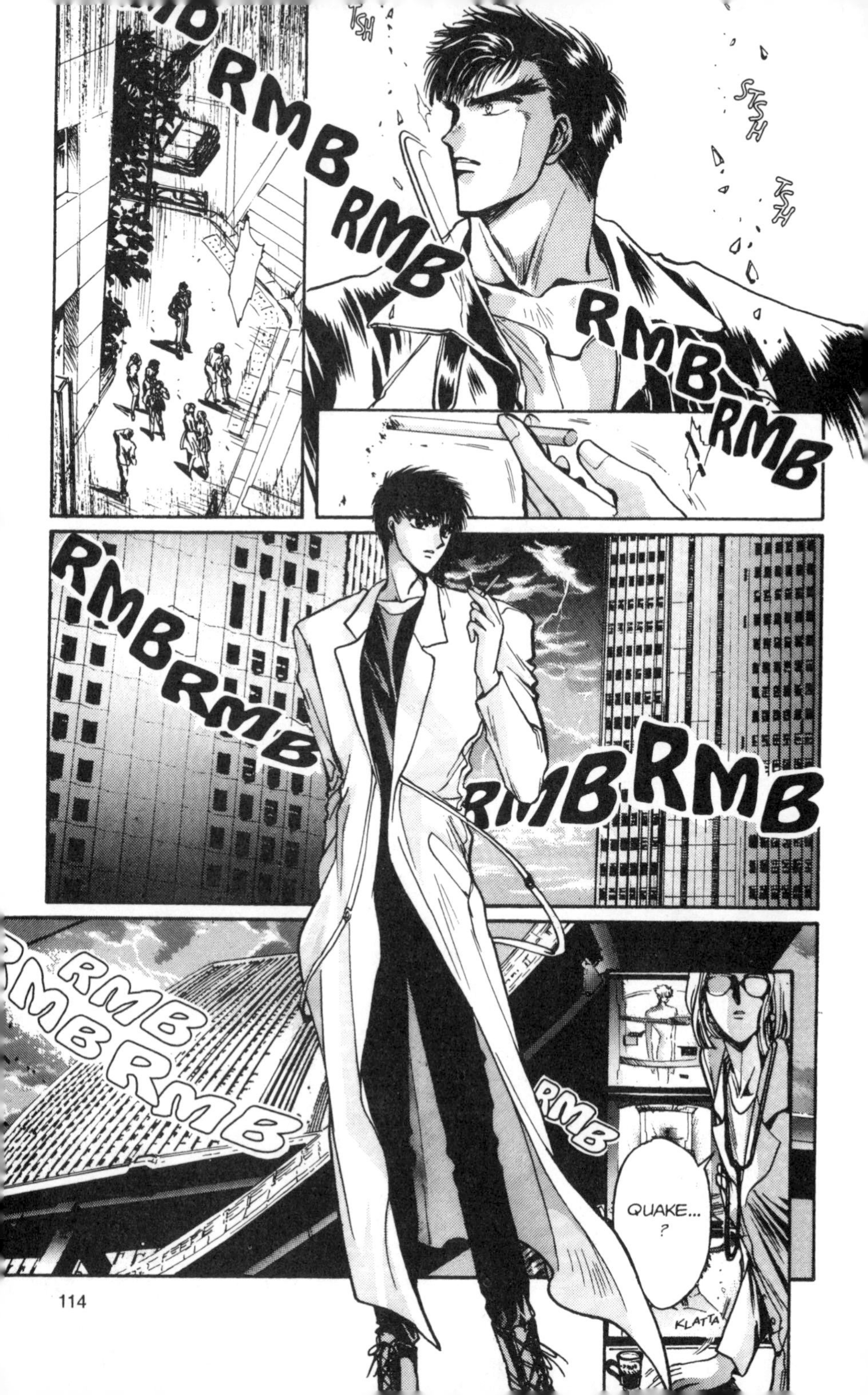
RMB RMB RMB
TSH
STSH
TSH
RMB RMB RMB
RMBRMBRMB
RMB RMB
RMB RMB RMB
RMB
QUAKE...?
KLATTA

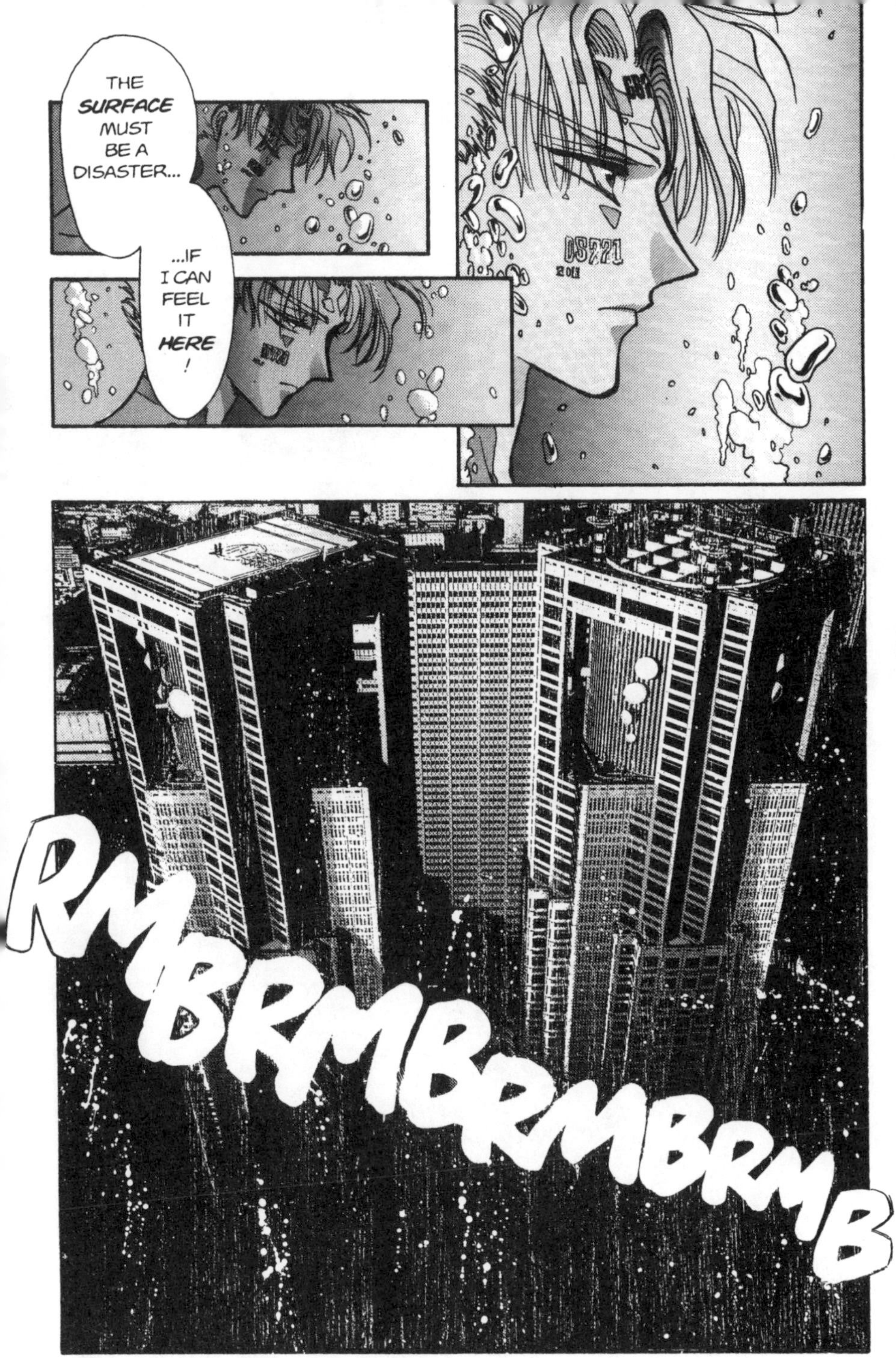
THE **SURFACE** MUST BE A DISASTER...
...IF I CAN FEEL IT **HERE**!
DS721
RMBRMBRMBRMBRMB

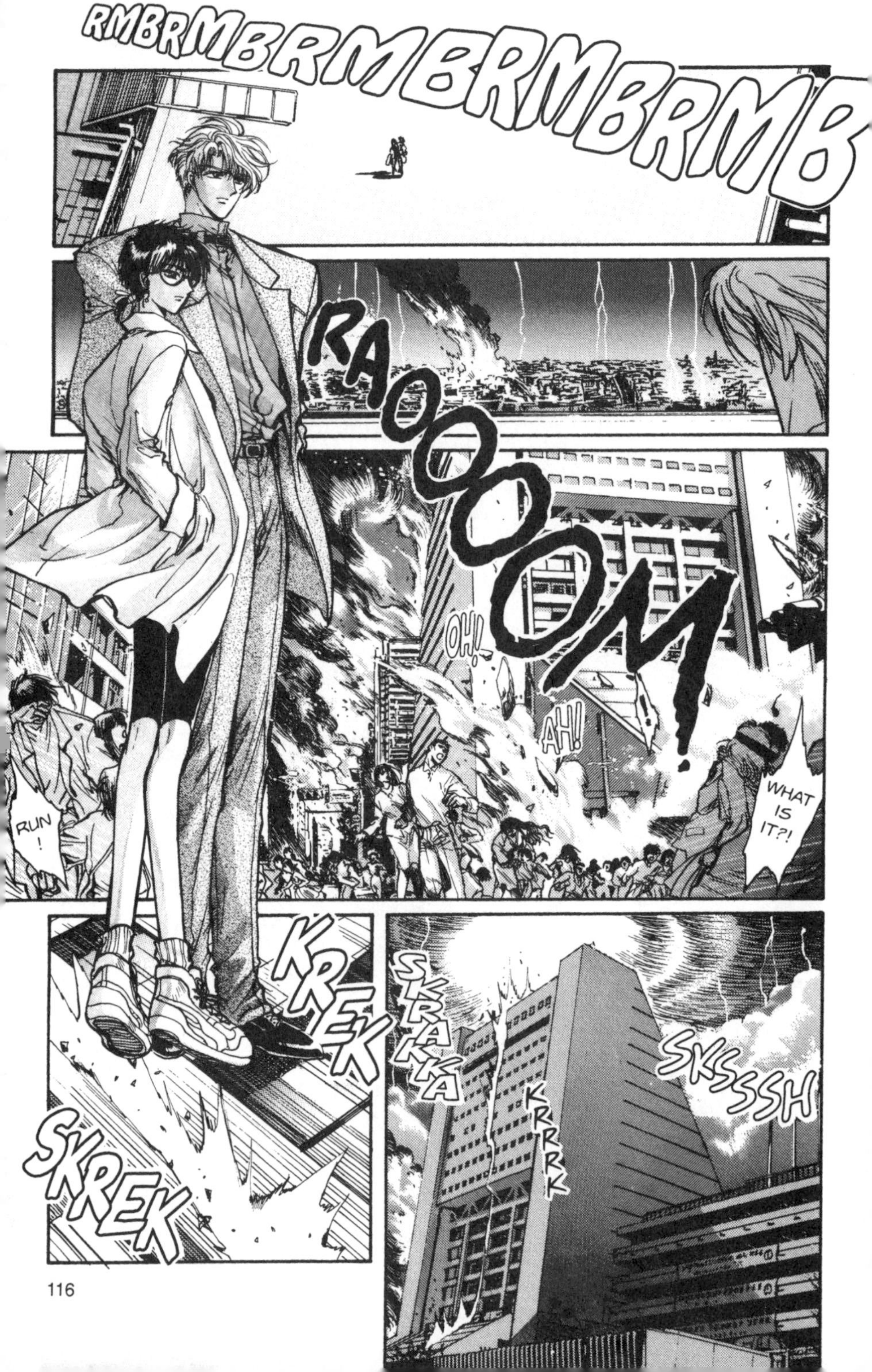
RMBRMBRMBRMBRMBRMB
RAOOOOM!
RUN!
OH!
AH!
WHAT IS IT?!
KREK
SKREK
SKRAKKA
KRRRK
SKSSSH

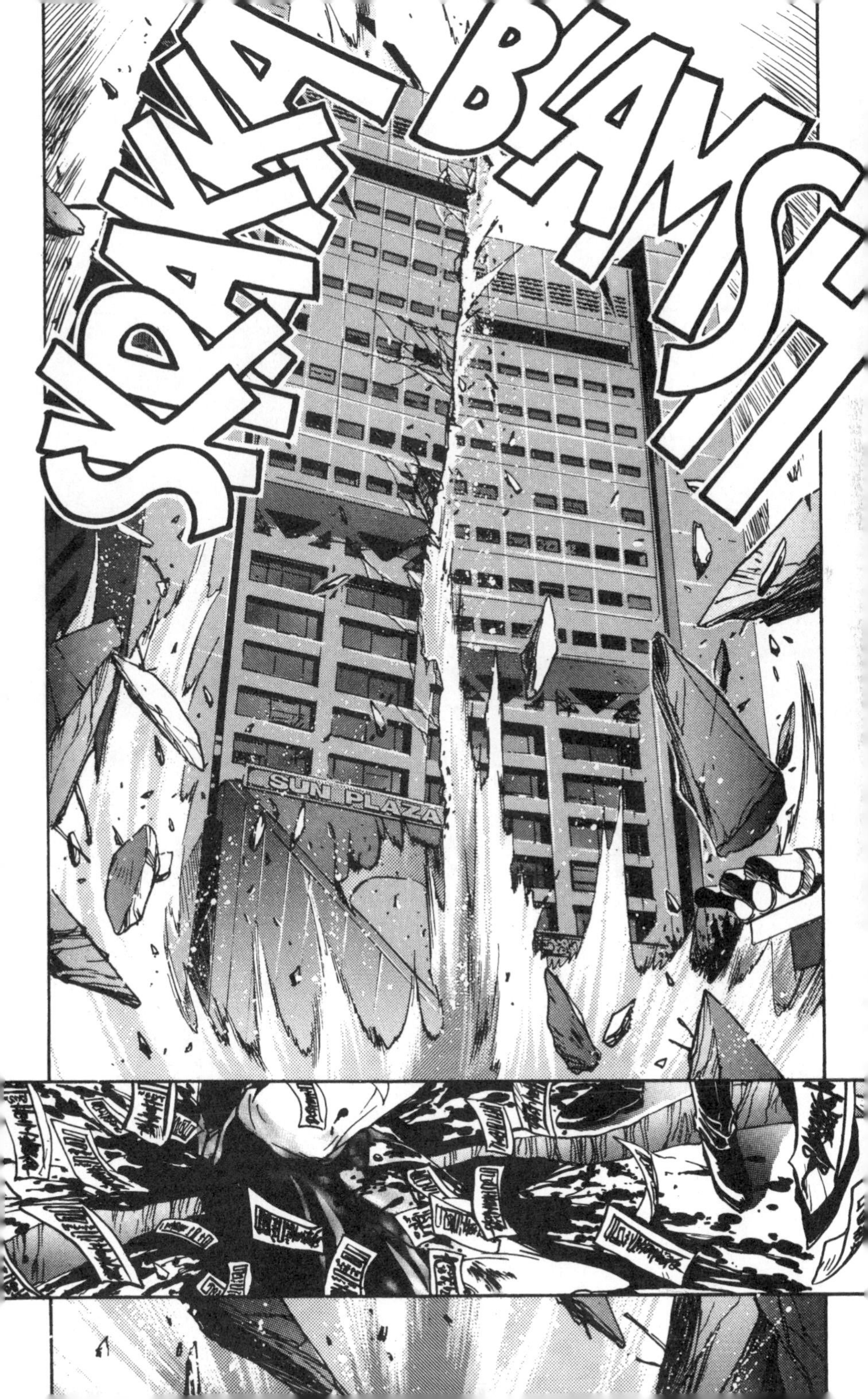
SKAKA
BLAMSH
SUN PLAZA

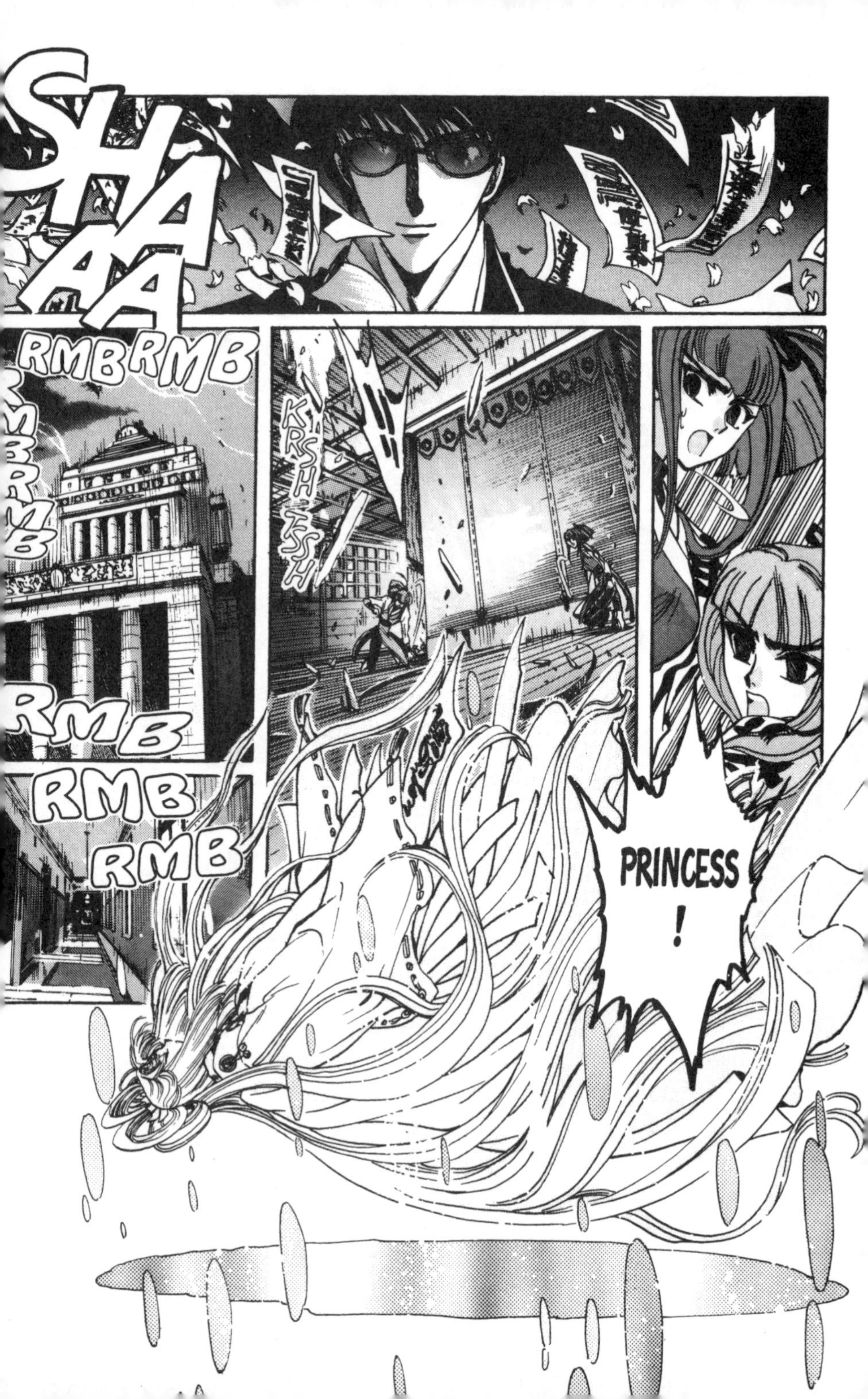
SHAAA
RMB RMB
RMBRMB
KRSH TSSH
RMB
RMB
RMB
PRINCESS!

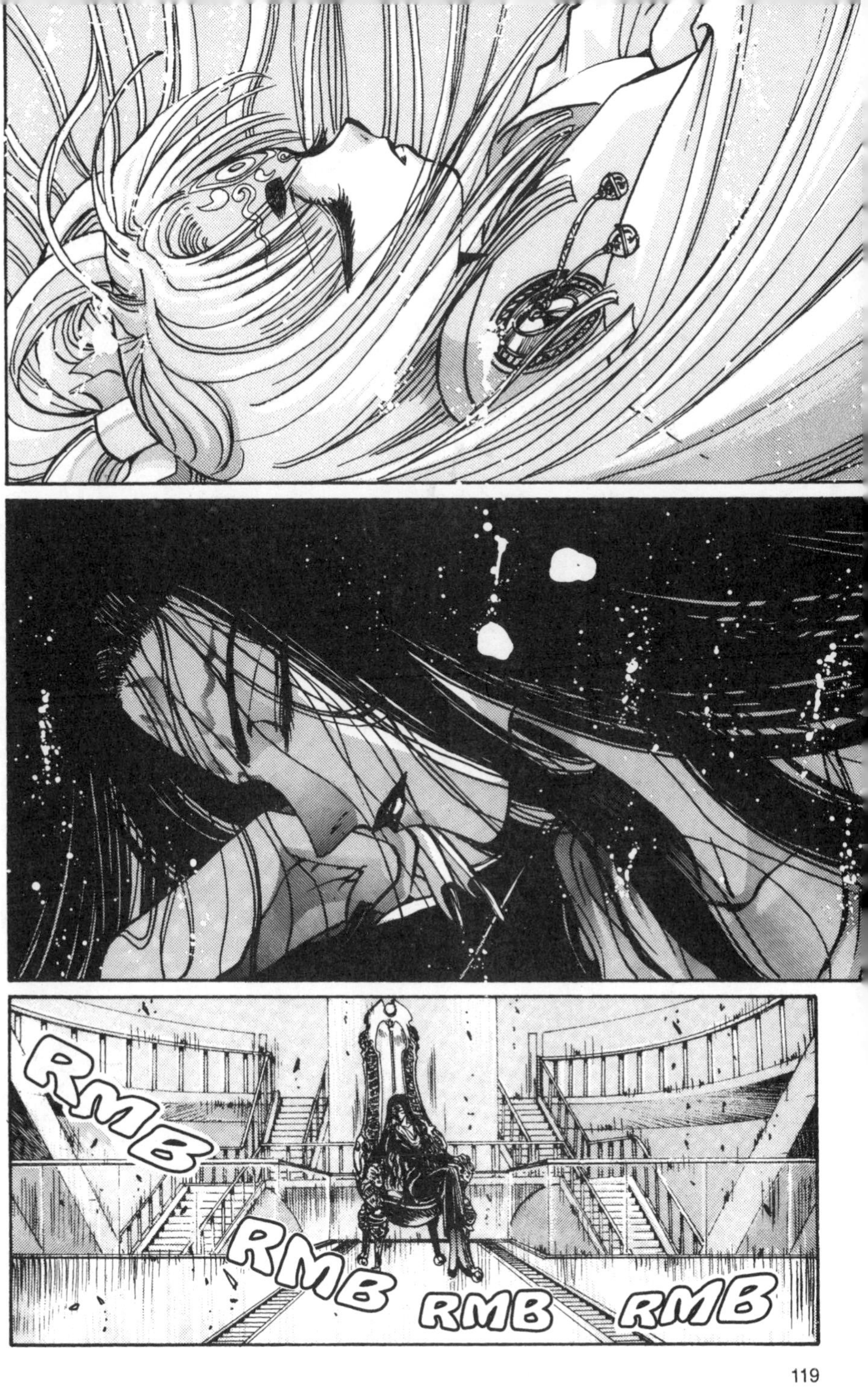
RMB
RMB
RMB
RMB

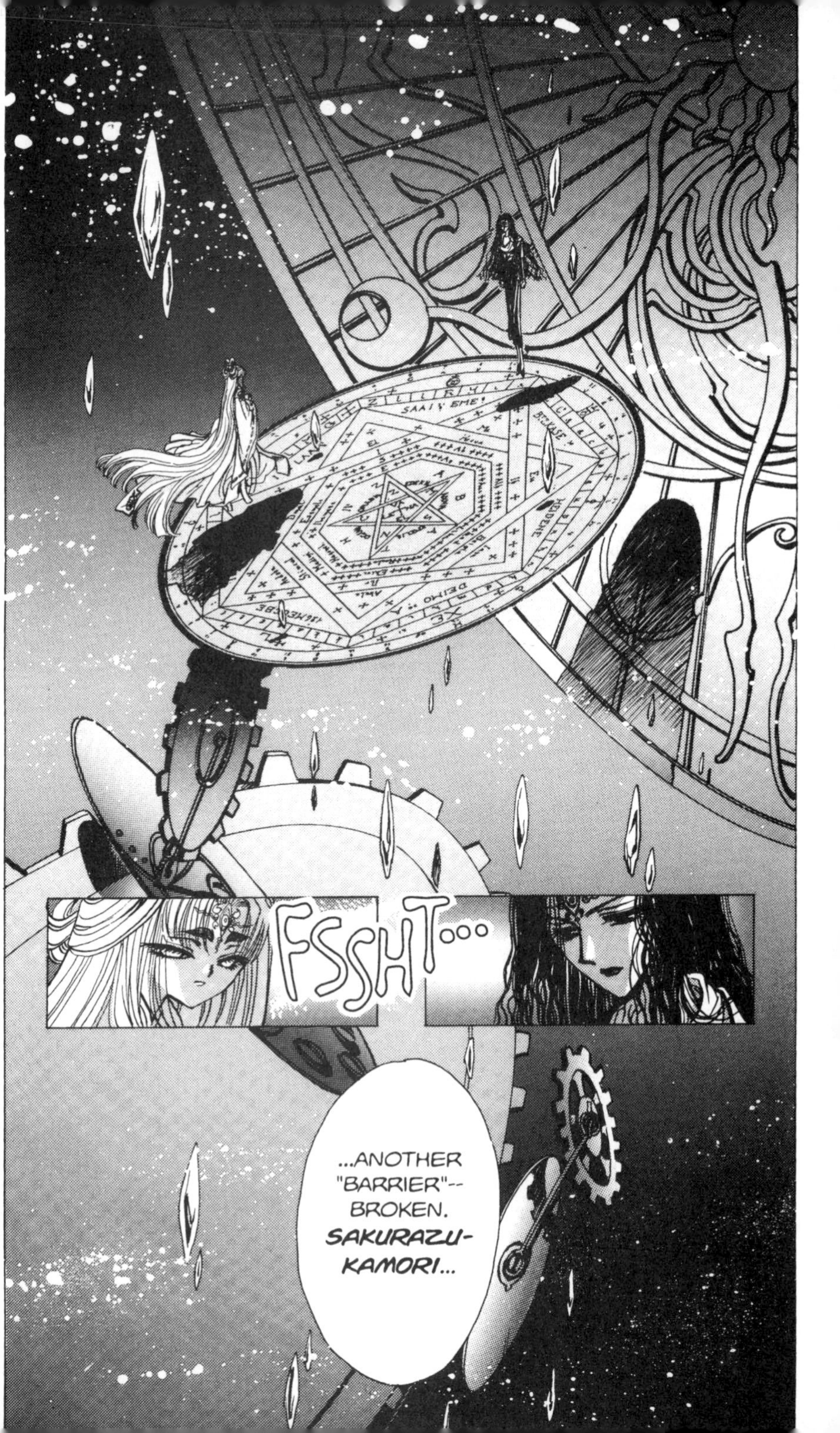
FSSHT...
...ANOTHER "BARRIER"-- BROKEN. SAKURAZUKAMORI...

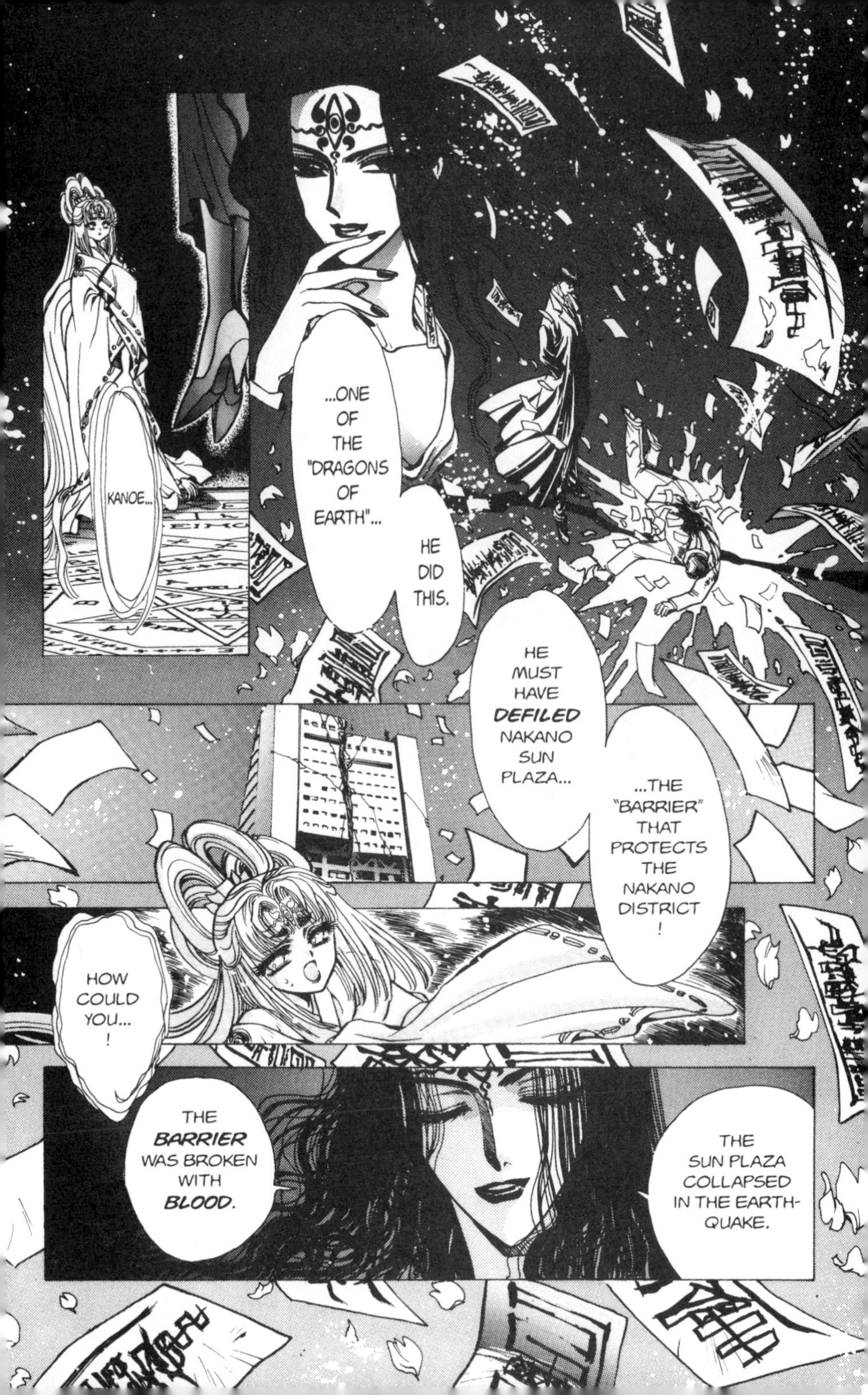
KANOE...
...ONE OF THE "DRAGONS OF EARTH"...
HE DID THIS.
HE MUST HAVE **DEFILED** NAKANO SUN PLAZA...
...THE "BARRIER" THAT PROTECTS THE NAKANO DISTRICT !
HOW COULD YOU... !
THE **BARRIER** WAS BROKEN WITH **BLOOD**.
THE SUN PLAZA COLLAPSED IN THE EARTH-QUAKE.

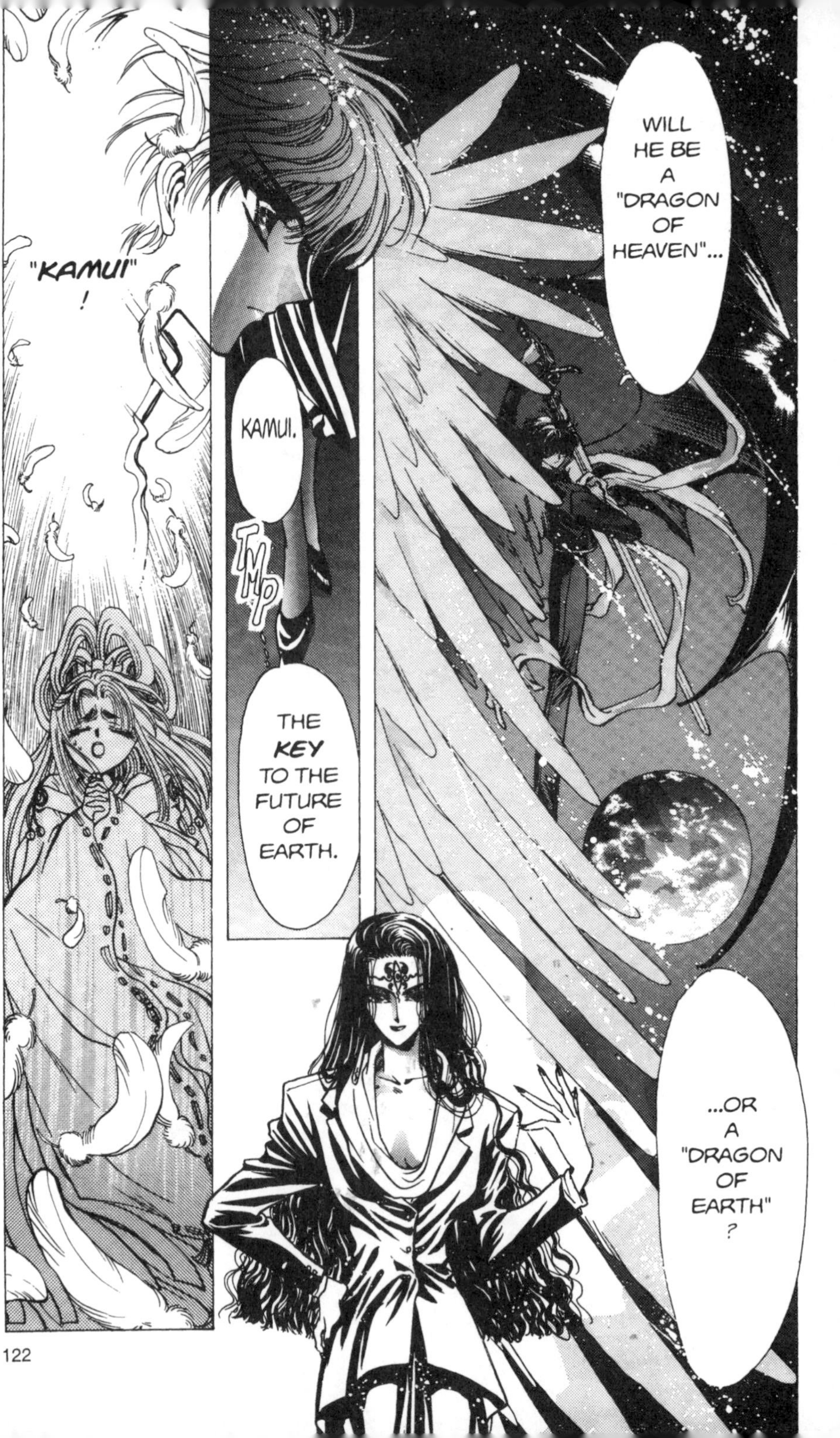
"KAMUI"!
KAMUI.
TMP
THE KEY TO THE FUTURE OF EARTH.
WILL HE BE A "DRAGON OF HEAVEN"...
...OR A "DRAGON OF EARTH"?

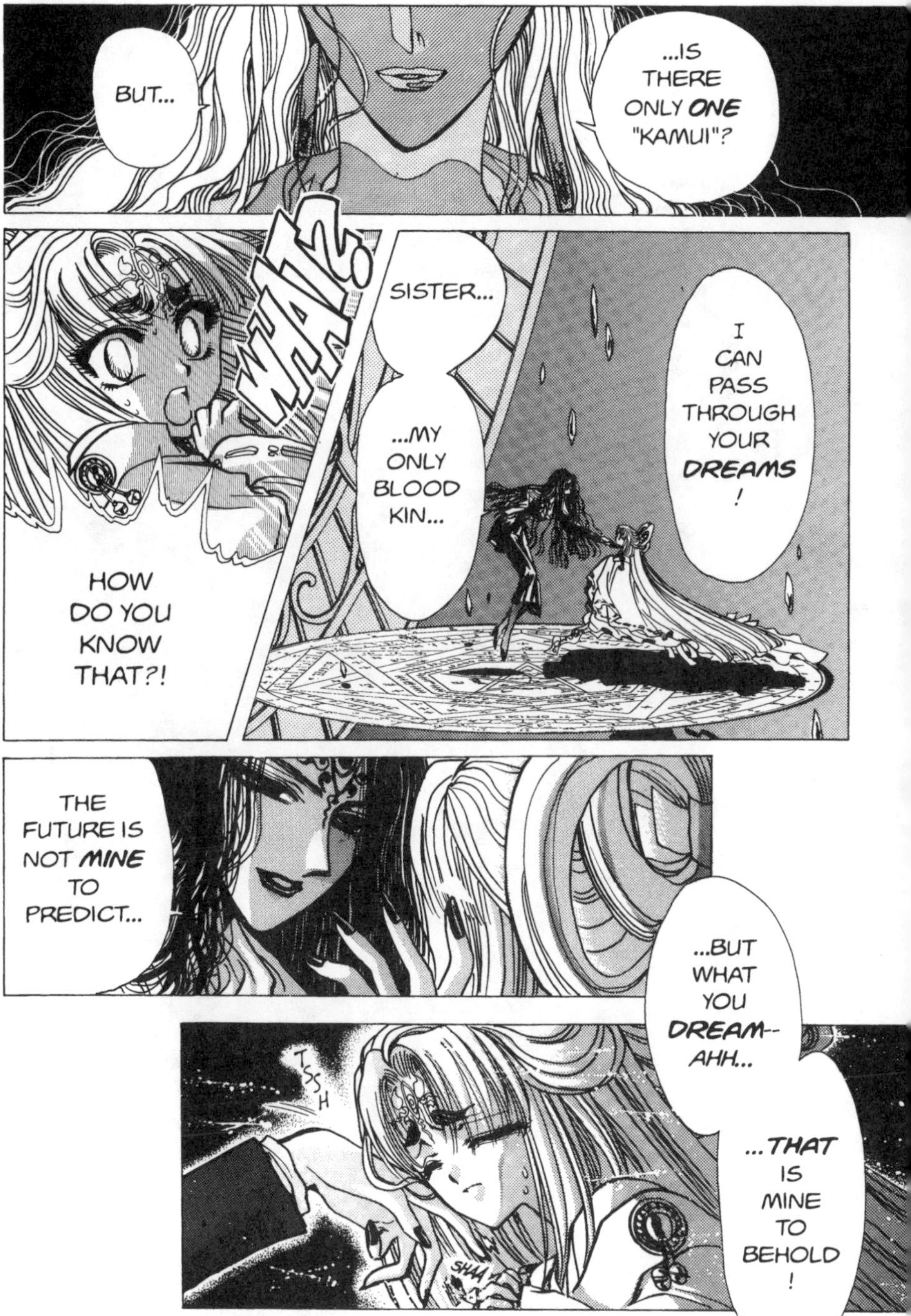
BUT...
...IS THERE ONLY **ONE** "KAMUI"?
WHA?!
HOW DO YOU KNOW THAT?!
SISTER...
...MY ONLY BLOOD KIN...
I CAN PASS THROUGH YOUR **DREAMS**!
THE FUTURE IS NOT **MINE** TO PREDICT...
...BUT WHAT YOU **DREAM**-- AHH...
TSSSH
...**THAT** IS MINE TO BEHOLD!
SHAA

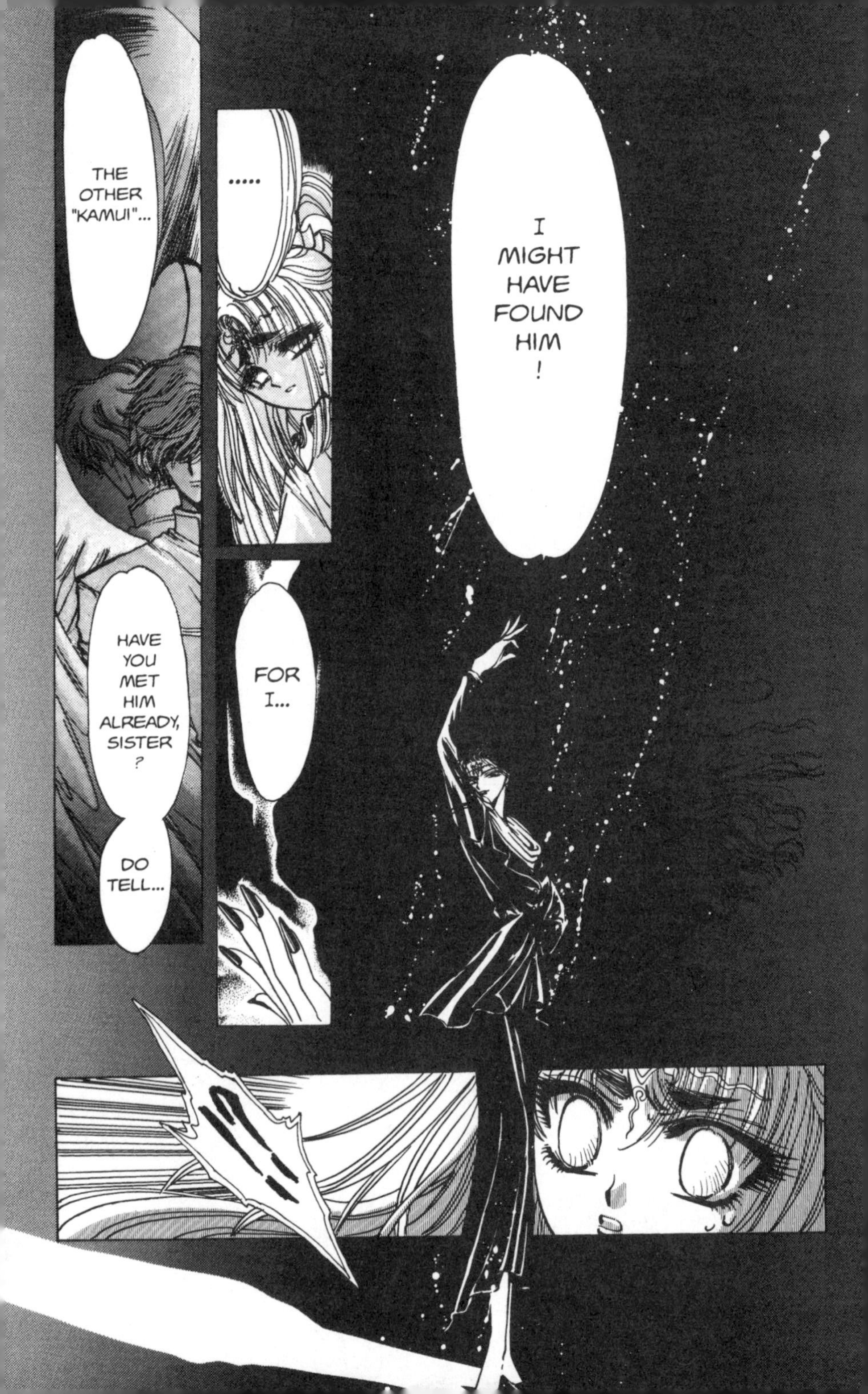
THE OTHER "KAMUI"...
HAVE YOU MET HIM ALREADY, SISTER?
DO TELL...
.....
FOR I...
I MIGHT HAVE FOUND HIM!

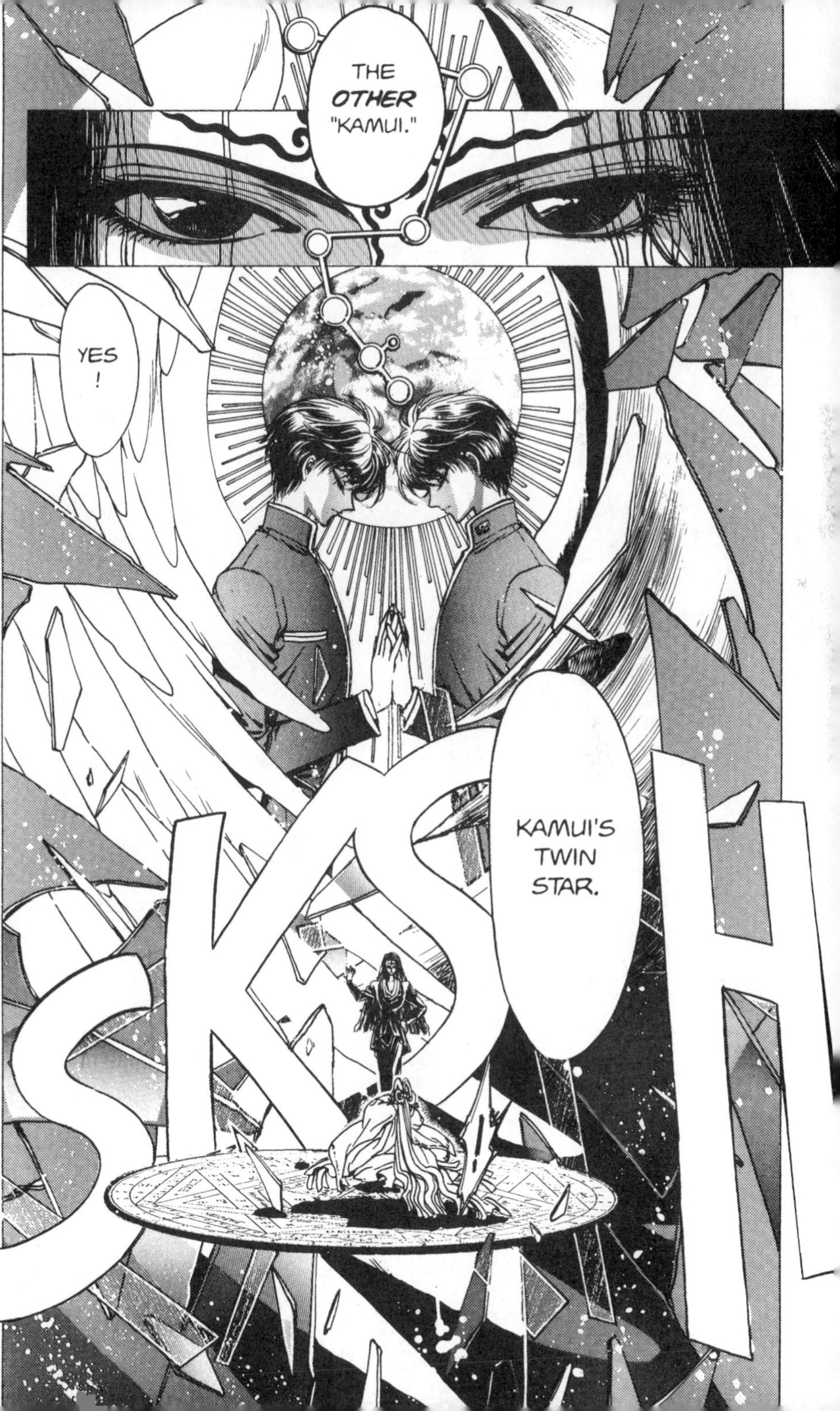
THE *OTHER* "KAMUI."
YES!
KAMUI'S TWIN STAR.
SKSH

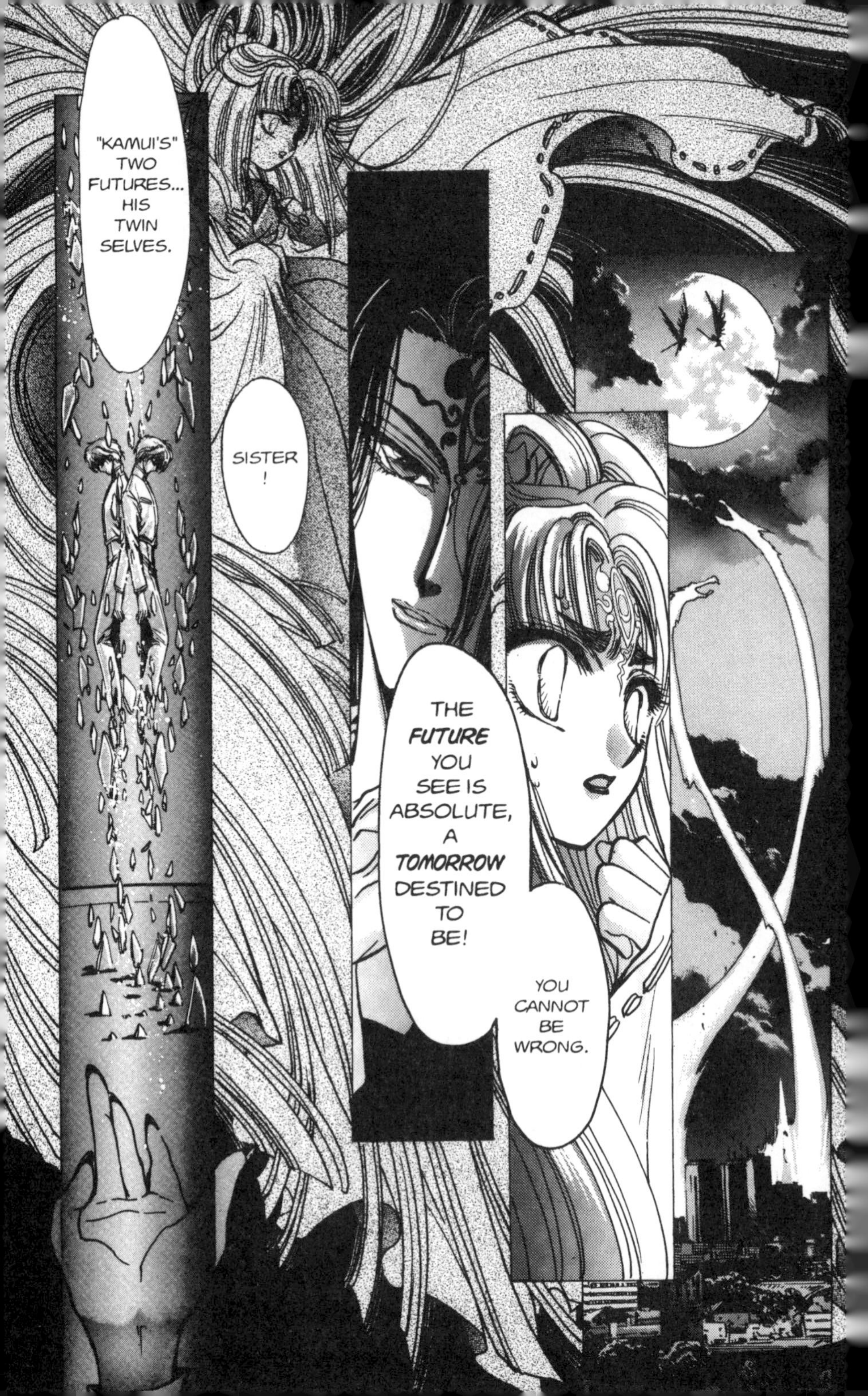
"KAMUI'S" TWO FUTURES... HIS TWIN SELVES.
SISTER!
THE FUTURE YOU SEE IS ABSOLUTE, A TOMORROW DESTINED TO BE!
YOU CANNOT BE WRONG.

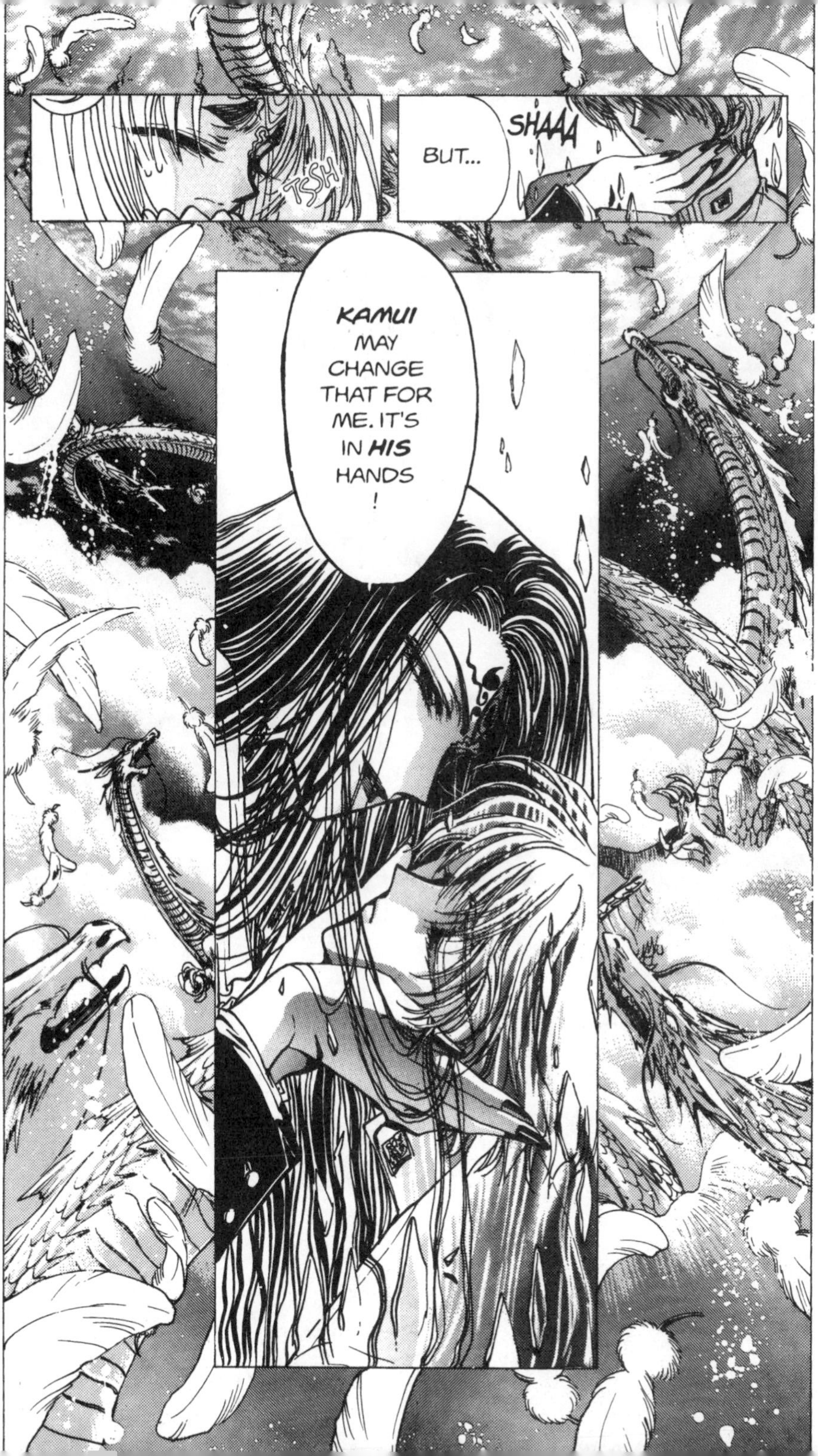
TSSH
BUT...
SHAAA
KAMUI MAY CHANGE THAT FOR ME. IT'S IN HIS HANDS!

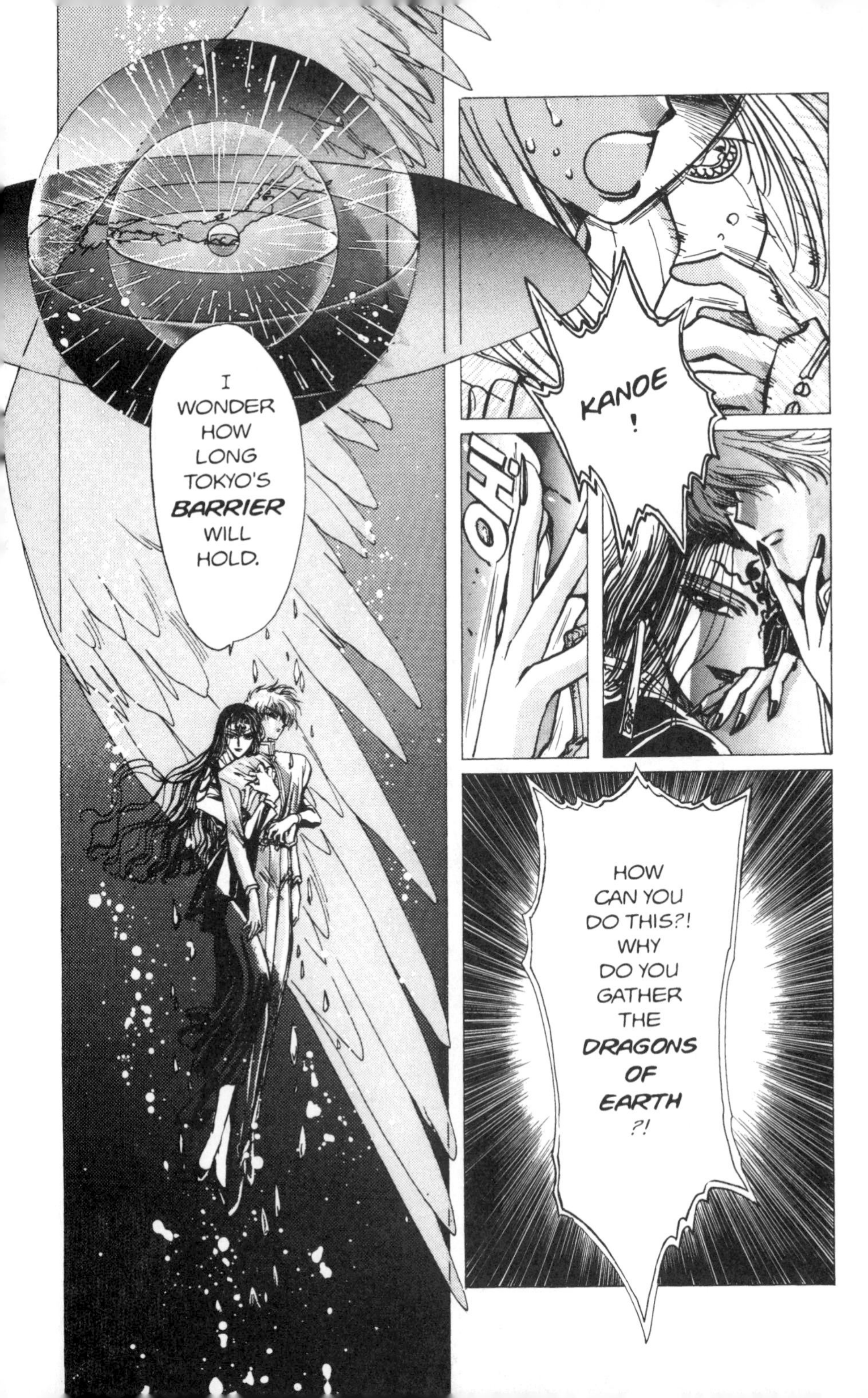
I WONDER HOW LONG TOKYO'S **BARRIER** WILL HOLD.
KANOE!
OH!
HOW CAN YOU DO THIS?! WHY DO YOU GATHER THE **DRAGONS OF EARTH**?!

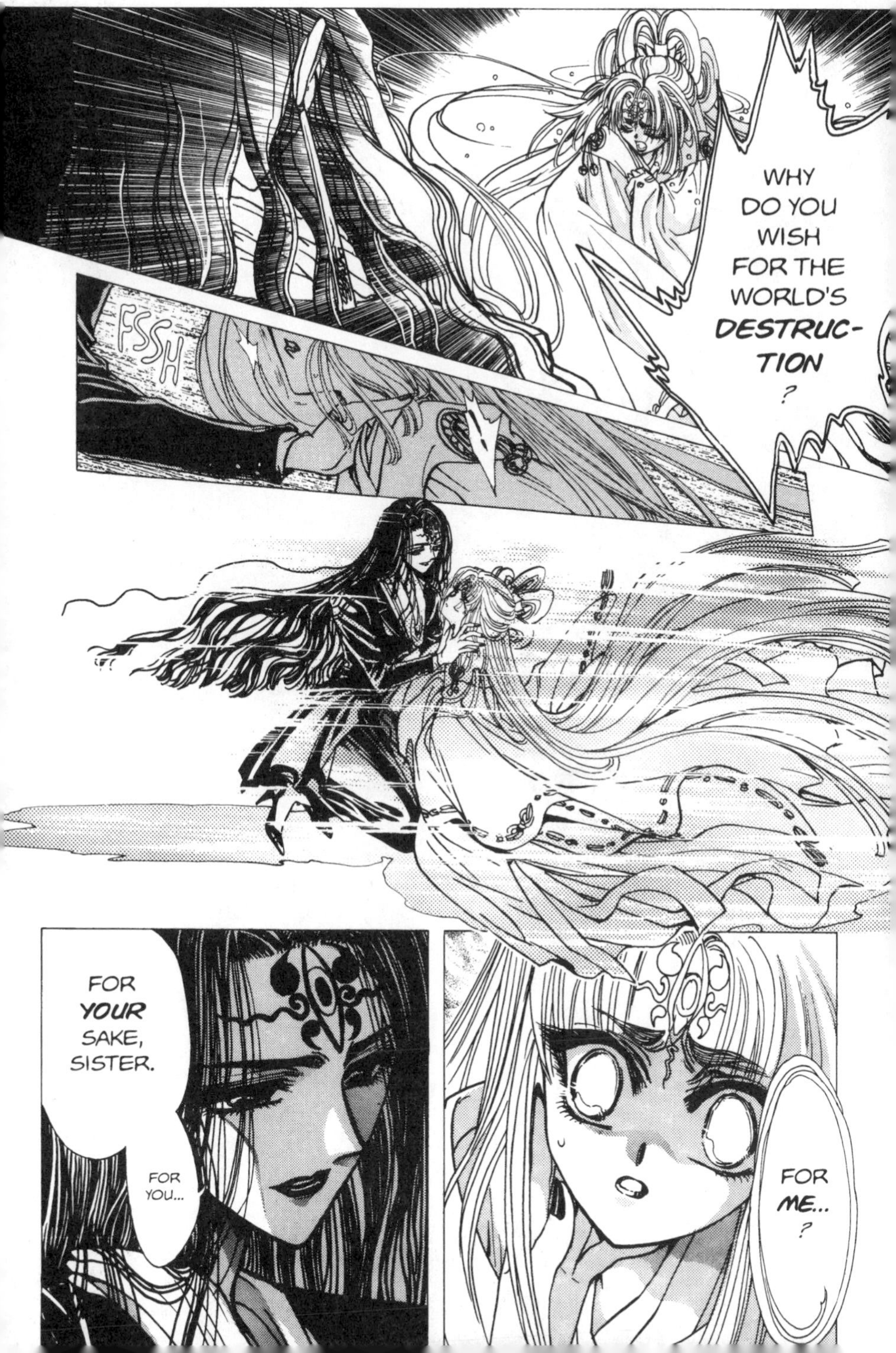
WHY DO YOU WISH FOR THE WORLD'S DESTRUCTION?
FSSH
FOR YOUR SAKE, SISTER.
FOR YOU...
FOR ME...?

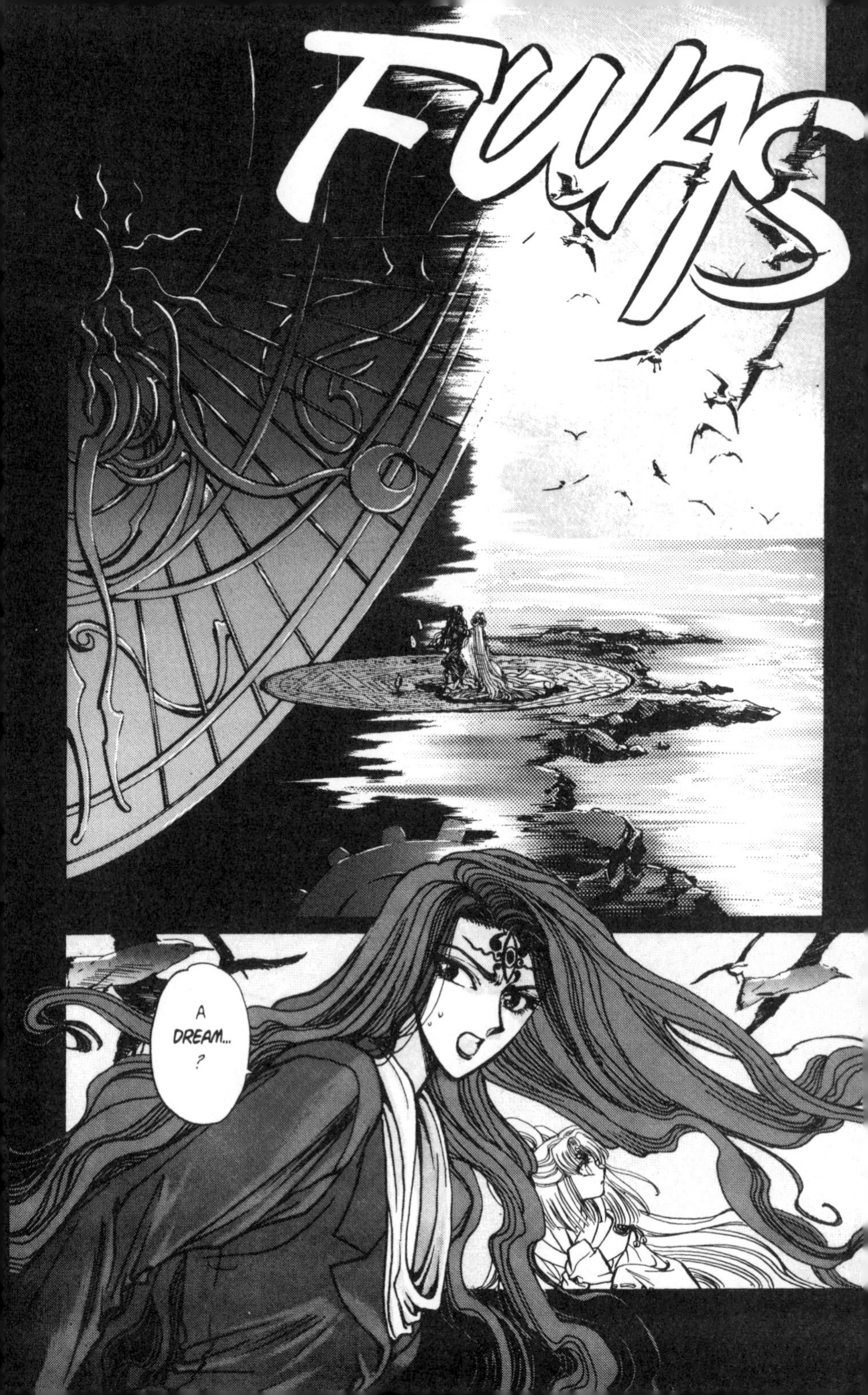
A DREAM... ?

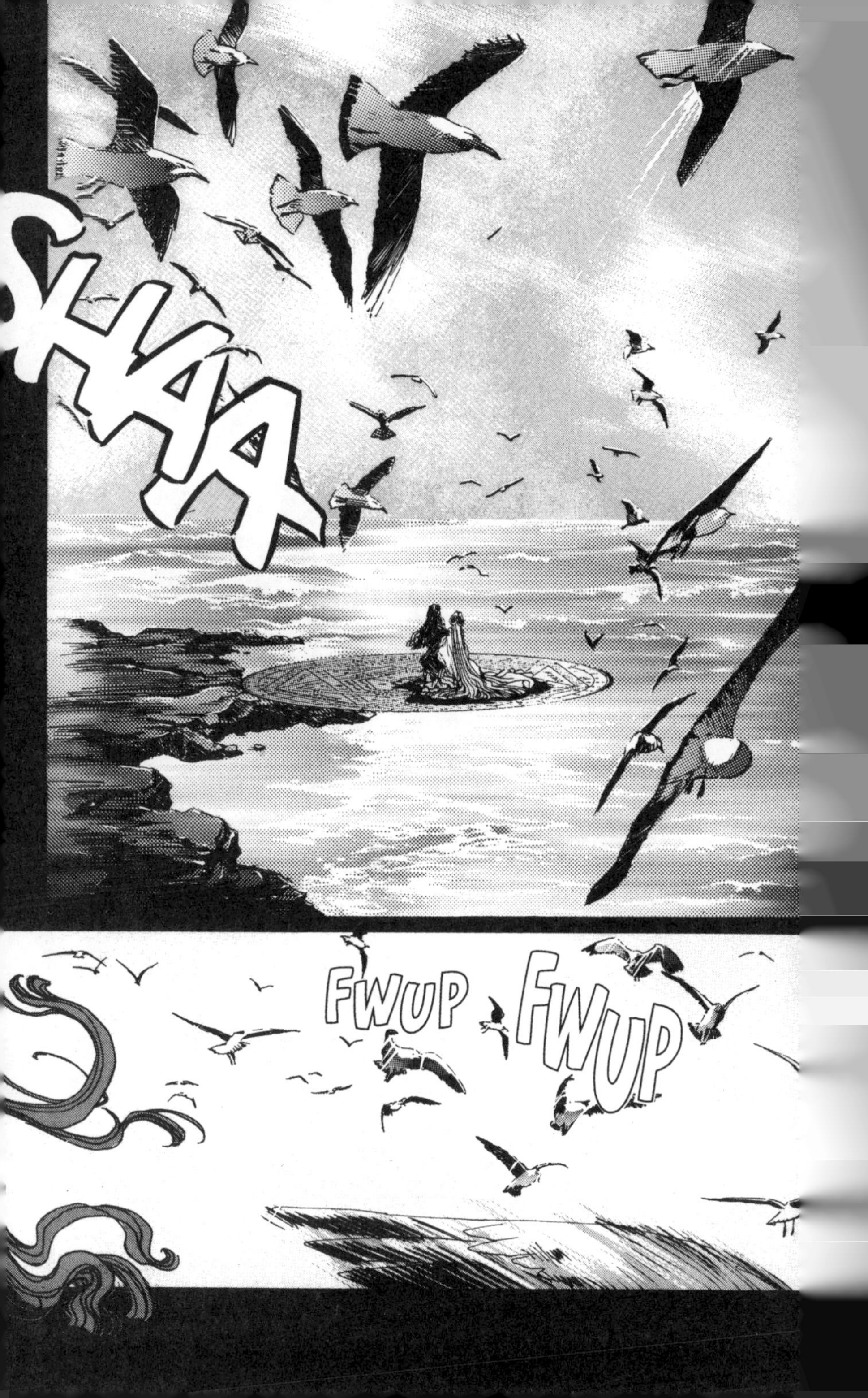
SHAA
FWUP
FWUP

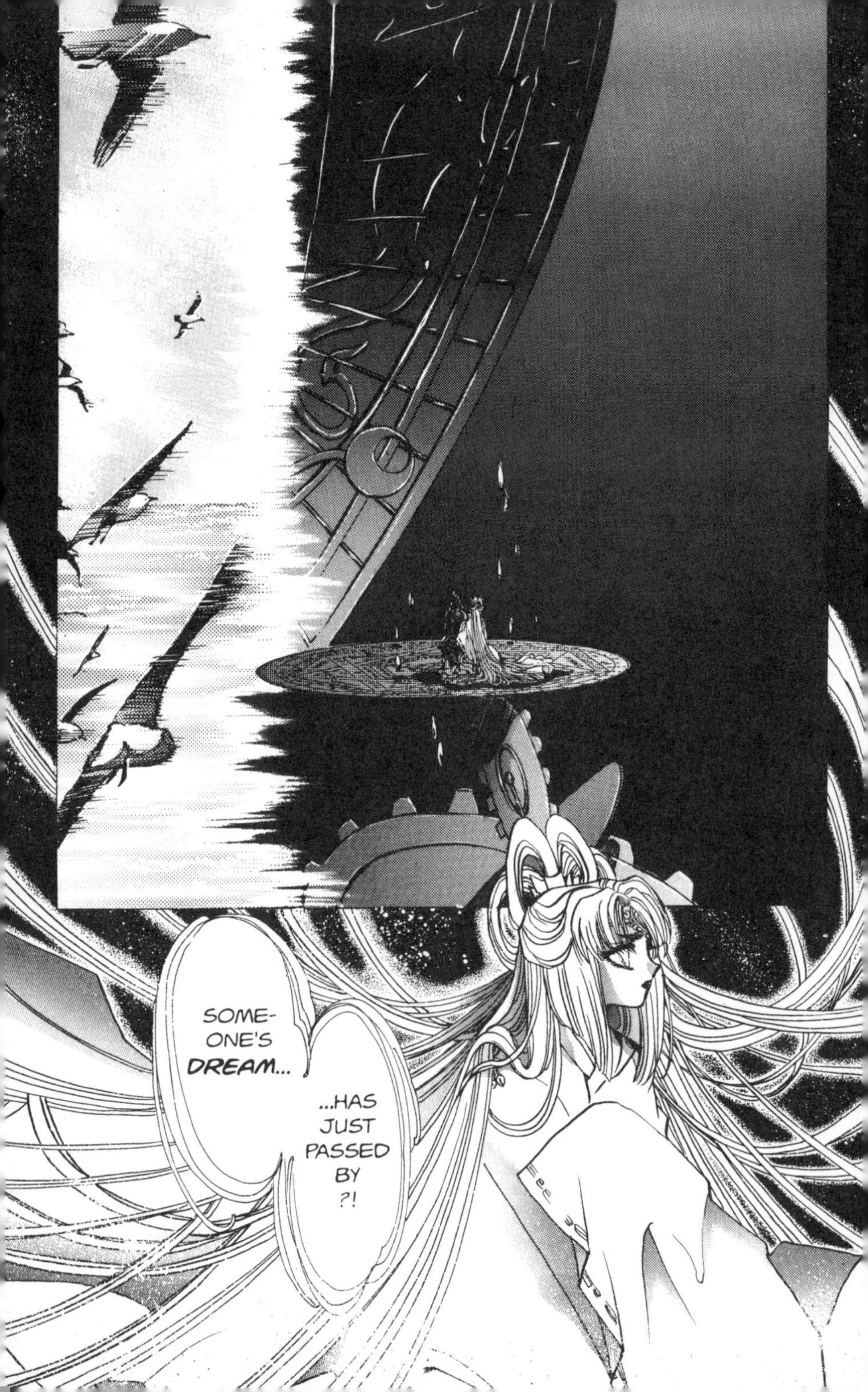
SOME-ONE'S **DREAM...**
...HAS JUST PASSED BY ?!

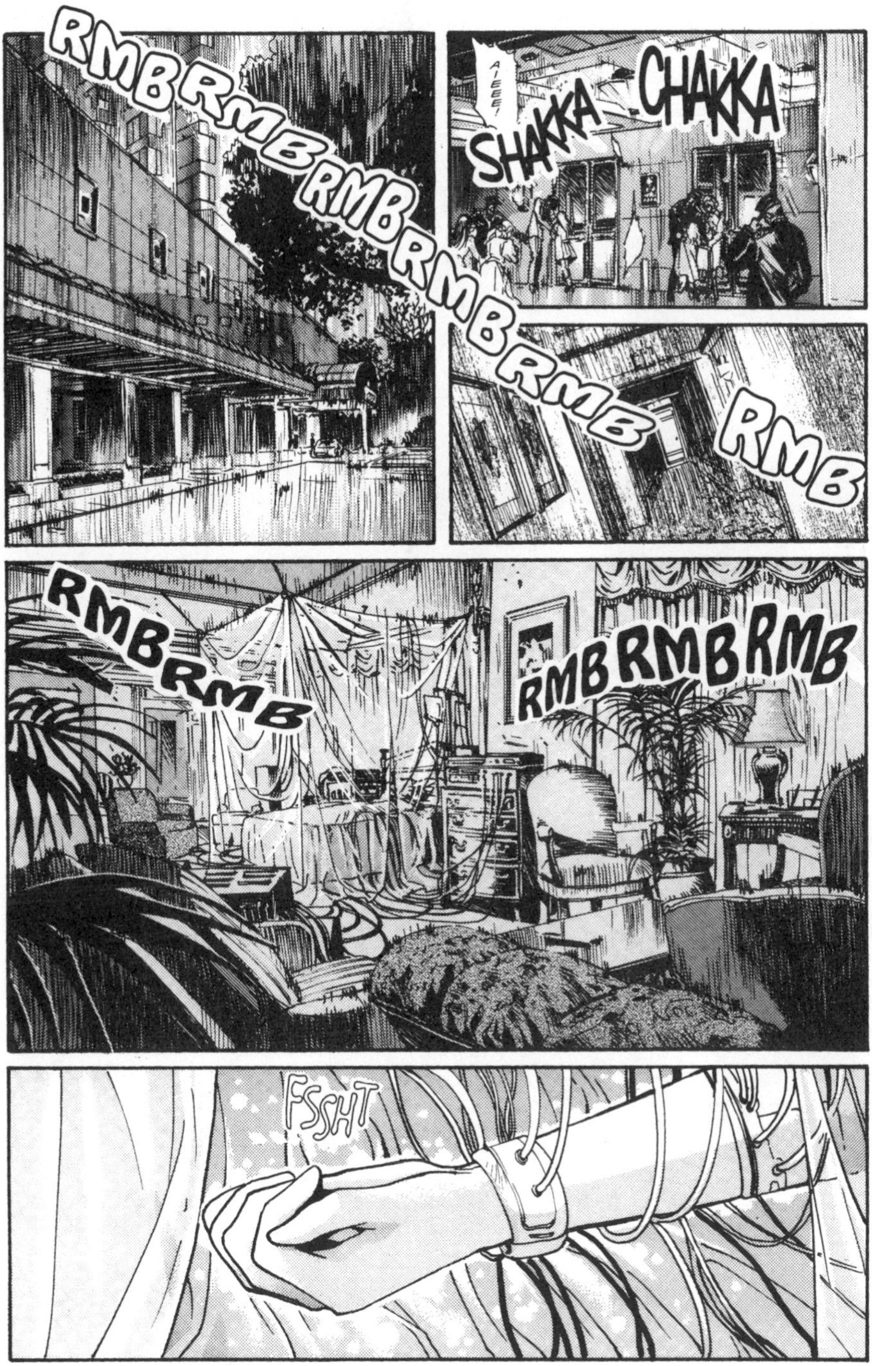
RMBRMBRMBRMBRMB
AIEEE!
SHAKKA CHAKKA
RMB
RMBRMB
RMBRMBRMB
FSSHT

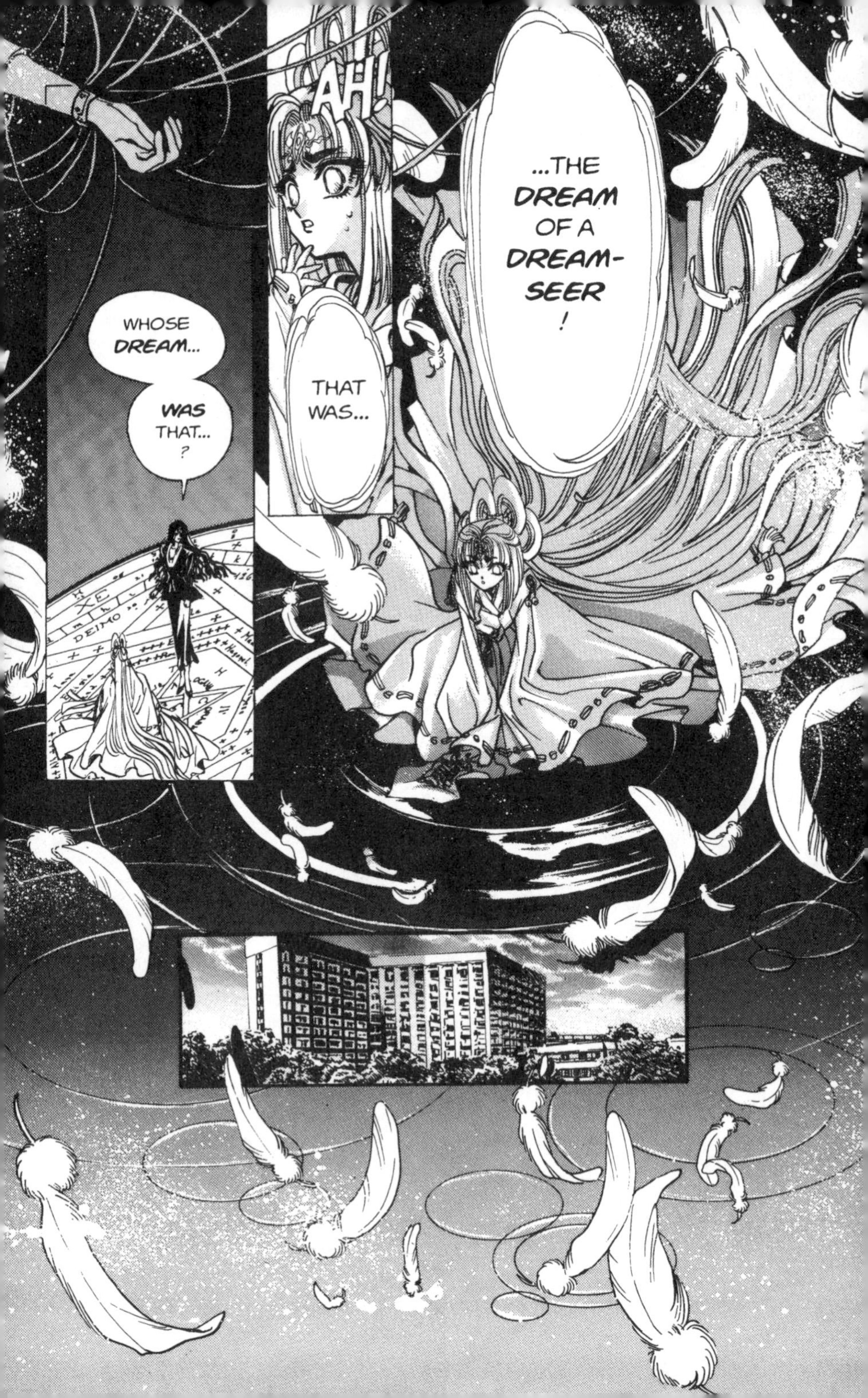

WHOSE DREAM...
WAS THAT...?
AH!
THAT WAS...
...THE DREAM OF A DREAM-SEER!

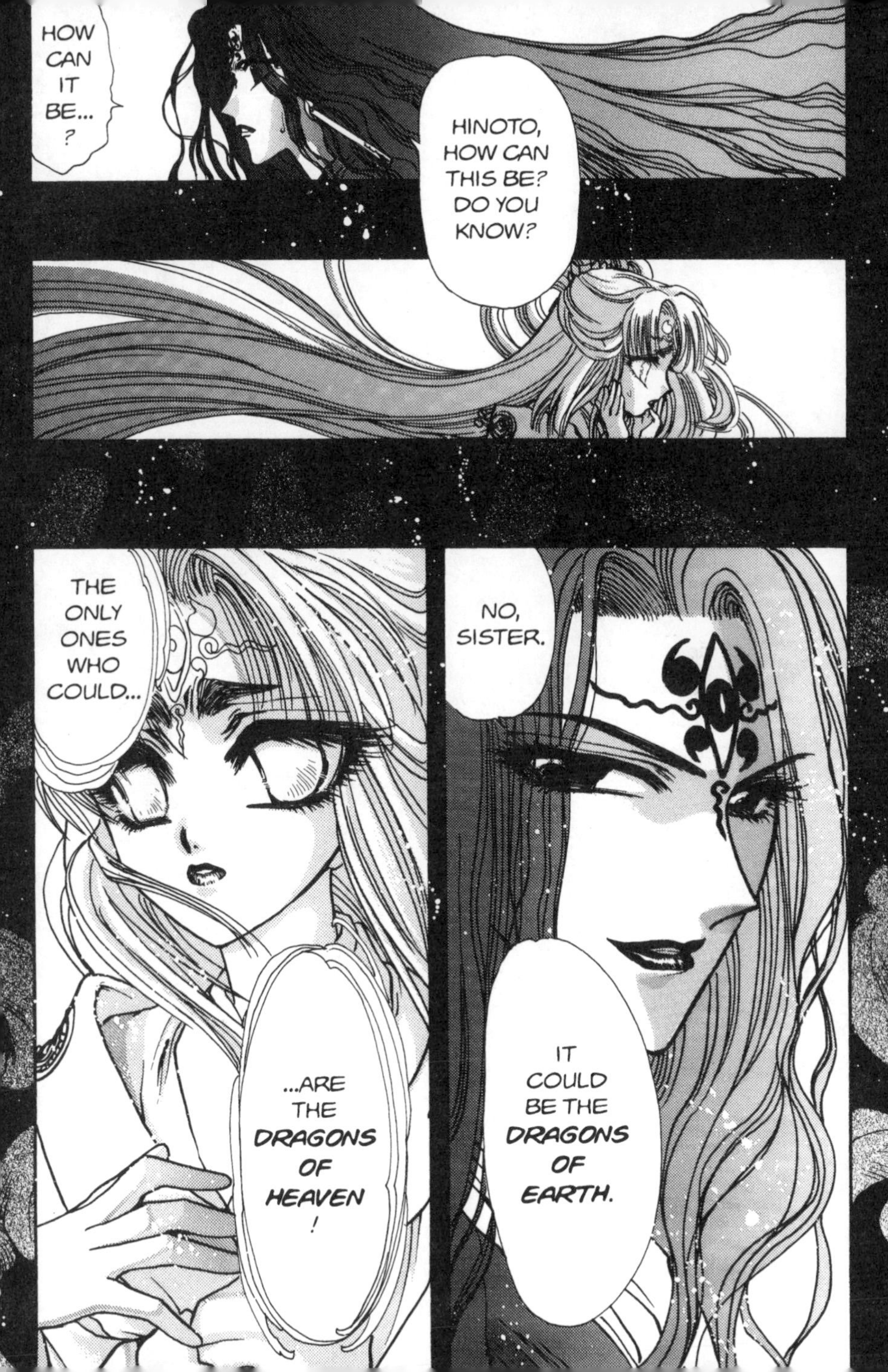
HOW CAN IT BE...?
HINOTO, HOW CAN THIS BE? DO YOU KNOW?
THE ONLY ONES WHO COULD...
...ARE THE DRAGONS OF HEAVEN!
NO, SISTER.
IT COULD BE THE DRAGONS OF EARTH.

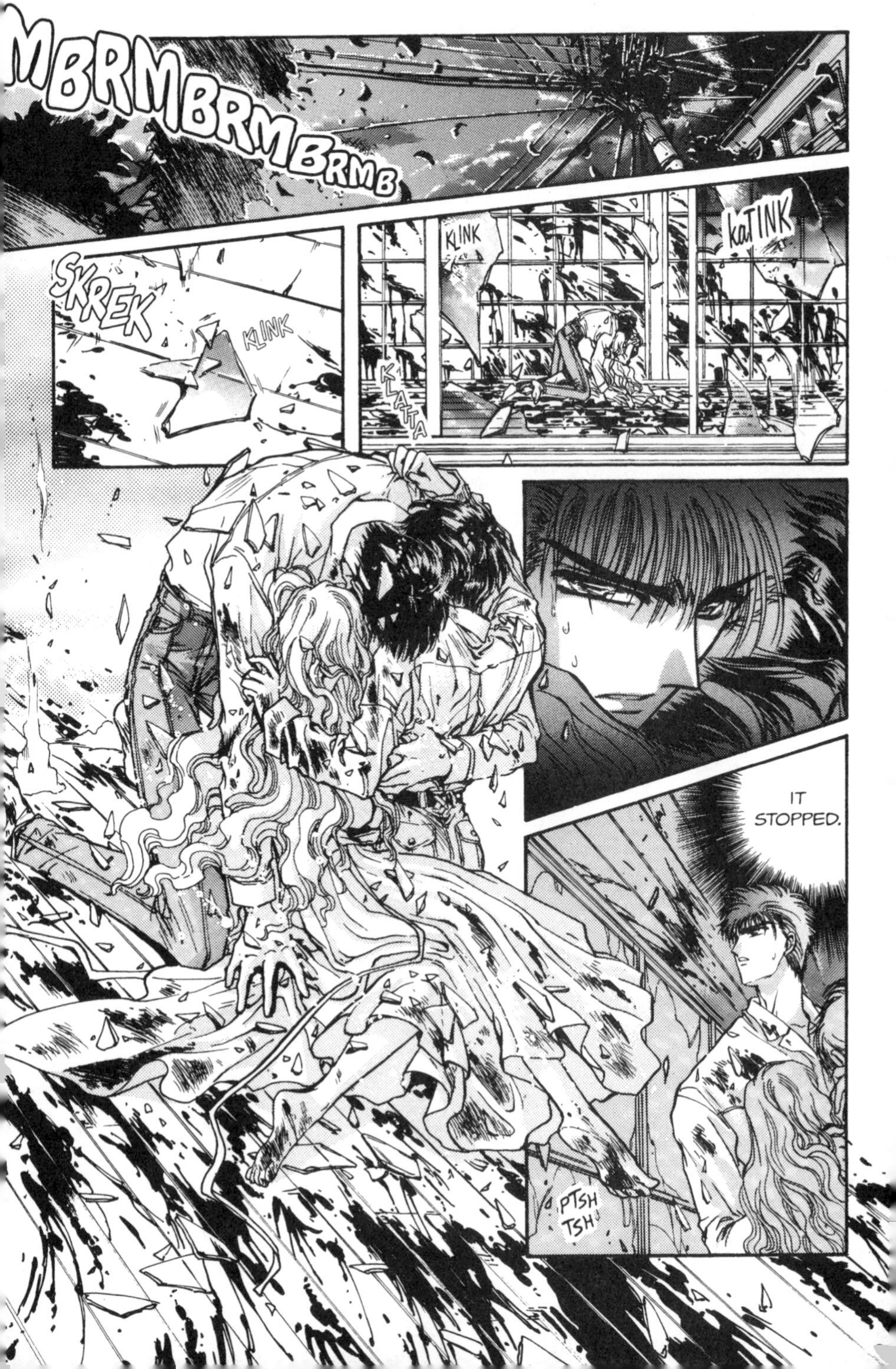

MBRMBRMBRMBRMB
SKREK
KLINK
KLINK
KLATTA
kaTINK
IT STOPPED.
PTSH TSH

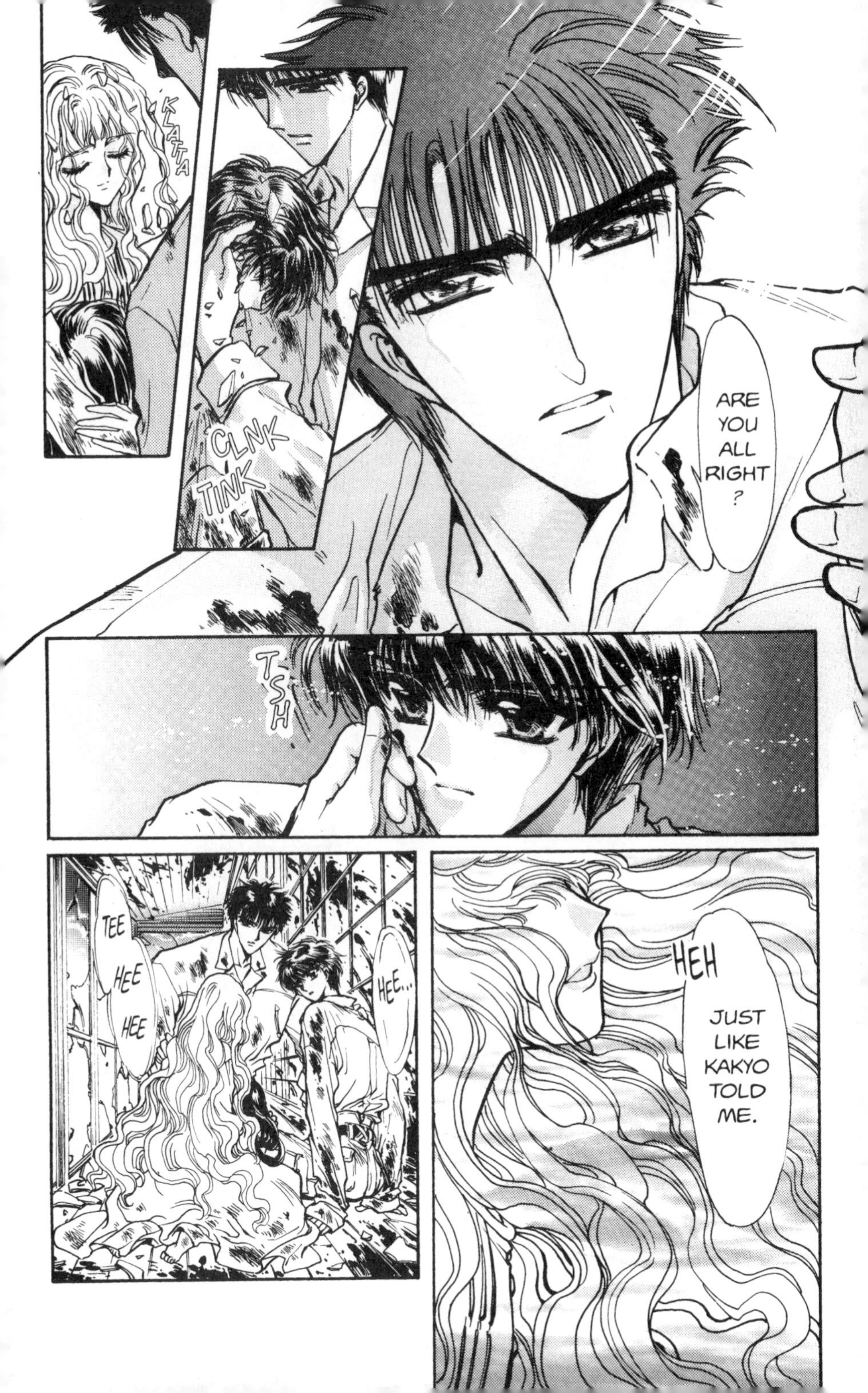
KLATTA
CLNK
TINK
ARE YOU ALL RIGHT?
TSH
TEE HEE HEE
HEE...
HEH
JUST LIKE KAKYO TOLD ME.

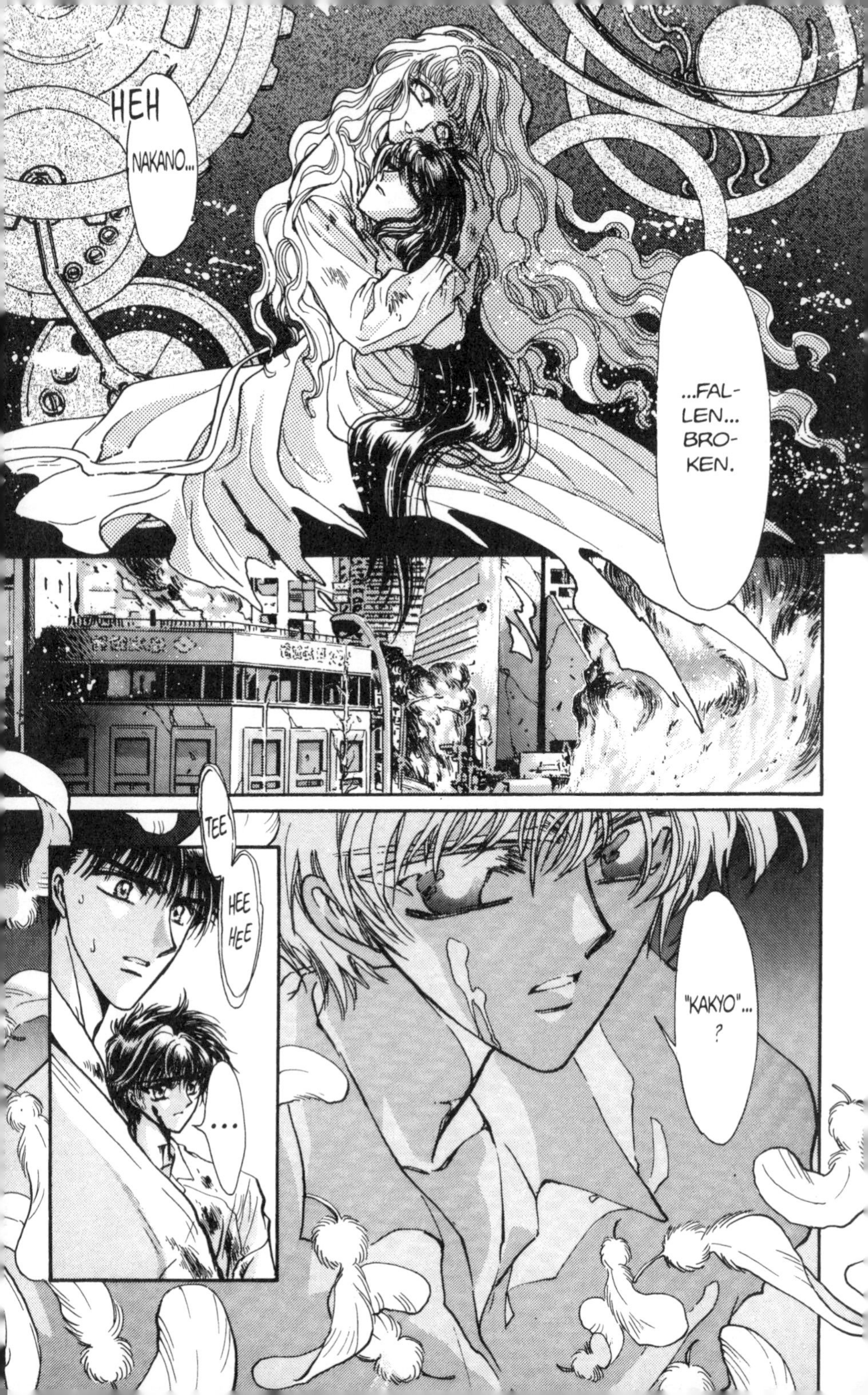
HEH
NAKANO...
...FALLEN... BROKEN.
TEE HEE HEE
...
"KAKYO"...?

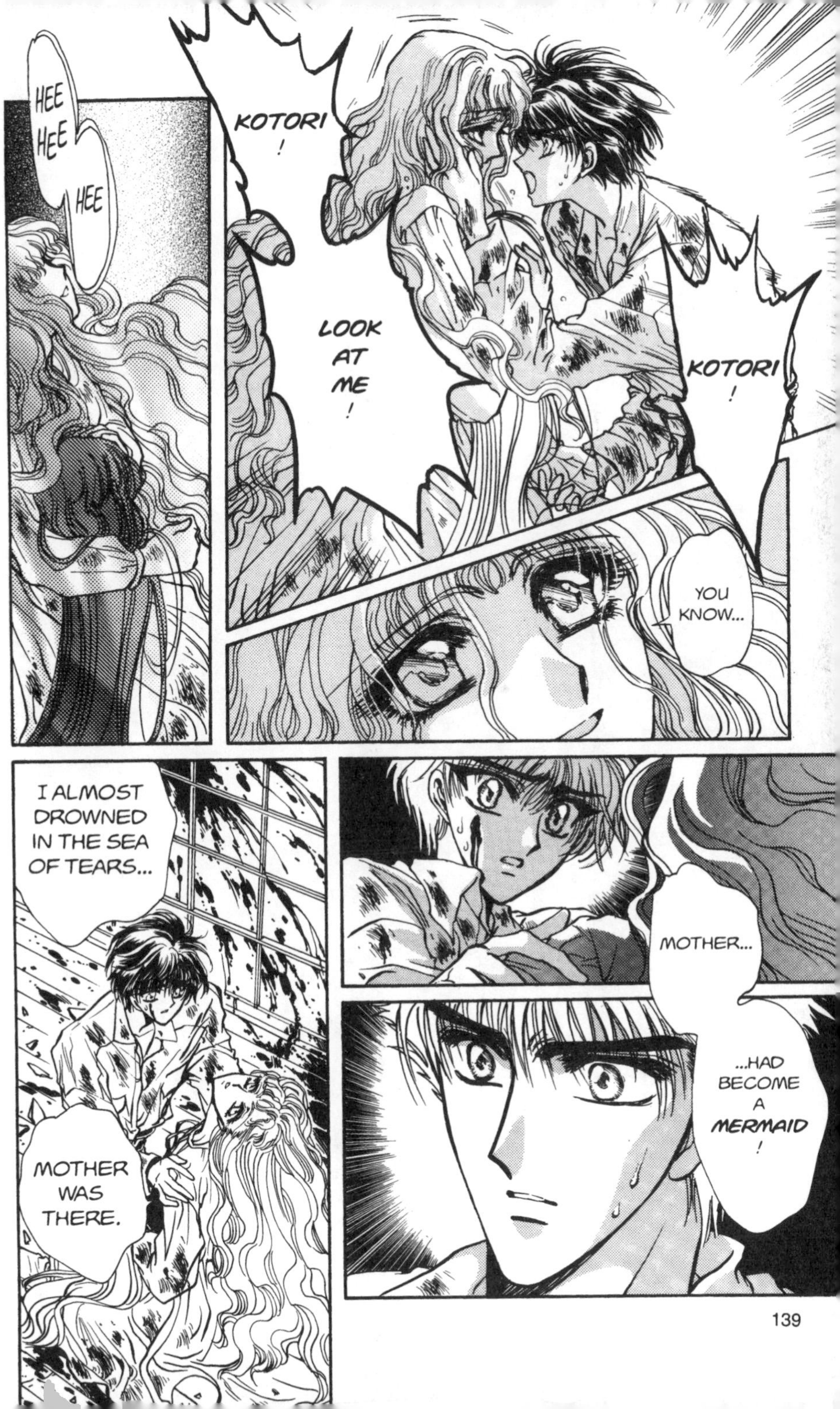
HEE HEE HEE
KOTORI!
LOOK AT ME!
KOTORI!
YOU KNOW...
I ALMOST DROWNED IN THE SEA OF TEARS...
MOTHER WAS THERE.
MOTHER...
...HAD BECOME A MERMAID!

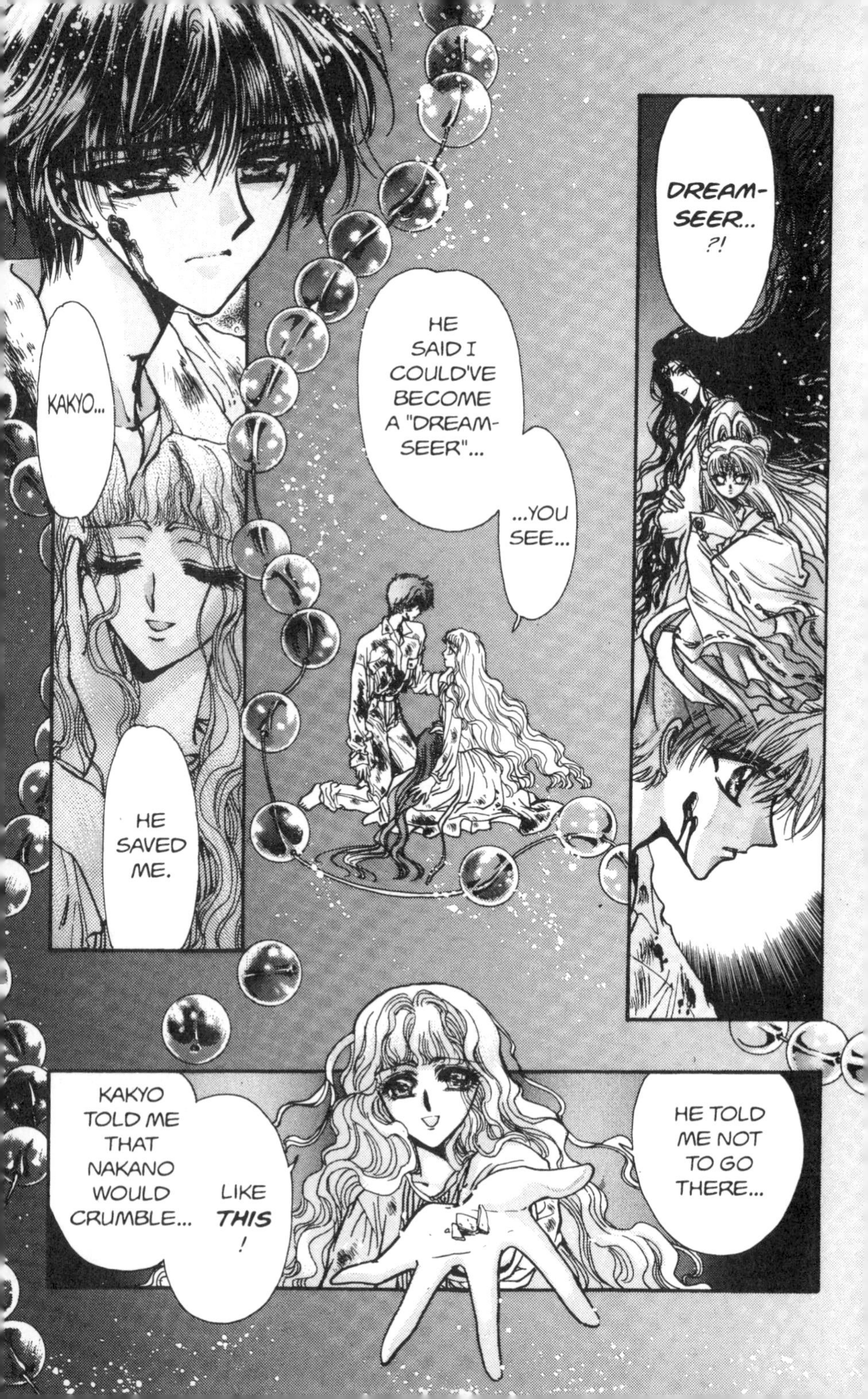
KAKYO...
HE SAVED ME.
HE SAID I COULD'VE BECOME A "DREAM-SEER"...
...YOU SEE...
DREAM-SEER... ?!
KAKYO TOLD ME THAT NAKANO WOULD CRUMBLE...
LIKE **THIS**!
HE TOLD ME NOT TO GO THERE...

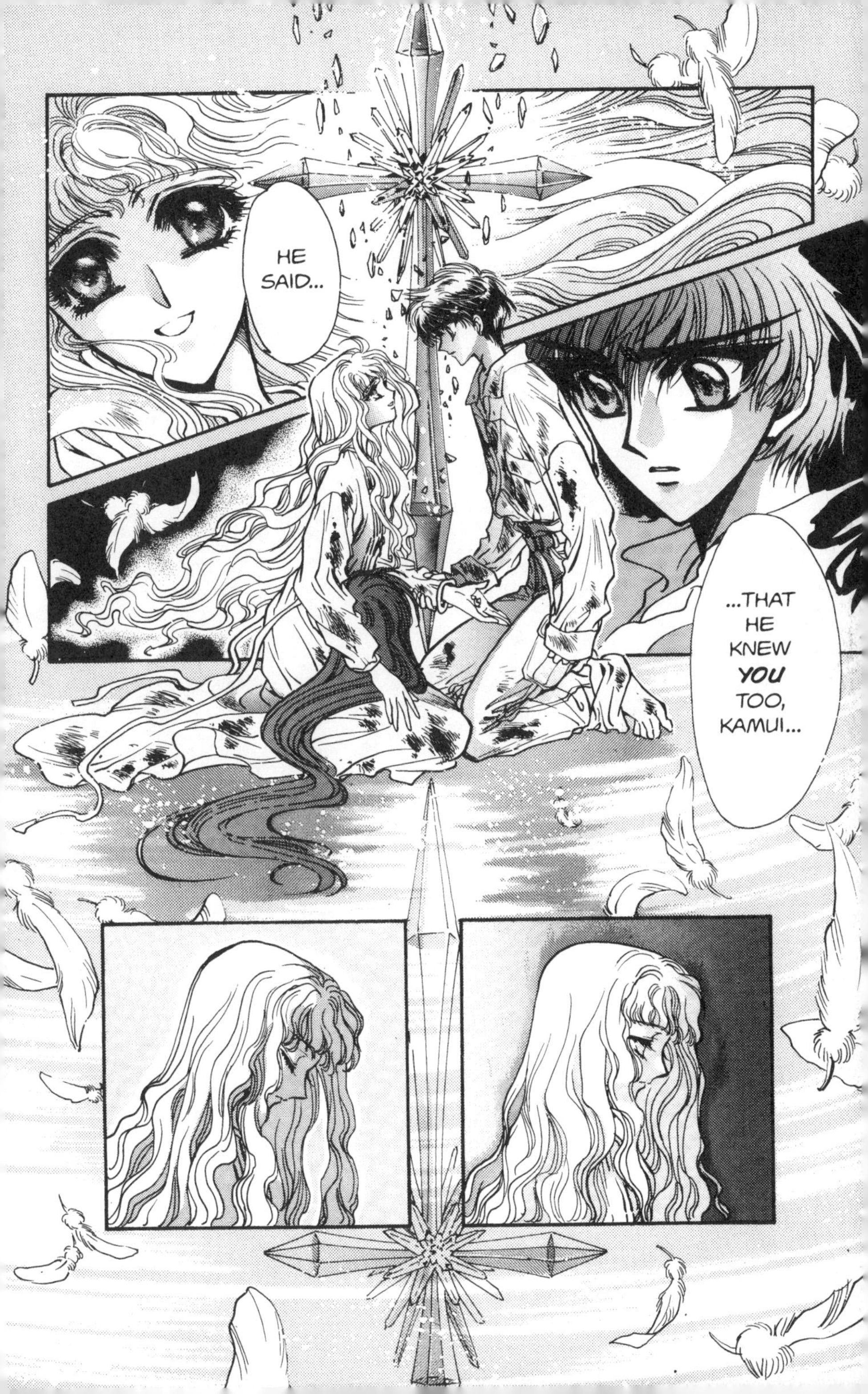
HE SAID...
...THAT HE KNEW **YOU** TOO, KAMUI...

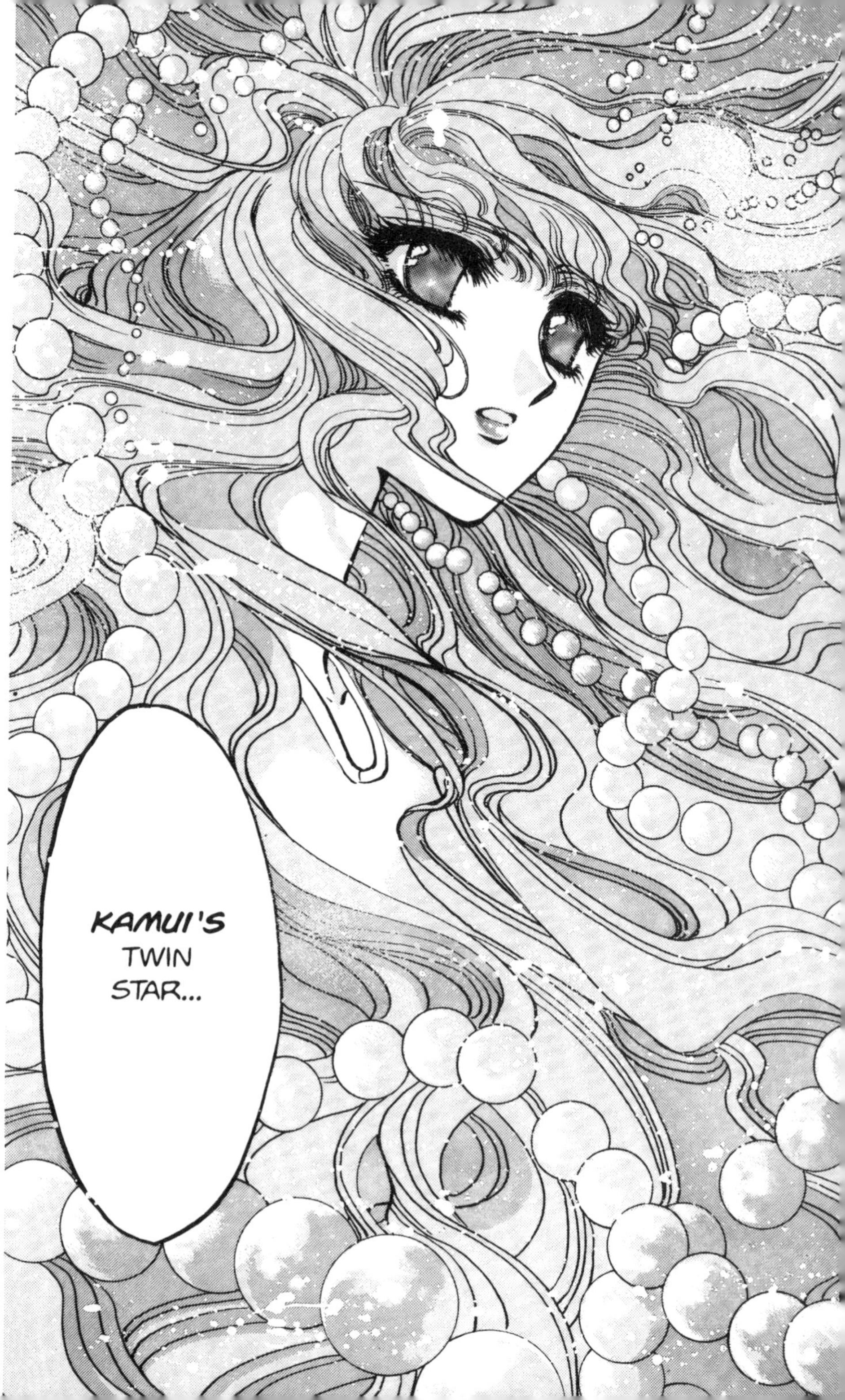
KAMUI'S TWIN STAR...

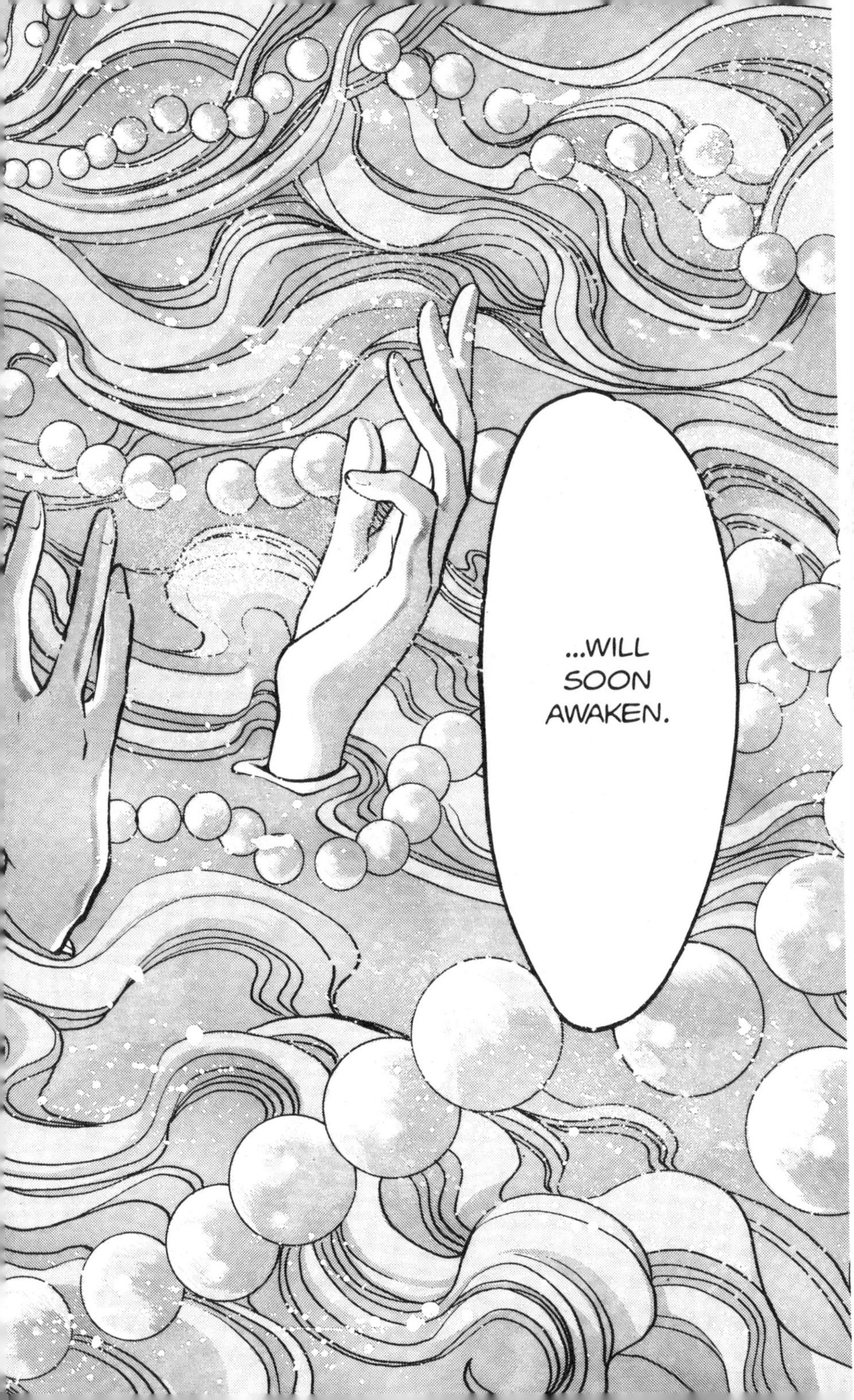
...WILL SOON AWAKEN.

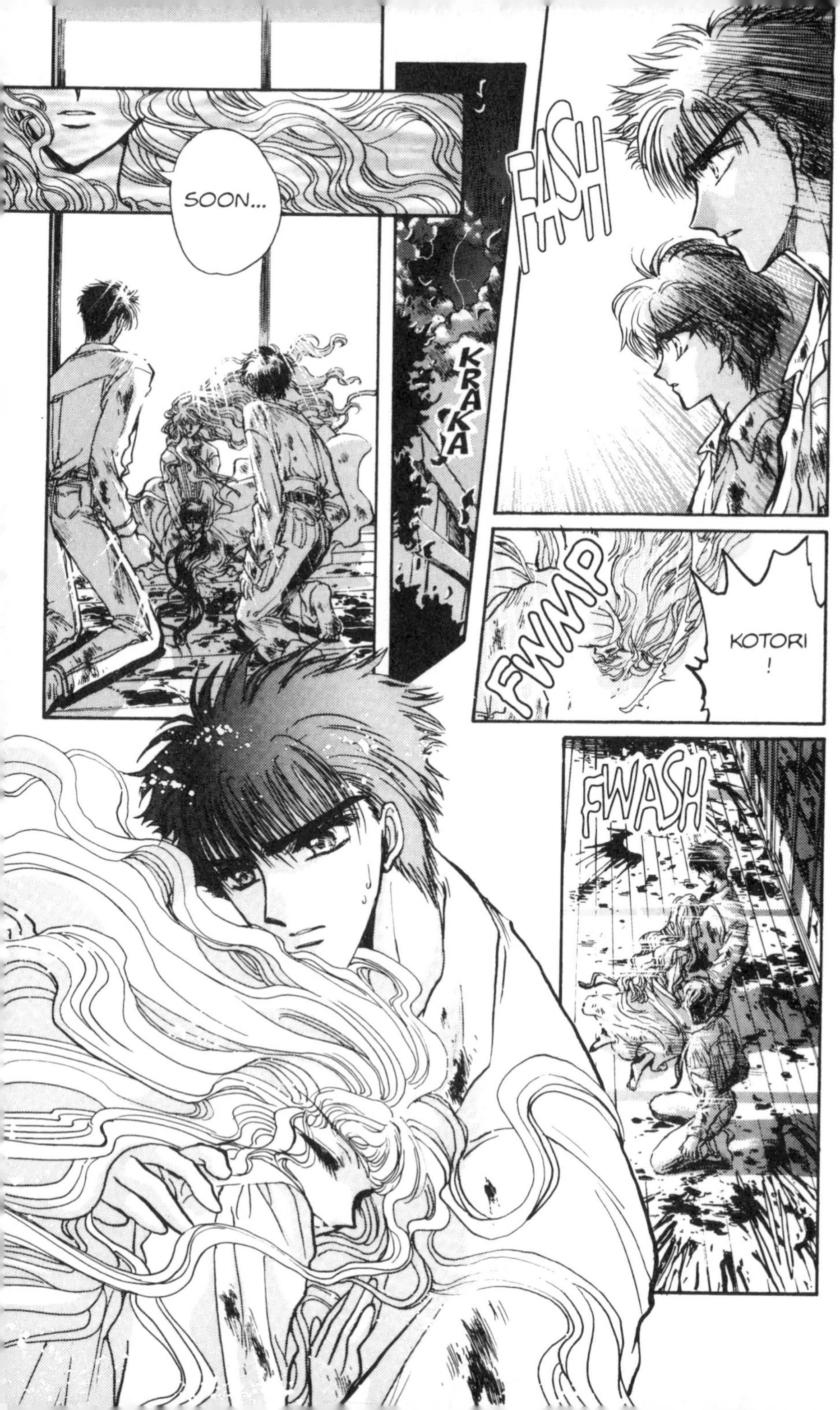
SOON...
KRAKA
FASH
FWMP
KOTORI!
FWASH

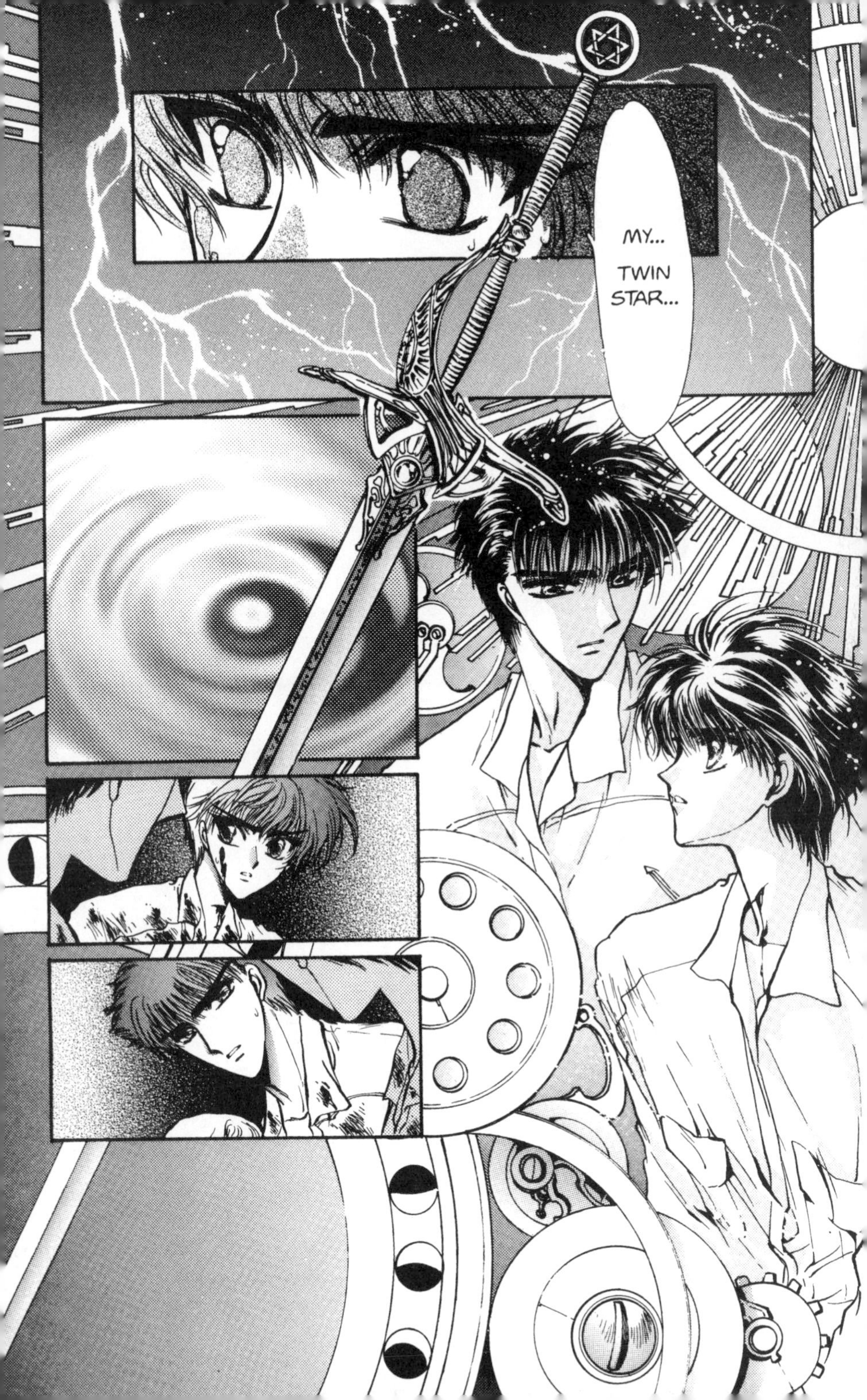
MY... TWIN STAR...

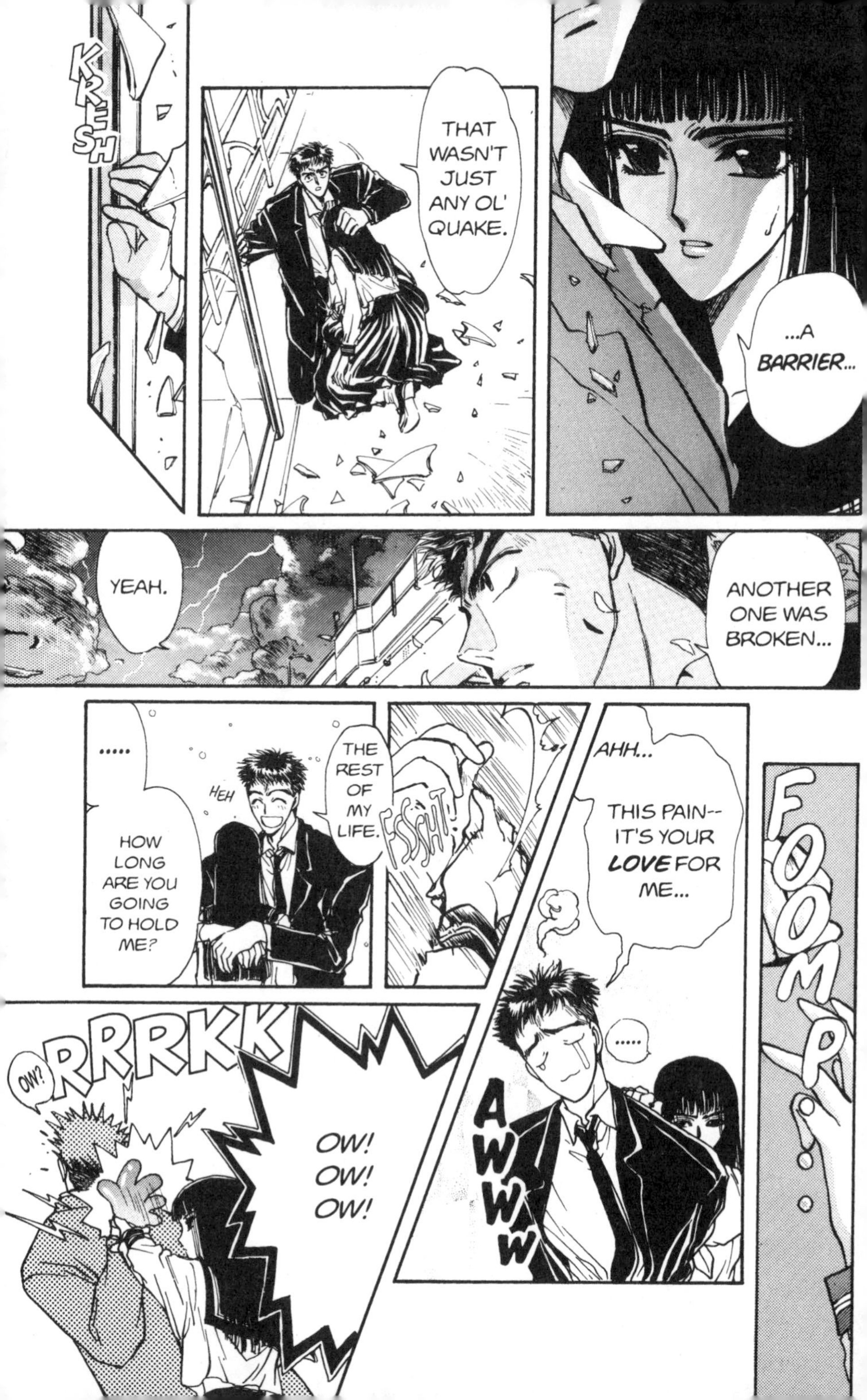
KRESH
THAT WASN'T JUST ANY OL' QUAKE.
...A *BARRIER*...
YEAH.
ANOTHER ONE WAS BROKEN...
.....
HOW LONG ARE YOU GOING TO HOLD ME?
HEH
THE REST OF MY LIFE.
FSSSHT!
OW?
RRRKK
OW! OW! OW!
AHH...
THIS PAIN-- IT'S YOUR **LOVE** FOR ME...
.....
AWWWW
FOOMP

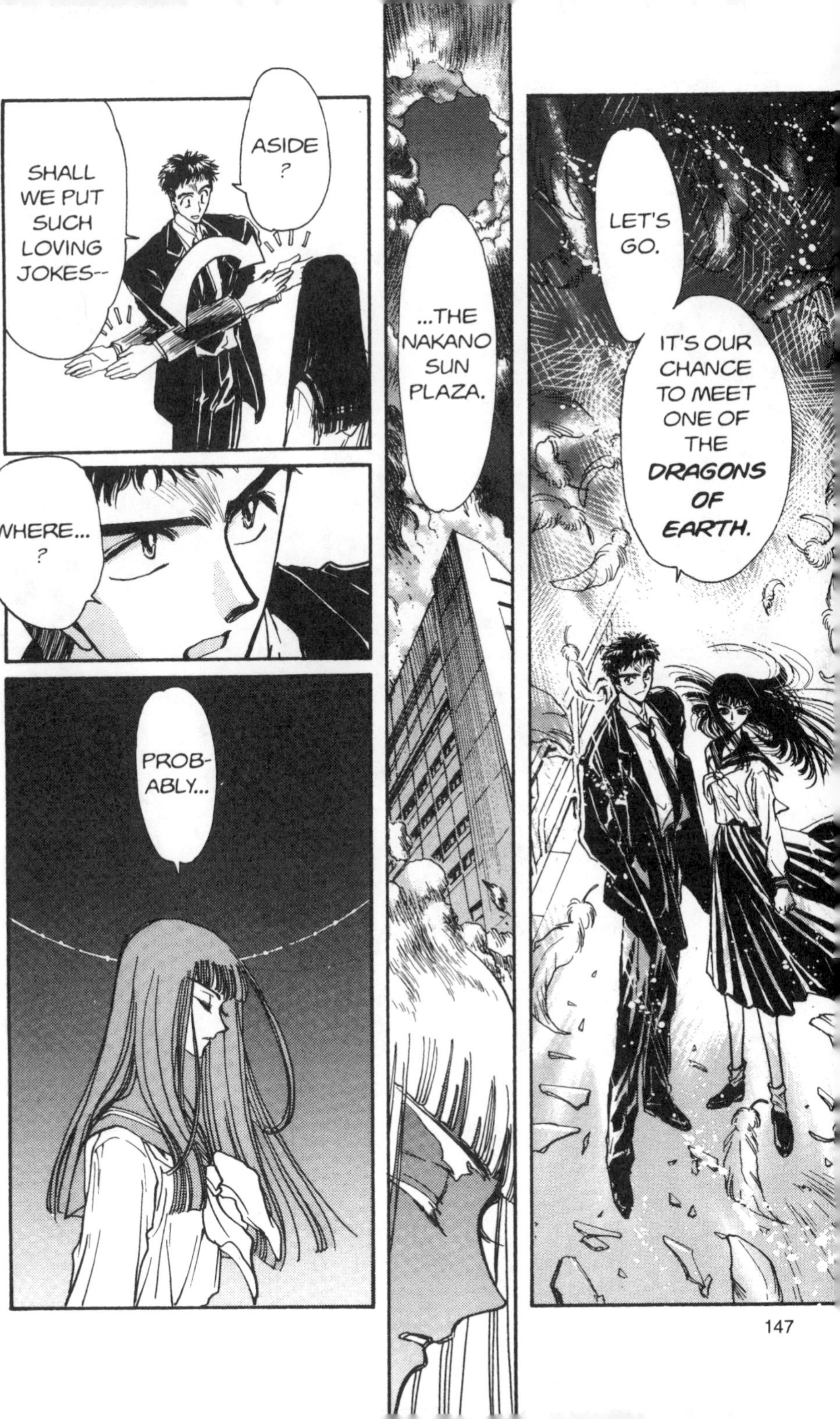

SHALL WE PUT SUCH LOVING JOKES--
ASIDE ?
WHERE... ?
PROB-ABLY...
...THE NAKANO SUN PLAZA.
LET'S GO.
IT'S OUR CHANCE TO MEET ONE OF THE ***DRAGONS OF EARTH.***

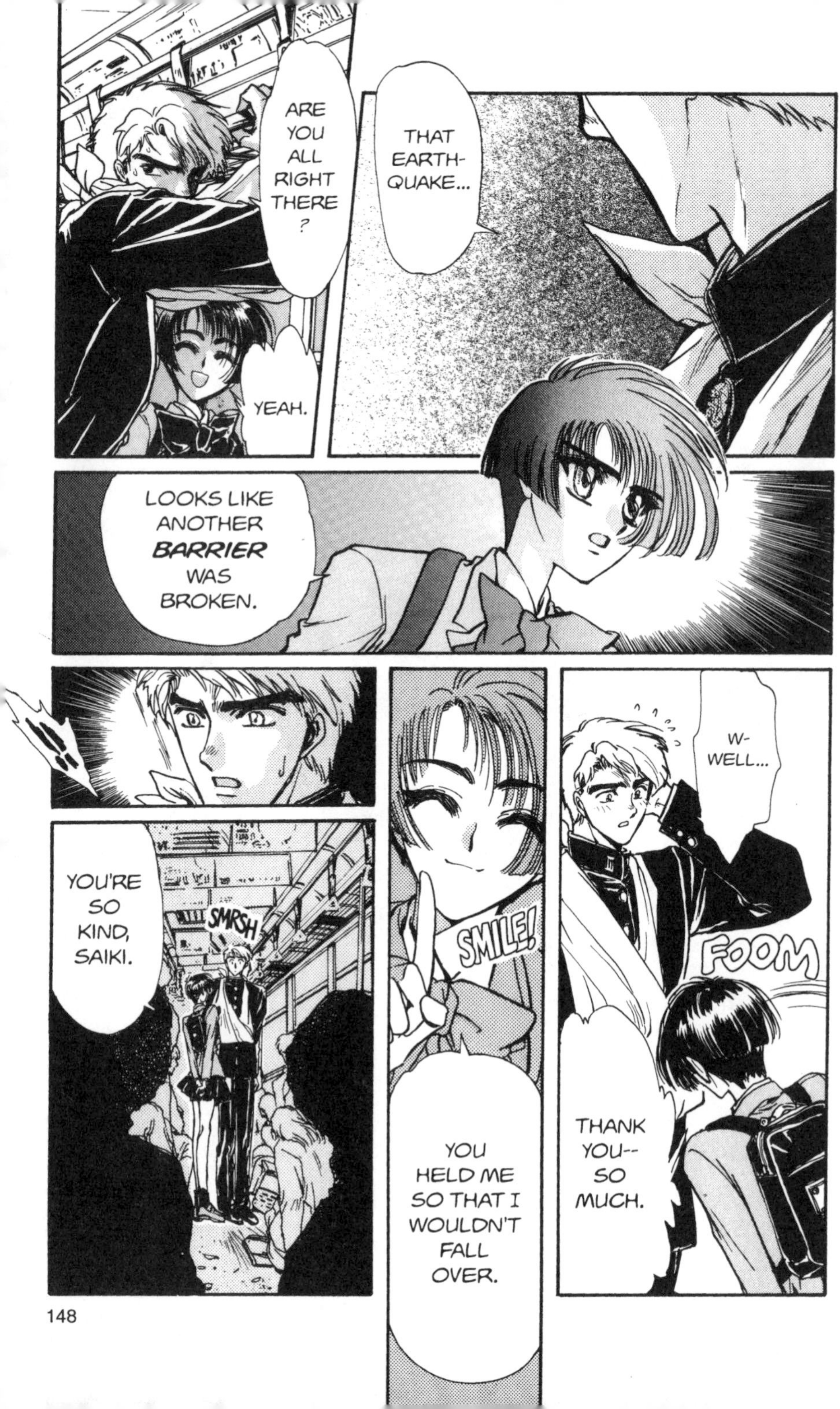
ARE YOU ALL RIGHT THERE?
YEAH.
THAT EARTHQUAKE...
LOOKS LIKE ANOTHER **BARRIER** WAS BROKEN.
YOU'RE SO KIND, SAIKI.
SMRSH
SMILE!
YOU HELD ME SO THAT I WOULDN'T FALL OVER.
W-WELL...
FOOM
THANK YOU--SO MUCH.

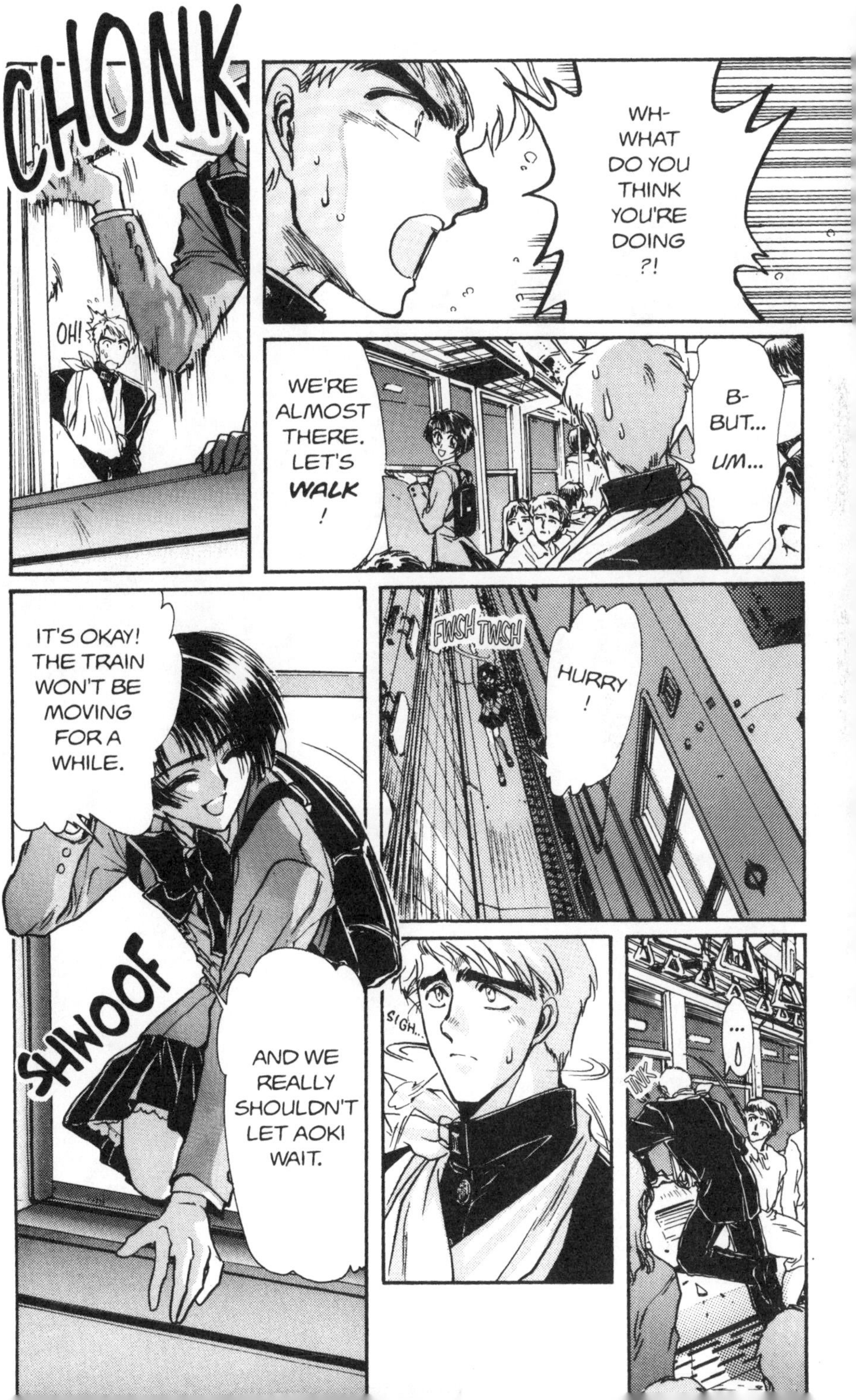
CHONK
OH!
WH- WHAT DO YOU THINK YOU'RE DOING ?!
WE'RE ALMOST THERE. LET'S **WALK** !
B- BUT... UM...
IT'S OKAY! THE TRAIN WON'T BE MOVING FOR A WHILE.
SHWOOF
AND WE REALLY SHOULDN'T LET AOKI WAIT.
FWSH TWSH
HURRY !
SIGH...
TNK
...

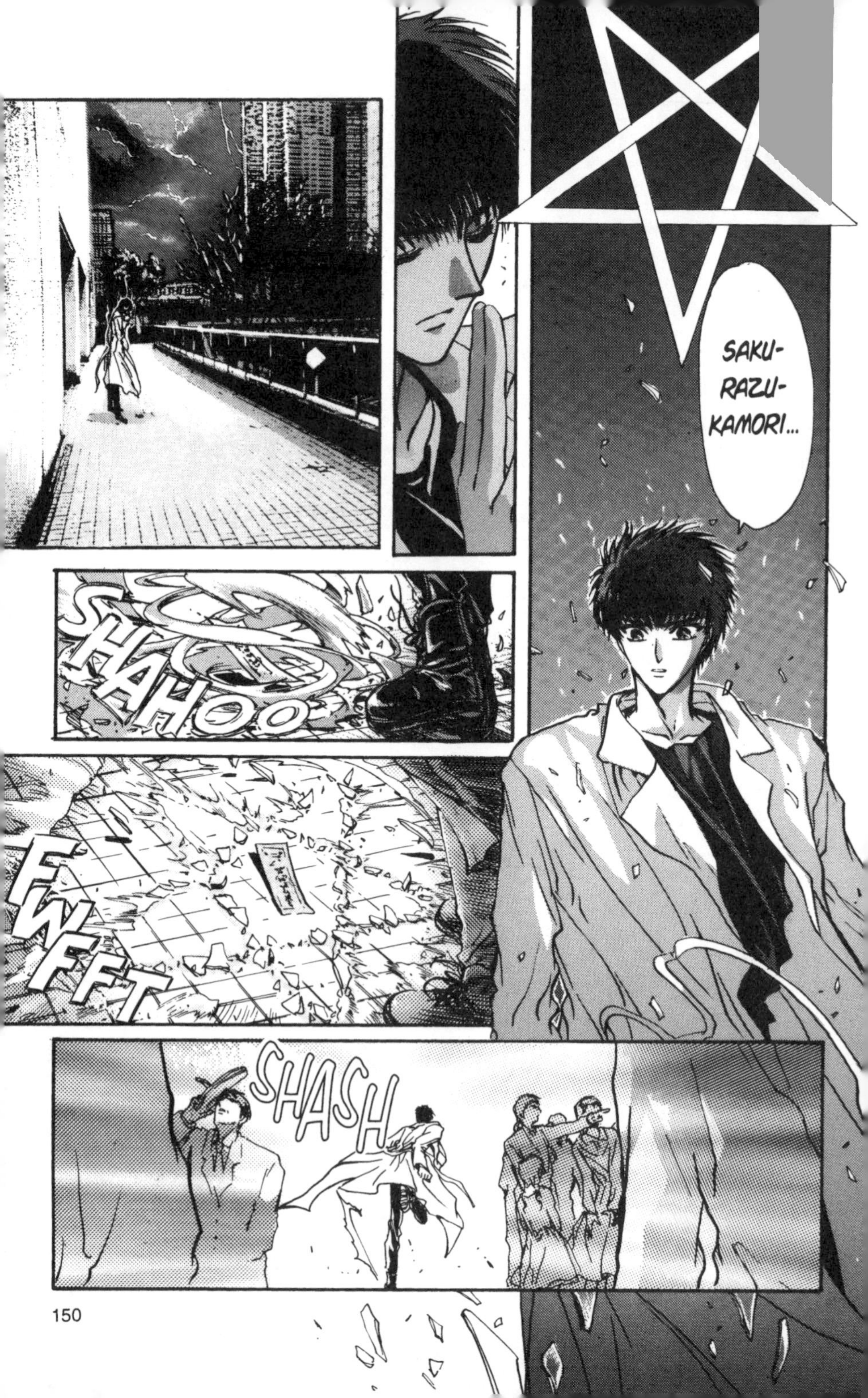
SHAHOO
FWFFT
SHASH
SAKU-RAZU-KAMORI...

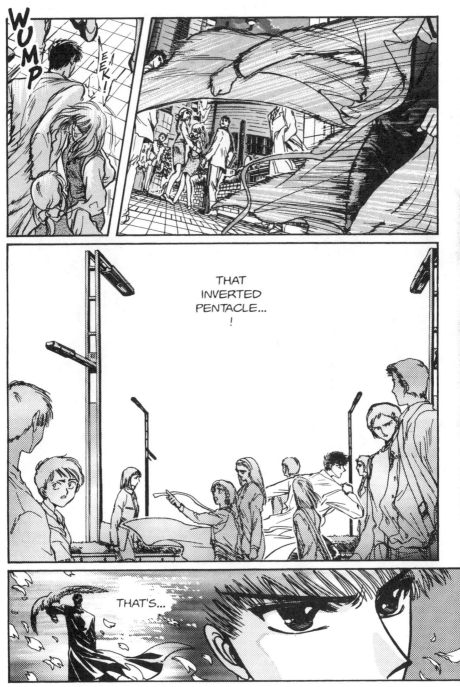

THAT
INVERTED
PENTACLE...
!

THAT'S...

151

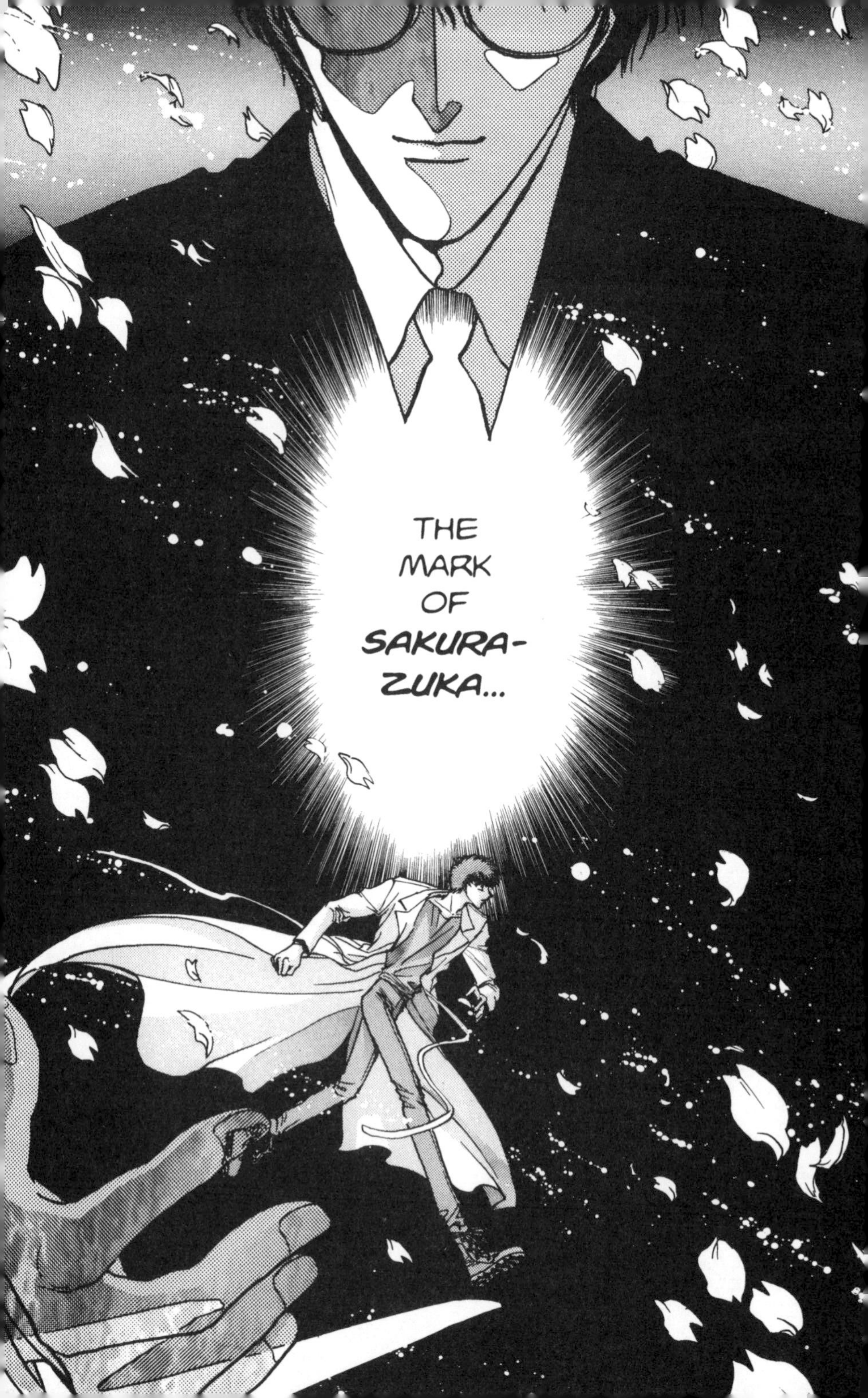
THE MARK OF SAKURA-ZUKA...

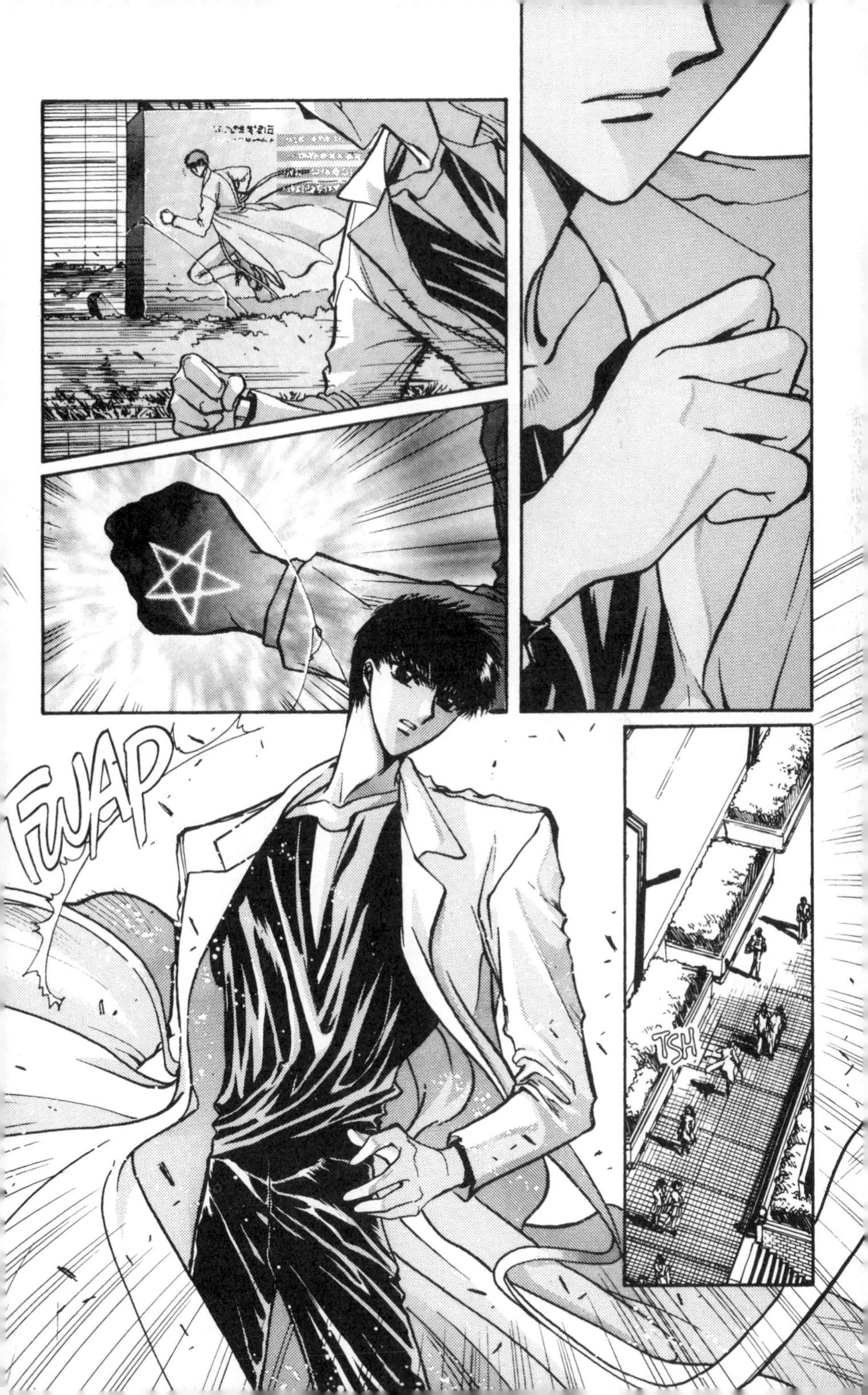
FWAP
TSH

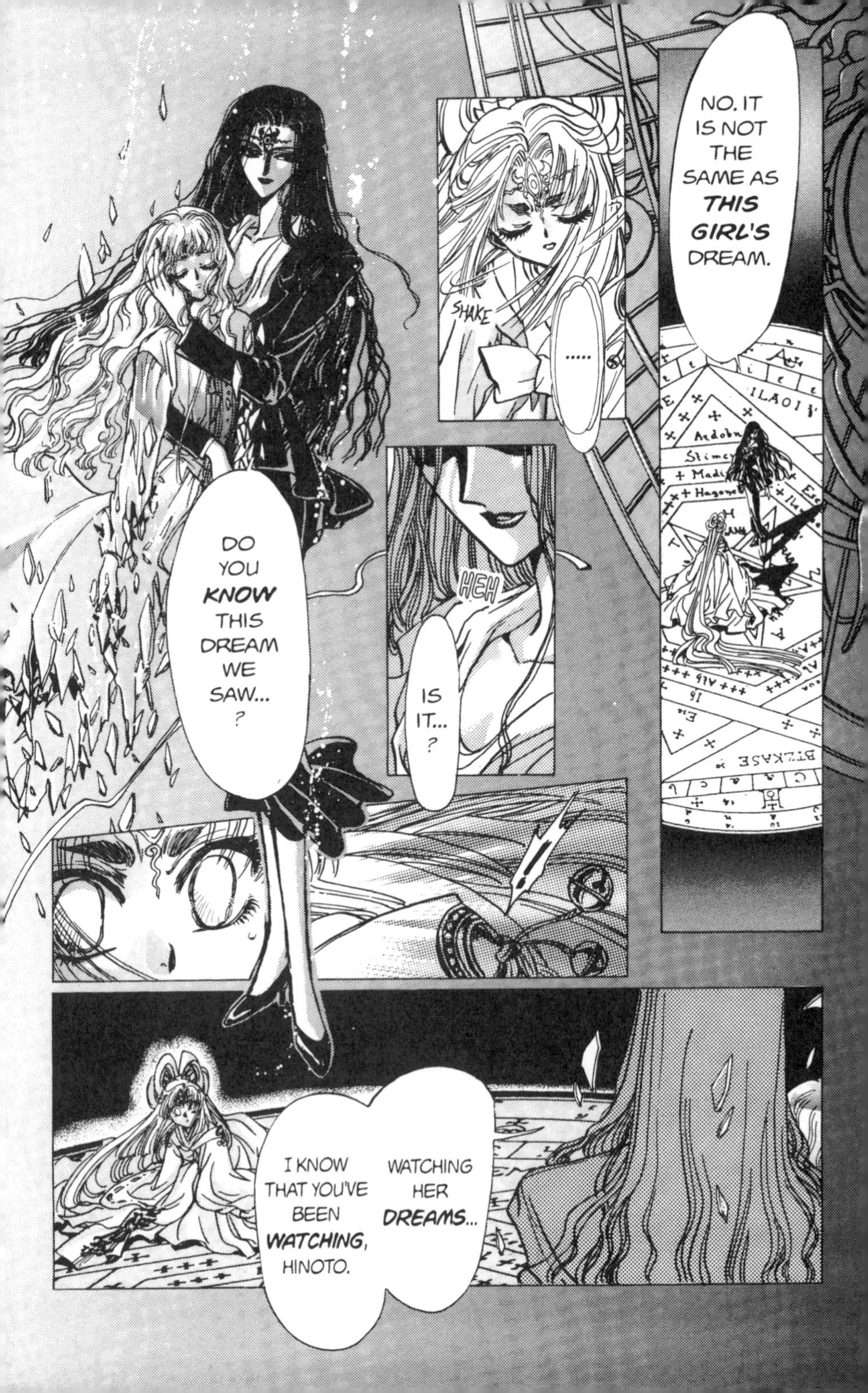
DO YOU KNOW THIS DREAM WE SAW... ?
SHAKE
.....
NO. IT IS NOT THE SAME AS THIS GIRL'S DREAM.
HEH
IS IT... ?
I KNOW THAT YOU'VE BEEN WATCHING, HINOTO.
WATCHING HER DREAMS...

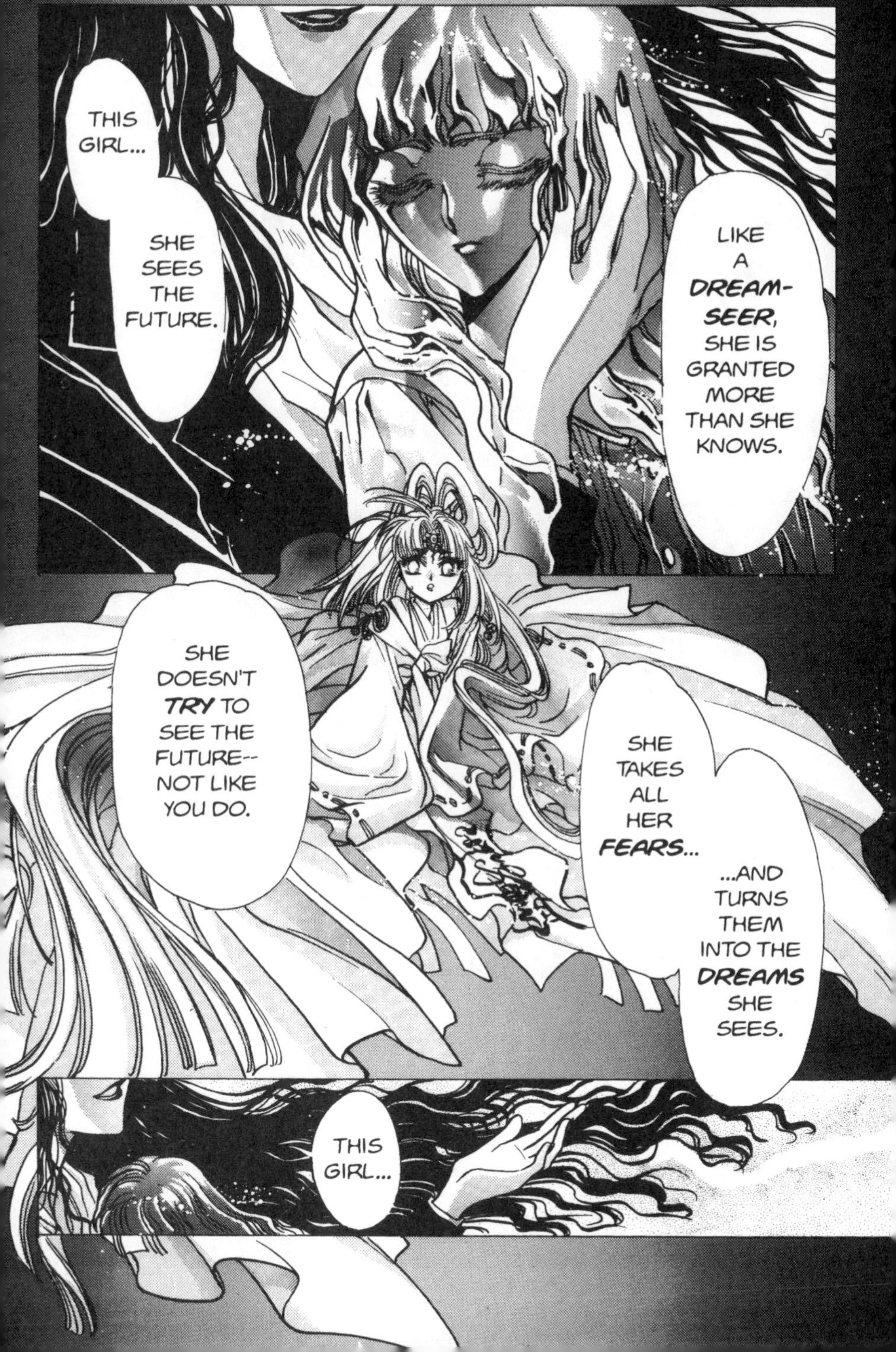
THIS GIRL...
SHE SEES THE FUTURE.
LIKE A DREAM-SEER, SHE IS GRANTED MORE THAN SHE KNOWS.
SHE DOESN'T TRY TO SEE THE FUTURE--NOT LIKE YOU DO.
SHE TAKES ALL HER FEARS...
...AND TURNS THEM INTO THE DREAMS SHE SEES.
THIS GIRL...

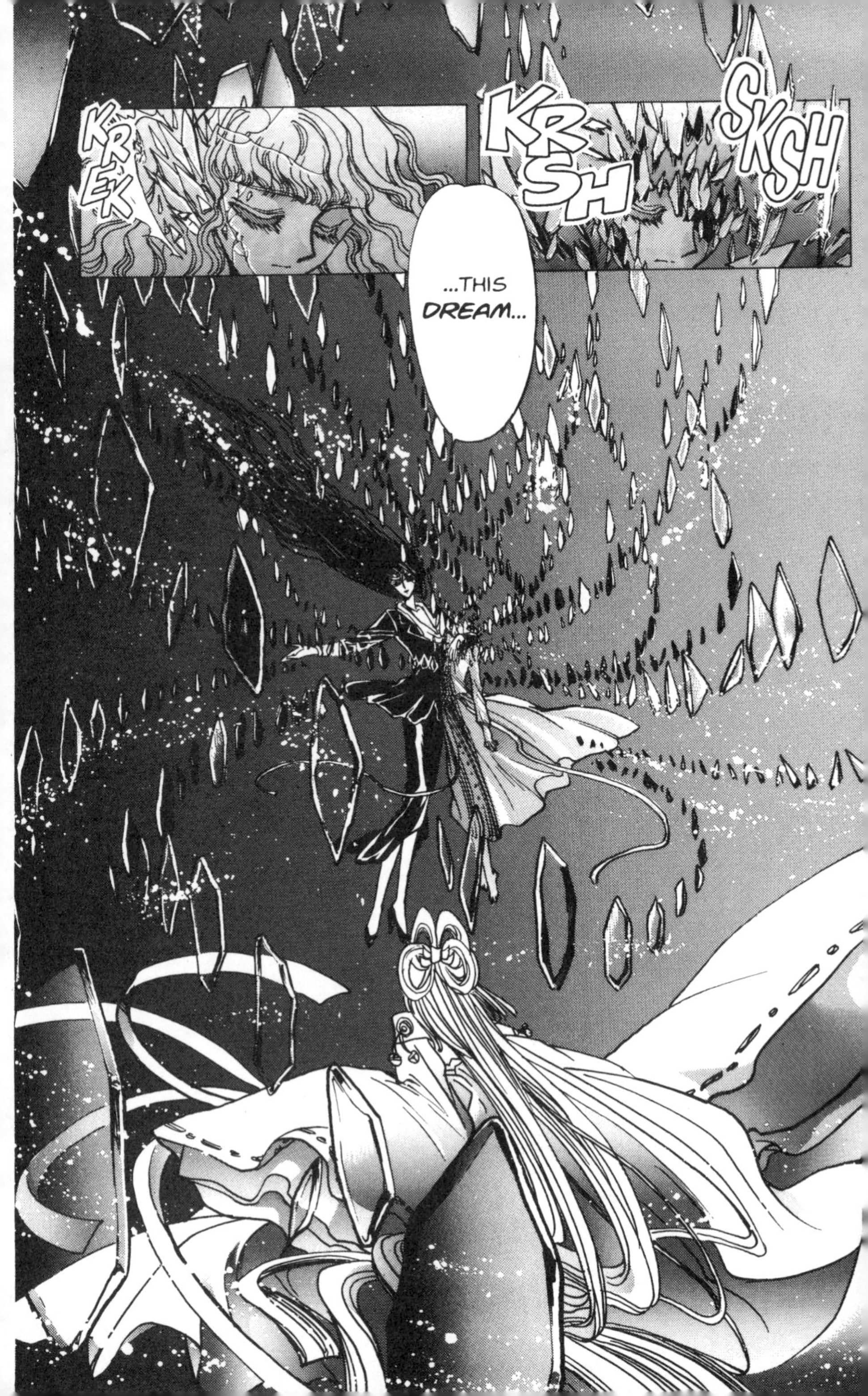
KREK
KR-SH
SKSH
...THIS DREAM...

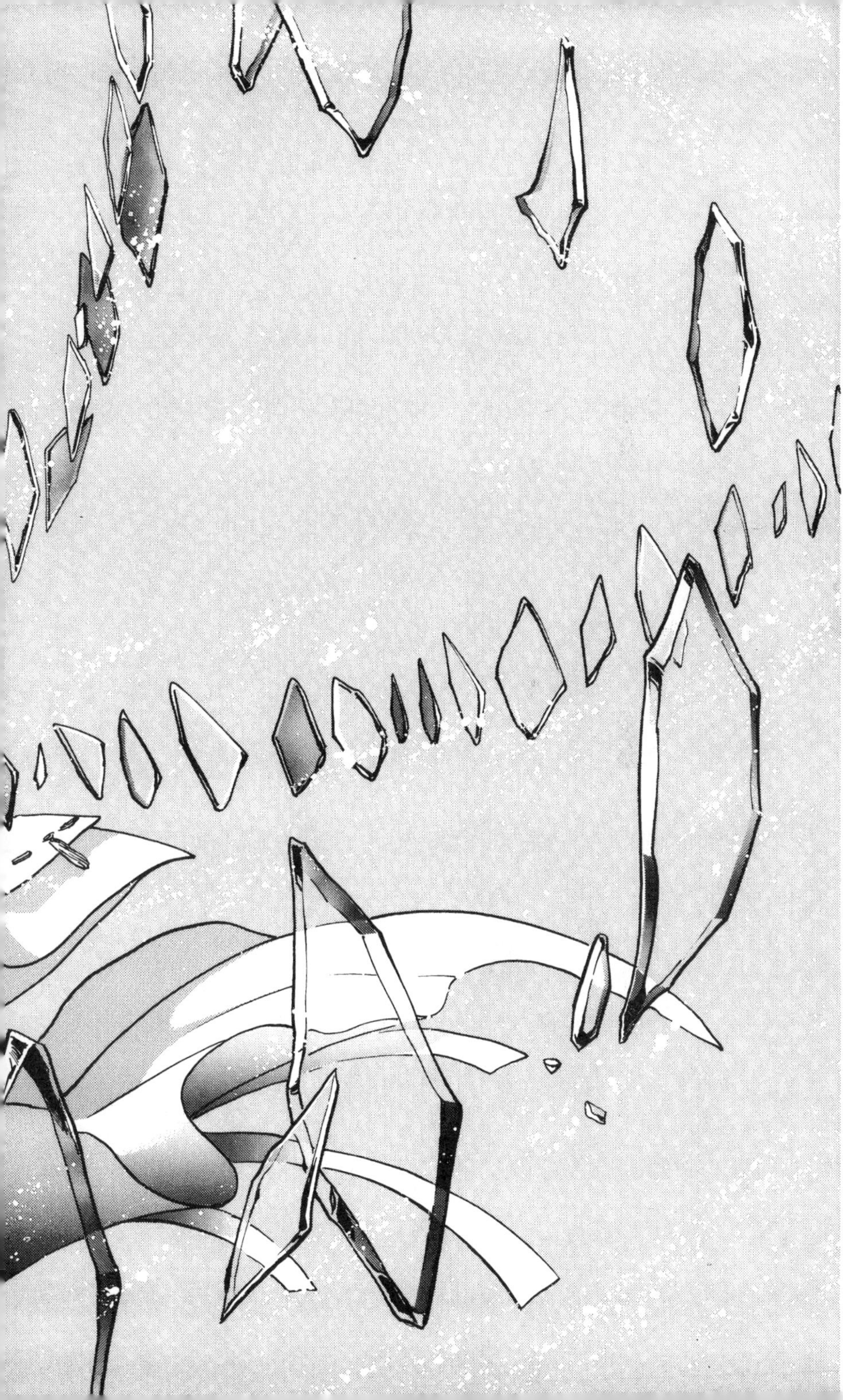

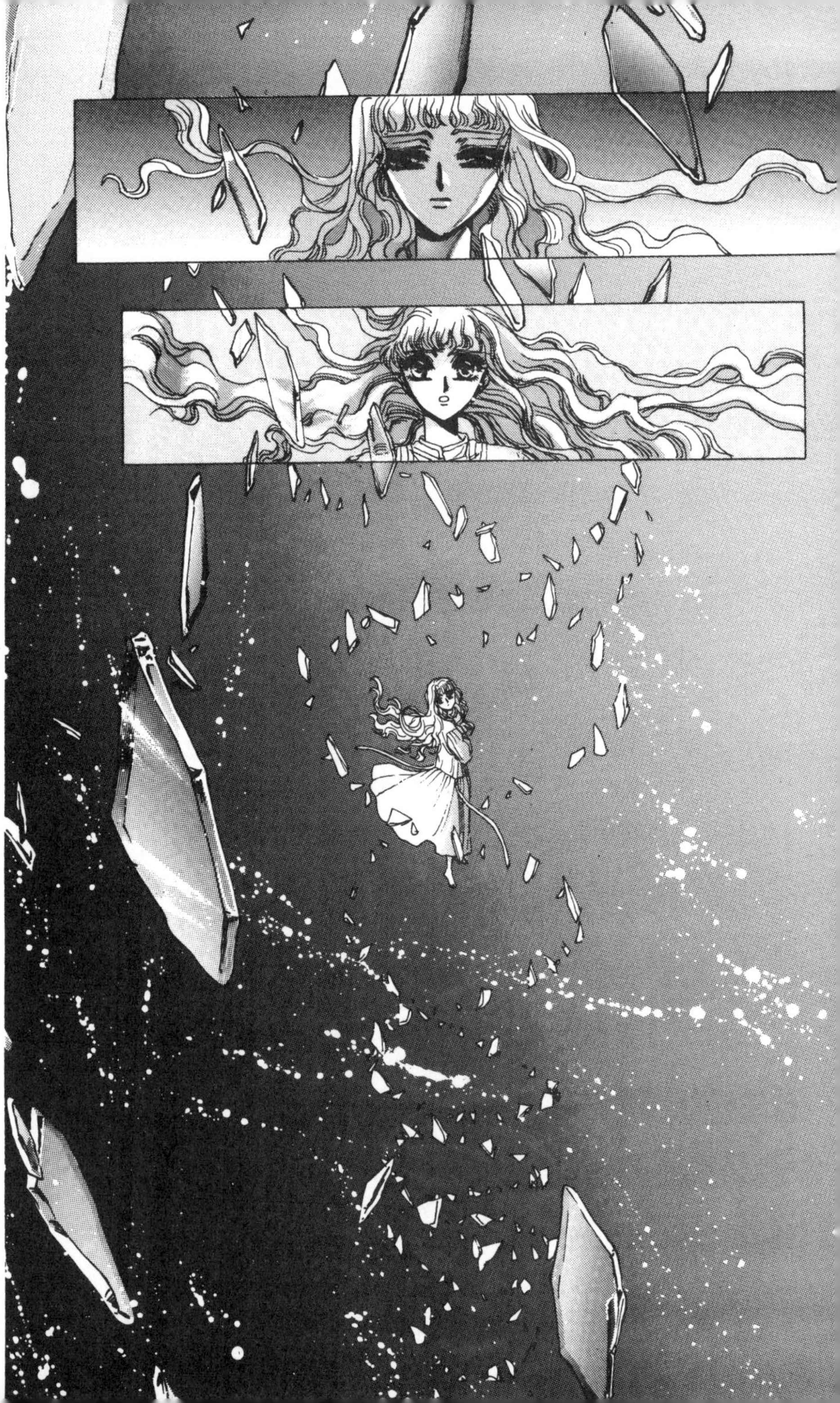

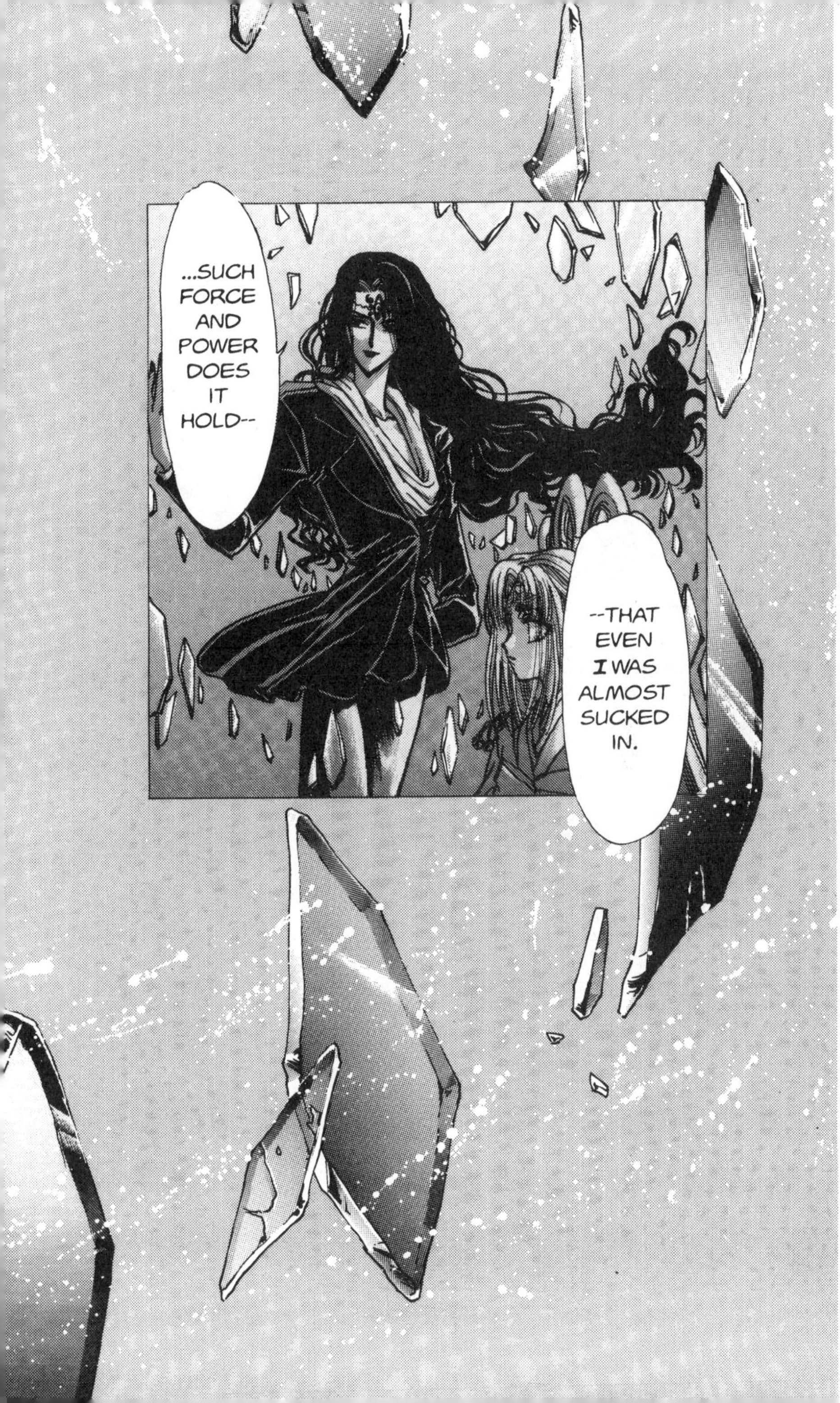
...SUCH FORCE AND POWER DOES IT HOLD--
--THAT EVEN I WAS ALMOST SUCKED IN.

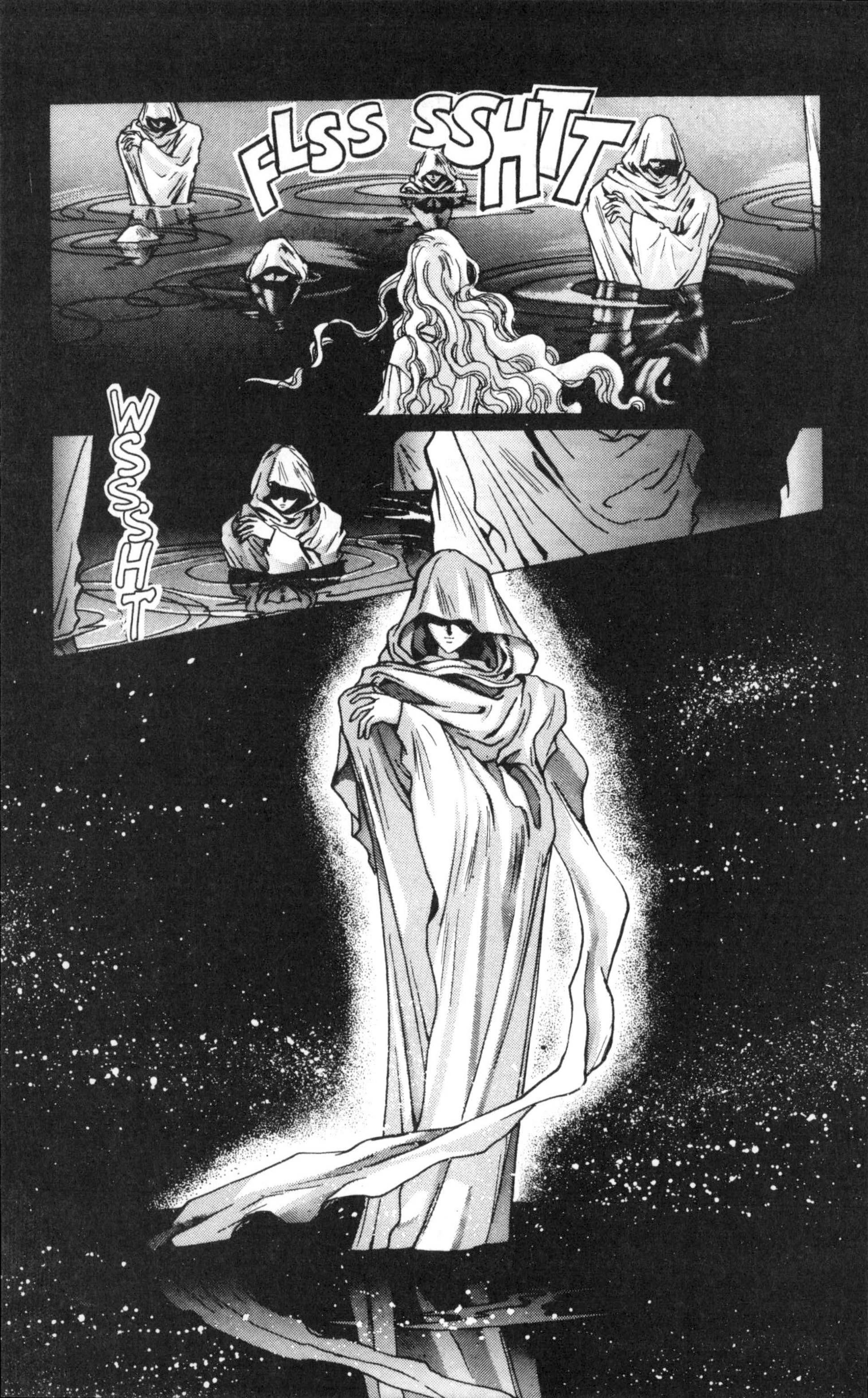
FLSS SSHTT
WSSSHT

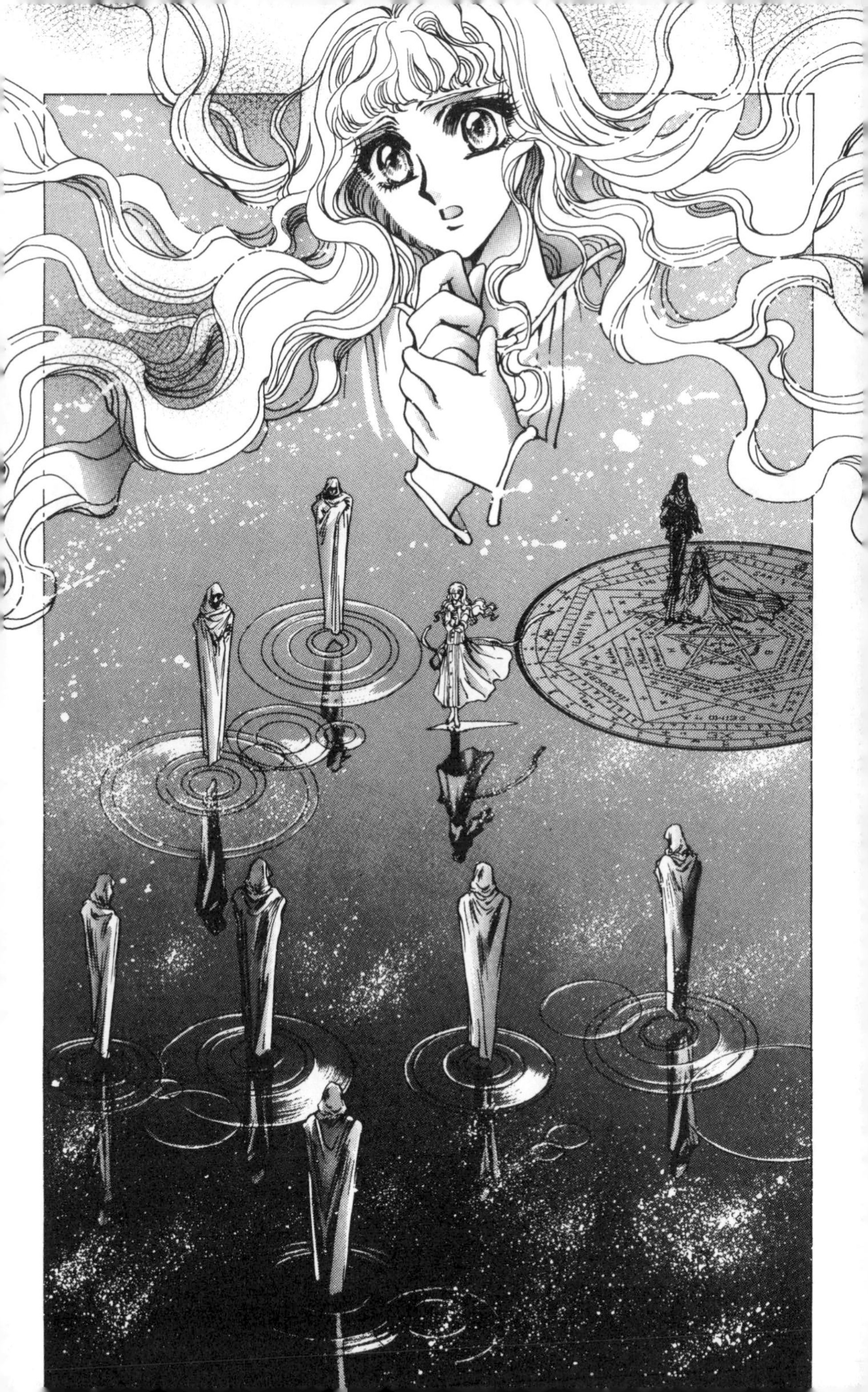

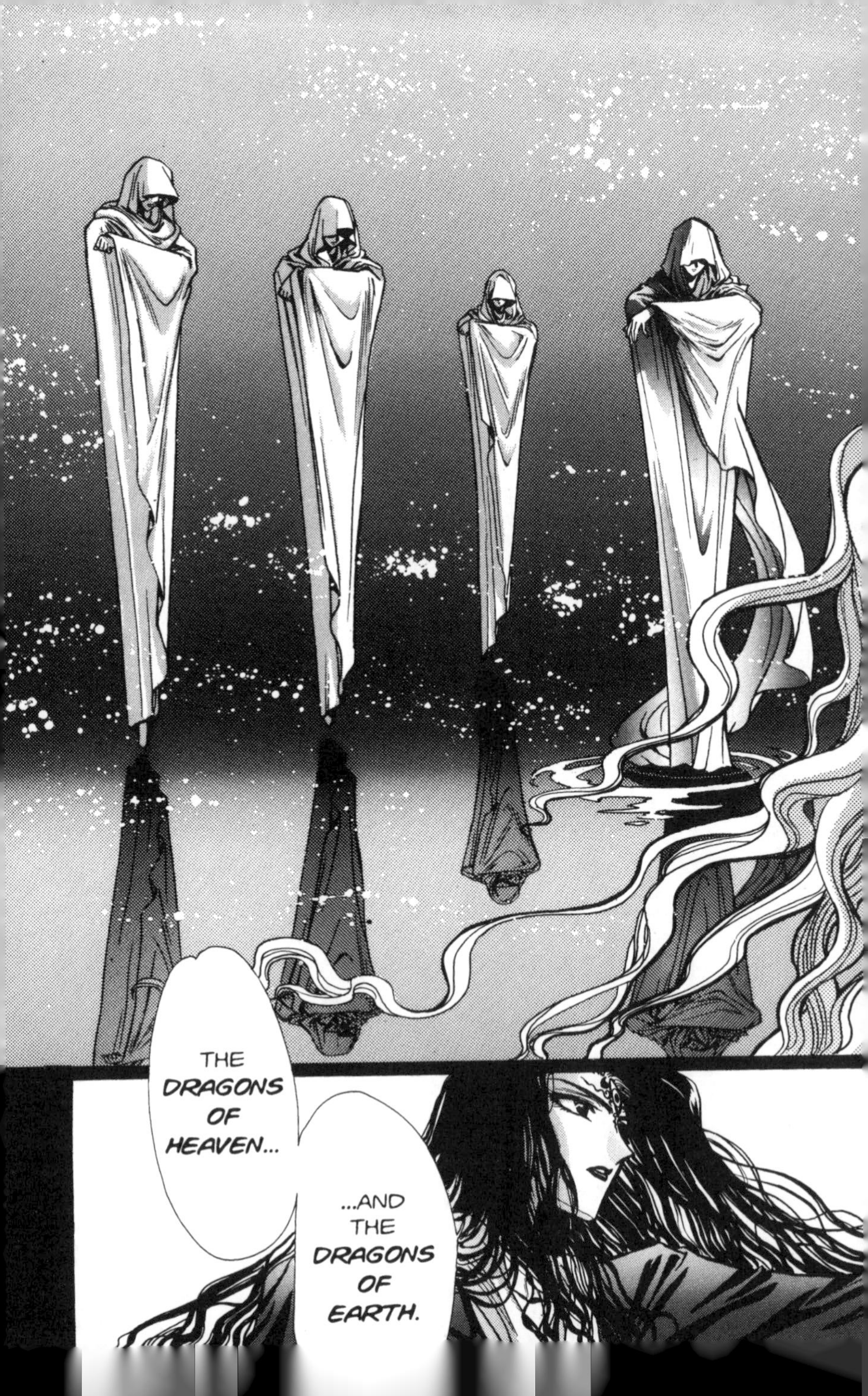
THE DRAGONS OF HEAVEN...
...AND THE DRAGONS OF EARTH.

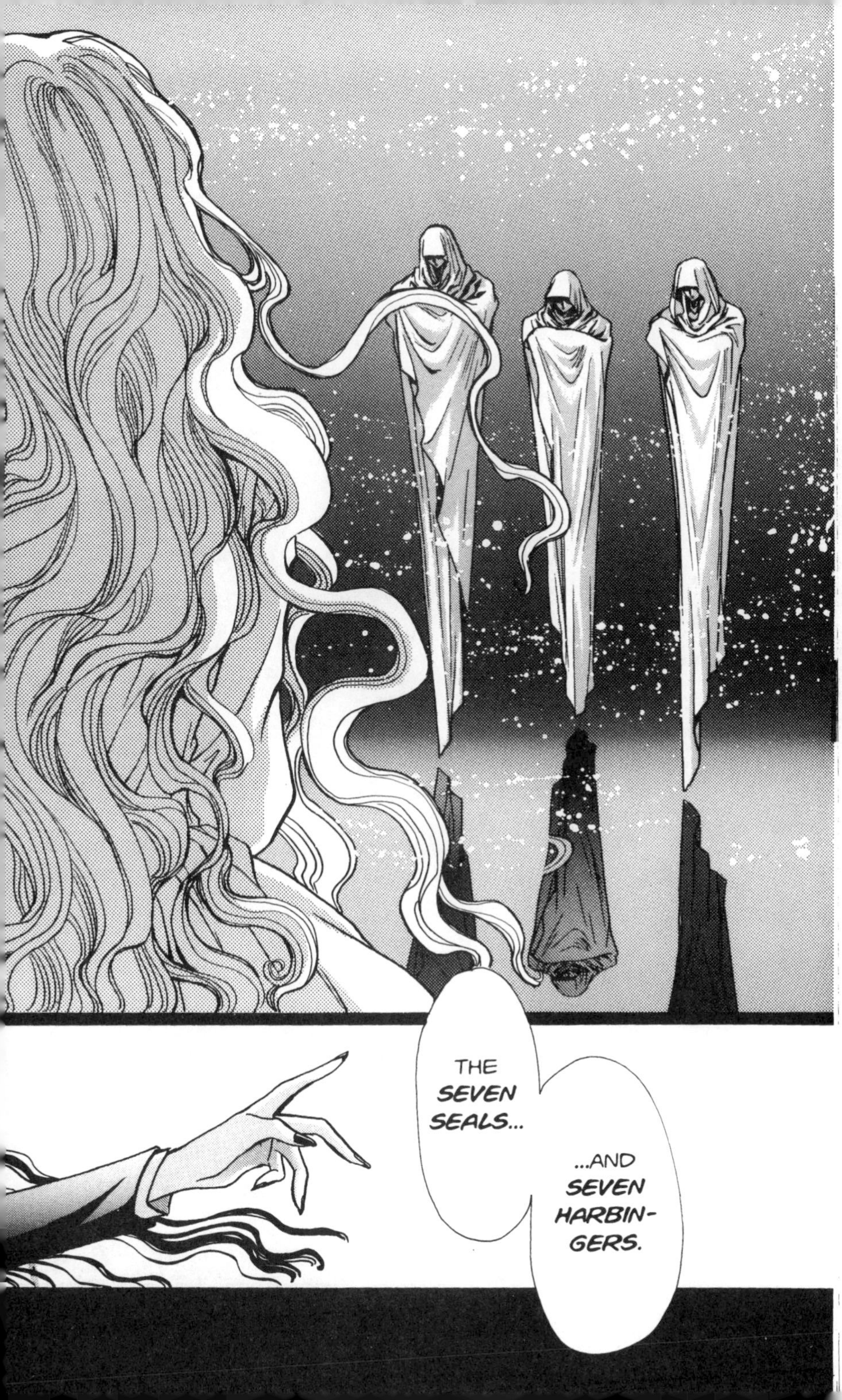
THE SEVEN SEALS...
...AND SEVEN HARBIN- GERS.

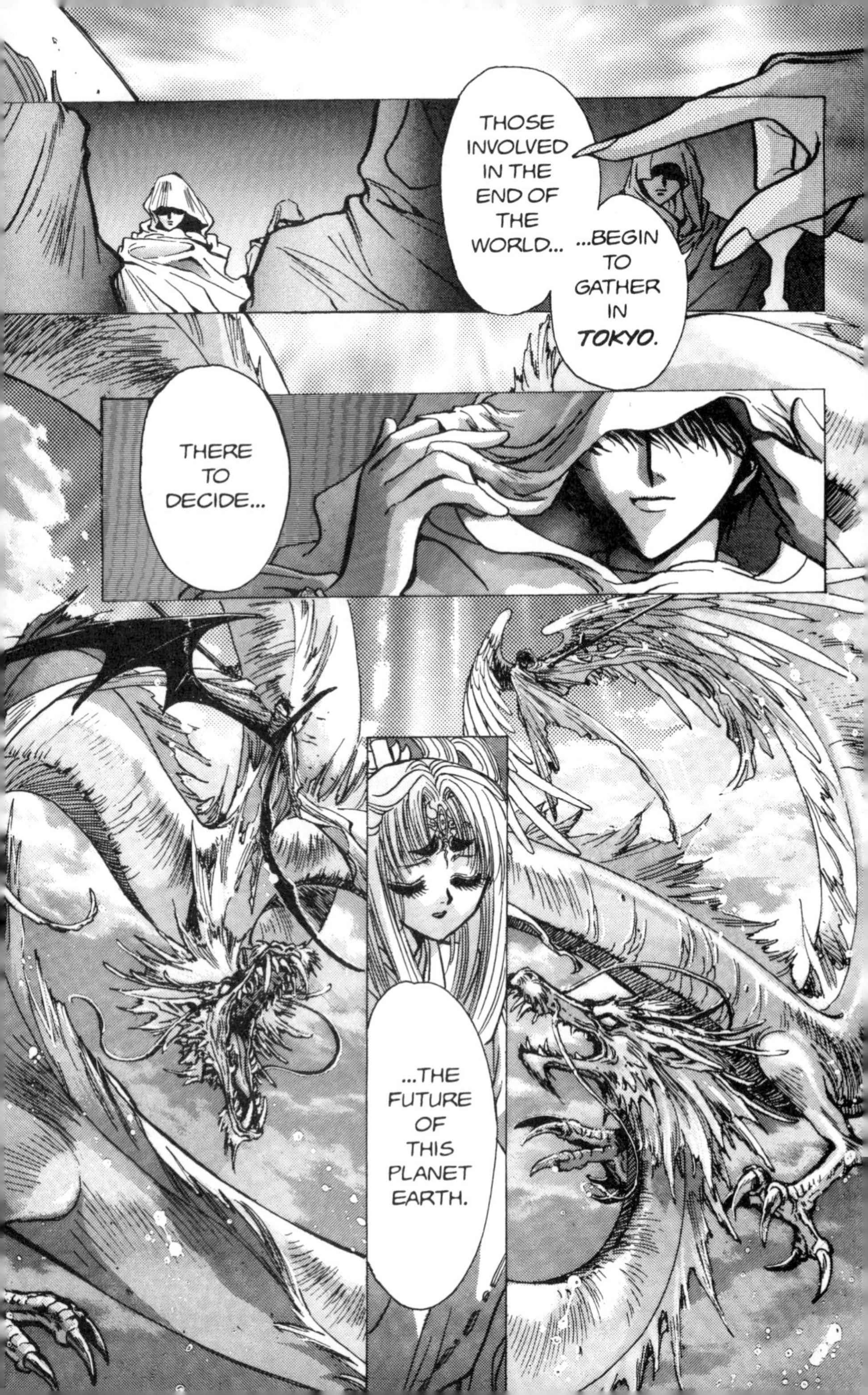
THOSE INVOLVED IN THE END OF THE WORLD...
...BEGIN TO GATHER IN **TOKYO**.
THERE TO DECIDE...
...THE FUTURE OF THIS PLANET EARTH.

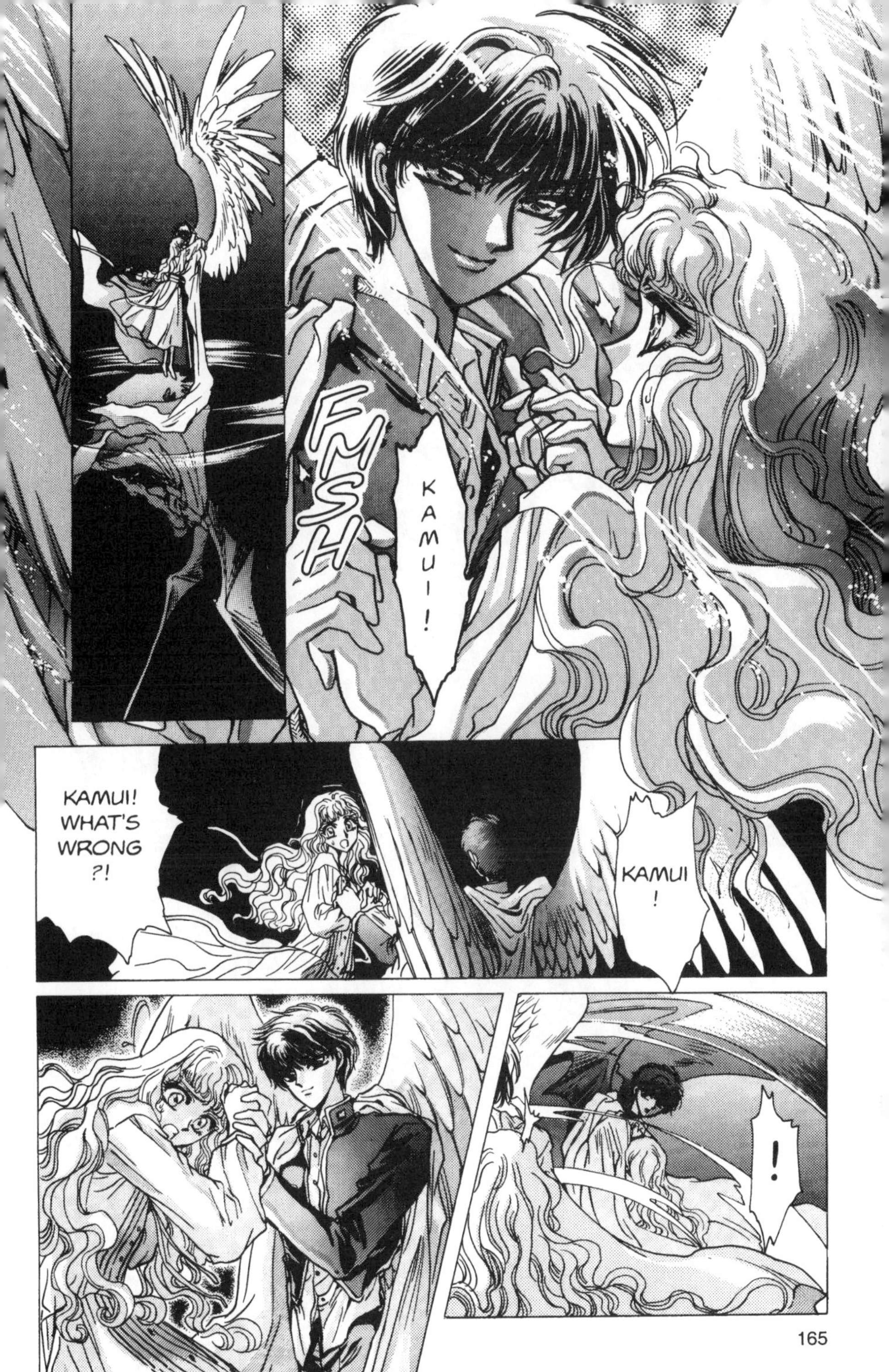
FMSH
KAMUI!
KAMUI! WHAT'S WRONG ?!
KAMUI!
!

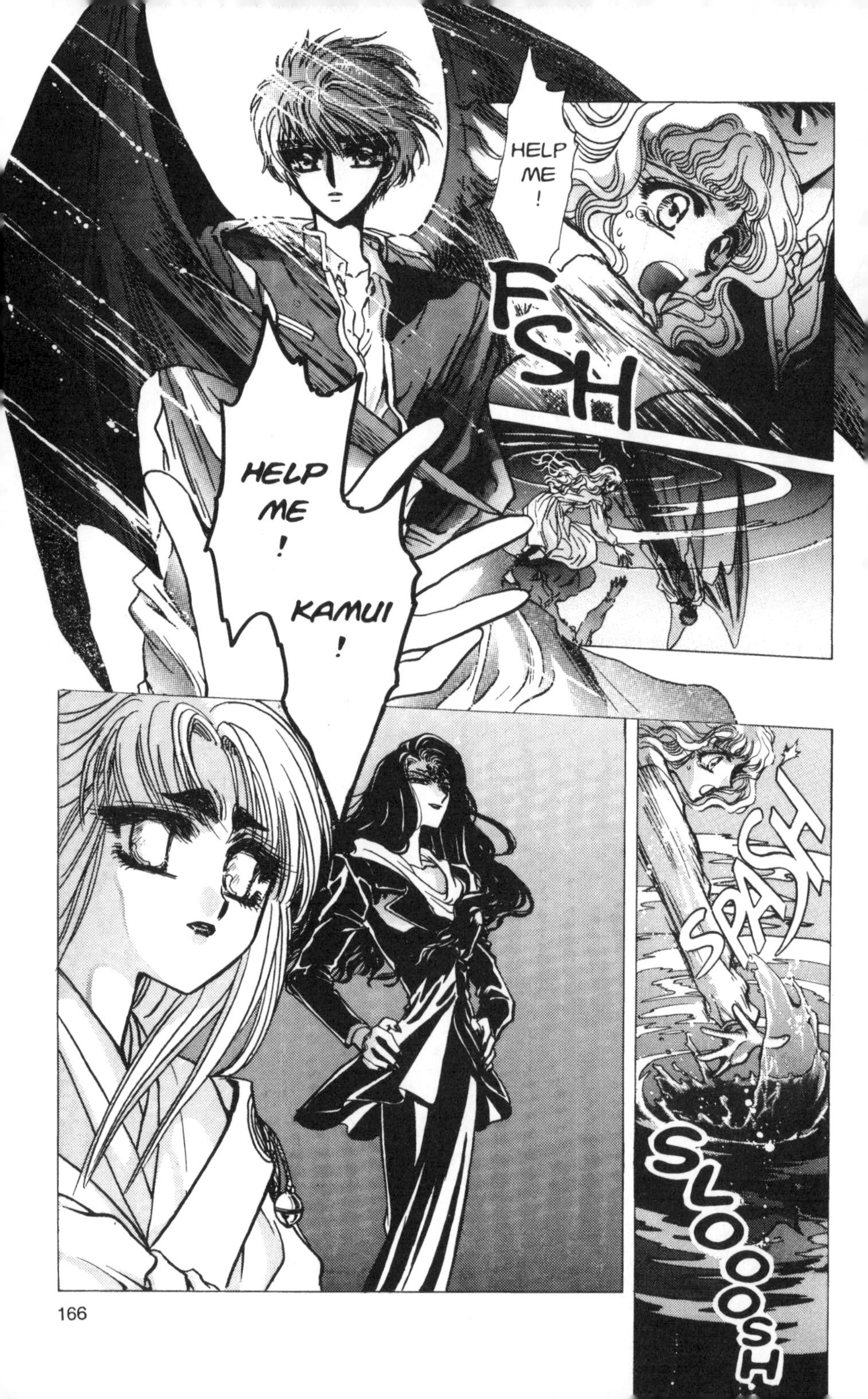
HELP ME !
FSH
HELP ME !
KAMUI !
SPLASH
SLOOOSH

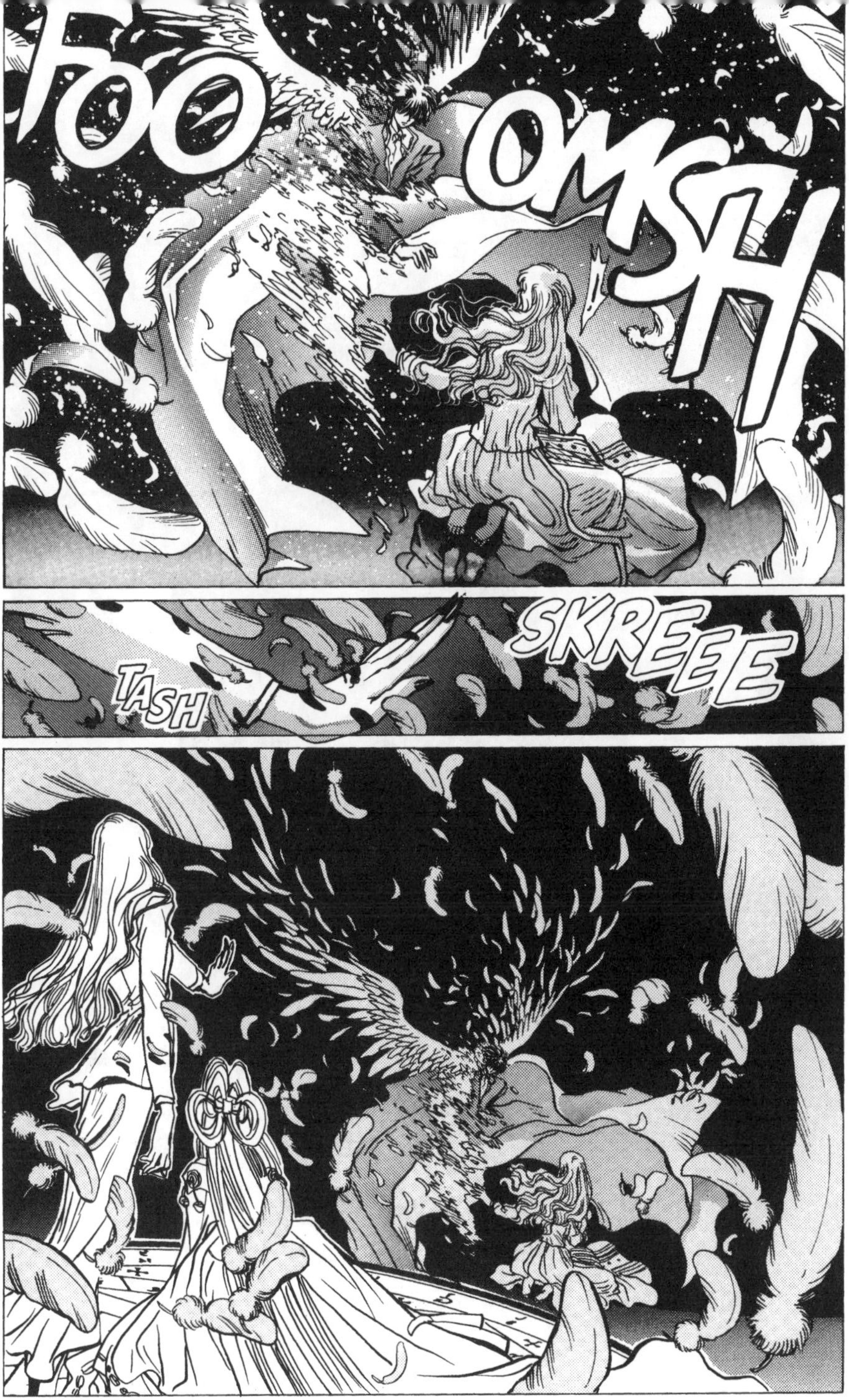
FOOOMSH
TASH
SKREEEE

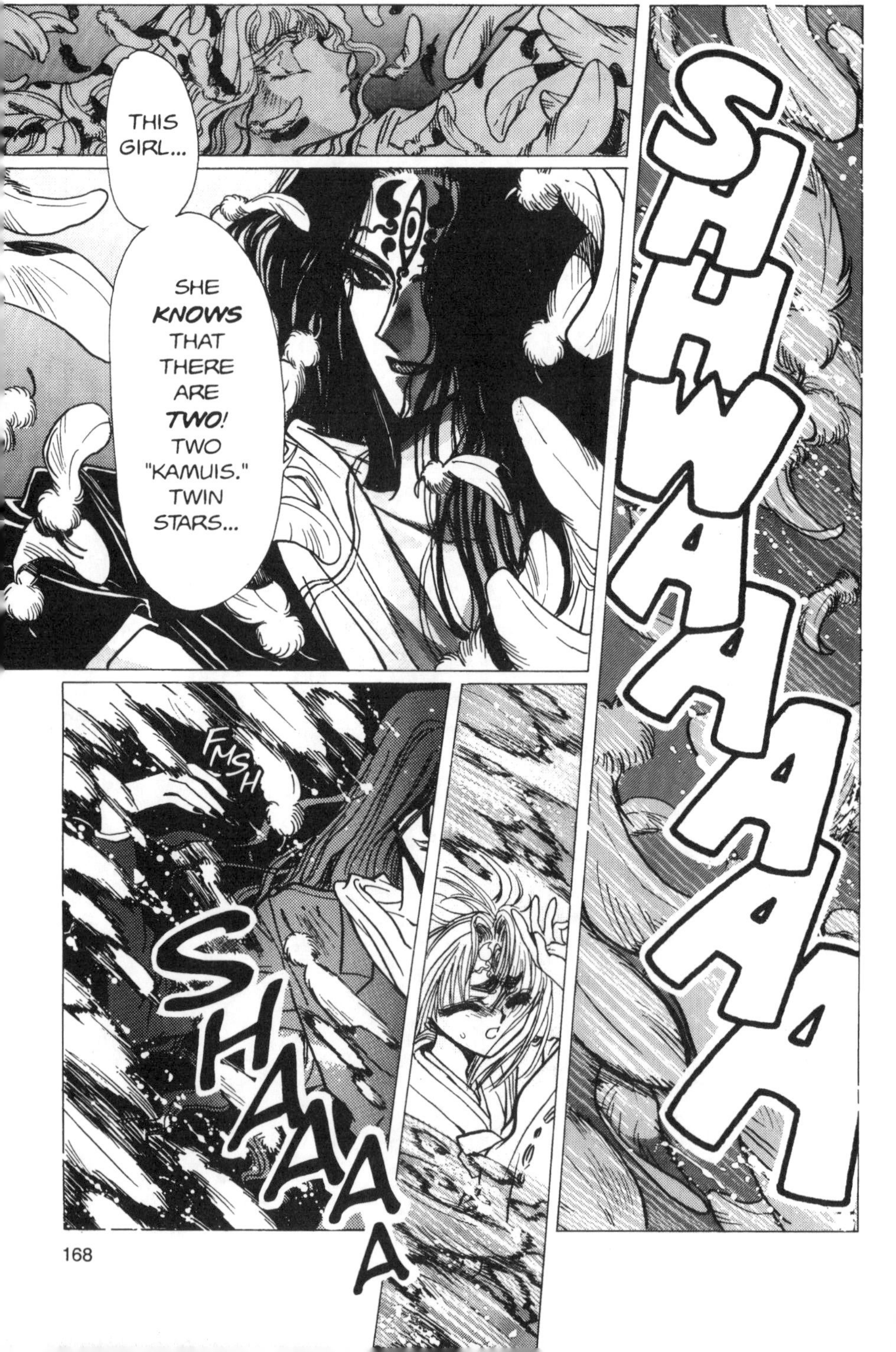
THIS GIRL...
SHE **KNOWS** THAT THERE ARE **TWO!** TWO "KAMUIS." TWIN STARS...
SHHWAAAAAAA
FMSH
SHAAAA

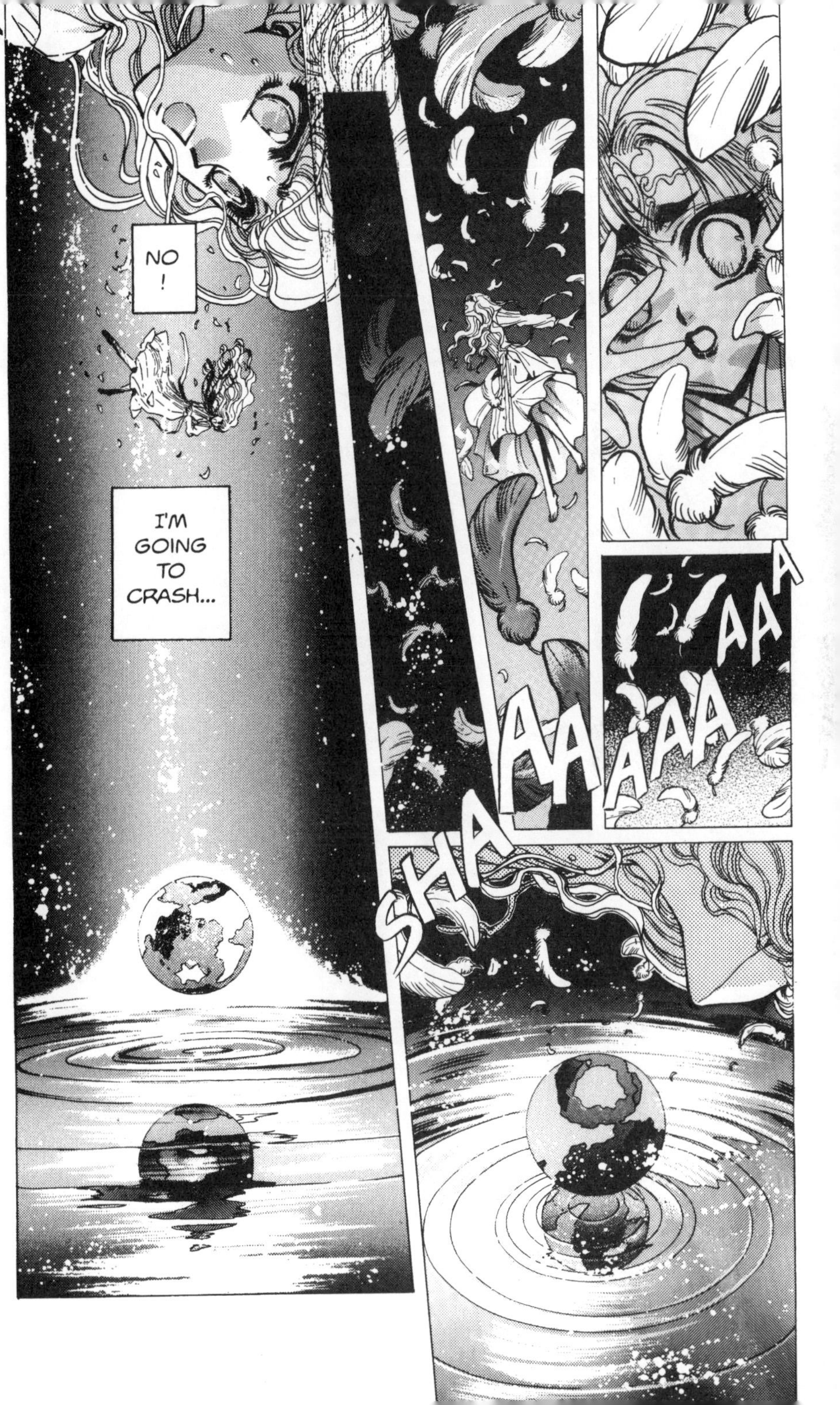
NO !
I'M GOING TO CRASH...
AAAAAAAAAA
SHA

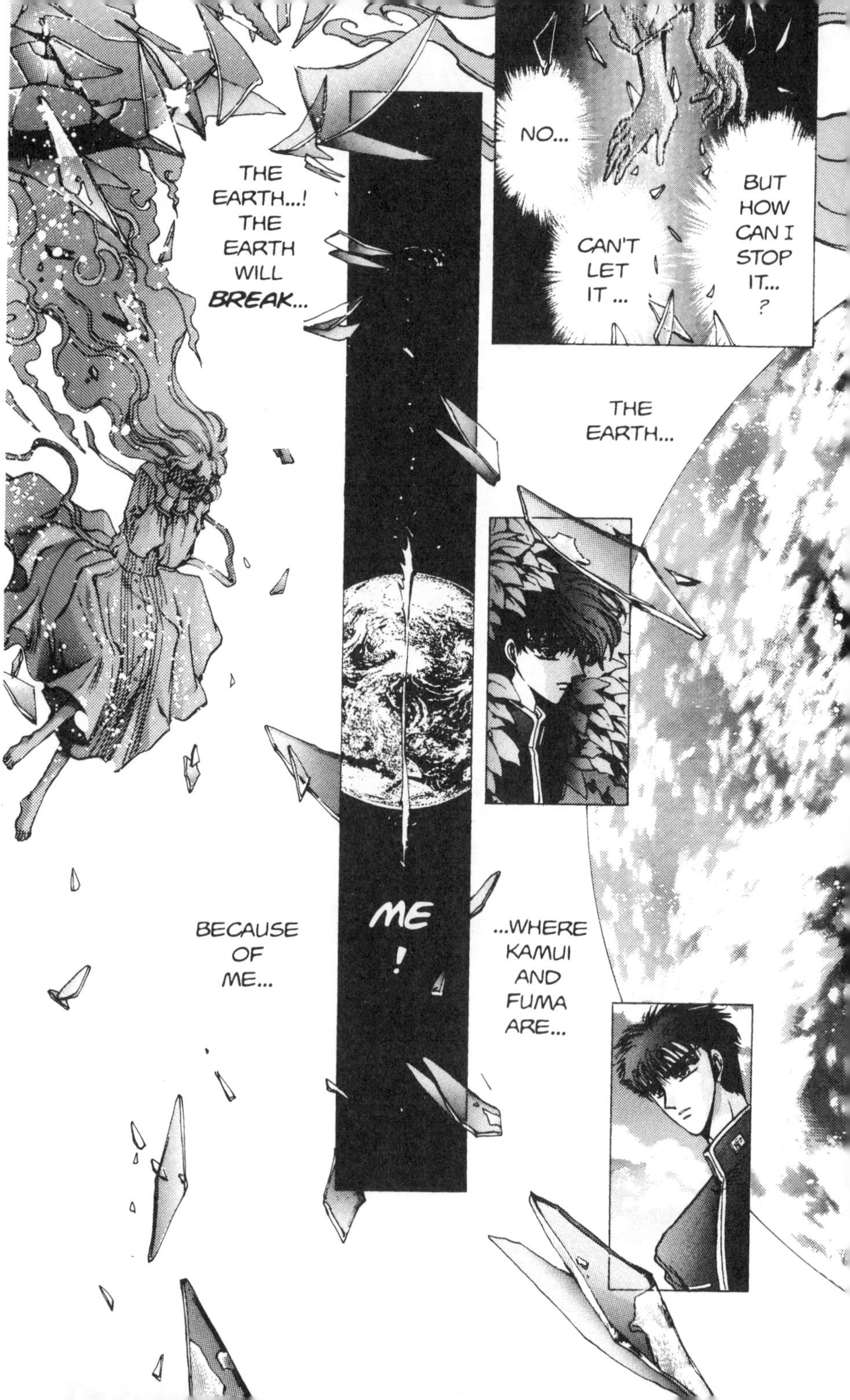
THE EARTH...! THE EARTH WILL BREAK...
BECAUSE OF ME...
ME!
NO...
CAN'T LET IT ...
BUT HOW CAN I STOP IT... ?
THE EARTH...
...WHERE KAMUI AND FUMA ARE...

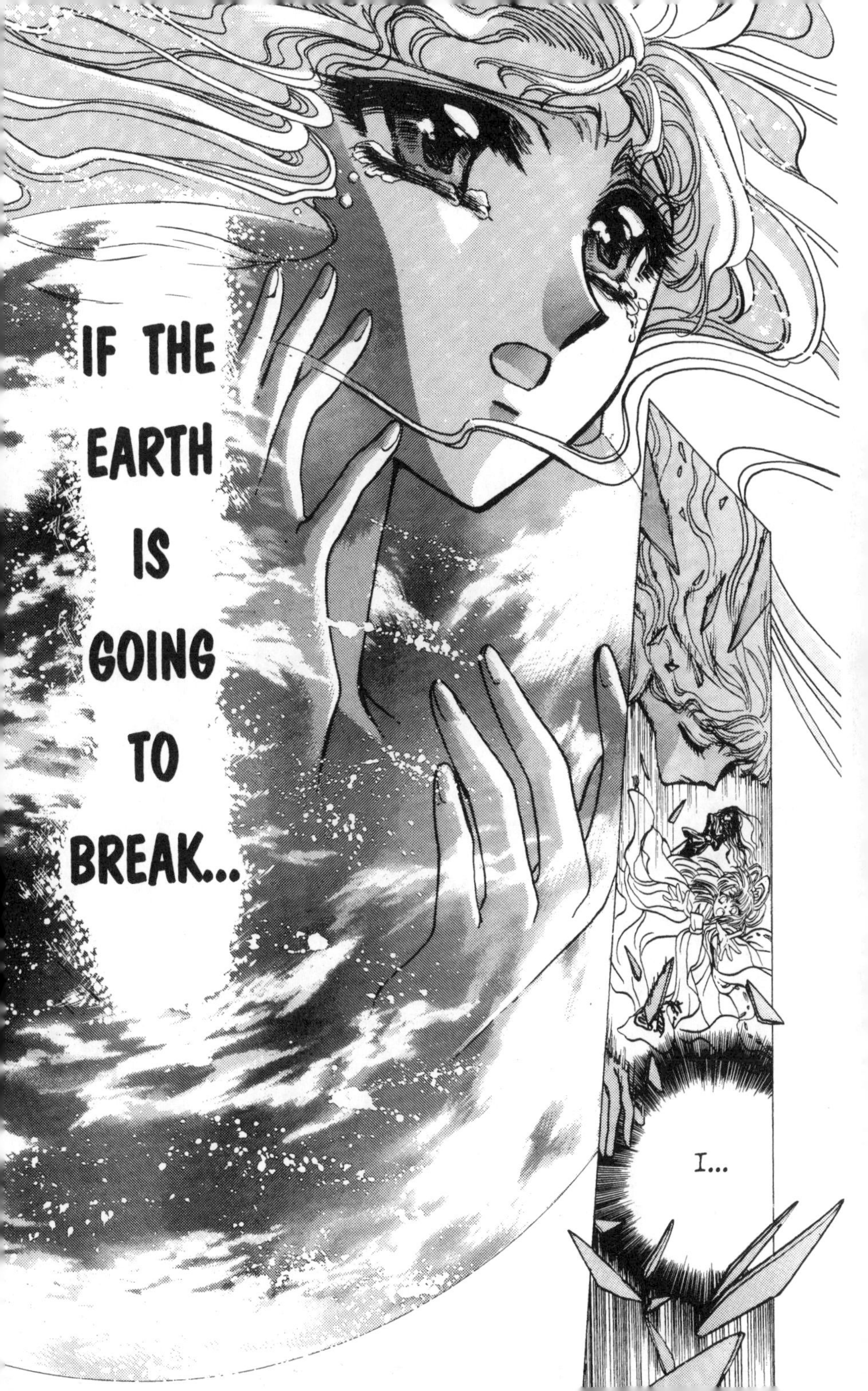
IF THE EARTH IS GOING TO BREAK...
I...

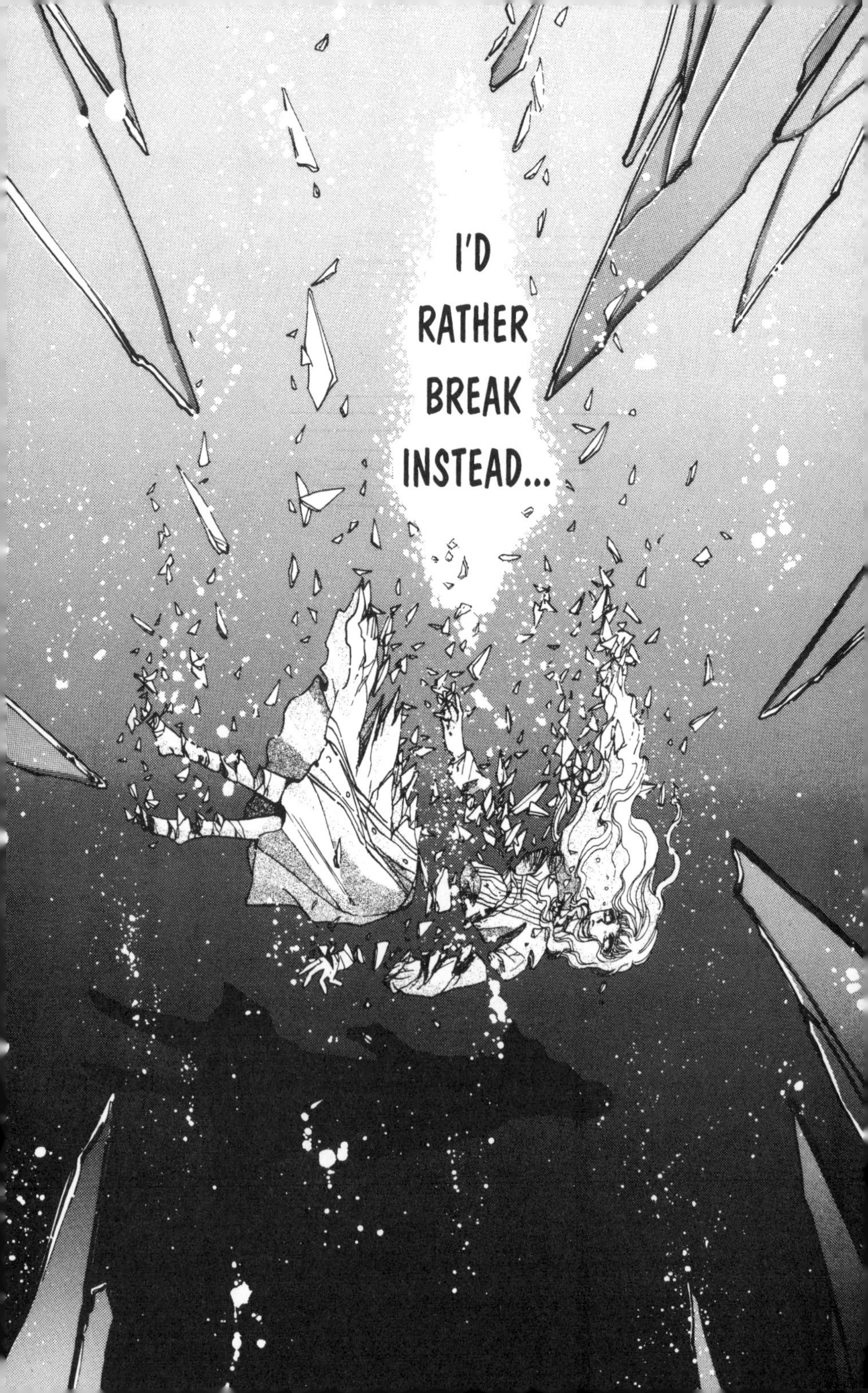
I'D RATHER BREAK INSTEAD...

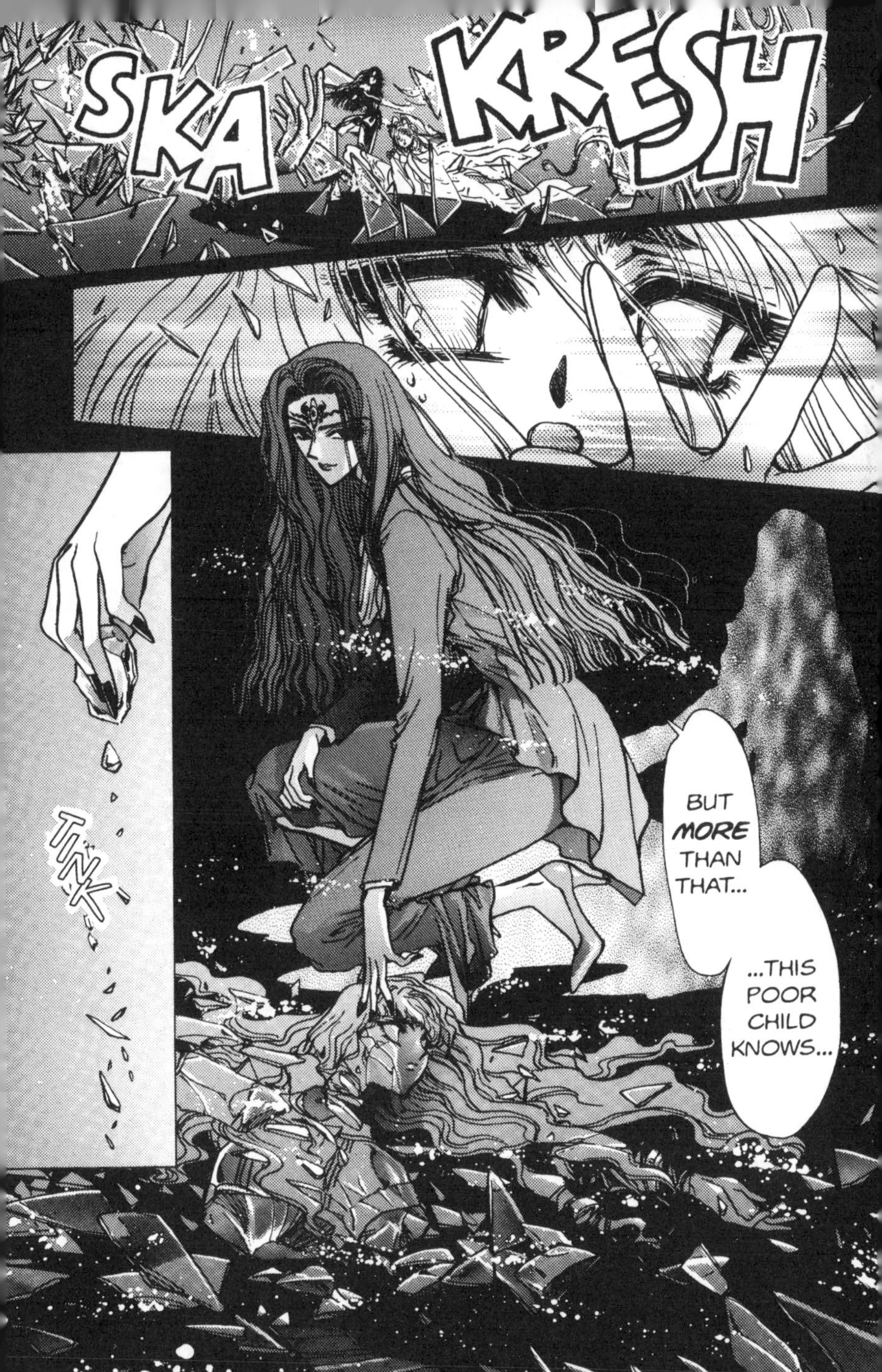
SKA KRESH
TINK
BUT MORE THAN THAT...
...THIS POOR CHILD KNOWS...

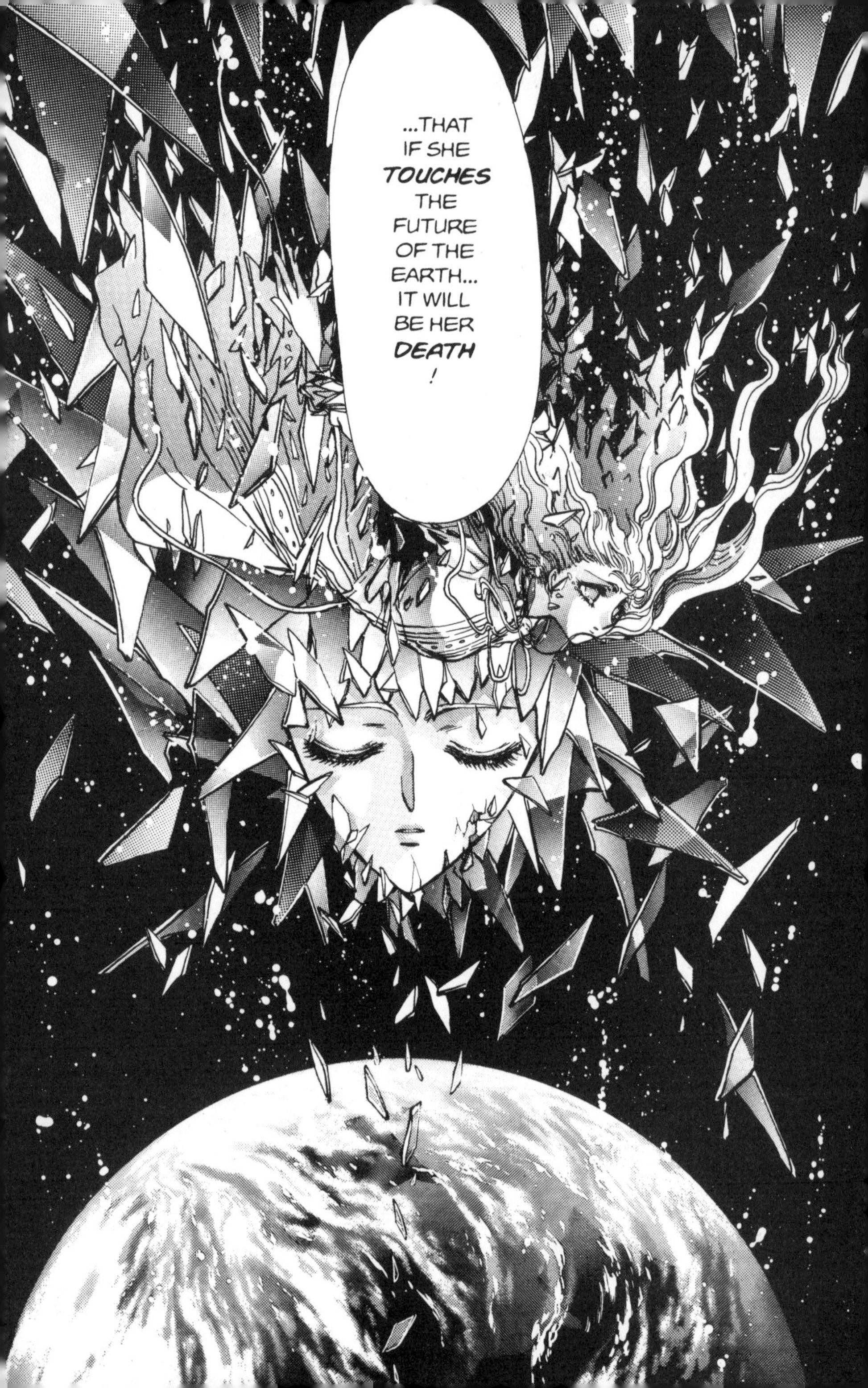
...THAT IF SHE *TOUCHES* THE FUTURE OF THE EARTH... IT WILL BE HER *DEATH*!

X

SATSUKI YATŌJI

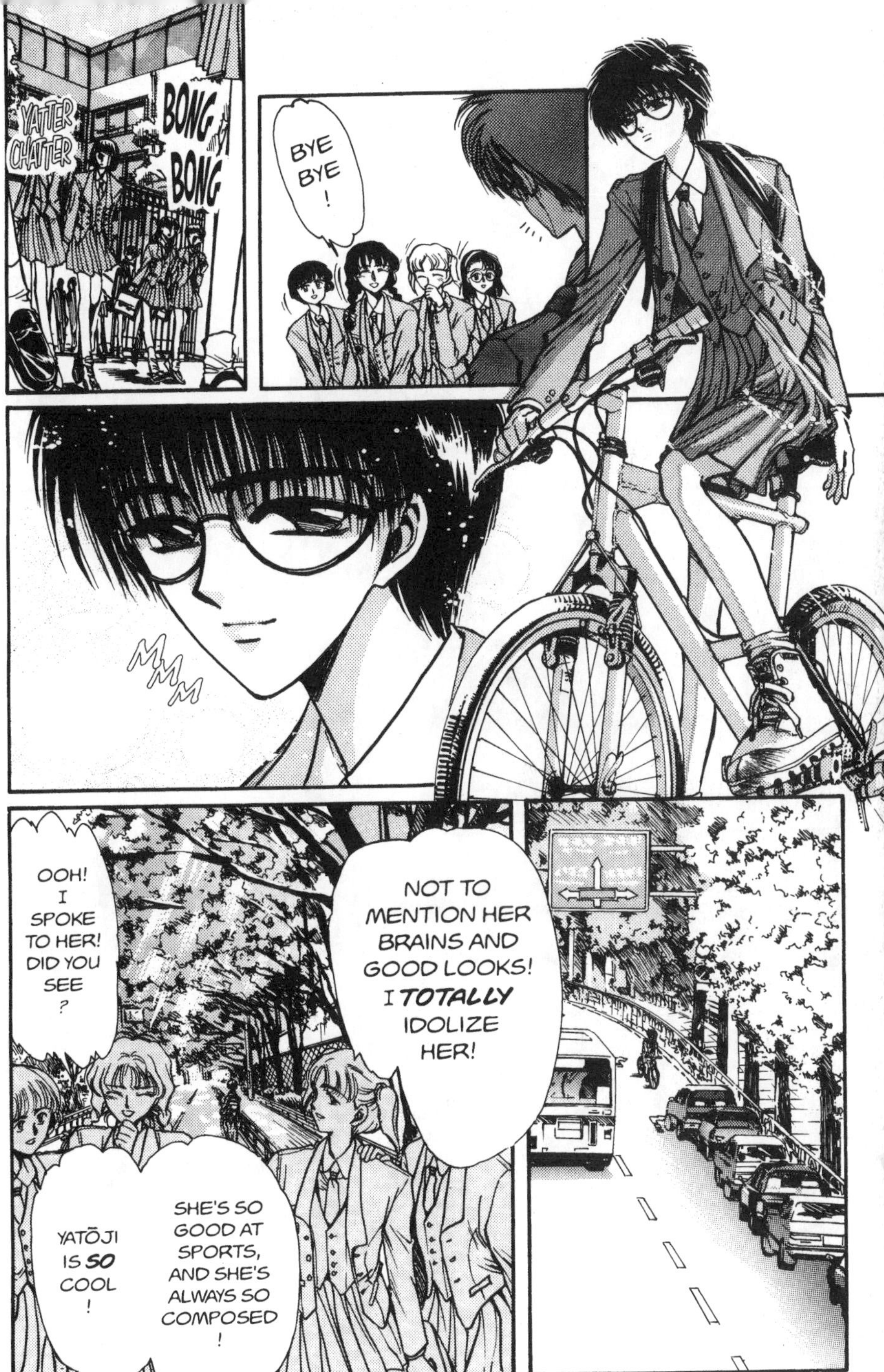

YATTER CHATTER
BONG BONG
BYE BYE !
MMM
OOH! I SPOKE TO HER! DID YOU SEE ?
NOT TO MENTION HER BRAINS AND GOOD LOOKS! I ***TOTALLY*** IDOLIZE HER!
YATŌJI IS ***SO*** COOL !
SHE'S SO GOOD AT SPORTS, AND SHE'S ALWAYS SO COMPOSED !

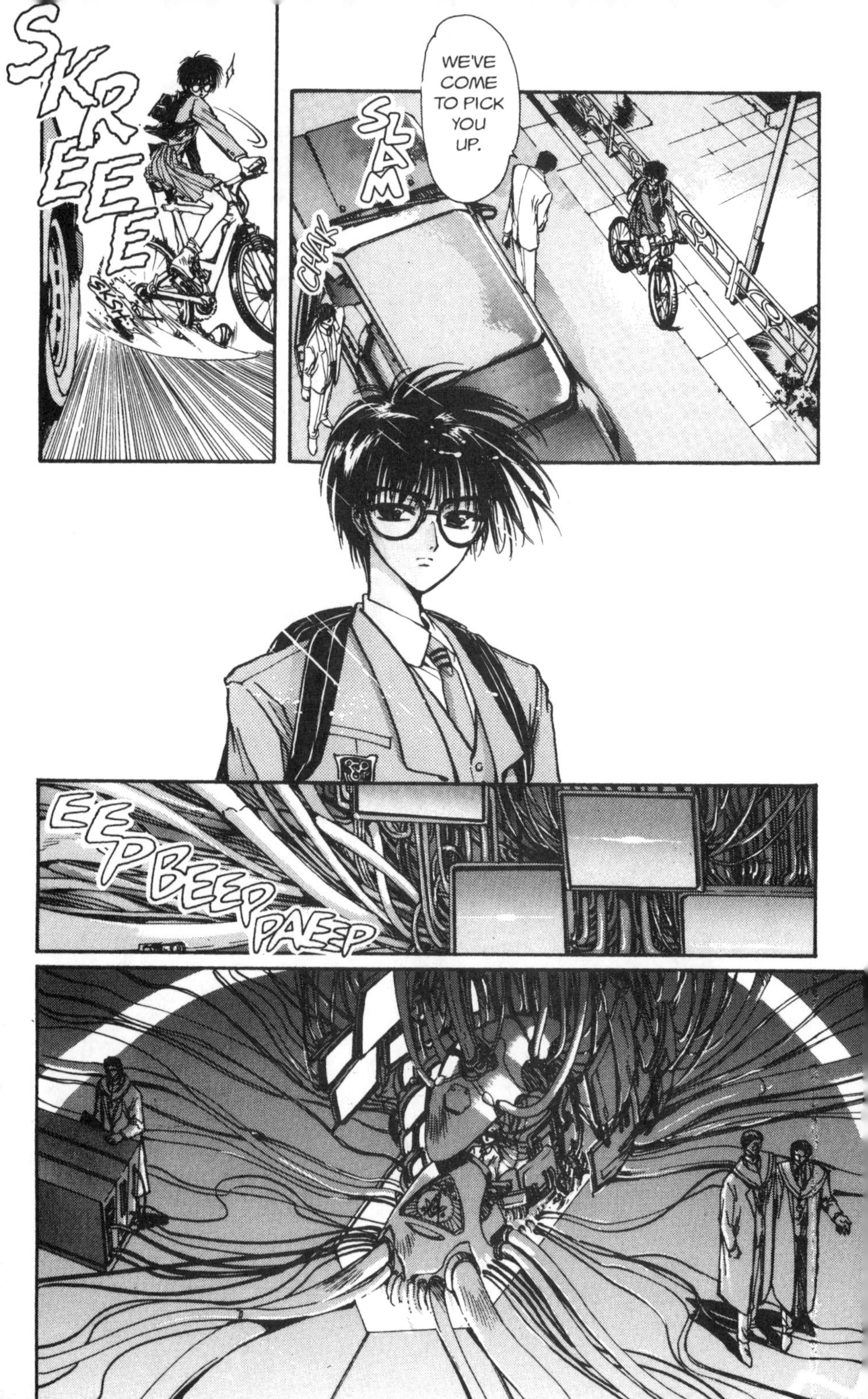
SKREEEE
SKSH
SLAM
WE'VE COME TO PICK YOU UP.
CHAK
EEEP BEEEP PAEEP

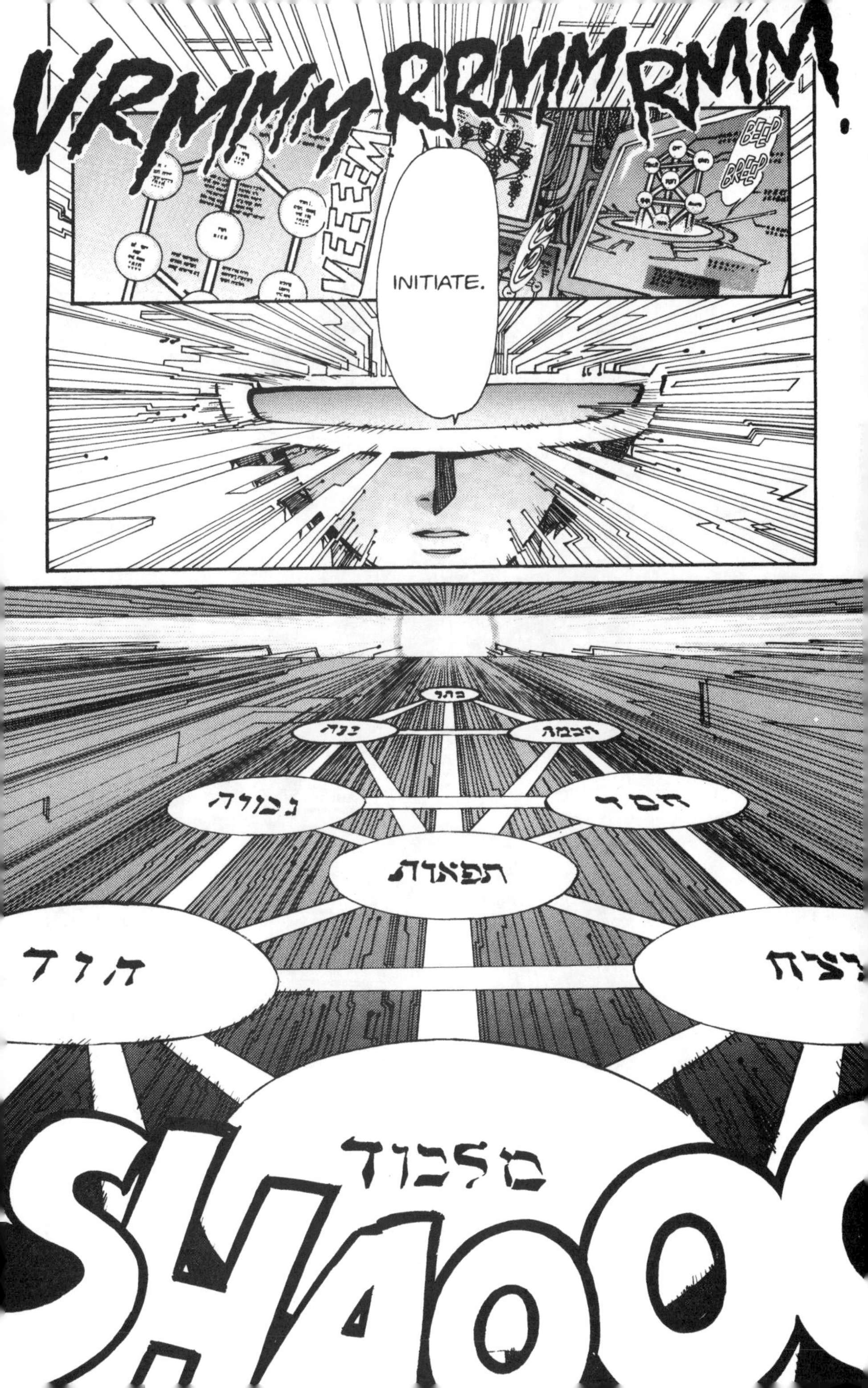
VRMMM RRMMM RMM
VEEEM
BEEP
BREEP
INITIATE.
כתר
בינה
חכמה
גבורה
חסד
תפארת
הוד
מלכות
SHAOO

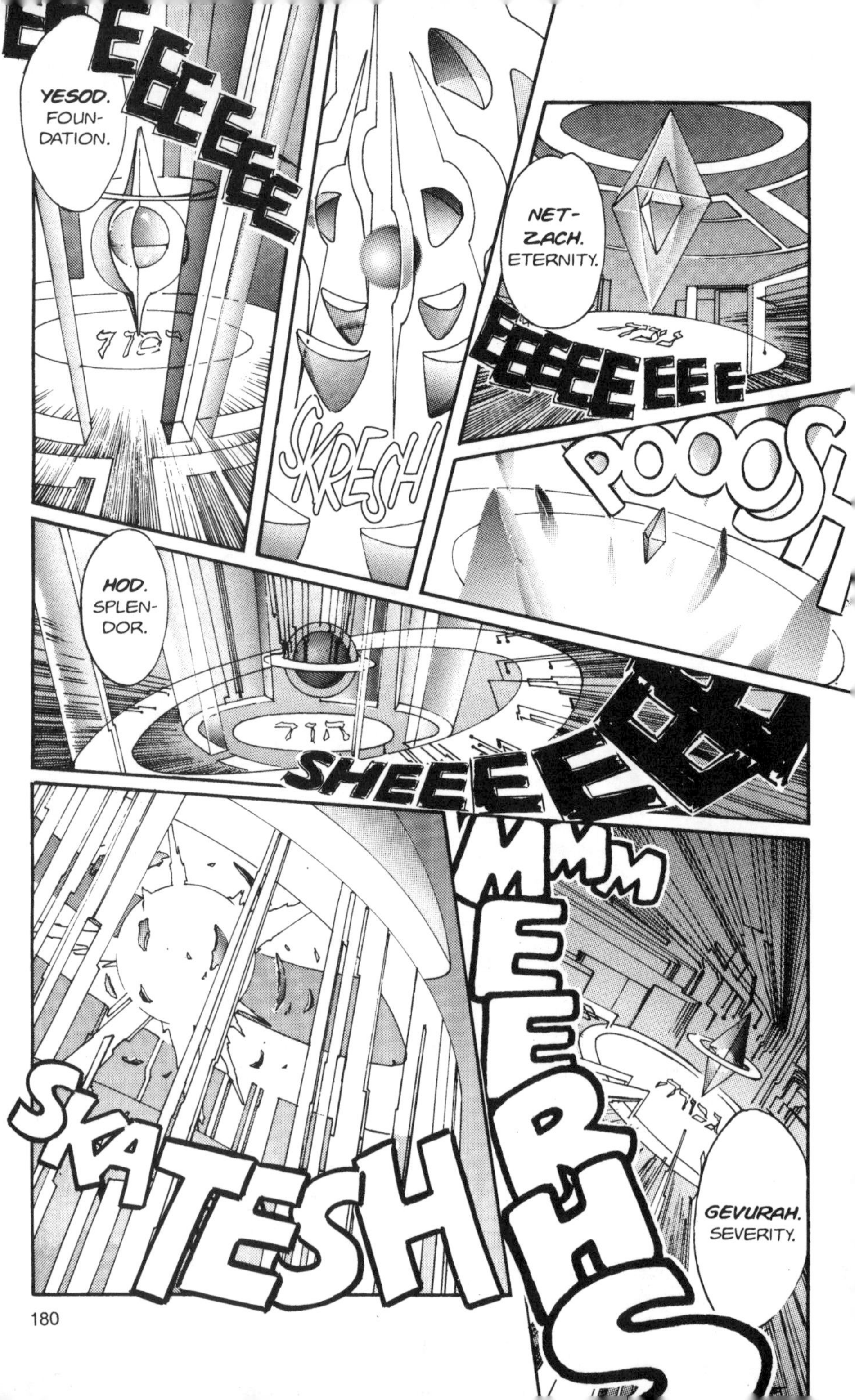
YESOD. FOUN-DATION.
SKRESCH
NET-ZACH. ETERNITY.
EEEEEEE
POOOSH
HOD. SPLEN-DOR.
SHEEEE
SKATESH
GEVURAH. SEVERITY.

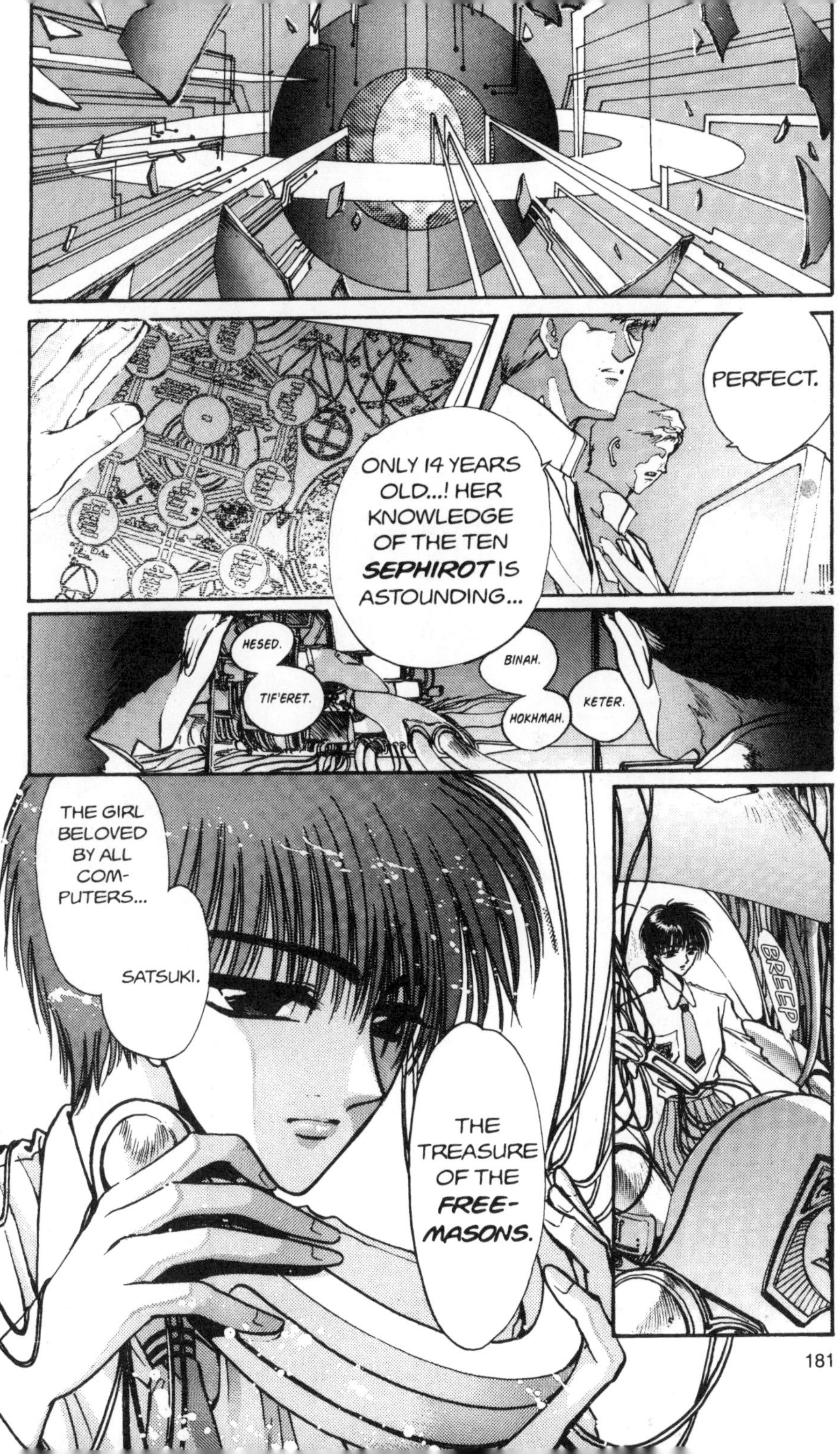
PERFECT.
ONLY 14 YEARS OLD...! HER KNOWLEDGE OF THE TEN *SEPHIROT* IS ASTOUNDING...
HESED.
TIF'ERET.
BINAH.
HOKHMAH.
KETER.
THE GIRL BELOVED BY ALL COM-PUTERS...
SATSUKI.
THE TREASURE OF THE *FREE-MASONS*.
BREEP

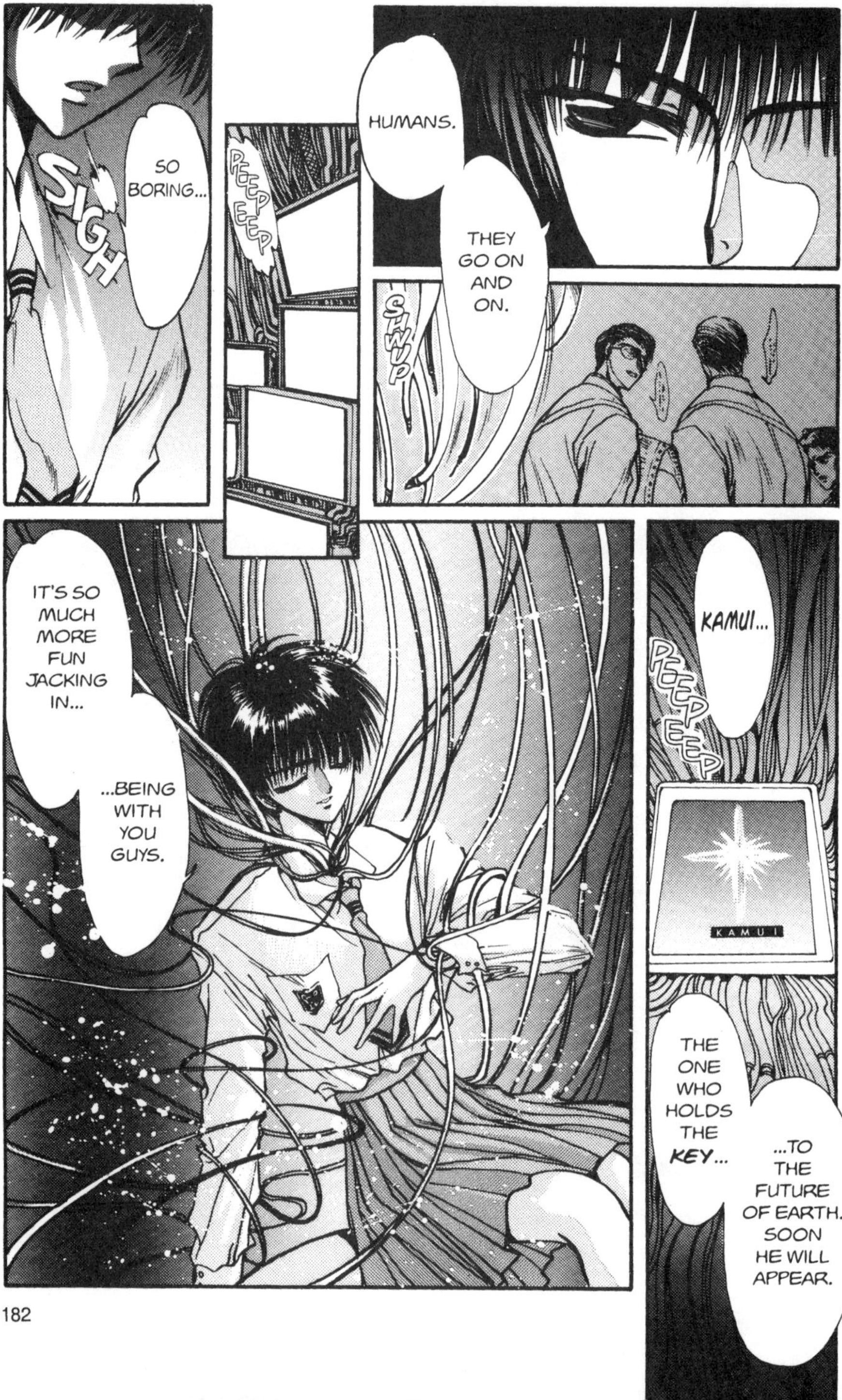
SO BORING...
SIGH
PEEEP EEEP
HUMANS.
THEY GO ON AND ON.
SHWUP
IT'S SO MUCH MORE FUN JACKING IN...
...BEING WITH YOU GUYS.
KAMUI...
PEEEP EEEP
KAMUI
THE ONE WHO HOLDS THE KEY...
...TO THE FUTURE OF EARTH. SOON HE WILL APPEAR.

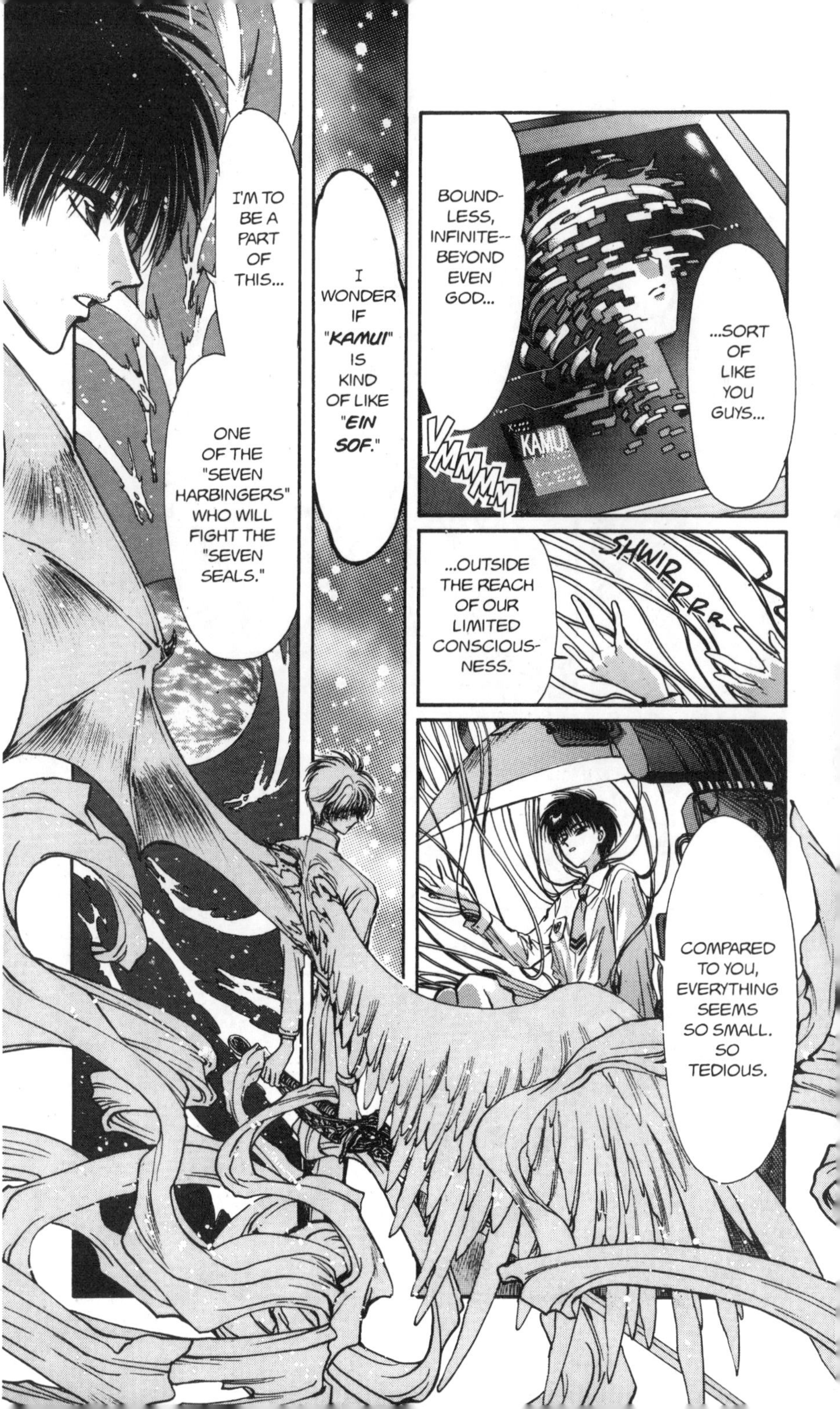
I'M TO BE A PART OF THIS...
ONE OF THE "SEVEN HARBINGERS" WHO WILL FIGHT THE "SEVEN SEALS."
I WONDER IF "KAMUI" IS KIND OF LIKE "EIN SOF."
BOUNDLESS, INFINITE--BEYOND EVEN GOD...
...SORT OF LIKE YOU GUYS...
VMMMM
KAMUI
...OUTSIDE THE REACH OF OUR LIMITED CONSCIOUSNESS.
SHWIRRRR
COMPARED TO YOU, EVERYTHING SEEMS SO SMALL. SO TEDIOUS.

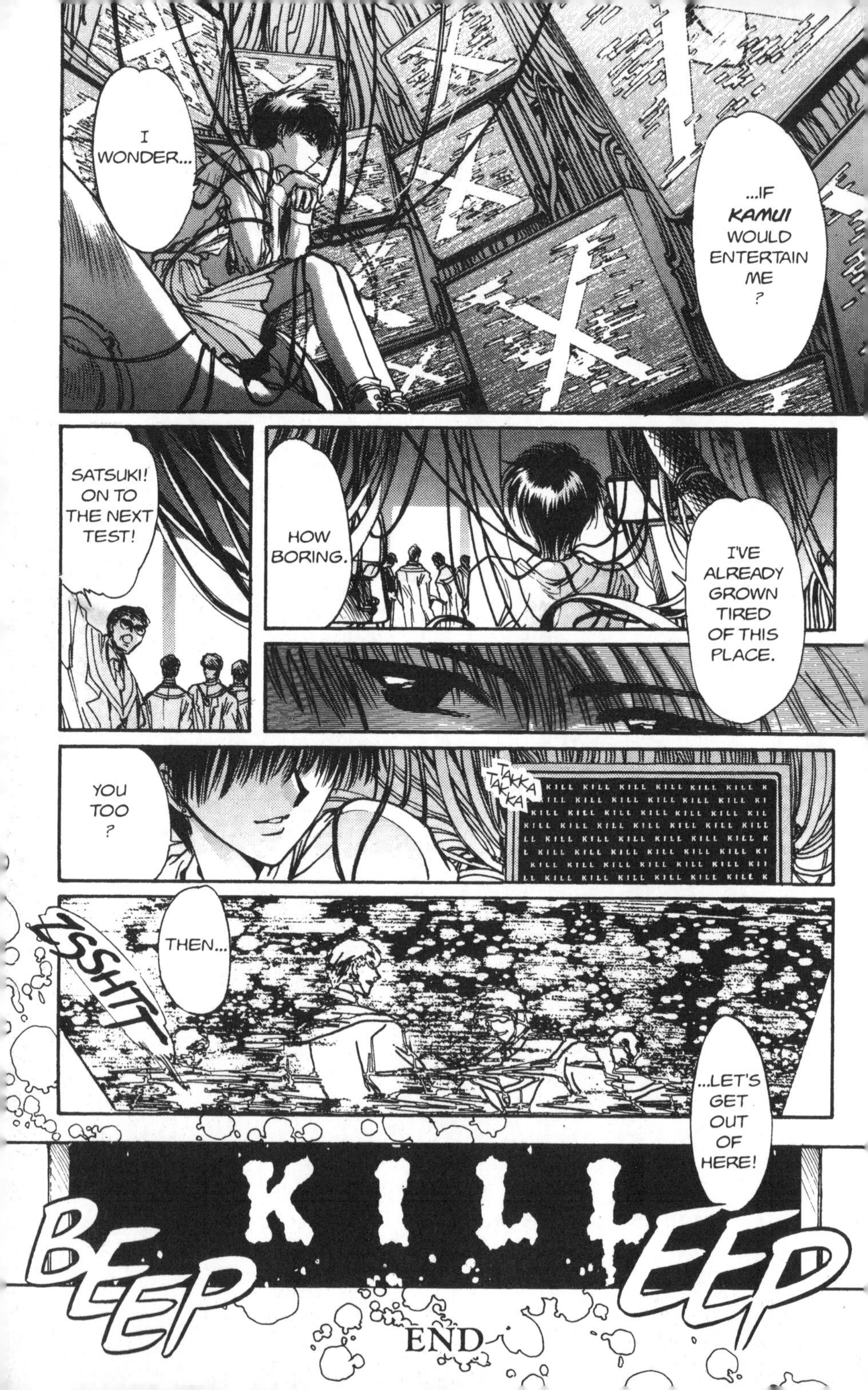
I WONDER...
...IF KAMUI WOULD ENTERTAIN ME?
SATSUKI! ON TO THE NEXT TEST!
HOW BORING.
I'VE ALREADY GROWN TIRED OF THIS PLACE.
YOU TOO?
TAKKA TAKKA
ZSSHT
THEN...
...LET'S GET OUT OF HERE!
BEEP
KILL
EEP
END